C000110982

DAILY WITH GOD

With the Festivals and Saints Days kept by the Church

USING THE
REVISED STANDARD VERSION OF THE BIBLE

Compilation and Prayers
by
JOHN PITCHFORD
Vicar of Emmanuel Church Sutton Coldfield

with a Foreword by
Bishop Mark Santer

The Canterbury Press
Norwich

First published 1991 by The Canterbury Press Norwich
(a publishing imprint of Hymns Ancient & Modern Limited which is a Registered Charity)
St Mary's Works, St Mary's Plain,
Norwich, Norfolk, NR3 3BH

British Library Cataloguing in Publication Data
A catalogue record for this book is available
from the British Library

ISBN 1–85311–028–0

*Typeset by Cambridge Composing (UK) Ltd
and printed in Great Britain by
William Clowes Ltd, Beccles, Suffolk*

Foreword

by The Right Reverend Mark Santer Bishop of Birmingham

One of the Church's needs today is for a pattern of prayer which people can actually use day by day. We need words and forms, following the rhythm of the week and of the year and its festivals, which help us to offer our lives to God. John Pitchford offers us a pattern of prayer and praise which I gladly commend – not just for dipping or reading, but for daily use.

+Mark Birmingham

ACKNOWLEDGEMENTS

I would like to thank all who have helped me to reach this stage in my spiritual pilgrimage, and who have thus indirectly helped me to write the 397 new prayers in this book.

Two priests read the typescript, and I much appreciate their helpful comments. First, the Reverend Michael Ainsworth, Chaplain of the Northern Ordination Course (now Vicar of St Christopher's Church, Withington, Manchester). He read the manuscript in the early stages. Secondly, the Reverend Alan Amos, O.B.E, Vice Principal of Westcott House (Theological College), Cambridge, (now the Principal of the Canterbury Ministerial Training Course).

I am grateful to the Right Reverend Mark Santer, Bishop of Birmingham, for the Foreword, and for his helpful suggestions.

I also thank the following: Mrs Kath Parker and Mrs Alison Alp for their comments on the 31 Day Cycle of Prayer. Jean and Wally Allman, and Jenny Clemens for help with the word-processing. Dr Harry Butterworth read the typescripts, and Mr Rex Tillson read the printer's proofs. Father Malcolm Gray, Vicar of Holy Trinity, Winchmore Hill, London, suggested the title 'Daily with God' on a journey from Walsingham to London.

The hymns used are now in the 'public domain' but I would like to acknowledge that they come from the English Hymnal, and Hymns Ancient & Modern.

I express my gratitude to Mr Kenneth Baker, Project Development Manager of The Canterbury Press Norwich. He was a great help to me originally on *The ABC for the PCC*, and now he has helped me again with *Daily with God*.

The cross on the front cover is reproduced from a detail from fol. 291v of the Book of Kells with permission of The Board of Trinity College Dublin.

The Scripture readings and Psalms are from The Revised Standard Version of the Bible (RSV), copyright 1946, 1952, © 1971, 1973 by The Division of Christian Education of the National Council of the Churches of Christ in the USA and reproduced with permission.

The texts of the Canticles: Benedictus, Te Deum and Magnificat are copyright © 1970, 1971, 1975 International Consultation on English Texts (ICET). Great and Wonderful, Glory and Honour, and Saviour of the World derive from the Daily Office of the Joint Liturgical Group. The Song of Christ's Glory is from the South African Daily Office, the copyright of which is held by the Church of the Province of Southern Africa. All the above are reproduced with permission from The Alternative Service Book 1980, copyright © The Central Board of Finance of the Church of England.

Contents

Preface

Aim of this book

The aim is to help people with their daily prayers and Bible reading, and to use the Scriptures to give a new vitality and freshness to their prayers.

This prayer book is based on the traditional faith and calender of the Church. It is designed for the use of Anglicans, but it is hoped that many other Christians may also find it helpful. It is intended for use by regular worshippers, and all who are serious in their search for God and his Kingdom, and who are also interested in the life and mission of their local church.

Structure and contents

Each day is limited to one page. For this reason, some Scripture passages and Psalms have been shortened, and the abbreviated passages are usually marked with an asterisk (*) after the Scripture reference. The Closing Prayers have also been limited to two lines (see pages 402–403).

SCRIPTURE READINGS. Most of the four Gospels and some of the Epistles are used in consecutive order, and are based on the secular calendar. The scheme for the main reading is as follows:

2 January – 28 March	St Matthew's Gospel
29 March – 30 May	St Mark's Gospel
1 June – 19 August	St Luke's Gospel
20 August – 28 September	St John's Gospel
2 October – 31 October	Acts of the Apostles
3 November – 14 November	The Letter to the Romans
15 November – 29 November	The Letters to the Corinthians
1 December – 18 December	Various Old Testament readings
19 December – 31 December	Mainly St Luke, chapters 1 and 2

An appropriate second reading has been chosen for use with the main reading. A few selected verses from most of the Psalms are used in consecutive order in the course of the year.

MOVABLE FESTIVALS. The date of Easter and the other Festivals change each year, and for this reason, provision has been made to keep these movable festivals at the correct liturgical time. It may happen that Holy Week and Easter as kept by the Church will be close to the same events as they occur in the daily reading scheme of this prayer book. It all depends on the date of Easter each year. The Baptism of the Lord comes on the Sunday after the Epiphany. In *Daily with God* it has been fixed on 4 January.

SAINTS DAYS, as celebrated by Anglicans and Roman Catholics, are kept on the correct date, with appropriate readings and Psalms. Two feasts of St Mary are included, on 15 August and 8 December. These are not at present kept by the Church of England, but are observed in some Anglican Provinces and by Roman Catholics.

How to use this prayer book

TIME AND PLACE. Plan when to pray. Choose a quiet place where you are not likely to be disturbed (eg. your bedroom?) It is possible to pray anywhere, especially by using short 'Arrow Prayers'. And it is a good idea to offer a prayer at an appropriate time during the day or night, or on a journey. However, in addition to these occasional prayers, long experience has proved that a regular time for prayer is needed for Christian formation and growth. Try to pray at the same time each day.

HOW TO BEGIN. The first step is to become aware of God's presence. Think what you are actually doing in your prayers before you begin. Many people make the Sign of the Cross, to remind them in a shorthand way of God's whole act of salvation, as they say: 'In the name of the Father and of the Son and of the Holy Spirit'. The Sign of the Cross is the crossing out of the letter 'I' (your selfish interests) as you turn to God in prayer.

Some people close their eyes, to shut out noise and external thoughts, and others like to look at a Crucifix or Cross. You need to pause, and be still, and learn to relax. Feel the floor supporting you, and be aware of your feet, head and body. Listen to your breathing. Be aware of God's presence. 'Be still and know that I am God.' Do not begin until you have an inner calm and stillness, whatever method you use to achieve this.

OPENING PRAYERS. The 'Glory be . . .' is used each day, except in Lent and Advent. 'Glory be to the Father, and to the Son, and to the Holy Spirit, as it was in the beginning, is now and ever shall be, world without end. Amen.'

ASH WEDNESDAY is found on page 370

THE SEASON OF LENT. The ordinary calendar 'date' is used, together with the Lenten Opening Prayer on the Bookmark (or see page 370). The 'Glory be . . .' is not used in Lent and Holy Week, as Lent and Holy Week are penitential seasons.

HOLY WEEK AND EASTER WEEK. These are found on pages 371–384.

EASTERTIDE. An Easter Opening Prayer (on the Bookmark, or see page 384) is provided for the remainder of the Great Forty Days of Easter, using the ordinary calendar 'date' until Ascension Day.

OTHER FESTIVALS: Ascension Day page 385
Pentecost (Whitsun) page 386
Trinity Sunday page 387
Corpus Christi page 388

THE SEASON OF ADVENT. The Church keeps Advent from the fourth Sunday before Christmas. To make it easier to use, Advent is kept in this Prayer Book from 1 to 24 December, but with a 'change of flavour' for the pre-Christmas period 17–24 December.

SUGGESTIONS FOR A 31 DAY CYCLE OF PRAYER (see Intercessions pages 390–393). All four sets can be used each day. Alternatively, Set A can be used during month one (e.g. January), Set B in month two (e.g. February), and Set C in month three. Or A and B could be used in month one, and A and C in month two, and A and D in month three. The sick are prayed for on Day 21, but you may feel it appropriate to pray for them each day. In set C you may wish to add 'We pray for the Church throughout the world, and especially for the Church in . . .' (e.g. 'Japan').

Set D has been left blank, so that you can make your own cycle of prayer. Some suggestions are – (1) Your relatives, friends, work and leisure. (2) Individual members of your church. (3) Roads in the parish. *Members of other Christian churches could use set D for intercessions appropriate for their own church.*

CANTICLES (see pages 396–399) can be used after the Intercession Prayers and before the Closing Prayers.

USE OF SILENCE. Silence has been called 'the gateway to the spiritual life', and it is periods of silence which make your prayers come alive. Silence is more than an absence of noise, and it is an essential part of the spiritual life. Silence can be uncomfortable, especially if sin or some other problem comes between you and God. When distracting thoughts and worries come into your mind, one way to deal with them is to turn them into prayer, and then return to the silence.

WHEN TO HAVE A PERIOD OF SILENCE IN YOUR PRAYERS? A short time before you begin is helpful, or after the 'Glory be . . .' Other suggestions are in the middle of each verse of the Psalm, during or after the Scripture readings, or during the prayers. Use of silence is not always easy, but try to have a silence, and gradually increase it over the years.

PRAYING THE PRAYERS. Instead of just reading the prayers each day, try to pray them. These prayers are the response of the author to the Scripture. In due course, you may wish to make your own additional responses.

SCRIPTURE READINGS. Read them slowly, pausing to think about the meaning. What is God wanting to say to you through the passage? It is a good idea to read each passage more than once, if you can make time to do this. Try to understand what God wants to say to you through the Scriptures.

Thoughts about the spiritual life

Your prayer life is a major part of your response to God's love for you in Jesus Christ. Prayer is not easy. It requires commitment of time for God each day, and a determination to succeed, with God's help. 'You shall love the Lord your God with all your heart, and with all your mind, and with all your soul, and with all your strength.' Once daily prayer is well established, you will not want to be without it.

The spiritual life has been likened to a three legged stool. One leg is the regular and prayerful reading of the Scriptures. The second leg is receiving Holy Communion, and at least on the 'first day of the week'. The third leg is your own prayers. There are different ways of praying, but you will not make much progress without a proper balance between all three legs.

Our prayers are affected by the practical side of being a Christian disciple, and trying to live the Gospel day by day. Most people fail often, and our sins can be a problem for our spiritual lives. All sin creates a barrier between us and God. The Holy Spirit makes us aware of our sins. To grow, we need to be open to the Spirit, and to repent and be truly sorry for all our sins. We need to ask for God's forgiveness, and to show ourselves that we have accepted God's forgiveness by our good works.

'Love your neighbour as yourself.' Not always easy! But it is important to learn what that means in our lives. Try to bring your daily living into line with your faith. Live to please God.

If you use this Prayer Book in the morning, then it is a good idea to have another short time of prayer in the evening. Or *vice versa*.

Our prayers are offered to God the Father, through Jesus Christ, and in the power of the Holy Spirit. You may be completely alone when you are praying. But your prayers are always offered with the worship of the whole Church, on earth, and with the worship of the angels and archangels and all the heavenly host. We are never alone in our prayers. For this reason, 'we' is used instead of 'I' in the prayers.

Daily Prayers and Scripture Readings

1 January *Mary and the Naming of Jesus*

OPENING PRAYER Almighty God, all praise and glory belong to you. You sent your Son to take flesh in the womb of Mary and to be the Redeemer of the world. Hear our prayer and fill us with your Spirit . . . Glory be . . .

PSALMODY Let them praise the name of the Lord!
For he commanded and they were created.
Let them praise the name of the Lord,
for his name alone is exalted;
his glory is above earth and heaven. Psalm 148.6–13*

SCRIPTURE READINGS

The Lord said to Moses, 'Say to Aaron and his sons,
Thus you shall bless the people of Israel:
you shall say to them,
The Lord bless you and keep you:
The Lord make his face to shine upon you,
and be gracious to you:
The Lord lift up his countenance upon you,
and give you peace.'

Numbers 6. 22–28

When the time had fully come, God sent his Son, born of woman, born under the Law, to redeem those who were under the Law, so that we might receive adoption as sons. And because we are sons, God has sent the Spirit of his Son into our hearts, crying, 'Abba, Father!' So through God you are no longer a slave but a son, and if a son then an heir. Galatians 4. 4–7

The shepherds said, 'Let us go over to Bethlehem, and see this thing that has happened, which the Lord has made known to us'. And they went with haste, and found Mary and Joseph, and the babe lying in a manger. And when they saw it they made known the saying which had been told them concerning this child; and all who heard it wondered at what the shepherds told them. But Mary kept all these things, pondering them in her heart. And the shepherds returned, glorifying and praising God for all they had heard and seen, as it had been told them. And at the end of eight days, when he was circumcised, he was called Jesus, the name given by the angel before he was conceived in the womb. St Luke 2.15–31

RESPONSE 'Let all creation join in one to bless the sacred name of him who sits upon the throne, and to adore the Lamb.'

Almighty God, you bring joy and salvation to the world through your Son – we praise you for the Word made flesh in the womb of Mary . . .
You gave the name of Jesus to the child of Mary – we pray that his sacred name may be glorified and praised in all the world . . .
You make all things new in Christ – Lord, help us to enter this new year with courage and faith, trusting in your unfailing love . . .

INTERCESSIONS *pages 390–393* CLOSING PRAYERS *page 402–403*

OPENING PRAYER Almighty God, all praise and glory belong to you. You sent your Son to take flesh in the womb of Mary and to be the Redeemer of the world. Hear our prayer and fill us with your Spirit . . . Glory be . . .

PSALMODY Blessed is the man
who walks not in the counsel of the wicked,
nor stands in the way of sinners,
but his delight is in the law of the Lord,
and on his law he meditates day and night.
He is like a tree planted by streams of water,
that yields its fruit in its season,
and its leaf does not wither.
In all that he does he prospers.
The wicked are not so,
but are like chaff which the wind drives away.
Therefore the wicked will not stand in the judgement.
For the Lord knows the way of the righteous,
but the way of the wicked will perish. Psalm 1.1–6*

SCRIPTURE READINGS In those days came John the Baptist, preaching in the wilderness of Judea, 'Repent, for the Kingdom of Heaven is at hand.' For this is he who was spoken of by the prophet Isaiah when he said:

'The voice of one crying in the wilderness:
prepare the way of the Lord,
make his paths straight.'

John wore a garment of camel's hair, and a leather girdle around his waist; and his food was locusts and wild honey. Then went out to him Jerusalem and all Judea and all the region about the Jordan, and they were baptized by him in the river Jordan, confessing their sins. St Matthew 3.1–6

The Pharisees asked John, 'Why are you baptizing, if you are neither the Christ, nor Elijah, nor the prophet?' John answered, 'I baptize with water; but among you stands one whom you do not know, even he who comes after me, the thong of whose sandal I am not worthy to untie.' St John 1.24

RESPONSE 'Your kingdom come on earth, as it is in heaven.'

Almighty God, your Kingdom is the union of all who accept your authority – we praise you for all the blessings you give us in your Son . . .
'Among you stands one whom you do not know' – Lord, help us by your grace to grow in knowledge and love of your eternal Son . . .
'Repent, for the Kingdom of Heaven is at hand' – help us by the Spirit to be sorry for our sins, and to grow into union with Christ . . .

INTERCESSIONS *pages 390–393* CLOSING PRAYERS *page 402–403*

3 January *Baptism with the Holy Spirit and with Fire*

OPENING PRAYER Almighty God, all praise and glory belong to you. You sent your Son to take flesh in the womb of Mary and to be the Redeemer of the world. Hear our prayer and fill us with your Spirit . . . Glory be . . .

PSALMODY O Lord, how many are my foes!
Many are rising against me.
But thou, O Lord, art a shield about me,
my glory, and the lifter of my head.
I cry aloud to the Lord,
and he answers me from his holy hill.
Deliverance belongs to the Lord;
thy blessing be upon thy people! Psalm 3.1–8*

SCRIPTURE READINGS King Nebuchadnezzar said, 'Is it true, O Shadrach, Meshack, and Abednego, that you do not serve my gods or worship the golden image which I have set up? Now if you are ready to fall down and worship, well and good; but if you do not worship, you shall immediately be cast into a burning fiery furnace.' Daniel 3.14–15

When John saw many of the Pharisees and Sadducees coming for baptism, he said, 'You brood of vipers! Who warned you to flee from the wrath to come? Bear fruit that befits repentance, and do not presume to say to yourselves, "We have Abraham as our father"; for I tell you, God is able from these stones to raise up children to Abraham. Even now the axe is laid to the root of the trees; every tree therefore that does not bear good fruit is cut down and thrown into the fire. I baptize you with water for repentance, but he who is coming after me is mightier than I, whose sandals I am not worthy to carry; he will baptize you with the Holy Spirit and with fire. His winnowing fork is in his hand, and he will clear his threshing floor and gather his wheat into the granary, but the chaff he will burn with unquenchable fire.' St Matthew 3.7–12*

RESPONSE 'Just as I am, without one plea, but that thy blood was shed for me, O Lamb of God, I come.'

Eternal God, you speak to Christians in every generation through the prophets – we thank you and praise you for their faithful witness . . .
'Bear fruit that befits repentance' – help us by your grace to overcome our sins, and to be active in the service of your Kingdom . . .
'He will baptize you with the Holy Spirit and with fire' – Lord, kindle the fire of your love in all who have been baptized into Christ . . .

INTERCESSIONS *pages 390–393* CLOSING PRAYERS *page 402–403*

OPENING PRAYER Almighty God, all praise and glory belong to you. You sent your Son to take flesh in the womb of Mary and to be the Redeemer of the world. Hear our prayer and fill us with your Spirit . . . Glory be . . .

PSALMODY The Lord reigns; let the earth rejoice.
The heavens proclaim his righteousness.
For thou, O Lord, art most high over all the earth;
thou art exalted far above all gods.
Light dawns for the righteous,
and joy for the upright in heart.
Rejoice in the Lord, O you righteous,
and give thanks to his holy name! Psalm 97.1–12*

SCRIPTURE READINGS
Behold my servant, whom I uphold,
my chosen, in whom my soul delights;
I have put my spirit upon him,
he will bring forth justice to the nations.
'I have given you as a convenant to the people,
a light to the nations,
to open the eyes that are blind,
to bring out the prisoners from the dungeon,
from the prison those who sit in darkness.' Isaiah 42.1–7*

Jesus came from Galilee to the Jordan to John, to be baptized by him. John would have prevented him, saying, 'I need to be baptized by you, and do you come to me?' But Jesus answered him, 'Let it be so now; for thus it is fitting for us to fulfil all righteousness.' Then he consented. And when Jesus was baptized, he went up immediately from the water, and behold, the heavens were opened and he saw the Spirit of God descending like a dove, and alighting on him; and lo, a voice from heaven, saying, 'This is my beloved Son, with whom I am well pleased.' St Matthew 3.13–17

RESPONSE 'The Lord is my strength and my song,
he has become my salvation.'

Heavenly Father, you revealed Jesus as your Beloved Son at his baptism – we praise you for anointing him with the Holy Spirit and with power . . .
'I need to be baptized by you' – Lord, we thank you for our baptism into Christ, and for making us your adopted sons and daughters . . .
'This is my beloved son, with whom I am well pleased' – Blessed and praised be Jesus Christ, for time and for eternity, alleluia, alleluia . . .

INTERCESSIONS *pages 390–393* CLOSING PRAYERS *page 402–403*

OPENING PRAYER Almighty God, all praise and glory belong to you. You sent your Son to take flesh in the womb of Mary and to be the Redeemer of the world. Hear our prayer and fill us with your Spirit . . . Glory be . . .

PSALMODY Answer me when I call, O God of my right!
Be gracious to me, and hear my prayer.
But know that the Lord has set apart
the godly for himself;
the Lord hears when I call to him.
Be angry, but sin not;
commune with your own hearts on your beds,
and be silent.
Offer right sacrifices,
and put your trust in the Lord. Psalm 4.1–5*

SCRIPTURE READINGS Jesus was led up by the Spirit into the wilderness to be tempted by the devil. And he fasted forty days and forty nights, and afterwards he was hungry. The tempter came and said, 'If you are the Son of God, command these stones to be loaves of bread.' But he answered, 'It is written, "man shall not live by bread alone, but by every word that proceeds from the mouth of God."' Then the devil took him to the holy city, and set him on the pinnacle of the temple, and said, 'If you are the Son of God, throw yourself down; for it is written, "He will give his angels charge of you," and "on their hands they will bear you up, lest you strike your foot against a stone."' Jesus said, 'Again it is written, "you shall not tempt the Lord your God."' Again the devil took him to a very high mountain, and showed him all the kingdoms of the world and the glory of them; and he said, 'All these I will give you, if you will fall down and worship me.' Jesus said, 'Begone, Satan! for it is written, "You shall worship the Lord your God and him only shall you serve."' The devil left him, and angels came and ministered to him. St Matthew 4. 1–11*

As by one man's disobedience many were made sinners, so by one man's obedience many will be made righteous. Romans 5.19

RESPONSE 'Crown him as your captain in temptations's hour;
let his will enfold you in its light and power.'

Eternal God, your Son was tempted but did not fall to temptation – we praise you for his faithfulness and love . . .
'Man shall not live by bread alone' – we thank you for feeding us with your Word in the Scriptures and in the Sacrament of the Eucharist . . .
'He will give his angels charge of you' – Lord, send your holy angels to guard and protect us in all times of trouble and temptation . . .

INTERCESSIONS *pages 390–393* CLOSING PRAYERS *page 402–403*

6 January *The Feast of the Epiphany*

OPENING PRAYER Blessed is your name, O Lord God, for the light of your glory has shone forth in all the world in your Son Jesus Christ. Come to us as we think about the mystery of your love . . . Glory be . . .

PSALMODY May he have dominion from sea to sea,
and from the River to the ends of the earth!
May the kings of Tarshish and of the isles
render him tribute,
may the kings of Sheba and Seba bring gifts!
May all kings fall down before him, all nations serve him!
All nations call him blessed! Psalm 72.8–17*

SCRIPTURE READINGS You can perceive my insight into the mystery of Christ, which was not made known to the sons of men in other generations as it has now been revealed to his holy apostles and prophets by the Spirit; that is, how the Gentiles are fellow heirs, members of the same body, and partakers of the promise in Christ Jesus through the Gospel.
Ephesians 3. 4–6

Wise men from the East came to Jerusalem, saying, 'Where is he who has been born king of the Jews? We have seen his star in the East, and have come to worship him.' When Herod the king heard this, he was troubled, and all Jerusalem with him; and assembling all the chief priests and scribes, he enquired where the Christ was to be born. They told him, 'In Bethlehem of Judea; for it is written by the prophet: "you, O Bethlehem, in the land of Judah, are by no means least among the rulers of Judah; for from you shall come a ruler who will govern my people Israel."' Herod summoned the wise men secretly and ascertained from them what time the star appeared; and he sent them to Bethlehem, saying, 'Go and search diligently for the child, and when you have found him bring me word, that I too may come and worship him.' When they had heard the king they went their way; and the star went before them, till it came to rest over the place where the child was. When they saw the star, they rejoiced exceedingly with great joy; and going into the house they saw the child with Mary his mother, and they fell down and worshipped him. Then, opening their treasures, they offered him gifts, gold and frankincense and myrrh. St Matthew 2.1–12*

RESPONSE 'From the rising of the sun to its setting,
my name is great among the nations, says the Lord.'

Heavenly Father, you revealed the glory of your Son to the nations – on this Feast of the Epiphany, we praise you for your redeeming love . . .
Your Son was revealed to the Wise Men – Lord, grant that the brightness of his glory may shine through our lives and be seen in the world . . .
The Wise Men offered costly gifts – accept our sacrifice of praise . . .

INTERCESSIONS *pages 390–393* CLOSING PRAYERS *page 402–403*

7 January *Fishers of Men*

OPENING PRAYER Eternal Father, you reveal your love for us in your Son. Help us by the Spirit to draw near with faith, and in your mercy, accept our prayers offered through Jesus Christ our Lord . . . Glory be . . .

PSALMODY Give ear to my words, O Lord;
give heed to my groaning.
Harken to the sound of my cry,
my King and my God, for to thee do I pray.
O Lord, in the morning thou dost hear my voice;
in the morning I prepare a sacrifice for thee, and watch.
For thou are not a God who delights in wickedness;
evil may not sojourn with thee. Psalm 5.1–4

SCRIPTURE READINGS King Nebuchadnezzar to all peoples, nations, and languages, that dwell in all the earth: Peace be multiplied to you! It seemed good to me to show the signs and wonders that the Most High God has wrought toward me. How great are his signs, how mighty his wonders! His kingdom is an everlasting kingdom, and his dominion is from generation to generation. Daniel 4.1–3

As Jesus walked by the Sea of Galilee, he saw two brothers, Simon who is called Peter and Andrew his brother, casting a net into the sea; for they were fishermen. And he said to them, 'Follow me, and I will make you fishers of men.' Immediately they left their nets and followed him. And going on from there he saw two other brothers, James the son of Zebedee and John his brother, in the boat with Zebedee their father, mending their nets, and he called them. Immediately they left the boat and their father and followed him. And he went about all Galilee, teaching in their synagogues and preaching the gospel of the Kingdom and healing every disease and every infirmity among the people. So his fame spread throughout all Syria, and they brought him all the sick, those afflicted with various diseases and pain, demoniacs, epileptics, and paralytics, and he healed them. Great crowds followed him. St Matthew 4. 18–25*

RESPONSE 'Saviour, may we hear thy call,
serve and love thee best of all.'

Eternal God, you sent your Son to preach the Good News of your Kingdom – we praise you for all who respond to your love in Jesus Christ . . .
'Follow me, and I will make you fishers of men' – equip your Church and give it courage to witness to the resurrection of your Son . . .
The bishops are the successors of the Apostles – Lord, bless the bishops and priests of the Church, and fill them with your Spirit . . .

INTERCESSIONS *pages 390–393* CLOSING PRAYERS *page 402–403*

OPENING PRAYER Eternal Father, you reveal your love for us in your Son. Help us by the Spirit to draw near with faith, and in your mercy, accept our prayers, offered through Jesus Christ our Lord . . . Glory be . . .

PSALMODY The boastful may not stand before thy eyes;
thou hatest all evildoers.
But I through the abundance of thy steadfast love
will enter thy house,
I will worship towards thy holy temple in the fear of thee.
But let all who take refuge in thee rejoice,
let them ever sing for joy;
and do thou defend them,
that those who love thy name may exult in thee.

Psalm 5.5–11*

SCRIPTURE READINGS Beloved, let us love one another; for love is of God, and he who loves is born of God and knows God. 1 John 4.7

Seeing the crowds, Jesus went up on the mountain, and when he sat down his disciples came to him, and he taught them, saying,
'Blessed are the poor in spirit, for theirs is the Kingdom of heaven.
Blessed are those who mourn, for they shall be comforted.
Blessed are the meek, for they shall inherit the earth.
Blessed are those who hunger and thirst for righteousness, for they shall be satisfied.
Blessed are the merciful, for they shall obtain mercy.
Blessed are the pure in heart, for they shall see God.
Blessed are the peacemakers, for they shall be called sons of God.
Blessed are those who are persecuted for righteousness' sake, for theirs is the Kingdom of heaven.
Blessed are you when men revile you and persecute you and utter all kinds of evil against you falsely on my account. Rejoice and be glad, for your reward is great in heaven, for so men persecuted the prophets who were before you.' St Matthew 5.1–12

RESPONSE 'Give me a pure and lowly heart,
a temple meet for thee.'

Blessed be God, Father, Son and Holy Spirit – Alleluia, Alleluia . . .
You are the source of all comfort and hope – Lord, we praise you . . .
You satisfy those who hunger for righteousness – Lord, we thank you . . .
You reward the meek and humble – Lord, we bless your holy name . . .
You are merciful to all who come to you – Lord, we worship you . . .
You are the source of all peace – Lord, we thank you for your love . . .

INTERCESSIONS *pages 390–393* CLOSING PRAYERS *page 402–403*

9 January *Let your Light be Seen*

OPENING PRAYER Eternal Father, you reveal your love for us in your Son. Help us by the Spirit to draw near with faith, and in your mercy, accept our prayers, offered through Jesus Christ our Lord . . . Glory be . . .

PSALMODY Be gracious to me, O Lord, for I am languishing;
O Lord, heal me, for my bones are troubled.
My soul also is sorely troubled.
But thou, O Lord – how long?
Turn, O Lord, save my life;
deliver me for the sake of thy steadfast love.
For in death there is no remembrance of thee;
in Sheol who can give thee praise?
The Lord has heard my supplication;
the Lord accepts my prayer. Psalm 6. 2–9*

SCRIPTURE READINGS No man has ever seen God; if we love one another, God abides in us and his love is perfected in us. 1 John 4. 12

Jesus said, 'You are the salt of the earth; but if salt has lost its taste, how shall its saltness be restored? It is no longer good for anything but to be thrown out and trodden under foot by men. You are the light of the world. A city set on a hill cannot be hid. Nor do men light a lamp and put it under a bushel, but on a stand, and it gives light to all in the house. Let your light so shine before men, that they may see your good works and give glory to your Father who is in heaven. Think not that I have come to abolish the law and the prophets; I have come not to abolish them but to fulfil them. For truly, I say to you, till heaven and earth pass away, not an iota, not a dot, will pass from the law until all is accomplished. Whoever then relaxes one of the least of these commandments and teaches men so, shall be called least in the kingdom of heaven; but he who does them and teaches them shall be called great in the kingdom of heaven. For I tell you, unless your righteousness exceeds that of the scribes and Pharisees, you will never enter the kingdom of heaven.' St Matthew 5.13–20

RESPONSE 'Lift high the Cross, the love of Christ proclaim,
till all the world adore his sacred name.

Eternal God, you reveal the light of your truth in your Son – we praise you for the presence and light of Christ in the Church today . . .
'You are the light of the world – Lord, enlighten our minds with the light of Christ and help us to reflect His light in our lives . . .
'I have not come to abolish the law and the prophets but to fulfil them' – we rejoice that all things will be gathered up in Christ . . .

INTERCESSIONS *pages 390–393* CLOSING PRAYERS *page 402–403*

OPENING PRAYER Eternal Father, you reveal your love for us in your Son. Help us by the Spirit to draw near with faith, and in your mercy, accept our prayers offered through Jesus Christ our Lord . . . Glory be . . .

PSALMODY O Lord my God, in thee do I take refuge;
save me from all my pursuers, and deliver me.
Arise, O Lord, in thy anger,
lift thyself up against the fury of my enemies;
Let the assembly of the peoples be gathered about thee;
and over it take thy seat on high.
O let the evil of the wicked come to an end,
but establish thou the righteous,
thou who triest the minds and hearts,
thou righteous God. Psalm 7.1–9*

SCRIPTURE READINGS To this day whenever Moses is read a veil lies over their minds; but when a man turns to the Lord the veil is removed. Now the Lord is the Spirit, and where the Spirit of the Lord is, there is freedom. And we all, with unveiled face, beholding the glory of the Lord, are being changed into his likeness from one degree of glory to another; for this comes from the Lord who is the Spirit. 2 Corinthians 3.15–18

'You have heard that it was said to the men of old, "You shall not kill; and whoever kills shall be liable to judgement." But I say to you that everyone who is angry with his brother shall be liable to judgement; whoever insults his brother shall be liable to the council, and whoever says, "You fool!" shall be liable to the hell of fire. So if you are offering your gift at the altar, and there remember that your brother has something against you, leave your gift there before the altar and go; first be reconciled to your brother, and then come and offer your gift. Make friends quickly with your accuser, while you are going with him to court, lest your accuser hands you over to the judge, and the judge to the guard, and you be put in prison; truly, I say to you, you will never get out till you have paid the last penny.'
St Matthew 5.21-26

RESPONSE 'Changed from glory into glory, till in heaven we take our place, till we cast our crowns before thee, lost in wonder, love and praise.'

Eternal Father, you change our values and standards through the teaching of your Son – we praise you for your gifts of forgiveness and love . . .
'Everyone who is angry with his brother shall be liable to the judgement' – Lord, help us to control our anger, and use our energy wisely . . .
'First, be reconciled to your brother' – help us to be reconciled to all whom we have offended, and to love others as you love us . . .

INTERCESSIONS *pages 390–393* CLOSING PRAYERS *page 402–403*

11 January *Divorce*

OPENING PRAYER Eternal Father, you reveal your love for us in your Son. Help us by the Spirit to draw near with faith, and in your mercy, accept our prayers offered through Jesus Christ our Lord . . . Glory be . . .

PSALMODY The Lord judges the peoples;
judge me, O Lord, according to my righteousness
and according to the integrity that is in me.
My shield is with God,
who saves the upright in heart.
God is a righteous judge,
and a God who has indignation every day.
Behold, the wicked man conceives evil,
and is pregnant with mischief, and brings forth lies.
His mischief returns upon his own head,
and on his own pate his violence descends.
I will give to the Lord,
the thanks due to his righteousness;
and I will sing praise to the name of the Lord,
the Most High. Psalm 7. 8–17*

SCRIPTURE READINGS When you make a vow to the Lord your God, you shall not be slack to pay it. Deuteronomy 23.21

'You have heard that it was said, "You shall not commit adultery." But I say to you that every one who looks at a woman lustfully has already committed adultery with her in his heart. If your right eye causes you to sin, pluck it out and throw it away; it is better that you lose one of your members than that your whole body be thrown into hell. And if your right hand causes you to sin, cut it off and throw it away; it is better that you lose one of your members than that your whole body go into hell. It was also said, "Whoever divorces his wife, let him give her a certificate of divorce." But I say to you that every one who divorces his wife, except on the ground of unchastity, makes her an adulteress; and whoever marries a divorced woman commits adultery.' St. Matthew 5.27–32

RESPONSE 'O for a heart to praise my God, a heart from sin set free;
a heart that's sprinkled with the Blood, so freely shed for me.'

Heavenly Father, you create us in your own image and our bodies are a dwelling place for your Holy Spirit – we praise you for your love . . .
'Let him that is without sin throw the first stone' – Lord, have mercy on us, and forgive us all our sins . . .
'Your grace alone is sufficient for us' – bring your healing into all our relationships, and fill us with your grace . . .

INTERCESSIONS *pages 390–393* CLOSING PRAYERS *page 402–403*

12 January *Love your Enemies*

OPENING PRAYER Eternal Father, you reveal your love for us in your Son. Help us by the Spirit to draw near with faith, and in your mercy, accept our prayers offered through Jesus Christ our Lord . . . Glory be . . .

PSALMODY O Lord, our Lord,
how majestic is thy name in all the earth!
Thou whose glory above the heavens is chanted
by the mouth of babes and infants.
When I look at thy heavens, the work of thy fingers,
the moon and the stars which thou hast established;
what is man that thou art mindful of him
and the son of man that thou dost care for him? Psalm 8.1–4

SCRIPTURE READINGS You shall not take vengeance or bear any grudge against the sons of your own people, but you shall love your neighbour as yourself. I am the Lord. Leviticus 19.21

'You have heard that it was said, "An eye for an eye and a tooth for a tooth." But I say to you, Do not resist one who is evil. But if anyone strikes you on the right cheek, turn to him the other also; and if anyone would sue you and take your coat, let him have your cloak as well; and if anyone forces you to go one mile, go with him two miles. Give to him who begs from you, and do not refuse him who would borrow from you. You have heard that it was said, "You shall love your neighbour and hate your enemy." But I say to you, Love your enemies and pray for those who persecute you, so that you may be sons of your Father who is in heaven, for he makes his sun rise on the evil and on the good, and sends rain on the just and on the unjust. For if you love those who love you, what reward have you? Do not even the tax collectors do the same? And if you salute only your brethren, what more are you doing than others? Do not even the Gentiles do the same? You, therefore, must be perfect, as your heavenly Father is perfect.' St Matthew 5.38–48

RESPONSE 'Mine is an unchanging love, higher than the heights above, deeper than the depths beneath, free and faithful, strong as death.'

Heavenly Father, you command us through your Son to love our enemies – we praise you for your perfect love in Christ . . .
'You must be perfect' – Lord, help us to respond to this challenge and to unite our wills with your perfect will . . .
Your Son forgave the soldiers who nailed him to the Cross – teach us to forgive those who hurt us, and give your blessing to them and to us . . .

INTERCESSIONS *pages 390–393* CLOSING PRAYERS *page 402–403*

OPENING PRAYER Eternal Father, you reveal your love for us in your Son. Help us by the Spirit to draw near with faith, and in your mercy, accept our prayers offered through Jesus Christ our Lord . . . Glory be . . .

PSALMODY What is man that thou art mindful of him,
and the son of man that thou dost care for him?
Yet thou hast made him little less than God,
and dost crown him with glory and honour.
Thou hast given him dominion over the works of thy hands.
O Lord, our Lord,
how majestic is thy name in all the earth. Psalm 8.4–9*

SCRIPTURE READINGS He said, 'The saints of the Most High shall receive the kingdom, and possess the kingdom for ever, for ever and ever.' Daniel 7.18

'When you pray, go into your room and shut the door and pray to your Father who is in secret; and your Father who sees in secret will reward you. In praying do not heep up empty phrases as the Gentiles do; for they think that they will be heard for their many words. Do not be like them, for your Father knows what you need before you ask him. Pray then like this:

Our Father who art in heaven;
Hallowed by thy name.
Thy Kingdom come,
Thy will be done, on earth as it is in heaven.
Give us this day our daily bread;
and forgive us our debts,
as we also have forgiven our debtors;
and lead us not into temptation,
but deliver us from evil.

For if you forgive men their trespasses, your heavenly Father also will forgive you; but if you do not forgive men their trespasses, neither will your Father forgive your trespasses.' St Matthew 6.6–15

RESPONSE 'Before thy throne we sinners bend;
grace, pardon, life to us extend.'

Gracious God, you release your power into the world through our prayers – we open our hearts to your glory and we praise you . . .
'Go into your room and shut the door and pray to your Father' – Lord, teach us how to pray, and help us to grow in holiness and love . . .
'They think that they will be heard for their many words' – help us to be still in your presence, and open to the leading of the Spirit . . .

INTERCESSIONS *pages 390–393* CLOSING PRAYERS *page 402–403*

14 January *Heavenly Riches*

OPENING PRAYER Eternal Father, you reveal your love for us in your Son. Help us by the Spirit to draw near with faith, and in your mercy, accept our prayers offered through Jesus Christ our Lord . . . Glory be . . .

PSALMODY I will give thanks to my Lord with my whole heart;
I will tell of all thy wonderful deeds.
I will be glad and exult in thee,
I will sing praise to thy name, O Most High.
For thou hast maintained my just cause;
thou hast sat on the throne giving righteous judgement.
Thou hast rebuked the nations,
thou hast destroyed the wicked.
But the Lord sits enthroned for ever,
he has established his throne for judgement;
and he judges the world with righteousness,
he judges the peoples with equity.
The Lord is a stronghold for the oppressed,
a stronghold in times of trouble.
Those who know thy name put their trust in thee.
Psalm 9.1–10*

SCRIPTURE READINGS 'Let not the rich man glory in his riches; but let him who glories glory in this, that he understands and knows me, that I am the Lord, who practise kindness, justice and righteousness on earth; for in these things I delight, says the Lord.' Jeremiah 9.23-24*

'Do not lay up for yourselves treasures on earth, where moth and rust consume and where thieves break in and steal, but lay up for yourselves treasures in heaven, where neither moth nor rust consumes and where thieves do not break in and steal. For where your treasure is, there will your heart be also. The eye is the lamp of the body. So, if your eye is sound, your whole body will be full of light; but if your eye is not sound, your whole body will be full of darkness. If the light in you is darkness, how great is the darkness! No one can serve two masters; for either he will hate the one and love the other, or he will be devoted to the one and despise the other. You cannot serve God and mammon.' St Matthew 6.19–24

RESPONSE 'Unto thee be glory given, holy, holy, holy Lord.'

Heavenly Father, in your Son you give us spiritual riches which money cannot buy – we praise you for your gift of faith to the Church . . .
'Where your treasure is, there will your heart be also' – Lord, help us to seek true happiness in promoting the justice of your Kingdom . . .
'No one can serve two masters' – inspire us to be wise stewards of all you have entrusted to us, and help us to seek your will in all things . . .

INTERCESSIONS *pages 390–393* CLOSING PRAYERS *page 402–403*

OPENING PRAYER Eternal Father, you reveal your love for us in your Son. Help us by the Spirit to draw near with faith, and in your mercy, accept our prayers offered through Jesus Christ our Lord . . . Glory be . . .

PSALMODY Why does the wicked man renounce God,
and say in his heart, 'Thou wilt not call to account?'
Thou dost see; Yea, thou dost note trouble and vexation,
that thou mayest take it into thy hands.
Break thou the arm of the wicked and evildoer;
seek out his wickedness until thou find none.
The Lord is king for ever and ever. Psalm 10.13–16*

SCRIPTURE READINGS The Spirit of God took possession of Zechariah, and he stood above the people and said, 'Thus says God, "Why do you transgress the commandments of the Lord, so that you cannot prosper? Because you have forsaken the Lord, the Lord has forsaken you."'
2 Chronicles 24.20

'Therefore I tell you, do not be anxious about your life, what you shall eat or what you shall drink, nor about your body, what you shall put on. Is not life more than food, and the body more than clothing? Look at the birds of the air: they neither sow nor reap nor gather into barns, and yet your heavenly Father feeds them. Are you not of more value than they? Which of you by being anxious can add one cubit to his span of life? And why are you anxious about clothing? Consider the lilies of the field, how they grow; they neither toil nor spin; yet I tell you, even Solomon in all his glory was not arrayed like one of these. If God so clothes the grass of the field, which today is alive and tomorrow is thrown into the oven, will he not much more clothe you, O men of little faith? Therefore do not be anxious, saying, "What shall we eat?" or "What shall we drink?" or "What shall we wear?" For the Gentiles seek all these things; and your heavenly Father knows that you need them all. Seek first his Kingdom and his righteousness, and all these things shall be yours as well. Therefore do not be anxious about tomorrow, for tomorrow will be anxious for itself. Let the day's own trouble be sufficient for the day. St Matthew 6.25–34

RESPONSE 'Who like thyself my guide and stay can be?
Through cloud and sunshine, O abide with me.'

Eternal Father, you give us peace and joy and hope in the promises of your Son – we rejoice that nothing can separate us from your love . . .
'O men of little faith' – Lord, purify our hearts, and help us to grow in faith and love . . .
'Seek first his Kingdom and his righteousness' – Lord, help us by your grace to put your will before our own desires . . .

INTERCESSIONS *pages 390–393* CLOSING PRAYERS *page 402–403*

16 January *Do Not Judge*

OPENING PRAYER Eternal Father, you reveal your love for us in your Son. Help us by the Spirit to draw near with faith, and in your mercy, accept our prayers offered through Jesus Christ our Lord . . . Glory be . . .

PSALMODY In the Lord I take my refuge;
how can you say to me,
'Flee like a bird to the mountains;
for lo, the wicked bend the bow,
they have fitted their arrow to the string,
to shoot in the dark at the upright in heart;
if the foundations are destroyed,
what can the righteous do'?
The Lord is in his holy temple,
the Lord's throne is in heaven.
His eyes behold, his eyelids test, the children of men.
The Lord tests the righteous and the wicked,
and his soul hates him that loves violence.
For the Lord is righteous, he loves righteous deeds;
the upright shall behold his face. Psalm 11.1–7*

SCRIPTURE READINGS The Lord is our judge, the Lord is our ruler, the Lord is our king; he will save us. Isaiah 33.22

'Judge not, that you be not judged. For with the judgement you pronounce you will be judged, and the measure you give will be the measure you get. Why do you see the speck that is in your brother's eye, but do not notice the log that is in your own eye? Or how can you say to your brother, "Let me take the speck out of your eye," when there is the log in your own eye? You hypocrite, first take the log out of your own eye, and then you will see clearly to take the speck out of your brother's eye. Do not give dogs what is holy; and do not throw your pearls before swine, lest they trample them under foot and turn to attack you.' St Matthew 7.1–6

RESPONSE 'Blessed is the man who walks not in the counsel of sinners;
but his delight is in the way of the Lord.'

All-powerful Father, you are generous with your forgiveness and love – we praise you for all your compassion and mercy and love . . .
'Judge not' – Lord, help us to see the good in all people, and help us to love the sinner and to hate the sin . . .
It is your will for all people to be saved – pour out your Spirit into the Church, and help us to share the Good News of your Kingdom . . .

INTERCESSIONS *pages 390–393* CLOSING PRAYERS *page 402–403*

OPENING PRAYER Eternal Father, you reveal your love for us in your Son. Help us by the Spirit to draw near with faith, and in your mercy, accept our prayers offered through Jesus Christ our Lord . . . Glory be . . .

PSALMODY Help, Lord; for there is no longer any that is godly;
for the faithful have vanished from among the sons of men.
Every one utters lies to his neighbour;
with flattering lips and a double heart they speak.
May the Lord cut off all flattering lips,
the tongue that makes great boasts,
those who say, 'With our tongue we will prevail,
our lips are with us; who is our master?'
The promises of the Lord are promises that are pure,
silver refined in a furnace on the ground,
purified seven times.
Do thou, O Lord, protect us,
guard us ever from this generation. Psalm 12.1–7

SCRIPTURE READINGS If any of you lacks wisdom, let him ask God who gives to all men generously and without reproaching, and it will be given him. But let him ask in faith, with no doubting. St James 1.5–6

'Ask, and it will be given you; seek, and you will find; knock, and it will be opened to you. For every one who asks receives, and he who seeks finds, and to him who knocks it will be opened. Or what man of you, if his son asks him for bread, will give him a stone? Or if he asks for a fish, will give him a serpent? If you then, who are evil, know how to give good gifts to your children, how much more will your Father who is in heaven give good things to those who ask him! So whatever you wish that men would do to you, do so to them; for this is the law and the prophets. Enter by the narrow gate; for the gate is wide and the way is easy, that leads to destruction, and those who enter by it are many. For the gate is narrow and the way is hard, that leads to life, and those who find it are few.'
St Matthew 7.7–14

RESPONSE 'Guard us, guide us, keep us, feed us,
for we have no help but thee.'

God our Father, you know our needs before we turn to you in prayer – we rejoice that you always hear our prayers and we praise you . . .
'Ask and it will be given to you' – Lord, teach us to ask those things which are agreeable to your holy will . . .
'Seek and you will find' – guide us on our journey through this earthly life, and in your mercy, bring us to your eternal Kingdom . . .

INTERCESSIONS *pages 390–393* CLOSING PRAYERS *page 402–403*

18 January *Good and Bad Fruit*

OPENING PRAYER Eternal Father, you reveal your love for us in your Son. Help us by the Spirit to draw near with faith, and in your mercy, accept our prayers offered through Jesus Christ our Lord . . . Glory be . . .

PSALMODY How long, O Lord? Wilt thou forget me for ever?
How long wilt thou hide thy face from me?
How long must I bear pain in my soul,
and have sorrow in my heart all the day?
How long shall my enemy be exalted over me?
Consider and answer me, O Lord my God;
Lighten my eyes, lest I sleep in the path of death.
But I have trusted in thy steadfast love;
my heart shall rejoice in thy salvation.
I will sing to the Lord,
because he has dealt bountifully with me. Psalm 13.1–6*

SCRIPTURE READINGS The Lord made a covenant with Abram, saying, 'To your descendants I give this land, from the river of Egypt to the great river, the river Euphrates. Genesis 15.18

'Beware of false prophets, who come to you in sheep's clothing but inwardly are ravenous wolves. You will know them by their fruits. Are grapes gathered from thorns, or figs from thistles? So, every sound tree bears good fruit, but the bad tree bears evil fruit. A sound tree cannot bear evil fruit, nor can a bad tree bear good fruit. Every tree that does not bear good fruit is cut down and thrown into the fire. Thus you will know them by their fruits. Not every one who says to me, "Lord, Lord," shall enter the Kingdom of heaven, but he who does the will of my Father who is in heaven. On that day many will say to me, "Lord, Lord, did we not prophesy in your name, and cast out demons in your name, and do many mighty works in your name?" And then will I declare to them, "I never knew you; depart from me, you evildoers."' St Matthew 7.15–23

RESPONSE 'The Church's one foundation is Jesus Christ, her Lord;
she is his new creation, by water and the Word.'

Eternal God, you are the source of all goodness and truth – we praise you for your faithful servants in every generation . . .
'A good tree brings forth good fruit' – help us to work and pray for the extension of your Kingdom in our hearts and in the world . . .
'Not every one who says to me, Lord, Lord, will enter the Kingdom of heaven' – Lord, assist us to unite our will with your divine will . . .
(*Unity Week*) 'There is one Lord, one faith, one baptism' – help us by the Spirit to heal the wounds that divide your Body the Church . . .

INTERCESSIONS *pages 390–393* CLOSING PRAYERS *page 402–403*

19 January *The House on the Rock*

OPENING PRAYER Eternal Father, you reveal your love for us in your Son. Help us by the Spirit to draw near with faith, and in your mercy, accept our prayers offered through Jesus Christ our Lord . . . Glory be . . .

PSALMODY The fool says in his heart, 'There is no God.'
They are corrupt, they do abominable deeds,
there is none that does good.
They have all gone astray, they are all alike corrupt;
There is none that does good, no, not one.
There they shall be in great terror,
for God is with the generation of the righteous.
O that deliverance for Israel would come out of Zion!
When the Lord restores the fortunes of his people,
Jacob shall rejoice, Israel shall be glad. Psalm 14.1–7*

SCRIPTURE READINGS Jehoiachin was eighteen years old when he became king. He did what was evil in the sight of the Lord. The servants of Nebuchadnezzar king of Babylon came up to Jerusalem, and beseiged the city. The king of Babylon took him prisoner and carried off all the treasures of the house of the Lord, and of the king's house. He carried away all Jerusalem, and all the princes and all the mighty men of valour; none remained, except the poorest in the land. 2 Kings 24.8–14

'Every one then who hears these words of mine and does them will be like a wise man who built his house upon the rock; and the rain fell, and the floods came, and the winds blew and beat upon that house, but it did not fall, because it had been founded on the rock. And every one who hears these words of mine and does not do them will be like a foolish man who built his house upon the sand; and the rain fell, and the floods came, and the winds blew and beat against that house, and it fell; and great was the fall of it.' And when Jesus finished these sayings, the crowds were astonished at his teaching, for he taught them as one who had authority, and not as their scribes. St Matthew 7.24–29

RESPONSE 'Serve the Lord with fear.
Blessed are all who take refuge in him.'

Eternal God, you built the Church on the firm foundation of your risen Son – we praise you for the faith of the Church through the ages . . .
The power of your living Word supports the church and gives it energy – Lord, help us to build our lives on the Gospel of Christ . . .
(*Unity Week*) Your Son prayed for the unity of the Church on the night before he died – we pray for that same unity in Christ . . .

INTERCESSIONS *pages 390–393* CLOSING PRAYERS *page 402–403*

20 January *Healing the Leper*

OPENING PRAYER Eternal Father, you reveal your love for us in your Son. Help us by the Spirit to draw near with faith, and in your mercy, accept our prayers offered through Jesus Christ our Lord . . . Glory be . . .

PSALMODY O Lord, who shall sojourn in thy tent?
Who shall dwell on thy holy hill?
He who walks blamelessly, and does what is right,
and speaks truth from his heart;
who does not slander with his tongue,
and does no evil to his friend,
nor takes up a reproach against his neighbour;
in whose eyes a reprobate is despised,
but who honours those who fear the Lord;
who swears to his own hurt and does not change;
who does not put out his money at interest,
and does not take a bribe against the innocent.
He who does these things shall never be moved. Psalm 15.1–6

SCRIPTURE READINGS 'Therefore say to the house of Israel, Thus says the Lord God: I will sprinkle clean water upon you, and you shall be clean from all your uncleanness. A new heart I will give you, and a new spirit I will put within you; and I will take out of your flesh the heart of stone and give you a heart of flesh. And I will put my spirit within you, and cause you to walk in my statutes and be careful to observe my ordinances. You shall dwell in the land which I gave to your fathers; and you shall be my people, and I will be your God.' Ezekiel 36.25–28*

A leper came and knelt before Jesus, saying, 'Lord, if you will, you can make me clean.' He stretched out his hand and touched him, saying, 'I will; be clean.' Immediately his leprosy was cleansed. Jesus said, 'See that you say nothing to any one; but go, show yourself to the priest, and offer the gift that Moses commanded for a proof to the people.' St Matthew 8.1–4

RESPONSE 'Before thy throne we sinners bend:
to us thy saving grace extend.'

Heavenly Father, your love is eternal – we praise you and glorify you for your love for us in your Son . . .
'Lord, if you will, you can make me clean' – Lord, cleanse us from our sins, and give us grace to overcome all temptation . . .
(*Unity Week*) Your Son died for the sins of the world – forgive our sins of disunity, and help us to grow in love for you and for each other . . .

INTERCESSIONS *pages 390–393* CLOSING PRAYERS *page 402–403*

21 January *The Centurion's Servant*

OPENING PRAYER Eternal Father, you reveal your love for us in your Son. Help us by the Spirit to draw near with faith, and in your mercy, accept our prayers offered through Jesus Christ our Lord . . . Glory be . . .

PSALMODY Preserve me, O God, for in thee I take refuge.
I say to the Lord, 'Thou art my Lord;
I have no good apart from thee.'
As for the saints in the land, they are the noble,
in whom is all my delight.
The Lord is my chosen portion and my cup;
thou holdest my lot.
the lines have fallen for me in pleasant places;
yea, I have a goodly heritage. Psalm 16.1–6*

SCRIPTURE READINGS From the rising of the sun to its setting my name is great among the nations, and in every place incense is offered to my name, and a pure offering; for my name is great among the nations, says the Lord of hosts. Malachi 1.11

As Jesus entered Capernaum, a centurion came forward to him, beseeching him and saying, 'Lord, my servant is lying paralysed at home, in terrible distress.' And he said to him, 'I will come and heal him.' But the centurion answered him, 'Lord, I am not worthy to have you come under my roof; but only say the word, and my servant will be healed. For I am a man under authority, with soldiers under me; and I say to one, "Go," and he goes, and to another, "Come," and he comes, and to my slave, "Do this," and he does it.' When Jesus heard him, he marvelled, and said to those who followed him, 'Truly, I say to you, not even in Israel have I found such faith. I tell you, many will come from east and west, and sit at table with Abraham, Isaac, and Jacob in the Kingdom of Heaven, while the sons of the kingdom will be thrown into the outer darkness; there men will weep and gnash their teeth.' And to the centurion Jesus said, 'Go; be it done for you as you have believed.' And the servant was healed at that very moment.
St Matthew 8.5–13

RESPONSE 'All hail the power of Jesu's name: let angels prostrate fall;
bring forth thy royal diadem to crown him Lord of all.'

Almighty God, your power and might are past our understanding – we praise you and bless you for your power and eternal love . . .
'Many will sit at table with Abraham, Isaac and Jacob in the Kingdom of Heaven' – we rejoice that your salvation is offered to all people . . .
(*Unity Week*) Your will is for the unity of all Christians – bless the work of all who seek the unity of your Church according to your will . . .

INTERCESSIONS *pages 390–393* CLOSING PRAYERS *page 402–403*

22 January *The Peace of God*

OPENING PRAYER Eternal Father, you reveal your love for us in your Son. Help us by the Spirit to draw near with faith, and in your mercy, accept our prayers offered through Jesus Christ our Lord . . . Glory be . . .

PSALMODY I bless the Lord who gives me counsel;
in the night also my heart instructs me.
I keep the Lord always before me;
because he is at my right hand, I shall not be moved.
Therefore my heart is glad, and my soul rejoices;
my body also dwells secure.
For thou dost not give me up to Sheol,
or let thy godly one see the Pit.
Thou dost show me the path of life;
in thy presence there is fullness of joy,
in thy right hand are pleasures for evermore. Psalm 16.7–11*

SCRIPTURE READINGS
Agree with God, and be at peace;
thereby good will come to you. Job 22.21

Who shall separate us from the love of Christ? Shall tribulation, or distress, or persecution, or famine, or nakedness, or peril, or sword? As it is written, 'For thy sake we are being killed all the day long; we are regarded as sheep to be slaughtered.' No, in all these things we are more than conquerors through him who loved us. Romans 8.35–37

And when he got into the boat, his disciples followed him. And behold, there arose a great storm on the sea, so that the boat was being swamped by the waves; but he was asleep. And they went and woke him, saying, 'Save, Lord; we are perishing.' And he said to them, 'Why are you afraid, O men of little faith?' Then he rose and rebuked the winds and the sea; and there was a great calm. And the men marvelled, saying, 'What sort of man is this, that even the winds and sea obey him?' St Matthew 8.23–27

RESPONSE 'Peace, perfect peace, our future all unknown?
Jesus we know, and he is on the throne.'

Almighty God, peace is the gift of your Son to the Church – we praise you for all your perfect gifts to us in Jesus Christ . . .
Your Son brought peace to the disciples in the storm – give us your peace in our hearts, and make us instruments of your peace in the world . . .
(*Unity Week*) 'All will be gathered up into Christ' – help us to resolve those problems which still divide your Church on earth . . .

INTERCESSIONS *pages 390–393* CLOSING PRAYERS *page 402–403*

23 January *The Gadarene Swine*

OPENING PRAYER Eternal Father, you reveal your love for us in your Son. Help us by the Spirit to draw near with faith, and in your mercy, accept our prayers offered through Jesus Christ our Lord . . . Glory be . . .

PSALMODY If thou triest my heart, if thou visitest me by night,
if thou testest me, thou wilt find no wickedness in me.
My steps have held fast to thy paths,
My feet have not slipped. Psalm 17.3–5*

SCRIPTURE READINGS In that day the branch of the Lord shall be beautiful and glorious, and the fruit of the land shall be the pride and glory of the survivors of Israel. He who is left in Zion and remains in Jerusalem will be called holy, everyone who has been recorded for life in Jerusalem, when the Lord shall have washed away the filth of the daughters of Zion and cleansed the bloodstains of Jerusalem from its midst by a spirit of judgement and by a spirit of burning. Then the Lord will create over the whole site of Mount Zion and over her assemblies a cloud by day, and smoke and the shining of a flaming fire by night; for over all the glory there will be a canopy and a pavilion. It will be for a shade by day from the heat, and for a refuge from the storm and rain. Isaiah 4.2–6*

When Jesus came to the country of the Gadarenes, two demoniacs met him, coming out of the tombs, so fierce that no one could pass that way. They cried out, 'What have you to do with us, O Son of God? Have you come here to torment us before the time?' Now a herd of many swine was feeding at some distance from them. The demons begged him, 'If you cast us out, send us away into the herd of swine.' He said, 'Go.' So they came out and went into the swine, and the whole herd rushed down the steep bank into the sea, and perished in the waters. The herdsmen fled, and going into the city they told everything, and what had happened to the demoniacs. All the city came out to meet Jesus; and when they saw him, they begged him to leave their neighbourhood. St Matthew 8.28–34

RESPONSE 'Let not fears your courage impede,
great your strength, if great your need.'

Almighty God, great is the mystery of your love – we offer our praise to you in union with the perfect offering of your Son . . .
'What have you to do with us, O Son of God?' – we rejoice that you create us and sustain us and redeem us, and we belong to you . . .
'They perished in the water' – Lord, we thank you for our death and resurrection to new life in Christ through the waters of Baptism . . .
(*Unity Week*) The Church belongs to God – Lord, draw all Christians to yourself, and help us by your grace to grow in unity and love . . .

INTERCESSIONS *pages 390–393* CLOSING PRAYERS *page 402–403*

OPENING PRAYER Eternal Father, you reveal your love for us in your Son. Help us by the Spirit to draw near with faith, and in your mercy, accept our prayers offered through Jesus Christ our Lord . . . Glory be . . .

PSALMODY I call upon thee, for thou wilt answer me, O God;
incline thy ear to me, hear my words.
Wonderously show thy steadfast love,
O Saviour of those who seek refuge
from their adversaries at thy right hand.
Keep me as the apple of the eye;
hide me in the shadow of thy wings,
from the wicked who despoil me,
my deadly enemies who surround me.
They close their hearts to pity;
with their mouths they speak arrogantly.
As for me, I shall behold thy face in righteousness;
when I awake, I shall be satisfied
with beholding thy form. Psalm 17.6–15*

SCRIPTURE READINGS The saying is sure and worthy of full acceptance, that Christ Jesus came into the world to save sinners. 1 Timothy 1.15

And getting into a boat he crossed over and came to his own city. Behold, they brought him a paralytic, lying on his bed; and when Jesus saw their faith he said to the paralytic, 'Take heart, my son; your sins are forgiven.' And behold, some of the scribes said to themselves, 'This man is blaspheming.' But Jesus, knowing their thoughts, said, 'Why do you think evil in your hearts? For which is easier, to say, "Your sins are forgiven," or to say, "rise and walk"? But that you may know that the Son of Man has authority on earth to forgive sins' – he then said to the paralytic – 'Rise, take up your bed and go home.' And he rose and went home. When the crowds saw it they were afraid, and they glorified God, who had given such authority to men. St Matthew 9.1–8

RESPONSE 'Before thy throne we sinners bend;
to us thy pardoning love extend.'

God of eternal glory, you are a loving and forgiving Father in heaven – we praise you for your forgiveness of our sins . . .
'Your sins are forgiven' – look with mercy on all who are paralysed by sin, and draw them to yourself through the ministry of your Church . . .
(*Unity Week*) You call us to the fellowship of all who trust in your Son – grant to your Church that unity which is according to your will . . .

INTERCESSIONS *pages 390–393* CLOSING PRAYERS *page 402–403*

25 January *The Conversion of Saint Paul*

OPENING PRAYER Eternal Father, you reveal your love for us in your Son. Help us by the Spirit to draw near with faith, and in your mercy, accept our prayers offered through Jesus Christ our Lord . . . Glory be . . .

PSALMODY May God be gracious to us and bless us
and make his face to shine upon us,
that thy way may be known upon earth,
thy saving power among all nations.
The earth has yielded its increase;
God, our God, has blessed us. Psalm 67.1–6*

SCRIPTURE READINGS You have heard of my former life in Judaism, how I persecuted the church of God violently and tried to destroy it; and I advanced in Judaism beyond many of my own age among my people, so extremely zealous was I for the traditions of my fathers. Galatians 1.13–14

Paul said, 'I am a Jew, born at Tarsus, but brought up in this city at the feet of Gamaliel, educated according to the strict manner of the law. I persecuted this Way to the death, binding and delivering to prison both men and women, as the high priest and the whole council of elders bear me witness. From them I received letters to the brethren, and I journeyed to Damascus to take those who were there and bring them in bonds to Jerusalem to be punished. As I drew near to Damascus, about noon a great light from heaven suddenly shone above me. I fell to the ground and heard a voice saying, 'Saul, Saul, why do you persecute me?' I answered, 'Who are you, Lord?' He said, 'I am Jesus of Nazareth whom you are persecuting.' Those who were with me saw the light but did not hear the voice. I said, 'What shall I do, Lord?' The Lord said, 'Rise, and go to Damascus, and there you will be told all that is appointed for you to do.'
Acts 22.3–10*

Jesus said, 'Go into all the world and preach the Gospel to the whole creation. He who believes and is baptized will be saved.' St Mark 16.15–16

RESPONSE 'I live by faith in the Son of God,
who loved me and gave himself for me.'

Almighty God, you inspired Saint Paul to proclaim the Gospel – we celebrate this Feast of his conversion with joy and praise . . .
You called Saul the persecutor to become Paul the Apostle – Lord, we thank you and praise you for this miracle of your grace . . .
Your Church first received the faith through the Apostles – we pray with Saint Paul for the mission of your Church throughout the world . . .
(*Unity Week*) You call us into the unity of the one Body of Christ – Lord, help all Christians to grow together into unity in Christ . . .

INTERCESSIONS *pages 390–393* CLOSING PRAYERS *page 402–403*

OPENING PRAYER Eternal Father, you reveal your love for us in your Son. Help us by the Spirit to draw near with faith, and in your mercy, accept our prayers offered through Jesus Christ our Lord . . . Glory be . . .

PSALMODY I call upon the Lord,
who is worthy to be praised,
and I am saved from my enemies.
The cords of death encompassed me,
the torrents of perdition assailed me;
in my distress I called upon the Lord;
to my God I cried for help.
From his temple he heard my voice. Psalm 18.3–6*

SCRIPTURE READINGS The grace of God has dawned on the world with healing for all mankind. Titus 2.11

Paul, an apostle of Christ Jesus by the will of God according to the promise of the life which is in Christ Jesus, to Timothy, my beloved child: Grace, mercy and peace from God the Father and Christ Jesus our Lord. I thank God whom I serve with a clear conscience, as did my fathers, when I remember you constantly in my prayers. As I remember your tears, I long night and day to see you, that I may be filled with joy. I am reminded of your sincere faith, a faith that dwelt first in your grandmother Lois and your mother Eunice and now, I am sure, dwells in you. Hence I remind you to rekindle the gift of God that is within you through the laying on of my hands; for God did not give us a spirit of timidity but a spirit of power and love and self-control. Do not be ashamed of testifying to our Lord, nor of me his prisoner, but share in suffering for the gospel in the power of God, who saved us and called us with a holy calling, not in virtue of our works but in virtue of his own purpose and the grace which he gave us in Christ Jesus ages ago, and now has manifested through the appearing of our Saviour Christ Jesus, who abolished death and brought life and immortality to light through the gospel. 2 Timothy 1.1–10

RESPONSE 'Now, in God's most holy place,
blest they stand before his face.'

Eternal God, you raised up Timothy and Titus to be the companions of Saint Paul – on this day we rejoice and praise you for their faith . . .
'Grace, mercy and peace from God the Father and Christ Jesus our Lord' – we thank you for all the blessings you give to us in your Son . . .
'Do not be ashamed of testifying to our Lord' – we pray with Titus and Timothy for the mission of your Church in the world . . .

INTERCESSIONS *pages 390–393* CLOSING PRAYERS *page 402–403*

27 January *Mercy not Sacrifice*

OPENING PRAYER Eternal Father, you reveal your love for us in your Son. Help us by the Spirit to draw near with faith, and in your mercy, accept our prayers offered through Jesus Christ our Lord . . . Glory be . . .

PSALMODY All his ordinances were before me,
and his statutes I did not put away from me.
I was blameless before him, and I kept myself from guilt.
Therefore the Lord has recompensed me
according to my righteousness,
according to the cleanness of my hands in his sight.
With the loyal thou dost show thyself loyal;
with the blameless man thou dost show thyself blameless.
With the pure thou dost show thyself pure;
and with the crooked thou dost show thyself perverse.
Psalm 18.22–26

SCRIPTURE READINGS
Happy is the man who finds wisdom,
and for the man who gets understanding,
for the gain from it is better than gain from silver
and its profit better than gold.
She is more precious than jewels,
and nothing you desire can compare with her.
Her ways are ways of pleasantness,
and all her paths are peace. Proverbs 3.13–17*

Jesus saw a man called Matthew sitting at the tax office; and he said to him, 'Follow me.' He rose and followed him. As he sat at table in the house, behold, many tax collectors and sinners came and sat down with Jesus and his disciples. When the Pharisees saw this, they said to his disciples, 'Why does your teacher eat with tax collectors and sinners?' When he heard it, he said, 'Those who are well have no need of a physician, but those who are sick. Go and learn what this means, "I desire mercy and not sacrifice". For I came not to call the righteous, but sinners.' St Matthew 9.9–13

RESPONSE 'I will be glad and exult in thee,
I will sing praise to thy name, O Most High.'

Heavenly Father, your son came to bring forgiveness and healing to all who repent of their sins – we praise you for your mercy and love . . .
You call each of us for a special task in your Church – help us to respond and fulfil your will in our lives . . .
'He rose and followed him' – Lord, help us by your grace to learn more about the nature of Christian discipleship . . .

INTERCESSIONS *pages 390–393* CLOSING PRAYERS *page 402–403*

OPENING PRAYER Eternal Father, you reveal your love for us in your Son. Help us by the Spirit to draw near with faith, and in your mercy, accept our prayers offered through Jesus Christ our Lord . . . Glory be . . .

PSALMODY Thou dost deliver a humble people;
but the haughty eyes thou dost bring down.
Yea, thou dost light my lamp;
the Lord my God lightens my darkness.
Yes, by thee I can crush a troop;
and by my God I can leap over a wall.
This God – his way is perfect;
the promise of the Lord proves true;
he is a shield
for all those who take refuge in him. Psalm 18.27–30

SCRIPTURE READINGS It will be said on that day, 'Lo, this is our God; we have waited for him, that he might save us. This is the Lord; we have waited for him; let us be glad and rejoice in his salvation.' Isaiah 25.9

A ruler came in and knelt before Jesus, saying, 'My daughter has just died; but come and lay your hand on her, and she will live.' Jesus rose and followed him, with his disciples. Behold, a woman who had suffered from a haemorrhage for twelve years came up behind him and touched the fringe of his garment; for she said to herself, 'If I only touch his garment, I shall be made well.' Jesus turned, and seeing her he said, 'Take heart, daughter; your faith has made you well.' Instantly the woman was made well. When Jesus came to the ruler's house, and saw the flute players, and the crowd making a tumult, he said, 'Depart; for the girl is not dead but sleeping.' They laughed at him. When the crowd had been put outside, he went in and took her by the hand, and the girl arose. The report of this went through all that district. St Matthew 9.18–26

RESPONSE 'Death is conquered, man is free,
Christ has won the victory.'

Eternal God, your goodness and love embraces all people – we give you thanks and praise always and everywhere, and we rejoice in your love . . .
'A ruler knelt before him' – Lord, we pray that all people will come to acknowledge Christ as Redeemer and King . . .
'Come and lay hands on her' – bless the sick and dying, and all involved in the ministry of the laying on of hands and anointing with oil . . .

INTERCESSIONS *pages 390–393* CLOSING PRAYERS *page 402–403*

OPENING PRAYER Eternal Father, you reveal your love for us in your Son. Help us by the Spirit to draw near with faith, and in your mercy, accept our prayers offered through Jesus Christ our Lord . . . Glory be . . .

PSALMODY For who is God, but the Lord?
And who is a rock, except our God? –
the God who girded me with strength,
and made my way safe.
He made my feet like hinds' feet,
and set me secure on the heights.
Thou hast given me the shield of thy salvation,
and thy right hand supported me,
and thy help made me great.
Thou didst give a wide place for my steps under me,
and my feet did not slip.
The Lord lives; and blessed be my rock,
and exalted be the God of my salvation,
who delivered me from my enemies;
yea, thou didst exalt me above my adversaries;
thou didst deliver me from men of violence.
For this I will extol thee, O Lord, among the nations,
and sing praises to thy name. Psalm 18.31–49*

SCRIPTURE READINGS
In that day the deaf shall hear the words of a book,
and out of their gloom and darkness
the eyes of the blind shall see. Isaiah 28.18

As Jesus passed on from there, two blind men followed him, crying aloud, 'Have mercy on us, Son of David.' When he entered the house, the blind men came to him; and Jesus said, 'Do you believe that I am able to do this?' They said, 'Yes, Lord.' Then he touched their eyes, saying, 'According to your faith be it done to you.' Their eyes were opened. And Jesus sternly charged them, 'See that no one knows it.' But they went away and spread his fame through all that district. St Matthew 9.27–31

RESPONSE 'Through the world, far and wide,
let there be light.'

Eternal God, our faith is a gift from yourself through your Son – you are greatly to be exalted and praised . . .
'Have mercy on us, Son of David' – illuminate our minds and free us from spiritual blindness . . .
'He touched their eyes' – Lord, give your special blessing to all who are blind, their families and those who care for them . . .

INTERCESSIONS *pages 390–393* CLOSING PRAYERS *page 402–403*

OPENING PRAYER Eternal Father, you reveal your love for us in your Son. Help us by the Spirit to draw near with faith, and in your mercy, accept our prayers offered through Jesus Christ our Lord . . . Glory be . . .

PSALMODY The heavens are telling the glory of God,
and the firmament proclaims his handiwork.
Day to day pours forth speech,
and night to night declares knowledge.
There is no speech, nor are there words;
their voice is not heard;
yet their voice goes out through all the earth,
and their words to the end of the world.
In them he has set a tent for the sun,
which comes forth like a bridgroom leaving his chamber,
and like a strong man runs its course with joy.
Its rising is from the end of the heavens,
and its circuit to the end of them;
and there is nothing hid from its heat. Psalm 19.1–6

SCRIPTURE READINGS Jesus said, 'Do you not say, "There are yet four months, then comes the harvest"? I tell you, lift up your eyes, and see how the fields are already white for harvest.' St John 4.35

As they were going away, behold, a dumb demoniac was brought to him. When the demon had been cast out, the dumb man spoke, and the crowds marvelled, saying, 'Never was anything like this seen in Israel.' But the Pharisees said, 'He casts out demons by the prince of demons.' Jesus went about all the cities and villages, teaching in their synagogues and preaching the gospel of the kingdom, and healing every disease and every infirmity. When he saw the crowds, he had compassion for them, because they were harassed and helpless, like sheep without a shepherd. He said, 'The harvest is plentiful, but the labourers are few; pray therefore the Lord of the harvest to send out labourers into his harvest.' St Matthew 9.32–38

RESPONSE 'Hear my prayer, O God,
give ear to the words of my mouth.'

Gracious Father, you guided the Apostles to ordain bishops and priests and deacons to serve you in your Church – we praise you for your faithful servants in every generation . . .
'Never was anything like this seen in Israel' – Lord, we rejoice that you gave your only Son to be the Redeemer of the world . . .
All Christians are commissioned by their baptism to share in the mission of your Son – Lord, help us all to be channels of your love . . .

INTERCESSIONS *pages 390–393* CLOSING PRAYERS *page 402–403*

31 January *The Mission of the Twelve*

OPENING PRAYER Eternal Father, you reveal your love for us in your Son. Help us by the Spirit to draw near with faith, and in your mercy, accept our prayers offered through Jesus Christ our Lord . . . Glory be . . .

PSALMODY The law of the Lord is perfect, reviving the soul;
the testimony of the Lord is sure, making wise the simple.
In keeping them there is great reward. Psalm 19.7–11*

SCRIPTURE READINGS
When Israel was a child, I loved him,
and out of Egypt I called my son.
It was I who taught Ephraim to walk,
I took them up in my arms;
I led them with cords of compassion.
How can I hand you over, O Israel!
I will not again destroy Ephraim
for I am God and not man,
the Holy One in your midst. Hosea 11.1–9

Jesus called to him his twelve disciples and gave them authority over unclean spirits, to cast them out, and to heal every disease and every infirmity. These twelve Jesus sent out, charging them, 'Go nowhere among the Gentiles, and enter no town of the Samaritans, but go rather to the lost sheep of the house of Israel. Preach as you go, saying, "The Kingdom of Heaven is at hand." Heal the sick, raise the dead, cleanse lepers, cast out demons. You received without paying, give without paying. Take no gold, nor silver, nor copper in your belts, no bag for your journey, nor two tunics, nor sandals, nor a staff; for the labourer deserves his food. Whatever town or village you enter, find out who is worthy in it, and stay with him until you depart. As you enter the house, salute it. And if the house is worthy, let your peace come upon it; but if it is not worthy, let your peace return to you. If any one will not receive you or listen to your words, shake off the dust from your feet as you leave that house or town. Truly, I say to you, it shall be more tolerable on the day of judgement for the land of Sodom or Gomorrah than for that town. St Matthew 10.1–15*

RESPONSE 'Be strong, and let your heart take courage;
yea, wait for the Lord.'

Eternal God, your will is for all people to be saved – we bless you and we praise you for the power of Christ's redeeming love on the Cross . . .
'These twelve Jesus sent out' – pour out your Spirit on the Church, and equip it to share in the mission of your Son in the world . . .
'Jesus called to him his twelve disciples and gave them authority' – bless and guide the Bishops and all who hold office in your church . . .

INTERCESSIONS *pages 390–393* CLOSING PRAYERS *page 402–403*

1 February *Coming Persecution*

OPENING PRAYER O Lord, open our lips that we may proclaim your praise and glory. Fill us with your Spirit, that we may worship your holy name . . . Glory be . . .

PSALMODY But who can discern his errors?
Clear thou me from hidden faults.
Keep back thy servant also from presumptuous sins;
let them not have dominion over me!
Let the words of my mouth
and the meditation of my heart
be acceptable in thy sight,
O Lord, my rock and my redeemer. Psalm 19.12–14*

SCRIPTURE READINGS Bless those who persecute you; bless and do not curse them. Romans 12.14

Jesus said, 'Behold, I send you out as sheep in the midst of wolves; so be wise as serpents and innocent as doves. Beware of men; for they will deliver you up to councils, and flog you in their synagogues, and you will be dragged before governors and kings for my sake, to bear testimony before them and the Gentiles. When they deliver you up, do not be anxious how you are to speak or what you are to say; for what you are to say will be given to you in that hour; for it is not you who speak, but the Spirit of your Father speaking through you. Brother will deliver up brother to death, and the father his child, and children will rise against parents and have them put to death; and you will be hated by all for my name's sake. But he who endures to the end will be saved. When they persecute you in one town, flee to the next; for truly, I say to you, you will not have gone through all the towns of Israel, before the Son of man comes. A disciple is not above his teacher, nor a servant above his master; it is enough for the disciple to be like his teacher, and the servant like his master. If they have called the master of the house Beelzebul, how much more will they malign those of his household.' St Matthew 10.16–25

RESPONSE 'May the Lord give strength to his people!
May the Lord bless his people with peace.'

God of love, your Son suffered pain and loneliness on the Cross for our salvation – we praise you for the new life of grace in Christ . . .
'I send you out as sheep in the midst of wolves' – protect your Church from temptation and evil, and keep it faithful to the Gospel . . .
'Be wise as serpents and innocent as doves' – Lord, help us to use the wisdom you give us for the benefit of your Church and your Kingdom . . .

INTERCESSIONS *pages 390–393* CLOSING PRAYERS *page 402–403*

2 February *The Presentation of Christ in the Temple (Candlemas)*

OPENING PRAYER O Lord, open our lips that we may proclaim your praise and glory. Fill us with your Spirit, that we may worship your holy name . . . Glory be . . .

PSALMODY Great is the Lord
and greatly to be praised in the city of our God!
Within her citadels God has shown himself a sure defence.
We have thought on thy steadfast love, O God,
in the midst of thy temple.
As thy name, O God,
so thy praise reaches to the ends of the earth. Psalm 48.1–10*

SCRIPTURE READINGS 'I send my messenger to prepare the way before me, and the Lord whom you seek will suddenly come to his temple.'
Malachai 3.1

I appeal to you therefore, brethren, by the mercies of God, to present your bodies as a living sacrifice, holy and acceptable to God. Romans 12.1

When the time came for their purification according to the law of Moses, they brought Jesus to Jerusalem to present him to the Lord. Now there was a man in Jerusalem, whose name was Simeon, and this man was righteous and devout, looking for the consolation of Israel, and the Holy Spirit was upon him. And inspired by the Spirit he came into the temple; and when the parents brought in the child Jesus, he took him up in his arms and blessed God and said, 'Lord, now lettest thou thy servant depart in peace, according to thy word; for mine eyes have seen thy salvation which thou hast prepared in the presence of all peoples, a light for revelation to the Gentiles, and for glory to thy people Israel.' And his father and his mother marvelled at what was said about him; and Simeon blessed them and said to Mary his mother, 'Behold, this child is set for the fall and rising of many in Israel, and for a sign that is spoken against, (and a sword will pierce through your own soul also), that thoughts out of many hearts may be revealed.' St Luke 2.22–35*

RESPONSE 'Blessed be the Lord, the God of Israel,
from everlasting to everlasting. Amen and Amen.'

Heavenly Father, on this day Mary and Joseph presented your Son to you in the Temple – we praise you for revealing Christ as the Light of the world . . .
Simeon was led by the Spirit to recognise the infant Jesus as your Messiah – may all people come to accept him as Redeemer and Lord . . .
Jesus is the light of the world and the glory of your people Israel – Lord, purify your Church so that the light of Christ may be seen by all . . .

INTERCESSIONS *pages 390–393* CLOSING PRAYERS *page 402–403*

3 February *Not Peace but a Sword*

OPENING PRAYER O Lord, open our lips that we may proclaim your praise and glory. Fill us with your Spirit, that we may worship your holy name . . . Glory be . . .

PSALMODY The Lord answer you in the day of trouble!
The name of the God of Jacob protect you!
May he send you help from the sanctuary,
and give you support from Zion!
May he remember all your offerings.
May he grant you your heart's desire,
and fulfil all your plans! Psalm 20.1–4

SCRIPTURE READINGS Be strong and of a good courage; be not frightened, neither be dismayed; for the Lord your God is with you wherever you go. Joshua 1.9

Jesus said, 'Do not fear those who kill the body but cannot kill the soul; rather fear him who can destroy both soul and body in hell. Are not two sparrows sold for a penny? Not one of them will fall to the ground without your Father's will. Even the hairs of your head are all numbered. Fear not, therefore; you are of more value than many sparrows. So every one who acknowledges me before men, I also will acknowledge before my Father who is in heaven; but whoever denies me before men, I also will deny before my Father who is in heaven. Do not think that I have come to bring peace on earth; I have not come to bring peace, but a sword. For I have come to set a man against his father, and a daughter against her mother, and a daughter-in-law against her mother-in-law; and a man's foes will be those of his own household. He who loves father or mother more than me is not worthy of me; and he who loves son or daughter more than me is not worthy of me; and he who does not take his cross and follow me is not worthy of me. He who finds his life will lose it, and he who loses his life for my sake will find it.' St Matthew 10.28–39

RESPONSE 'Thou art my rock and my fortress;
for thy name's sake lead me and guide me.'

Heavenly Father, you are the source of all peace and love – we praise you for your Son's gift of perfect peace to the Church . . .
'I have not come to bring peace but a sword' – Lord, strenghten the Church and give us courage to proclaim the Gospel message in the world . . .
'Everyone who acknowledges me before men, I also will acknowledge before my Father who is in heaven' – Lord, equip us to do your work . . .

INTERCESSIONS *pages 390–393* CLOSING PRAYERS *page 402–403*

4 February *Messengers from St John the Baptist*

OPENING PRAYER O Lord, open our lips that we may proclaim your praise and glory. Fill us with your Spirit, that we may worship your holy name . . . Glory be . . .

PSALMODY Now I know that the Lord will help his anointed;
he will answer him from his holy heaven.
Some boast of chariots, and some of horses;
but we boast of the name of the Lord our God.
They will collapse and fall;
but we shall rise and stand upright. Psalm 20.6–8*

SCRIPTURE READINGS
What will one answer the messengers of the nation?
'The Lord has founded Zion, and in her
the afflicted of his people find refuge.' Isaiah 14.32

When John heard in prison about the deeds of the Christ, he sent word by his disciples and said to him, 'Are you he who is to come, or shall we look for another?' Jesus answered, 'Go and tell John what you hear and see: the blind receive their sight and the lame walk, lepers are cleansed and the deaf hear, and the dead are raised up, and the poor have good news preached to them. Blessed is he who takes no offence at me.' As they went away, Jesus began to speak to the crowds concerning John: 'What did you go out into the wilderness to behold? A reed shaken by the wind? Why then did you go out? To see a man clothed in soft raiment? Behold, those who wear soft raiment are in kings' houses. Why then did you go out? To see a prophet? Yes, I tell you, and more than a prophet. This is he of whom it is written, "Behold, I send my messenger before thy face, who shall prepare thy way before thee." Truly, I say to you, among those born of women there has risen no one greater than John the Baptist; yet he who is least in the kingdom of heaven is greater than he. From the days of John the Baptist until now the kingdom of heaven has suffered violence, and men of violence take it by force. For all the prophets and the law prophesied until John; and if you are willing to accept it, he is Elijah who is to come. He who has ears to hear, let him hear.' St Matthew 11.2–15

RESPONSE 'O give thanks to the Lord, for he is good;
for his steadfast love endures for ever.'

God of eternal love, you called John the Baptist to announce the coming of your Son – we acclaim your glory and we rejoice in your love . . .
You made a long preparation in Israel for the coming of your Son – we praise you for your faithful servants in every generation . . .
'He who has ears to hear, let him hear' – Lord, open our hearts and minds to receive your living Word in the Scriptures . . .

INTERCESSIONS *pages 390–393* CLOSING PRAYERS *page 402–403*

5 February *My Yoke is Easy*

OPENING PRAYER O Lord, open our lips that we may proclaim your praise and glory. Fill us with your Spirit, that we may worship your holy name . . . Glory be . . .

PSALMODY In thy strength the king rejoices, O Lord;
and in thy help how greatly he exults!
He asked life of thee; thou gavest it to him,
length of days for ever and ever.
Be exalted, O Lord, in thy strength!
We will sing and praise thy power. Psalm 21.1–13*

SCRIPTURE READINGS Moses was keeping the flock of his father-in-law, Jethro, and he came to Horeb the mountain of God. The angel of the Lord appeared to him in a flame of fire out of the midst of a bush; and he looked, and lo, the bush was burning, yet it was not consumed. Moses said, 'I will turn aside and see this great sight, why the bush is not burnt.' When the Lord saw that he turned aside to see, God called to him out of the bush, 'Moses, Moses!' He said, 'Here am I.' Then he said, 'Do not come near; put off your shoes from your feet, for the place on which you are standing is holy ground.' And he said, 'I am the God of your father, the God of Abraham, the God of Isaac, and the God of Jacob.' And Moses hid his face, for he was afraid to look at God. Exodus 3.1–6*

Jesus began to upbraid the cities where most of his mighty works had been done, because they did not repent. At that time Jesus declared, 'I thank thee, Father, Lord of heaven and earth, that thou hast hidden these things from the wise and understanding and revealed them to babes; yea, Father, for such was thy gracious will. All things have been delivered to me by my Father; and no one knows the Son except the Father, and no one knows the Father except the Son and any one to whom the Son chooses to reveal him. Come to me, all who labour and are heavy laden, and I will give you rest. Take my yoke upon you, and learn from me; for I am gentle and lowly in heart, and you will find rest for your souls. For my yoke is easy, and my burden is light.' St Matthew 11.20–36*

RESPONSE 'Only he who bears the Cross
may hope to wear the glorious crown.'

Eternal Father, you sent your Son to reveal the mysteries of your Kingdom – we respond to your love with praise and thanksgiving . . .
'Come to me all who labour and are heavy laden' – renew our souls and bodies by the power of your Spirit, and give us your peace . . .
'You will find rest for your souls' – Lord, help us and guide us in all things, and absorb our souls in your eternal love . . .

INTERCESSIONS *pages 390–393* CLOSING PRAYERS *page 402–403*

OPENING PRAYER O Lord, open our lips that we may proclaim your praise and glory. Fill us with your Spirit, that we may worship your holy name . . . Glory be . . .

PSALMODY My God, my God, why hast thou forsaken me?
Why art thou so far from helping me?
O my God, I cry by day, but thou dost not answer;
and by night, but find no rest.
Yet thou art holy, enthroned on the praises of Israel.
In thee our fathers trusted;
they trusted, and thou didst deliver them.
To thee they cried, and were saved.
But I am a worm, and no man;
scorned by men, and despised by the people.
All who see me mock at me,
they make mouths at me, they wag their heads;
'He committed his cause to the Lord; let him deliver him.
let him rescue him, for he delights in him!' Psalm 22.1–8*

SCRIPTURE READINGS Man does not live by bread alone, but by everything that proceeds out of the mouth of the Lord. Deuteronomy 8.3*

Jesus went through the grainfields on the sabbath; his disciples were hungry, and they began to pluck ears of grain and to eat. When the Pharisees saw it, they said, 'Look, your disciples are doing what is not lawful to do on the sabbath.' He said, 'Have you not read what David did, when he was hungry, and those who were with him: how he entered the house of God and ate the bread of the Presence, which it was not lawful for him to eat nor for those who were with him, but only for the priests? Or have you not read in the law how on the sabbath the priests in the temple profane the sabbath, and are guiltless? I tell you, something greater than the temple is here. If you had known what this means, "I desire mercy, and not sacrifice," you would not have condemned the guiltless. For the Son of man is lord of the sabbath.' St Matthew 12.1–8

RESPONSE 'Satisfy us in the morning with thy steadfast love,
that we may rejoice and be glad all our days.'

Gracious God, you provide corn to feed our bodies and the Eucharist to nourish our souls – we praise you for your redeeming love in your Son . . .
'The Son of Man is Lord of the Sabbath' – Lord, help us also to acknowledge Jesus as Lord in our daily lives . . .
'He entered the house of God' – Lord, we praise you and thank you for all the blessings you give to us through your holy Church . . .

INTERCESSIONS *pages 390–393* CLOSING PRAYERS *page 402–403*

7 February *Jesus and the Prince of Demons*

OPENING PRAYER O Lord, open our lips that we may proclaim your praise and glory. Fill us with your Spirit, that we may worship your holy name . . . Glory be . . .

PSALMODY Thou art he who took me from the womb;
thou didst keep me safe upon my mother's breasts.
Upon thee was I cast from my birth,
and since my mother bore me thou hast been my God.
Be not far from me,
for trouble is near and there is none to help.
But thou, O Lord, be not far off!
O thou my help, hasten to my aid. Psalm 22.9–19*

SCRIPTURE READINGS

Woe to those who devise wickedness.
When the morning dawns, they perform it,
because it is in the power of their hand. Micah 2.1*

Many followed Jesus, and he healed them all, and ordered them not to make him known. This was to fulfil what was spoken by the prophet Isaiah: 'Behold, my servant whom I have chosen, my beloved with whom my soul is well pleased. I will put my Spirit upon him, and he shall proclaim justice to the Gentiles. He will not wrangle or cry aloud, nor will any one hear his voice in the streets; he will not break a bruised reed, or quench a smouldering wick, till he brings justice to victory; and in his name will the Gentiles hope.' Then a blind and dumb demoniac was brought to him, and he healed him, so that the dumb man spoke and saw. All the people were amazed, and said, 'Can this be the Son of David?' When the Pharisees heard it they said, 'It is only by Beelzebul, the prince of demons, that this man casts out demons.' Knowing their thoughts, he said, 'Every kingdom divided against itself is laid waste, and no city or house divided against itself will stand; and if Satan casts out Satan, he is divided against himself; how then will his kingdom stand? And if I cast out demons by Beelzebul, by whom do your sons cast them out? Therefore they shall be your judges. But if it is by the Spirit of God that I cast out demons, then the kingdom of God has come upon you. St Matthew 12.15–19

RESPONSE 'Hail him as thy matchless King through all eternity.'

Eternal God, your glory fills both heaven and earth – we praise you in union with the perfect praise of your Son . . .
Your Son entrusted his universal mission of salvation to the Church – strengthen the Church to fulfil your purposes in the world . . .
'Behold, my servant whom I have chosen, my beloved with whom my soul is well pleased' – all praise to Jesus Christ, our Prophet, Priest and King . . .

INTERCESSIONS *pages 390–393* CLOSING PRAYERS *page 402–403*

8 February *The Tree is Known by its Fruit*

OPENING PRAYER O Lord, open our lips that we may proclaim your praise and glory. Fill us with your Spirit, that we may worship your holy name . . . Glory be . . .

PSALMODY All the ends of the earth shall remember and turn to the Lord;
and all the families of the nations shall worship before him.
For dominion belongs to the Lord, and he rules over the nations.
Yea, to him shall all the proud of the earth bow down;
before him shall bow all who go down to the dust,
and he who cannot keep himself alive.
Posterity shall serve him;
men shall tell of the Lord to the coming generation,
and proclaim his deliverance to a people yet unborn,
that he has wrought it. Psalm 22.27–31

SCRIPTURE READINGS

The fruit of the righteous is a tree of life,
but lawlessness takes away lives. Proverbs 11.30

Jesus said, 'How can one enter a strong man's house and plunder his goods, unless he first binds the strong man? Then indeed he may plunder his house. He who is not with me is against me, and he who does not gather with me scatters. Therefore I tell you, every sin and blasphemy will be forgiven men, but the blasphemy against the Spirit will not be forgiven. And whoever says a word against the Son of man will be forgiven; but whoever speaks against the Holy Spirit will not be forgiven, either in this age or in the age to come. Either make the tree good, and its fruit good; or make the tree bad, and its fruit bad; for the tree is known by its fruit. You brood of vipers! how can you speak good, when you are evil? For out of the abundance of the heart the mouth speaks. The good man out of his good treasure beings forth good, and the evil man out of his evil treasure brings forth evil. I tell you, on the day of judgement men will render account for every careless word they utter; for by your words you will be justified, and by your words you will be condemned.' St Matthew 12.29–37

RESPONSE 'The steadfast love of the Lord is from everlasting to everlasting upon those who fear him.'

Almighty Father, you alone are the source of all good – we rejoice with confidence in your goodness and mercy, and we praise you . . .
'He who does not gather with me scatters' – Lord, equip your Church to share effectively in the mission of your Son in the world . . .
'The tree is known by its fruit' – Lord, purify our hearts, and help us to bring forth the fruit of good works day by day . . .

INTERCESSIONS *pages 390–393* CLOSING PRAYERS *page 402–403*

9 February *A Sign for Unbelievers*

OPENING PRAYER O Lord, open our lips that we may proclaim your praise and glory. Fill us with your Spirit, that we may worship your holy name . . . Glory be . . .

PSALMODY The Lord is my shepherd, I shall not want;
he makes me lie down in green pastures.
He leads me beside still waters; he restores my soul.
He leads me in paths of righteousness for his name's sake.
Even though I walk through the valley of the shadow of death,
I fear no evil; for thou art with me;
thy rod and thy staff, they comfort me.
Thou preparest a table before me in the presence of my enemies,
thou anointest my head with oil, my cup overflows.
Surely goodness and mercy shall follow me
all the days of my life;
and I shall dwell in the house of the Lord for ever. Psalm 23

SCRIPTURE READINGS
The Lord has a controversy with his people.
'O my people, what have I done to you?
For I brought you up from the land of Egypt,
and I sent before you Moses, that you may know
the saving acts of the Lord. Micah 6.2–5*

The scribes and Pharisees said to Jesus, 'Teacher, we wish to see a sign from you.' He answered, 'An evil and adulterous generation seeks for a sign; but no sign shall be given to it except the sign of the prophet Jonah. For as Jonah was three days and three nights in the belly of the whale, so will the Son of man be three days and three nights in the heart of the earth. The men of Nineveh will arise at the judgement with this generation and condemn it; for they repented at the preaching of Jonah, and behold, something greater than Jonah is here. The queen of the South will arise at the judgement with this generation and condemn it; for she came from the ends of the earth to hear the wisdom of Solomon, and behold, something greater than Solomon is here.' St Matthew 12.38–42

RESPONSE 'Inscribed upon the cross we see
in shining letters, "God is love."'

Blessed are you, Eternal God and Father, for revealing the mysteries of your Kingdom through your Son – all praise to your holy name . . .
The Church is a sign and sacrament of your presence in the world – strengthen the Church to witness to your saving love in the risen Christ . . .

INTERCESSIONS *pages 390–393* CLOSING PRAYERS *page 402–403*

OPENING PRAYER O Lord, open our lips that we may proclaim your praise and glory. Fill us with your Spirit, that we may worship your holy name . . . Glory be . . .

PSALMODY The earth is the Lord's and the fulness thereof,
the world and those who dwell therein.
Who shall ascend the hill of the Lord,
and who shall stand in his holy place?
He who has clean hands and a pure heart,
who does not lift up his soul to what is false,
and does not swear deceitfully.
He will receive blessing from the Lord,
and vindication from the God of his salvation.
Such is the generation of those who seek him,
who seek the face of the God of Jacob. Psalm 24.1–6*

SCRIPTURE READINGS

Who is a God like thee, pardoning iniquity,
and passing over transgression
for the remnant of his inheritance?
He does not retain his anger for ever
because he delights in steadfast love. Micah 7.18

Jesus said, 'When the unclean spirit has gone out of a man, he passes through waterless places seeking rest, but he finds none. Then he says, "I will return to my house from which I came." When he comes he finds it empty, swept, and put in order. Then he goes and brings with him seven other spirits more evil than himself, and they enter and dwell there; and the last state of that man becomes worse than the first. So shall it be also with this evil generation.' While he was still speaking, behold, his mother and his brothers stood outside, asking to speak to him. He replied, 'Who is my mother, and who are my brothers?' And stretching out his hand toward his disciples, he said, 'Here are my mother and my brothers! For whoever does the will of my Father in heaven is my brother, and sister, and mother.'
St Matthew 12.43–50

RESPONSE 'Teach me, my God and King, in all things thee to see;
and what I do in any thing to do it as for thee.'

Eternal Father, you create us in your own image and our bodies are temples for your Holy Spirit – we praise you for your goodness and love . . .
'Who is my mother?' – Lord, we praise you for the Blessed Virgin Mary, and for her obedience to your will . . .
'Whoever does the will of my Father in heaven is my brother, and sister, and mother' – assist us in seeking and doing your will in all things . . .

INTERCESSIONS *pages 390–393* CLOSING PRAYERS *page 402–403*

11 February *The Parable of the Sower*

OPENING PRAYER O Lord, open our lips that we may proclaim your praise and glory. Fill us with your Spirit, that we may worship your holy name . . . Glory be . . .

PSALMODY Lift up your heads, O gates!
and be lifted up, O ancient doors!
that the King of glory may come in.
Who is the King of glory?
The Lord, strong and mighty, the Lord, mighty in battle!
Lift up your heads, O gates!
and be lifted up, O ancient doors!
that the King of glory may come in.
Who is this King of glory?
The Lord of hosts, he is the King of glory! Psalm 24.7–10

SCRIPTURE READINGS

For as the rain and the snow come down from heaven
and return not thither but water the earth,
making it bring forth and sprout,
giving seed to the sower and bread to the eater,
so shall my word be that goes forth from my mouth;
it shall not return to me empty,
but it shall accomplish that which I purpose,
and prosper in the thing for which I sent it. Isaiah 55.10–11

Jesus got into a boat, and the crowd stood on the beach. He said. 'A sower went out to sow. As he sowed, some seeds fell along the path, and the birds came and devoured them. Other seeds fell on rocky ground, where they had not much soil and immediately they sprang up, since they had no depth of soil, but when the sun rose they were scorched; since they had no root they withered away. Other seeds fell upon thorns, and the thorns grew up and choked them. Other seeds fell on good soil and brought forth grain, some a hundredfold, some sixty, some thirty. He who has ears to hear, let him hear.' St Matthew 13.1–9*

RESPONSE 'O taste and see that the Lord is good!
Happy is the man who takes refuge in him.'

Almighty God, your Son is the Sower – we praise you for all who share his mission and work to extend your Kingdom in the world . . .
'My word shall not return to me empty' – help us to overcome all that prevents spiritual growth, and make us channels of your grace . . .
'A sower went out to sow' – Lord, assist with your Holy Spirit all who proclaim the Gospel message in the world . . .

INTERCESSIONS *pages 390–393* CLOSING PRAYERS *page 402–403*

OPENING PRAYER O Lord, open our lips that we may proclaim your praise and glory. Fill us with your Spirit, that we may worship your holy name . . . Glory be . . .

PSALMODY To thee, O Lord, I lift up my soul.
O my God, in thee I trust, let me not be put to shame.
Yea, let none that wait for thee be put to shame.
Psalm 25.1–3*

SCRIPTURE READINGS

I brought you into a plentiful land
to enjoy its fruits and its good things.
But when you came in you defiled my land,
and made my heritage an abomination. Jeremiah 2.7

The disciples said to Jesus, 'Why do you speak to them in parables?' He answered, 'To you it has been given to know the secrets of the kingdom of heaven, but to them it has not been given. For to him who has will more be given, and he will have abundance; but from him who has not, even what he has will be taken away. This is why I speak to them in parables, because seeing they do not see, and hearing they do not hear, nor do they understand. With them is fulfilled the prophesy of Isaiah, which says:

"You shall indeed hear but never understand,
and you shall indeed see but never perceive.
For this people's heart has grown dull,
and their ears are heavy of hearing,
and their eyes they have closed,
lest they should preceive with their eyes,
and hear with their ears,
and understand with their heart,
and turn for me to heal them."

Blessed are your eyes, for they see, and your ears, for they hear. Many prophets and righteous men longed to see what you see, and did not see it, and to hear what you hear, and did not hear it. St Matthew 13.10–17*

RESPONSE 'I will give thanks to thee, O Lord, among the peoples;
I will sing to thee among the nations.'

Heavenly Father, you revealed the secrets of your Kingdom in your Son Jesus Christ – we praise you for your timeless love . . .
'This people's hearts are grown dull' – Lord, help us to remove all things in our lives that separate us from your love . . .
'To him who has will more be given' – give us generous hearts, and inspire us to share with others the riches of your grace . . .

INTERCESSIONS *pages 390–393* CLOSING PRAYERS *page 402–403*

13 February *Jesus Explains about the Sower*

OPENING PRAYER O Lord, open our lips that we may proclaim your praise and glory. Fill us with your Spirit, that we may worship your holy name . . . Glory be . . .

PSALMODY Lead me in thy truth, and teach me,
for thou art the God of my salvation;
for thee I wait all the day long.
Be mindful of thy mercy, O Lord, and of thy steadfast love.
Remember not the sins of my youth, or my transgressions;
according to thy steadfast love remember me,
for thy goodness' sake, O Lord!
Good and upright is the Lord;
therefore he instructs sinners in the way.
He leads the humble in what is right,
and teaches the humble his way.
All the paths of the Lord are steadfast love and faithfulness,
for those who keep his covenant and his testimonies.

Psalm 25.5–10

SCRIPTURE READINGS Jerusalem shall be called the throne of the Lord, and all nations shall gather to it, to the presence of the Lord, and they shall no more stubbornly follow their own evil heart. Jeremiah 2.17*

Jesus said, 'Hear the parable of the sower. When any one hears the word of the kingdom and does not understand it, the evil one comes and snatches away what is sown in his heart; this is what was sown along the path. As for what was sown on rocky ground, this is he who hears the word and immediately receives it with joy; yet he has no root in himself, but endures for a while, and when tribulation or persecution arises on account of the word, immediately he falls away. As for what was sown among thorns, this is he who hears the word, but the cares of the world and the delight in riches choke the word, and it proves unfruitful. As for what was sown on good soil, this is he who hears the word and understands it; he indeed bears fruit, and yields, in one case a hundredfold, in another sixty, and in another thirty.' St Matthew 13.18–23

RESPONSE 'Bless the Lord, O peoples,
let the sound of his praise be heard.'

Eternal God, you sow the seed of eternal life in our hearts – bring our souls into union with yourself, and accept our praise and love . . .
'Some seed fell along the path' – strengthen all who have recently been baptized and confirmed, and help them to grow in the faith . . .
'Some seed fell on rocky ground' – Lord, turn all hard hearted people to Christ, through the prayers and mission of your Church . . .

INTERCESSIONS *pages 390–393* CLOSING PRAYERS *page 402–403*

14 February *The Weeds and the Wheat*

OPENING PRAYER O Lord, open our lips that we may proclaim your praise and glory. Fill us with your Spirit, that we may worship your holy name . . . Glory be . . .

PSALMODY For thy name's sake, O Lord, pardon my guilt, for it is great.
Who is the man that fears the Lord?
Him will he instruct in the way that he should choose.
He himself shall abide in prosperity,
and his children shall possess the land.
The friendship of the Lord is for those who fear him,
and he makes known to them his covenant. Psalm 25.11–14

SCRIPTURE READINGS

How the faithful city has become a harlot,
she that was full of justice!
Righteousness lodged in her, but now murderers.
Your silver has become dross,
your wine mixed with water.
Your princes are rebels and companions of thieves.
Therefore the Lord says, the Lord of hosts:
'Ah, I will vent my wrath on my enemies,
and avenge myself on my foes.' Isaiah 1.21–24*

Another parable he put before them, saying, 'The Kingdom of Heaven may be compared to a man who sowed good seed in his field; but while men were sleeping his enemy came and sowed weeds among the wheat and went away. When the plants came up and bore grain, then the weeds appeared also. The servants of the householder came and said, "Sir, did you not sow good seed in your field? How then has it weeds?" He said, "An enemy has done this." The servants said, "Then do you want us to go and gather them?" He said, "No; lest in gathering the weeds you root up the wheat along with them. Let both grow together until the harvest; and at harvest time I will tell the reapers, Gather the weeds first and bind them in bundles to be burned, but gather the wheat into my barn."'

St Matthew 13.24–30

RESPONSE 'May those who love thy salvation
say evermore, "God is great."'

Eternal God, you create all things visible and invisible – we join our prayers with the continuous praise of all creation to glorify your name . . .
'Let both grow together until harvest' – Lord, strengthen all that is good in your Church, and guard it from evil and temptation . . .
'Gather my wheat into my barn' – in your mercy, gather your whole Church into your Kingdom with the Blessed Virgin Mary, the patriarchs, prophets, apostles, saints and martyrs, and all the company of heaven . . .

INTERCESSIONS *pages 390–393* CLOSING PRAYERS *page 402–403*

OPENING PRAYER O Lord, open our lips that we may proclaim your praise and glory. Fill us with your Spirit, that we may worship your holy name . . . Glory be . . .

PSALMODY Turn thou to me, and be gracious to me;
for I am lonely and afflicted.
Relieve the troubles of my heart. Psalm 25.16–17*

SCRIPTURE READINGS He who searches the hearts of men knows what is the mind of the Spirit, because the Spirit intercedes for the saints according to the will of God. Romans 8.27

Another parable Jesus put before them, saying, 'The kingdom of heaven is like a grain of mustard seed which a man took and sowed in his field; it is the smallest of all seeds, but when it has grown it is the greatest of shrubs and becomes a tree, so that the birds of the air come and make nests in its branches.' He told them another parable. 'The kingdom of heaven is like leaven which a woman took and hid in three measures of flour, till it was all leavened.' All this Jesus said to the crowds in parables; indeed he said nothing to them without a parable. This was to fulfil what was spoken by the prophet: 'I will open my mouth in parables, I will utter what has been hidden since the foundation of the world.' Then he left the crowds and went into the house. His disciples came to him, saying, 'Explain to us the parable of the weeds of the field.' He answered, 'He who sows the good seed is the Son of man; the field is the world, and the good seed means the sons of the kingdom; the weeds are the sons of the evil one, and the enemy who sowed them is the devil; the harvest is the close of the age, and the reapers are angels. Just as the weeds are gathered and burned with fire, so will it be at the close of the age. The Son of man will send his angels, and they will gather out of his kingdom all causes of sin and all evildoers, and throw them into the furnace of fire; there men will weep and gnash their teeth. Then the righteous will shine like the sun in the kingdom of their Father. He who has ears to hear, let him hear.' Matthew 13.31–43

RESPONSE 'Thou art my help and my deliverer;
O Lord, do not tarry.'

Eternal God, you established your Kingdom through your Son – we praise you for revealing the mystery of your perfect love . . .
The Kingdom is eternal and its glory will be seen at the end of time – we pray for the extension of your Kingdom in the Church and in the world . . .
'The Kingdom is like leaven' – Lord, we pray for all who are working to spread your justice and truth and love in the world . . .

INTERCESSIONS *pages 390–393* CLOSING PRAYERS *page 402–403*

16 February *Parables of the Kingdom*

OPENING PRAYER O Lord, open our lips that we may proclaim your praise and glory. Fill us with your Spirit, that we may worship your holy name . . . Glory be . . .

PSALMODY Oh guard my life, and deliver me;
let me not be put to shame, for I take refuge in thee.
Redeem Israel, O God, out of all his troubles.

Psalm 25.20–22*

SCRIPTURE READINGS The Lord appeared to Solomon in a dream by night; and God said, 'Ask what I shall give you.' Solomon said, 'Give thy servant an understanding mind to govern thy people, that I may discern between good and evil.' 1 Kings 3.5–9*

Jesus said, 'The kingdom of heaven is like treasure hidden in a field, which a man found and covered up; then in his joy he goes and sells all that he has and buys that field. Again, the kingdom of heaven is like a merchant in search of fine pearls, who, on finding one pearl of great value, went and sold all that he had and bought it. Again, the kingdom of heaven is like a net which was thrown into the sea and gathered fish of every kind; when it was full, men drew it ashore and sat down and sorted the good into vessels but threw away the bad. So it will be at the close of the age. The angels will come out and separate the evil from the righteous, and throw them into the furnace of fire; there men will weep and gnash their teeth. Have you understood all this?' They said, 'Yes.' When Jesus had finished these parables, he went away from there, and coming to his own country he taught in their synagogue, so that they were astonished, and said, 'Where did this man get this wisdom and these mighty works? Is not this the carpenter's son? Is not his mother called Mary? Are not his brothers James and Joseph and Simon and Judas? Are not all his sisters with us? Where then did this man get all this?' They took offence at him. Jesus said, 'A prophet is not without honour except in his own country and in his own house.' He did not do many mighty works there, because of their unbelief.

St Matthew 13.44–58*

RESPONSE 'I will praise the name of God with a song;
I will magnify him with thanksgiving.'

Eternal God, your Son taught us to pray for the coming of your Kingdom – we praise you for setting this great hope before us . . .
Your Kingdom is hidden from sight – Lord, we pray for an increase of your gift of faith in the Church . . .
Your Kingdom contains spiritual treasures – Lord, we praise you for the riches of your grace in Jesus Christ our Lord . . .

INTERCESSIONS *pages 390–393* CLOSING PRAYERS *page 402–403*

OPENING PRAYER O Lord, open our lips that we may proclaim your praise and glory. Fill us with your Spirit, that we may worship your holy name . . . Glory be . . .

PSALMODY Vindicate me, O Lord, for I have walked in my integrity,
and I have trusted in the Lord without wavering.
Sweep me not away with sinners,
nor my life with bloodthirsty men. Psalm 26.1–12*

SCRIPTURE READINGS The priests and prophets said, 'This man deserves the sentence of death, because he has prophesied against this city.' Then Jeremiah said, 'The Lord sent me to prophesy against this city. Amend your ways, and obey the voice of the Lord your God, and the Lord will repent of the evil which he has pronounced against you. But as for me, I am in your hands. Do with me as seems good and right to you. Only know for certain that if you put me to death, you will bring innocent blood upon yourselves and upon this city.' The princes said, 'This man does not deserve the sentence of death; for he has spoken to us in the name of the Lord our God.' The hand of Ahaikam was with Jeremiah so that he was not given over to be put to death. Jeremiah 26.11–24*

Herod the tetrarch heard about the fame of Jesus; and he said, 'This is John the Baptist, he has been raised from the dead; that is why these powers are at work in him.' For Herod had seized John and put him in prison, for the sake of Herodias, his brother Philip's wife; because John said, 'It is not lawful for you to have her.' Though he wanted to put him to death, he feared the people, because they held him to be a prophet. When Herod's birthday came, the daughter of Herodias danced before the company, and pleased Herod, so that he promised with an oath to give her whatever she might ask. Prompted by her mother, she said, 'Give me the head of John the Baptist here on a platter.' The king was sorry; but because of his oaths and his guests he commanded it to be given; he sent and had John beheaded, and his head was brought on a platter and given to the girl, and she brought it to her mother. St Matthew 14.1–12*

RESPONSE 'My flesh and my heart may fail,
but God is the strength of my heart and my portion for ever.'

Loving Father, your Son died slowly and painfully at Calvary for our salvation – we praise you for the love of Jesus on the Cross . . .
Your servant John the Baptist died suddenly at the request of a wicked woman – preserve us from sudden death and dying unprepared . . .
John died for the truth – give us courage and wisdom, and have mercy on us and on all prisoners, now and at the hour of our death . . .

INTERCESSIONS *pages 390–393* CLOSING PRAYERS *page 402–403*

18 February *Five Loaves and Fishes*

OPENING PRAYER O Lord, open our lips that we may proclaim your praise and glory. Fill us with your Spirit, that we may worship your holy name . . . Glory be . . .

PSALMODY I do not sit with false men,
I hate the company of evildoers,
and I will not sit with the wicked.
I wash my hands in innocence,
and go about thy altar, O Lord,
singing aloud a song of thanksgiving,
and telling all thy wondrous deeds.
O Lord, I love the habitation of thy house,
and the place where thy glory dwells.
My foot stands on level ground;
in the great congregation I will bless the Lord.

Psalm 26.4–12*

SCRIPTURE READINGS

'Ho, every one who thirsts, come to the waters.
And he who has no money, come, buy and eat!
Hearken diligently to me, and eat what is good.
Incline your ear, and come to me;
hear, that your soul may live;
and I will make you an everlasting covenant,
my steadfast, sure love for David.' Isaiah 55.1–3*

Jesus had compassion on the multitude, and healed their sick. The disciples said, 'This is a lonely place, and the day is now over; send the crowds away to go into the villages and buy food for themselves.' Jesus said, 'They need not go away; you give them something to eat.' They said, 'We have only five loaves here and two fish.' He said, 'Bring them here to me.' He ordered the crowds to sit down on the grass; and taking the five loaves and the two fish he looked up to heaven, and blessed, and broke and gave the loaves to the disciples, and the disciples gave them to the crowds. They all ate and were satisfied. They took up twelve baskets full of the broken pieces left over. Those who ate were about five thousand men, besides women and children. St Matthew 14.31–21*

RESPONSE 'My mouth will tell of thy righteous acts,
of thy deeds of salvation all the day.'

Eternal Father, you are the creator and giver of every good and perfect gift – with thanksgiving, we sing praises to your holy name . . .
Jesus fed the crowds in Galilee – Lord, we thank you for feeding us with the Eucharist and with your living Word in the Scriptures . . .
'They all ate and were satisfied' – Lord, fill us with your grace . . .

INTERCESSIONS *pages 390–393* CLOSING PRAYERS *page 402–403*

19 February *Walking by Faith*

OPENING PRAYER O Lord, open our lips that we may proclaim your praise and glory. Fill us with your Spirit, that we may worship your holy name . . . Glory be . . .

PSALMODY The Lord is my light and my salvation; whom shall I fear?
When evildoers assail me, uttering slanders against me,
my adversaries and foes, they shall stumble and fall.
Though war arise against me, yet I will be confident.

Psalm 27.1–3

SCRIPTURE READINGS Elijah came to a cave and lodged there; and the word of the Lord came to him, and said, 'Go forth, and stand upon the mount before the Lord.' Behold, the Lord passed by, and a great and strong wind rent the mountains, and broke in pieces the rocks before the Lord, but the Lord was not in the wind; and after the wind an earthquake, but the Lord was not in the earthquake; and after the earthquake a fire, but the Lord was not in the fire; and after the fire a still small voice. When Elijah heard it, he wrapped his face in his mantle and went out and stood at the entrance of the cave. 1 Kings 19.9–12

Jesus made the disciples get into the boat and go to the other side. After he had dismissed the crowds, he went up on the mountain by himself to pray. When evening came, he was there alone, but the boat by this time was many furlongs distant from the land, beaten by the waves; for the wind was against them. And in the fourth watch of the night he came to them, walking on the sea. When the disciples saw him walking on the sea, they were terrified, saying, 'It is a ghost!' They cried out for fear. Immediately he spoke, saying, 'Take heart, it is I; have no fear.' Peter answered, 'Lord, if it is you, bid me come to you on the water.' He said, 'Come.' So Peter got out of the boat and walked on the water and came to Jesus; but when he saw the wind, he was afraid, and beginning to sink he cried out, 'Lord, save me.' Jesus immediately reached out his hand and caught him, saying, 'O man of little faith, why did you doubt?' When they got into the boat, the wind ceased. Those in the boat worshipped him, saying, 'Truly you are the Son of God.' St Matthew 14.22–33

RESPONSE 'Thy steadfast love is before my eyes,
and I walk in faithfulness to thee.'

Almighty God, you create the galaxies of space and the depths of the oceans – we praise you for the greatness of your power and love . . .
'Take heart, it is I. Have no fear' – Lord, give us the blessing of knowing your presence with us, and fill us with your love . . .
'Truly, you are the Son of God' – Lord, we call on your name with faith, and we worship and adore you with all your saints in heaven . . .

INTERCESSIONS *pages 390–393* CLOSING PRAYERS *page 402–403*

20 February *The Canaanite Woman*

OPENING PRAYER O Lord, open our lips that we may proclaim your praise and glory. Fill us with your Spirit, that we may worship your holy name . . . Glory be . . .

PSALMODY One thing have I asked of the Lord, that will I seek after;
that I may dwell in the house of the Lord
all the days of my life,
to behold the beauty of the Lord, and to inquire in his temple.
For he will hide me in his shelter in the day of trouble;
he will conceal me under the cover of his tent. Psalm 27.4–5*

SCRIPTURE READINGS
'Keep justice, and do righteousness,
for soon my salvation will come,
and my deliverance be revealed.
and the foreigners who join themselves to the Lord,
to minister to him, to love the name of the Lord,
and to be his servants,
every one who keeps the sabbath,
and does not profane it,
and holds fast my covenant –
these will I bring to my holy mountain,
and make them joyful in my house of prayer;
for my house shall be called
a house of prayer for all peoples. Isaiah 56.1–7*

A Canaanite woman from that region came out and cried, 'Have mercy on me, O Lord, Son of David; my daughter is severely possessed by a demon.' But he did not answer her a word. His disciples came and begged him, saying, 'Send her away, for she is crying after us.' He answered, 'I was sent only to the lost sheep of the house of Israel.' But she came and knelt before him, saying, 'Lord, help me.' He answered, 'It is not fair to take the children's bread and throw it to the dogs.' She said, 'Yes, Lord, yet even the dogs eat the crumbs that fall from their masters' table.' Jesus answered, 'O woman, great is your faith! Be it done for you as you desire.' Her daughter was healed instantly. St Matthew 15. 22–28

RESPONSE 'Shine upon us, Saviour, shine, fill thy Church with light divine,
and thy saving health extend unto earth's remotest end.'

Heavenly Father, your Son removed the barrier which separated Jew from Gentile – we praise you for the new covenant made by your Son . . .
'Have mercy on me, O Lord, Son of David' – it is through your mercy and grace that we come to you, and we thank you for your love . . .
'Lord, help me' – you create us and sustain us, and without you we are nothing. We praise you for your goodness and love to all people . . .

INTERCESSIONS *pages 390–393* CLOSING PRAYERS *page 402–403*

21 February *The Sign of Jonah*

OPENING PRAYER O Lord, open our lips that we may proclaim your praise and glory. Fill us with your Spirit, that we may worship your holy name . . . Glory be . . .

PSALMODY Thou hast said, 'Seek ye my face.'
My heart says to thee, 'Thy face, Lord, do I seek.
Hide not thy face from me.' Psalm 27.9

SCRIPTURE READINGS The Preacher said, 'I have seen this example of wisdom under the sun, and it seemed great to me. There was a little city with few men in it; and a great king came against it and beseiged it, building great seigeworks against it. But there was found in it a poor wise man, and he by his wisdom delivered the city. Yet no one remembered that poor man. Wisdom is better than might, though the poor man's wisdom is despised, and his words are not heeded.' Ecclesiastes 9.12–16

The Pharisees and Sadducees came, and to test Jesus they asked him to show them a sign from heaven. He answered, 'When it is evening, you say, "It will be fair weather; for the sky is red." In the morning, "It will be stormy today, for the sky is red and threatening." You know how to interpret the appearance of the sky, but you cannot interpret the signs of the times. An evil and adulterous generation seeks for a sign, but no sign will be given to it except the sign of Jonah.' So he left them and departed. When the disciples reached the other side, they had forgotten to bring any bread. Jesus said, 'Take heed and beware of the leaven of the Pharisees and Sadducees.' They discussed it, saying, 'We brought no bread.' Jesus said, 'O men of little faith, why do you discuss the fact that you have no bread? Do you not yet perceive? Do you not remember the five loaves of the five thousand, and how many baskets you gathered? Or the seven loaves of the four thousand, and how many baskets you gathered? How is it that you fail to perceive that I did not speak about bread? Beware of the leaven of the Pharisees and Sadducees.' Then they understood that he did not tell them to beware of the leaven of bread, but of the teaching of the Pharisees and Sadducees. St Matthew 16.1–12*

RESPONSE 'O loving wisdom of our God! When all was sin and shame,
a second Adam to the fight and to the rescue came.'

Gracious God and Father, your Son is present with us in the Spirit – we praise you for making us a new creation in Christ . . .
Your Son created the Church to proclaim the Gospel – Lord, protect your Church from error and false teaching, and make it holy . . .
The love of your Son is like yeast rising in the Church – purify our motives, and help us to grow into union with Christ . . .

INTERCESSIONS *pages 390–393* CLOSING PRAYERS *page 402–403*

OPENING PRAYER O Lord, open our lips that we may proclaim your praise and glory. Fill us with your Spirit, that we may worship your holy name . . . Glory be . . .

PSALMODY Turn not thy servant away in anger,
thou who hast been my help.
Forsake me not, O God of my salvation!
For my father and my mother have forsaken me,
but the Lord will take me up.
Teach me thy way, O Lord.
Be strong, and let your heart take courage;
yea, wait for the Lord! Psalm 27.9–14*

SCRIPTURE READINGS Thus says the Lord God of Hosts, 'Go to this steward, to Shebna, who is over the household, and say to him: I will thrust you from your office. I will call my servant Eliakim, and I will clothe him with your robe, and bind your girdle on him, and commit your authority to his hand; and he shall be a father to the inhabitants of Jerusalem and to the house of Judah. I will place on his shoulder the key of the house of David; he shall open, and none shall shut; and he shall shut, and none shall open. I will fasten him like a peg in a sure place, and he will become a throne of honour to his father's house.' Isaiah 22.15–23*

When Jesus came to Caesarea Philippi, he asked, 'Who do men say that the Son of Man is?' They said, 'Some say John the Baptist, others Elijah, and others Jeremiah or one of the prophets.' He said, 'Who do you say that I am?' Simon Peter replied, 'You are the Christ, the Son of the living God.' Jesus answered, 'Blessed are you, Simon Bar-Jona! Flesh and blood has not revealed this to you, but my Father who is in heaven. I tell you, you are Peter, and on this rock I will build my Church, and the powers of death shall not prevail against it. I will give you the keys of the Kingdom of Heaven, and whatever you bind on earth shall be bound in heaven, and whatever you loose on earth shall be loosed in heaven.' He strictly charged the disciples to tell no one that he was the Christ. St Matthew 16.13–20*

RESPONSE 'The friendship of the Lord is for those who fear him,
and he makes known to them his covenant.'

Eternal God, your Son built his Church on Peter the rock – we praise you that Christ is both the founder and the foundation stone of the Church . . . 'Who do you say that I am?' – you are our Redeemer, Brother and Friend, and we praise and adore you with all the angels and saints in heaven . . . 'Whatever you loose on earth shall be loosed in heaven' – we rejoice that your Son entrusted the Church on earth with power to forgive sins . . .

INTERCESSIONS *pages 390–393* CLOSING PRAYERS *page 402–403*

23 February *Jesus Predicts his Death*

OPENING PRAYER O Lord, open our lips that we may proclaim your praise and glory. Fill us with your Spirit, that we may worship your holy name . . . Glory be . . .

PSALMODY To thee, O Lord, I call; my rock, be not deaf to me,
lest, if thou be silent to me,
I become like those who go down to the Pit.
Hear the voice of my supplication,
as I cry to thee for help,
as I lift up my hands toward thy most holy sanctuary.
Take me not off with the wicked,
with those who are workers of evil,
who speak peace with their neighbours,
while mischief is in their hearts.
Requite them according to their work;
render them their due reward. Psalm 28.1–4*

SCRIPTURE READINGS
O Lord, thou hast deceived me, and I was deceived;
thou art stronger than I, and thou hast prevailed.
I have become a laughing stock all the day;
everyone mocks me. Jeremiah 20.7

Jesus began to show his disciples that he must go to Jerusalem and suffer many things from the elders and chief priests and scribes, and be killed, and on the third day be raised. Peter began to rebuke him, saying, 'God forbid, Lord! This shall never happen to you.' He said to Peter, 'Get behind me, Satan! You are a hindrance to me; for you are not on the side of God, but of men.' Jesus told his disciples, 'If any man would come after me, let him deny himself and take up his cross and follow me. Whoever would save his life will lose it, and whoever loses his life for my sake will find it. What will it profit a man, if he gains the whole world and forfeits his life? What shall a man give in return for his life? For the Son of Man is to come with his angels in the glory of his Father, and then he will repay every man for what he has done.' St Matthew 16.21–27*

RESPONSE 'Behold, the eye of the Lord is on those who fear him,
on those who hope in his steadfast love.'

Almighty God, the Cross and the Crib of Bethlehem reveal the nature of your love for us – we praise you for your perfect love in your Son . . .
'Let him deny himself and take up his cross and follow me' – convert our hearts, and help us to surrender more of our lives to your will . . .
'The Son of Man is to come again with his angels in the glory of his Father' – have mercy on us, and lead us in the way of life eternal . . .

INTERCESSIONS *pages 390–393* CLOSING PRAYERS *page 402–403*

24 February *The Glory of God on the Mountain*

OPENING PRAYER O Lord, open our lips that we may proclaim your praise and glory. Fill us with your Spirit, that we may worship your holy name . . . Glory be . . .

PSALMODY The Lord is my strength and my shield;
in him my heart trusts;
so I am helped, and my heart exults,
and with my song I give thanks to him.
O save thy people, and bless thy heritage;
be thou their shepherd, and carry them for ever.

Psalm 28.6–9*

SCRIPTURE READINGS The Lord is the Spirit, and where the Spirit of the Lord is, there is freedom. We all, with unveiled face, beholding the glory of the Lord, are being changed into his likeness from one degree of glory to another; this comes from the Lord, who is Spirit. Corinthians 3.17–18

Jesus took with him Peter and James and John his brother, and led them up a high mountain apart. He was transfigured before them, and his face shone like the sun, and his garments became white as light. There appeared to them Moses and Elijah, talking with him. Peter said to Jesus, 'Lord, it is well that we are here; if you wish, I will make three booths here, one for you and one for Moses and one for Elijah.' He was still speaking, when a bright cloud overshadowed them, and a voice from the cloud said, 'This is my beloved Son, with whom I am well pleased; listen to him.' When the disciples heard this, they fell on their faces, and were filled with awe. Jesus came and touched them, saying, 'Rise, and have no fear.' When they lifted up their eyes, they saw no one but Jesus only. As they were coming down the mountain, Jesus commanded them, 'Tell no one the vision, until the Son of Man is raised from the dead.' The disciples asked, 'Then why do the scribes say that first Elijah must come?' He replied, 'Elijah does come, and he is to restore all things; but I tell you that Elijah has already come, and they did not know him, but did to him whatever they pleased. So also the Son of Man will suffer at their hands.' Then the disciples understood that he was speaking of John the Baptist. St Matthew 17.1–13

RESPONSE 'I will bless thee as long as I live;
I will lift up my hands and call on thy name.'

God our Father, you revealed your Son in his transfigured glory on the mountain – we rejoice that Christ is now in eternal glory, with you and the Holy Spirit, one God for ever and ever . . .
Your servant Moses represents the Jewish Law and Elijah represents the Prophets – help us to keep your law of love, and to live by your Word . . .
'This is my Beloved Son' – we rejoice in the knowledge of your love . . .

INTERCESSIONS *pages 390–393* CLOSING PRAYERS *page 402–403*

OPENING PRAYER O Lord, open our lips that we may proclaim your praise and glory. Fill us with your Spirit, that we may worship your holy name . . . Glory be . . .

PSALMODY Ascribe to the Lord, O heavenly beings,
ascribe to the Lord glory and strength.
Ascribe to the Lord the glory of his name;
worship the Lord in holy array.
The voice of the Lord is upon the waters;
the God of glory thunders, the Lord, upon many waters.
The voice of the Lord is powerful,
the voice of the Lord is full of majesty. Psalm 29.1–4

SCRIPTURE READINGS You see that faith was active along with his works, and faith was completed by works. James 2.22

When they came to the crowd, a man came up to Jesus and kneeling before him said, 'Lord, have mercy on my son, for he is an epileptic and he suffers terribly; for often he falls into the fire, and often into the water. I brought him to your disciples, and they could not heal him.' Jesus answered, 'O faithless and perverse generation, how long am I to be with you? How long am I to bear with you? Bring him here to me.' And Jesus rebuked him, and the demon came out of him, and the boy was cured instantly. Then the disciples came to Jesus privately and said, 'Why could we not cast it out?' He said, 'Because of your little faith. For truly, I say to you, if you have faith as a grain of mustard seed, you will say to this mountain, "Move from here to there," and it will move; and nothing will be impossible to you.' As they were gathering in Galilee, Jesus said to them, 'The Son of Man is to be delivered into the hands of men, and they will kill him, and he will be raised on the third day.' And they were greatly distressed.
St Matthew 17.14–23

RESPONSE 'I will strengthen you, I will help you.
I will uphold you with my victorious right hand.'

Loving Father, you are the glory of all who put their trust in you – we praise you for your precious gift of faith . . .
'Why could we not cast it out?' – forgive all our sins and help us to put our whole trust in Jesus Christ, our Creator and Redeemer . . .
'If you have faith as a grain of mustard seed' – Lord, build up your Church in the most holy faith of Jesus, and in your mercy, bring it to perfection in the fullness of time . . .

INTERCESSIONS *pages 390–393* CLOSING PRAYERS *page 402–403*

26 February *Who is the Greatest?*

OPENING PRAYER O Lord, open our lips that we may proclaim your praise and glory. Fill us with your Spirit, that we may worship your holy name . . . Glory be . . .

PSALMODY The voice of the Lord breaks the cedars,
The voice of the Lord flashes forth flames of fire.
The voice of the Lord shakes the wilderness,
The voice of the Lord makes the oaks to whirl,
and strips the forests bare;
and in his temple all cry, 'Glory!'
the Lord sits enthroned as king for ever.
May the Lord give strength to his people!
May the Lord bless his people with peace! Psalm 29.5–11*

SCRIPTURE READINGS

The reward for humility and fear of the Lord
is riches and honour and life. Proverbs 22.4

The disciples came to Jesus, saying, 'Who is the greatest in the Kingdom of Heaven?' Calling a child he put him in the midst of them, and said, 'Truly, I say to you, unless you turn and become like children, you will never enter the Kingdom of Heaven. Whoever humbles himself like this child, he is the greatest in the Kingdom of Heaven. Whoever receives one such child in my name receives me; but whoever causes one of these little ones who believe in me to sin, it would be better for him to have a great millstone fastened round his neck and to be drowned in the sea. Woe to the world for temptations to sin! For it is necessary that temptations come, but woe to the man by whom the temptation comes! If your hand or foot causes you to sin, cut it off and throw it away; it is better to enter life maimed or lame than with two hands or two feet to be thrown into the eternal fire. If your eye causes you to sin, pluck it out and throw it away; it is better for you to enter life with one eye than with two eyes to be thrown into the hell of fire. See that you do not despise one of these little ones; for I tell you that in heaven their angels always behold the face of my Father who is in heaven.'
St Matthew 18.1–11*

RESPONSE 'Still to the lowly soul he doth himself impart,
and for his dwelling and his throne chooseth the pure in heart.'

Eternal God, your Son emptied himself of his power and glory for our salvation – we worship and adore your holy name . . .
'Unless you change and become like children' – Lord help us by the Spirit to grow in love, and to change into the likeness of Christ . . .
'It is necessary that temptations come' – help us to defeat all temptation by prayer, and give us your gifts of joy and peace . . .

INTERCESSIONS *pages 390–393* CLOSING PRAYERS *page 402–403*

OPENING PRAYER O Lord, open our lips that we may proclaim your praise and glory. Fill us with your Spirit, that we may worship your holy name . . . Glory be . . .

PSALMODY I will extol thee, O Lord, for thou hast drawn me up,
and hast not let my foes rejoice over me.
O Lord my God, I cried to thee for help,
and thou hast healed me.
Sing praises to the Lord, O you his saints.
For his anger is but for a moment,
and his favour is for a lifetime.
Weeping may tarry for the night,
but joy comes with the morning. Psalm 30.1–5*

SCRIPTURE READINGS The word of the Lord came to me: 'You, son of man, I have made a watchman for the house of Israel; whenever you hear a word from my mouth, you shall give them warning from me. If I say to the wicked, O wicked man, you shall surely die, and you do not speak to warn the wicked to turn from his way, that wicked man shall die in his iniquity, but his blood I will require at your hand. But if you warn the wicked to turn from his way, and he does not turn from his way; he shall die in his iniquity, but you will have saved your life.' Ezekiel 33.7–9

Jesus said, 'If your brother sins against you, go and tell him his fault, between you and him alone. If he listens to you, you have gained your brother. If he does not listen, take one or two others along with you, that every word may be confirmed by the evidence of two or three witnesses. If he refuses to listen to them, tell it to the church; and if he refuses to listen even to the church, let him be to you as a Gentile and a tax collector. Truly, I say to you, whatever you bind on earth shall be bound in heaven, and whatever you loose on earth shall be loosed in heaven. Again I say to you, if two of you agree on earth about anything they ask, it will be done for them by my Father in heaven. For where two or three are gathered in my name, there am I in the midst of them.' St Matthew 18.12–20

RESPONSE 'Bringing all my burdens, sorrow, sin and care,
at thy feet I lay them, and I leave them there.'

God of eternal Love, you are our chief delight and joy – we praise you for calling us to live in the fellowship of your holy Church . . .
'If your brother sins against you' – give us grace to forgive others as you forgive us, and by your Spirit make us aware of our own sins . . .
'Where two or three are gathered together in my name' – Lord, give us the blessing of being aware of your presence with us . . .

INTERCESSIONS *pages 390–393* CLOSING PRAYERS *page 402–403*

OPENING PRAYER O Lord, open our lips that we may proclaim your praise and glory. Fill us with your Spirit, that we may worship your holy name . . . Glory be . . .

PSALMODY Thou hast established me as a strong mountain;
thou didst hide thy face, I was dismayed. Psalm 30.7

SCRIPTURE READINGS None of us lives to himself, and none of us dies to himself. If we live, we live to the Lord, and if we die, we die to the Lord; so then, whether we live or whether we die, we are the Lord's. For to this end Christ died and lived again, that he might be Lord both of the dead and of the living. Romans 14.7–9

Peter said to Jesus, 'Lord, how often shall my brother sin against me, and I forgive him? As many as seven times?' Jesus said, 'I do not say to you seven times, but seventy times seven. Therefore the Kingdom of Heaven may be compared to a king who wished to settle accounts with his servants. When he began the reckoning, one was brought to him who owed him ten thousand talents; and as he could not pay, his lord ordered him to be sold, with his wife and children and all that he had, and payment be made. The servant fell on his knees, imploring him, "Lord, have patience with me, and I will pay you everything." Out of pity for him the lord of that servant forgave him the debt. But that same servant, as he went out, came upon one of his fellow servants who owed him a hundred denarii; and seizing him by the throat he said, "Pay what you owe." His fellow servant fell down and besought him, "Have patience with me, and I will pay you." He refused and put him in prison till he should pay the debt. When his fellow servants saw what had taken place, they were greatly distressed, and they reported to their lord all that had taken place. His lord said, "You wicked servant! I forgave you all that debt because you besought me; should not you have had mercy on your fellow servant, as I had mercy on you?" In anger his lord delivered him to the jailers, till he should pay all his debt. So my heavenly Father will do to every one of you, if you do not forgive your brother from your heart.' St Matthew 18.21–35

RESPONSE 'Thou, Lord, art good and forgiving,
abounding in steadfast love to all who call on thee.'

Merciful Father, your Son heals the wounds of sin for those who are truly penitent – we praise you for your gift of pardon and peace in Christ . . .
To be unwilling to forgive is a sin and a personal offence against God – Lord, teach us to forgive others, as you forgive us, without limit . . .
'The servant fell on his knees' – Lord, we pray that all people will come to worship you with the angels and saints in glory . . .

INTERCESSIONS *pages 390–393* CLOSING PRAYERS *page 402–403*

29 February *Divorce*

OPENING PRAYER O Lord, open our lips that we may proclaim your praise and glory. Fill us with your Spirit, that we may worship your holy name . . . Glory be . . .

PSALMODY To thee, O Lord, I cried;
'What profit is there in my death,
if I go down to the Pit?
Hear, O Lord, and be gracious to me!'
Thou hast turned for me my mourning into dancing:
thou hast loosed my sackcloth and girded me with gladness,
that my soul may praise thee and not be silent.

Psalm 30.8–12*

SCRIPTURE READINGS Jesus said, 'As the Father has loved me, so have I loved you; abide in my love.' St John 15.9

Pharisees tested Jesus by asking, 'Is it lawful to divorce one's wife for any cause?' He answered, 'Have you not read that he who made them from the beginning made them male and female, and said, "For this reason a man shall leave his father and mother and be joined to his wife, and the two shall become one flesh"? They are no longer two but one flesh. What God has joined together, let not man put asunder.' They said, 'Why did Moses command one to give a certificate of divorce, and to put her away?' He said, 'For your hardness of heart Moses allowed you to divorce your wives, but from the beginning it was not so. I say to you: whoever divorces his wife, except for unchastity, and marries another, commits adultery.' The disciples said, 'If such is the case of a man with his wife, it is not expedient to marry.' He said, 'Not all men can receive this saying, but only those to whom it is given. There are eunuchs who have been so from birth, and there are eunuchs who have been made eunuchs by men, and there are eunuchs who have made themselves eunuchs for the sake of the kingdom of heaven. He who is able to receive this, let him receive it.'

St Matthew 19.3–12*

RESPONSE 'Help me, O Lord my God!
Save me according to thy steadfast love.'

Heavenly Father, you keep your promises from generation to generation – we rejoice that your love is eternal and we praise you . . .
We have all sinned and need your forgiveness – Lord, have mercy on us, and guard us against spiritual pride . . .
'What God has joined together let no man put asunder' – Lord, bless all who are separated or divorced, and their children, and heal all who are emotionally wounded, and by your Spirit, purify all our relationships . . .

INTERCESSIONS *pages 390–393* CLOSING PRAYERS *page 402–403*

1 March (St David) *The Rich Young Man*

OPENING PRAYER Eternal God, you alone are holy and the source of all holiness. Cleanse us from our sins and unite our prayers with the worship of your one Church, in heaven and on earth . . . Glory be . . .

PSALMODY In thee, O Lord, do I seek refuge;
in thy righteousness deliver me!
Incline thy ear to me, rescue me speedily! Psalm 31.1–2*

SCRIPTURE READINGS Every good endowment and every perfect gift is from above, coming down from the Father of lights with whom there is no variation or shadow due to change. James 1.17

One came up to Jesus, saying, 'Teacher, what good deed must I do, to have eternal life?' He said, 'Why do you ask me about what is good? One there is who is good. If you would enter life, keep the commandments.' He said, 'Which?' Jesus said, 'You shall not kill, You shall not commit adultery, You shall not steal, You shall not bear false witness, Honour your father and mother, and, You shall love your neighbour as yourself.' The young man said, 'All these I have observed; what do I still lack?' Jesus said, 'If you want to be perfect, go, sell what you possess and give to the poor, and you will have treasure in heaven; and come, follow me.' When the young man heard this he went away sorrowful; for he had great possessions. Jesus said, 'It will be hard for a rich man to enter the Kingdom of Heaven. I tell you, it is easier for a camel to go through the eye of a needle than for a rich man to enter the Kingdom of God.' When the disciples heard this they were greatly astonished, saying, 'Who then can be saved?' Jesus said, 'With men this is impossible, but with God all things are possible.' Peter said, 'We have left everything and followed you. What shall we have?' Jesus said, 'In the new world, when the Son of Man shall sit on his glorious throne, you who have followed me will sit on twelve thrones, judging the twelve tribes of Israel. Every one who has left houses or brothers or sisters, or father or mother or children or lands, for my name's sake, will receive a hundredfold, and inherit eternal life. Many that are first will be last, and the last first.'
St Matthew 19.16–30*

RESPONSE 'Blessed is the man who fears the Lord,
who greatly delights in his commandments.'

Loving Father, your Son gave his life on the Cross for us – we praise you in union with Saint David and all the saints for your generous love . . .
'You have entrusted to us everything that we have – help us to be responsible stewards of all your gifts, and give us ever-grateful hearts . . .
'It is hard for a rich person to enter the Kingdom of Heaven' – Lord, help all who seek your Kingdom to grow into union with Christ . . .

INTERCESSIONS *pages 390–393* CLOSING PRAYERS *page 402–403*

2 March *Workers in the Vineyard*

OPENING PRAYER Eternal God, you alone are holy and the source of all holiness. Cleanse us from our sins and unite our prayers with the worship of your one Church, in heaven and on earth . . . Glory be . . .

PSALMODY Into thy hands I commit my spirit;
thou hast redeemed me, O Lord, faithful God. Psalm 31.5

SCRIPTURE READINGS

Let the wicked forsake his way,
and the unrighteous man his thoughts.
For as the heavens are higher than the earth,
so are my ways higher than your ways
and my thoughts than your thoughts. Isaiah 55.7–9*

Jesus said, 'The Kingdom of Heaven is like a householder who went out early to hire labourers for his vineyard. After agreeing with the labourers for a denarius a day, he sent them into his vineyard. Going out about the third hour he saw others standing idle in the market place; he said, "You go into the vineyard too, and whatever is right I will give you." So they went. Going out again about the sixth hour and the ninth hour, he did the same. About the eleventh hour he found others standing; and he said, "Why do you stand here idle all day?" They said, "Because no one has hired us." He said, "You go into the vineyard too." When evening came, the owner of the vineyard said to his steward, "Call the labourers and pay them their wages, beginning with the last, up to the first." When those hired about the eleventh hour came, each of them received a denarius. When the first came, they thought they would receive more; but each of them received a denarius. On receiving it they grumbled at the householder, saying, "These last worked only one hour, and you have made them equal to us who have bourne the burden of the day and the scorching heat." He replied, "Friend, I am doing you no wrong; did you not agree with me for a denarius? Take what belongs to you, and go; I choose to give to this last as I give to you. Am I not allowed to do what I choose with what belongs to me? Do you begrudge my generosity? So the last will be first, and the first last.'
St Matthew 20.1–16

RESPONSE 'Thy steadfast love is great above the heavens,
thy faithfulness reaches to the clouds.'

Almighty God, your ways are past our understanding – we praise you for revealing the mystery of your Kingdom in your Son . . .
You create us in your own image and all are equal in your sight – Lord, sanctify us, and help us to worship you in holiness and truth . . .
'You have made them equal to us' – Lord, we praise you for the justice of your Kingdom, and for your eternal love for every individual . . .

INTERCESSIONS *pages 390–393* CLOSING PRAYERS *page 402–403*

3 March *The Sons of Zebedee*

OPENING PRAYER Eternal God, you alone are holy and the source of all holiness. Cleanse us from our sins and unite our prayers with the worship of your one Church, in heaven and on earth . . . Glory be . . .

PSALMODY Thou art my rock and my fortress;
for thy name's sake lead me and guide me,
for thou art my refuge.
Thou hatest those who pay regard to vain idols;
but I trust in the Lord.
I will rejoice and be glad for thy steadfast love,
because thou hast seen my affliction,
thou hast taken heed of my adversities,
and hast not delivered me into the hand of the enemy;
thou hast set my feet in a broad place. Psalm 31.3–8*

SCRIPTURE READINGS It has been granted to you that for the sake of Christ you should not only believe in him but also suffer for his sake.
Philippians 1.29

The mother of the sons of Zebedee came to Jesus, with her sons, and kneeling before him she asked him for something. He said, 'What do you want?' She said, 'Command that these two sons of mine may sit, one at your right hand and one at your left, in your Kingdom.' Jesus answered, 'You do not know what you are asking. Are you able to drink the cup that I am to drink?' They said, 'We are able.' He said, 'You will drink my cup, but to sit at my right hand and at my left is not mine to grant, but it is for those for whom it has been prepared by my Father.' When the ten heard it, they were indignant at the two brothers. Jesus said, 'You know that the rulers of the Gentiles lord it over them, and their great men exercise authority over them. It shall not be so among you; whoever would be great among you must be your servant, and whoever would be first among you must be your slave; even as the Son of Man came not to be served but to serve, and to give his life as a ransom for many.' St Matthew 20.20–28

RESPONSE 'Great is his steadfast love towards us;
and the faithfulness of the Lord endures for ever.'

Almighty God, you are just and true in all your ways – we praise you for the pure light of the knowledge of Christ to enlighten the Church . . .
'Are you able to drink the cup that I am to drink?' – help us to share the sufferings of your Son, and take up our cross and follow Christ . . .
'Whoever would be great among you must be your servant' – Lord, purify our motives and ambitions, and give us your joy and peace in our hearts . . .

INTERCESSIONS *pages 390–393* CLOSING PRAYERS *page 402–403*

4 March *Two Blind Men*

OPENING PRAYER Eternal God, you alone are holy and the source of all holiness. Cleanse us from our sins and unite our prayers with the worship of your one Church, in heaven and on earth . . . Glory be . . .

PSALMODY Be gracious to me, O Lord,
for I am in distress.
But I trust in thee, O Lord,
I say, 'Thou art my God.'
Deliver me from the hand of my enemies!
Let thy face shine on thy servant;
save me in thy steadfast love! Psalm 31.9–16*

SCRIPTURE READINGS The people of Israel came into the wilderness. There was no water for the congregation; and they assembled themselves together against Moses and Aaron. Then Moses and Aaron went from the presence of the assembly to the door of the tent of meeting, and fell on their faces. The glory of the Lord appeared to them, and the Lord said to Moses, 'Take the rod, and assemble the congregation, and tell the rock before their eyes to yield its water; so you shall bring water out of the rock for them.' Moses and Aaron gathered the assembly together before the rock, and he said, 'Hear now, you rebels; shall we bring forth water for you out of this rock?' Moses lifted up his hand and struck the rock with his rod twice; and water came forth abundantly. Numbers 20.1–11*

As they went out of Jericho, a great crowd followed him. Two blind men sitting by the roadside, when they heard that Jesus was passing by, cried out, 'Have mercy on us, Son of David!' The crowd rebuked them, telling them to be silent; but they cried out the more, 'Lord, have mercy on us, Son of David!' Jesus called them, saying, 'What do you want me to do for you?' They said, 'Lord, let our eyes be opened.' Jesus touched their eyes, and they received their sight and followed him. St Matthew 20.29–34*

Jesus said, 'I am the light of the world; he who follows me will not walk in darkness, but will have the light of life.' St John 8.12

RESPONSE 'Light rises in the darkness for the upright;
the Lord is gracious and righteous.'

Eternal God, you are the source of light for our souls – we praise you for the light of Christ in the Church through the centuries . . .
'What do you want me to do for you?' – Lord, give us grateful hearts for all the blessings we receive in your Son Jesus Christ . . .
Your Son healed the sick – Lord, be ever present with those who are blind, their families, and those who care for them . . .

INTERCESSIONS *pages 390–393* CLOSING PRAYERS *page 402–403*

5 March *Triumphal Entry into the Holy City*

OPENING PRAYER Eternal God, you alone are holy and the source of all holiness. Cleanse us from our sins and unite our prayers with the worship of your one Church, in heaven and on earth . . . Glory be . . .

PSALMODY Let me not be put to shame, O Lord, for I call on thee;
O how abundant is thy goodness,
which thou hast laid up for those who fear thee,
in the sight of the sons of men!
In the covert of thy presence thou hidest them
from the plots of men;
thou holdest them safe under thy shelter
from the strife of tongues. Psalm 31.17–20*

SCRIPTURE READINGS The word of the cross is folly to those who are perishing, but to us who are being saved it is the power of God.
1 Corinthians 1.18

When Jesus and the disciples drew near to Jerusalem and came to Bethphage, to the Mount of Olives, Jesus sent two disciples, saying, 'Go into the village opposite you, and immediately you will find an ass tied, and a colt with her; untie them and bring them to me. If any one says anything to you, you shall say, "The Lord has need of them," and he will send them immediately.' This took place to fulfil what was spoken by the prophet, saying,

> 'Tell the daughter of Zion, Behold, your king is coming to you, humble, and mounted on an ass, and on a colt, the foal of an ass.'

The disciples did as Jesus had directed; they brought the ass and the colt, and put their garments on them, and he sat thereon. Most of the crowd spread their garments on the road, and others cut branches from the trees and spread them on the road. The crowds that went before him and that followed him shouted, 'Hosanna to the Son of David! Blessed is he who comes in the name of the Lord! Hosanna in the highest!' When he entered Jerusalem, all the city was stirred, saying, 'Who is this?' The crowds said, 'This is the prophet Jesus from Nazareth of Galilee.' St Matthew 21.1–11

RESPONSE 'Blessed is he who enters in the name of the Lord.
We bless you from the house of the Lord.'

Eternal God, your Son entered Jerusalem in triumph as Messiah and King – we join our hosannas with the praise of the Church through the centuries . . .
'Behold, your king is coming to you' – Blessed and praised is our Redeemer and Lord, Jesus the King of the universe . . .
'Hosanna to the Son of David' – Lord, we rejoice that the Jewish Law and Prophets have been gloriously fulfilled in your divine Son . . .

INTERCESSIONS *pages 390–393* CLOSING PRAYERS *page 402–403*

6 March *Cleansing the Temple*

OPENING PRAYER Eternal God, you alone are holy and the source of all holiness. Cleanse us from our sins and unite our prayers with the worship of your one Church, in heaven and on earth . . . Glory be . . .

PSALMODY Blessed be the Lord,
for he has wondrously shown his steadfast love to me
when I was beset as in a beseiged city.
I had said in my alarm,
'I am driven far from thy sight.'
But thou didst hear my supplications,
when I cried to thee for help.
Love the Lord, all you his saints. Psalm 31.21–23

SCRIPTURE READINGS Jesus entered the temple of God and drove out all who sold and bought in the temple, and he overturned the tables of the money-changers and the seats of those who sold pigeons. He said to them, 'It is written, "My house shall be called a house of prayer"; but you make it a den of robbers.' St Matthew 21.12–13

I tell you, something greater than the temple is here. St Matthew 12.6

According to the Grace of God given to me, like a skilled master builder I laid a foundation, and another man is building upon it. Let each man take care how he builds upon it. For no other foundation can any one lay then that which is laid, which is Jesus Christ. Now if any one builds on the foundation with gold, silver, precious stones, wood, hay, straw – each man's work will become manifest; for the Day will disclose it, because it will be revealed with fire, and the fire will test what sort of work each one has done. If the work which any man has built on the foundation survives, he will receive a reward. If any man's work is burned up, he will suffer loss, though he himself will be saved, but only as through fire. Do you not know that you are God's temple and that God's Spirit dwells in you? If any one destroys God's temple, God will destroy him. For God's temple is holy, and that temple you are. I Corinthians 3.10–17

RESPONSE 'Hear, O Lord, and be gracious to me.
O Lord, be thou my helper.'

Eternal God, your Son cleansed the Temple at Jerusalem – we rejoice that Christ is present as Judge and Redeemer in the Church today . . .
'Jesus drove out all who sold and bought in the temple' – cleanse your Church, and unite our praises with the perfect worship of your Son . . .
'You are God's temple and God's Spirit dwells in you' – purify us from greed and the love of money, and make us worthy of your eternal love . . .

INTERCESSIONS *pages 390–393* CLOSING PRAYERS *page 402–403*

7 March *The Wicked Tenants*

OPENING PRAYER Eternal God, you alone are holy and the source of all holiness. Cleanse us from our sins and unite our prayers with the worship of your one Church, in heaven and on earth . . . Glory be . . .

PSALMODY Blessed is the man to whom the Lord imputes no iniquity,
and in whose spirit there is no deceit. Psalm 32.2

SCRIPTURE READINGS When his brothers saw that their father loved Joseph more than all his brothers, they hated him. Now his brothers went to pasture their father's flock. They saw Joseph afar off, and they conspired to kill him. They said, 'Here comes the dreamer. Let us kill him.' They took him and cast him into a pit. Then they saw a caravan with their camels on their way to Egypt. They drew Joseph up and sold him to the Ishmaelites, and they took Joseph to Egypt. Genesis 37.3–28*

Jesus said, 'Hear another parable. There was a householder who planted a vineyard, and let it out to tenants, and went into another country. When the season of fruit drew near, he sent his servants to get his fruit; and the tenants took his servants and beat one, killed another, and stoned another. He sent other servants; and they did the same to them. Afterward he sent his son, saying, "They will respect my son". When the tenants saw the son, they said, "This is the heir; come, let us kill him and have his inheritance." They cast him out, and killed him. When the owner of the vineyard comes, what will he do to those tenants?' They said, 'He will put those wretches to a miserable death, and let out the vineyard to other tenants who will give him the fruits in their seasons.' Jesus said, 'Have you never read in the scriptures:

"The very stone which the builders rejected
has become the head of the corner;
this was the Lord's doing, and it is marvellous in our eyes"?

I tell you, the Kingdom of God will be taken away from you and given to a nation producing the fruits of it.' St Matthew 21.33–44

RESPONSE 'Our help is in the name of the Lord,
who made heaven and earth.'

Heavenly Father, the Church is your beloved vineyard – we praise you for all who have produced fruits for your honour and glory through the ages . . .
'They will respect my son' – Lord, we pray that the sacred name of Jesus may be honoured and loved by all people . . .
'The very stone which the builders rejected has become the head of the corner' – we rejoice at the glorious resurrection of your Son . . .

INTERCESSIONS *pages 390–393* CLOSING PRAYERS *page 402–403*

OPENING PRAYER Eternal God, you alone are holy and the source of all holiness. Cleanse us from our sins and unite our prayers with the worship of your one Church, in heaven and on earth . . . Glory be . . .

PSALMODY When I declared not my sin, my body wasted away.
For day and night thy hand was heavy upon me;
my strength was dried up as by the heat of summer.
I acknowledged my sin to thee, and I did not hide my iniquity;
I said, 'I will confess my transgressions to the Lord';
then thou didst forgive the guilt of my sin. Psalm 32.3–5*

SCRIPTURE READINGS My God will supply every need of yours according to his riches in glory in Christ Jesus. Philippians 4.19*

Jesus spoke in parables, saying, 'The Kingdom of Heaven may be compared to a king who gave a marriage feast for his son, and sent his servants to call those who were invited to the marriage feast; but they would not come. Again he sent other servants, saying, "Tell those who are invited, Behold, I have made ready my dinner, my oxen and my fat calves are killed, and everything is ready; come to the marriage feast." But they made light of it and went off, one to his farm, another to his business, while the rest seized his servants, treated them shamefully, and killed them. The king was angry, and he sent his troops and destroyed those murderers and burned their city. Then he said to his servants, "The wedding is ready, but those invited were not worthy. Go therefore to the thoroughfares, and invite to the marriage feast as many as you find." And those servants went out into the streets and gathered all whom they found, both bad and good; so the wedding hall was filled with guests. But when the king came in to look at the guests, he saw there a man who had no wedding garment; and he said to him, "Friend, how did you get in here, without a wedding garment?" And he was speechless. Then the king said to the attendants, "Bind him hand and foot, and cast him into the outer darkness; there men will weep and gnash their teeth." For many are called, but few are chosen.'
St Matthew 22.1–14

RESPONSE 'The Lord has done great things for us;
we are glad.'

Heavenly Father, you give us the Eucharist as a foretaste of your heavenly banquet – we rejoice and thank you for inviting us to the feast . . .
'The wedding is ready, but those invited were not worthy' – Lord, cleanse us from our sins, and make us worthy to be your guests . . .
'Go to the thoroughfares, and invite to the marriage feast as many as you find' – Lord, bless and prosper the work and mission of your Church . . .

INTERCESSIONS *pages 390–393* CLOSING PRAYERS *page 402–403*

9 March *God and Caesar*

OPENING PRAYER Eternal God, you alone are holy and the source of all holiness. Cleanse us from our sins and unite our prayers with the worship of your one Church, in heaven and on earth . . . Glory be . . .

PSALMODY Thou art a hiding place for me,
thou preservest me from trouble;
thou dost encompass me with deliverance.
I will instruct you and teach you the way you should go;
I will counsel you with my eye upon you.
Be not like a horse or a mule, without understanding,
which must be curbed with bit and bridle.
Many are the pangs of the wicked;
but steadfast love surrounds him who trusts in the Lord.
Be glad in the Lord, and rejoice, O righteous,
and shout for joy, all you upright in heart! Psalm 32.6–11*

SCRIPTURE READINGS

Thus says the Lord, to his anointed, to Cyrus:
'For the sake of my servant Jacob, and Israel my chosen,
I call you by name.
I gird you, though you do not know me,
that men may know, from the rising of the sun
and from the west, that there is none besides me;
I am the Lord, and there is no other. Isaiah 45.1–6*

The Pharisees took counsel how to entangle Jesus in his talk. They sent their disciples to him, along with the Herodians, saying, 'Teacher, we know that you are true, and teach the way of God truthfully, and care for no man; for you do not regard the position of men. Tell us, then, what you think. Is it lawful to pay taxes to Caesar, or not?' Jesus, aware of their malice, said, 'Why put me to the test, you hypocrites? Show me the money for the tax.' They brought him a coin. Jesus said, 'Whose likeness and inscription is this?' They said, 'Caesar's.' He said, 'Render therefore to Caesar the things that are Caesar's, and to God the things that are God's.' When they heard it, they marvelled, and they left him.

St Matthew 22.15–22

RESPONSE 'Blessed is everyone who fears the Lord,
who walks in his ways.'

All-powerful Father, you call us to live both as citizens of heaven and as citizens of this world – to you alone be the praise and the glory . . .
'Render to Caesar the things that are Caesar's' – inspire all Christians to play a responsible part in the life of the local community . . .
'Render to God the things that are God's' – Lord, help us to worship you with all our heart and mind and soul and strength . . .

INTERCESSIONS *pages 390–393* CLOSING PRAYERS *page 402–403*

OPENING PRAYER Eternal God, you alone are holy and the source of all holiness. Cleanse us from our sins and unite our prayers with the worship of your one Church, in heaven and on earth . . . Glory be . . .

PSALMODY Rejoice in the Lord, O you righteous!
Praise befits the upright.
Praise the Lord with the lyre,
make melody to him with the harp of ten strings!
Sing to him a new song,
play skilfully on the strings, with loud shouts.
For the word of the Lord is upright;
and all his work is done in faithfulness.
He loves righteousness and justice;
the earth is full of the steadfast love of the Lord. Psalm 33.1–5

SCRIPTURE READINGS Blessed be the God and Father of our Lord Jesus Christ! By his great mercy we have been born anew to a living hope through the resurrection of Jesus Christ from the dead to an inheritance which is imperishable, undefiled, and unfading, kept in heaven for you.
1 Peter 1.3–4

Some Sadducees, who say that there is no resurrection, came to Jesus; and they asked him a question, saying, 'Teacher, Moses said, "If a man dies, having no children, his brother must marry the widow, and raise up children for his brother." Now there were seven brothers among us; the first married, and died, and having no children left his wife to his brother. So too the second and third, down to the seventh. After them all, the woman died. In the resurrection, to which of the seven will she be wife? For they all had her.' Jesus answered, 'You are wrong, because you know neither the scriptures nor the power of God. For in the resurrection they neither marry nor are given in marriage, but are like angels in heaven. As for the resurrection of the dead, have you not read what was said to you by God, "I am the God of Abraham, and the God of Isaac, and the God of Jacob"? He is not God of the dead, but of the living.' When the crowd heard it, they were astonished at his teaching. St Matthew 22.23–33

RESPONSE 'Praise the Lord, for the Lord is good;
sing to his name, for he is gracious.'

God of Abraham, Isaac and Jacob, you raised your Son from the dead – we praise you for His victory over sin and death on the Cross . . .
Your Son opened the gate of everlasting life to all who put their trust in him – Lord, we praise you for your redeeming love . . .
'The Lord is risen indeed' – help us by your grace to share in his risen life through the life and worship of your Church on earth . . .

INTERCESSIONS *pages 390–393* CLOSING PRAYERS *page 402–403*

OPENING PRAYER Eternal God, you alone are holy and the source of all holiness. Cleanse us from our sins and unite our prayers with the worship of your one Church, in heaven and on earth . . . Glory be . . .

PSALMODY By the word of the Lord the heavens were made,
and all their host by the breath of his mouth.
He gathered the waters of the sea as in a bottle;
he put the deeps in storehouses.
Let all the earth fear the Lord,
let all the inhabitants of the world
stand in awe of him!
For he spoke and it came to be;
he commanded, and it stood forth.
The counsel of the Lord stands for ever,
the thoughts of his heart to all generations.
Blessed is the nation whose God is the Lord,
the people whom he has chosen as his heritage!
The Lord looks down from heaven,
and sees all the sons of men;
from where he sits enthroned he looks forth
on all the inhabitants of the earth. Psalm 33.6–14*

SCRIPTURE READINGS You know what kind of men we proved to be among you for your sake. You became imitators of us and of the Lord, for you received the word in much affliction, with joy inspired by the Holy Spirit; so that you became an example to all believers in Macedonia.
1 Thessalonians 1.5–6

When the Pharisees heard that Jesus had silenced the Sadducees, they came together. One of them, a lawyer, asked him a question, to test him. 'Teacher, which is the great commandment in the law?' He said, 'You shall love the Lord your God with all your heart, and with all your soul, and with all you mind. This is the great and first commandment. A second is like it, You shall love your neighbour as yourself. On these two commandments depend all the law and the prophets.' St Matthew 22.34–40

RESPONSE 'My tongue will sing of thy word,
for all thy commandments are right.'

Heavenly Father, you revealed your perfect love by sending your Son to redeem us – we rejoice and exult in his sacrificial love . . .
'You shall love the Lord your God' – Lord, give us grace to respond to your love throughout our earthly lives . . .
'You shall love your neighbour as yourself' – Lord, guide us and help us to reflect your pure love in all our relationships . . .

INTERCESSIONS *pages 390–393* CLOSING PRAYERS *page 402–403*

OPENING PRAYER Eternal God, you alone are holy and the source of all holiness. Cleanse us from our sins and unite our prayers with the worship of your one Church, in heaven and on earth . . . Glory be . . .

PSALMODY A king is not saved by his great army;
a warrior is not delivered by his great strength.
Behold, the eye of the Lord is on those who fear him,
that he may deliver their soul from death.
Our soul waits for the Lord; he is our help and shield.
Let thy steadfast love, O Lord, be upon us,
even as we hope in thee. Psalm 33.16–22*

SCRIPTURE READINGS We would not have you ignorant concerning those who are asleep, that you may not grieve as others do who have no hope. Since we believe that Jesus died and rose again, even so, through Jesus, God will bring with him those who have fallen asleep. For this we declare to you by the word of the Lord, that we who are alive, who are left until the coming of the Lord, shall not precede those who have fallen asleep.
1 Thessalonians 4.13–15

Jesus said, 'The Kingdom of heaven shall be compared to ten maidens who took their lamps and went to meet the bridegroom. Five of them were foolish, and five were wise. For when the foolish took their lamps, they took no oil with them; but the wise took flasks of oil with their lamps. As the bridegroom was delayed, they all slept. At midnight there was a cry, "Behold, the bridegroom! Come out to meet him." Then all those maidens rose and trimmed their lamps. The foolish said to the wise, "Give us some of your oil, for our lamps are going out." The wise replied, "Perhaps there will not be enough for us and for you; go rather to the dealers and buy for yourselves." While they went to buy, the bridegroom came, and those who were ready went into the marriage feast; and the door was shut. Afterward the other maidens came, saying, "Lord, Lord, open to us." He replied, "Truly, I say to you, I do not know you." Watch therefore, for you know neither the day nor the hour.' St Matthew 25. 1–13

RESPONSE 'The Lord will keep your going out and coming in
from this time forth and for evermore.'

Father of our Lord Jesus Christ, you have prepared a place for us in the Kingdom of your Son – we rejoice that your love is eternal, and we praise you . . .
Your Son will come again to judge the living and the dead. . . Lord, have mercy on us now, and at the hour of our death . . .
'Of that day and hour no one knows' – Lord, give us grace to be wise and vigilant, and help us to prepare for the coming of your Son . . .

INTERCESSIONS *pages 390–393* CLOSING PRAYERS *page 402–403*

OPENING PRAYER Eternal God, you alone are holy and the source of all holiness. Cleanse us from our sins and unite our prayers with the worship of your one Church, in heaven and on earth . . . Glory be . . .

PSALMODY I will bless the Lord at all times;
his praise shall continually be in my mouth.
My soul makes its boast in the Lord;
let the afflicted hear and be glad.
O magnify the Lord with me, and let us exalt his name together!
I sought the Lord, and he answered me,
and delivered me from all my fears.
Look at him, and be radiant;
so your faces shall never be ashamed.
This poor man cried, and the Lord heard him,
and saved him out of all his troubles.
The angel of the Lord encamps around those who fear him,
and delivers them.
O taste and see that the Lord is good!
Happy is the man who takes refuge in him! Psalm 34.1–8

SCRIPTURE READINGS
'Touch not my anointed ones,
do my prophets no harm.' 1 Chronicles 16.22

When Jesus was at Bethany in the house of Simon the leper, a woman came up to him with an alabaster flask of very expensive ointment, and she poured it on his head, as he sat at table. When the disciples saw it, they were indignant, saying, 'Why this waste? For this ointment might have been sold for a large sum, and given to the poor.' But Jesus, aware of this, said, 'Why do you trouble this woman? For she has done a beautiful thing to me. You always have the poor with you, but you will not always have me. In pouring this ointment on my body she has done it to prepare me for burial. Truly, I say to you, wherever this gospel is preached in the whole world, what she has done will be told in memory of her.'

St Matthew 26.6–13

RESPONSE 'Turn to me and be gracious to me,
as is thy wont towards those who love thy name.'

Almighty God, you ordained that your Son should enter his Kingdom through his death on the Cross – we praise you for his redeeming love . . .
You anointed your Son with the Spirit and with power at his Baptism – Lord, renew your gift of the Spirit in all who have been baptized . . .
Your Son was anointed with precious oil to prepare for his burial – help us to die to sin, and live in newness of life in the Spirit . . .

INTERCESSIONS *pages 390–393* CLOSING PRAYERS *page 402–403*

OPENING PRAYER Eternal God, you alone are holy and the source of all holiness. Cleanse us from our sins and unite our prayers with the worship of your one Church, in heaven and on earth . . . Glory be . . .

PSALMODY Come, O sons, listen to me,
I will teach you the fear of the Lord.
Keep your tongue from evil,
and your lips from speaking deceit.
Depart from evil, and do good;
seek peace, and pursue it. Psalm 34.11–14*

SCRIPTURE READINGS As often as you eat this bread and drink the cup, you proclaim the Lord's death until he comes. 1 Corinthians 11.26

On the first day of Unleavened Bread the disciples came to Jesus, saying, 'Where will you have us prepare for you to eat the passover?' He said, 'Go into the city to a certain one, and say to him, "The Teacher says, My time is at hand; I will keep the passover at your house with my disciples."' The disciples did as Jesus had directed, and prepared the passover. When it was evening, he sat at table with the twelve disciples; as they were eating, he said, 'Truly, I say to you, one of you will betray me.' They were very sorrowful, and began to say, one after another, 'Is it I, Lord?' He answered, 'He who has dipped his hand in the dish with me, will betray me. The Son of Man goes as it is written of him, but woe to that man by whom the Son of Man is betrayed! It would have been better for that man if he had not been born.' Judas, who betrayed him, said, 'Is it I, Master?' He said, 'You have said so.' As they were eating, Jesus took bread, and blessed, and broke it, and gave it to the disciples and said, 'Take, eat; this is my body.' And he took a cup, and when he had given thanks he gave it to them, saying, 'Drink of it, all of you; for this is my blood of the covenant, which is poured out for many for the forgiveness of sins. I tell you I shall not drink again of this fruit of the vine until that day when I drink it new with you in my Father's Kingdom.' When they had sung a hymn, they went out to the Mount of Olives. St Matthew 26.17–30*

RESPONSE 'O how abundant is thy goodness,
which thou hast laid up for those who fear thee.'

Gracious God, your Son commanded his apostles to celebrate the Eucharist as a memorial of his death – we praise you for your eternal love . . .
You provide the Eucharist as an everlasting gift to the Church – we praise you for the benefits which you give to us through this sacrament . . .
'This is my body' – Lord, we thank you for feeding us with the Body and Blood of your Son in this sacrament of the altar . . .

INTERCESSIONS *pages 390–393* CLOSING PRAYERS *page 402–403*

15 March *The Garden of Gethsemane*

OPENING PRAYER Eternal God, you alone are holy and the source of all holiness. Cleanse us from our sins and unite our prayers with the worship of your one Church, in heaven and on earth . . . Glory be . . .

PSALMODY The eyes of the Lord are toward the righteous,
and his ears toward their cry. Psalm 34.15

SCRIPTURE READINGS He who did not spare his own Son but gave him up for us all, will he not also give us all things with him? Romans 8.32

Jesus said, 'You will all fall away because of me this night; for it is written, "I will strike the shepherd, and the sheep of the flock will be scattered." But after I am raised up, I will go before you to Galilee.' Peter declared, 'Though they all fall away because of you, I will never fall away.' Jesus said, 'Truly, I say to you, this very night, before the cock crows, you will deny me three times.' Peter said, 'Even if I must die with you, I will not deny you.' So said all the disciples. Then Jesus went with them to a place called Gethsemane, and he said to his disciples, 'Sit here, while I go yonder and pray.' Taking with him Peter and the two sons of Zebedee, he began to be sorrowful and troubled. Then he said, 'My soul is very sorrowful, even to death; remain here, and watch with me.' Going a little further he fell on his face and prayed, 'My Father, if it be possible, let this cup pass from me; nevertheless, not as I will, but as thou wilt.' He came to the disciples and found them sleeping; and he said to Peter, 'Could you not watch with me one hour? Watch and pray that you may not enter into temptation; the spirit indeed is willing, but the flesh is weak.' Again, for the second time, he went away and prayed, 'My Father, if this cannot pass unless I drink it, thy will be done.' Again he came and found them sleeping, for their eyes were heavy. So, leaving them again, he went away and prayed for the third time, saying the same words. He came to the disciples and said, 'Are you still sleeping and taking your rest? Behold, the hour is at hand, and the Son of Man is betrayed into the hands of sinners. Rise, let us be going; see, my betrayer is at hand.' St Matthew 26.31–46

RESPONSE 'Blessed be the Lord,
for he has wondrously shown his steadfast love for me.'

Heavenly Father, your Son suffered spiritual agony for our salvation – we praise you for his obedience and love . . .
'Let this cup pass from me' – Lord, give a sense of discipline to your Church and help us to share in the sufferings of Christ . . .
'The Spirit is willing but the flesh is weak' – help us to overcome all our weaknesses through prayer, and fill us with your love . . .

INTERCESSIONS *pages 390–393* CLOSING PRAYERS *page 402–403*

16 March *Jesus is Arrested*

OPENING PRAYER Eternal God, you alone are holy and the source of all holiness. Cleanse us from our sins and unite our prayers with the worship of your one Church, in heaven and on earth . . . Glory be . . .

PSALMODY Contend, O Lord, with those who contend with me;
fight against those who fight against me!
Take hold of shield and buckler, and rise for my help!
Draw the spear and javelin against my pursuers!
Say to my soul, 'I am your deliverance!'
Let them be put to shame and dishonour
who seek after my life!
Let them be turned back and confounded
who devise evil against me!
Without cause they dug a pit for my life. Psalm 35.1–7*

SCRIPTURE READINGS I therefore, a prisoner for the Lord, beg you to lead a life worthy of the calling to which you have been called. Ephesians 4.1

Judas came, one of the twelve, and with him a great crowd with swords and clubs, from the chief priests and the elders of the people. Now the betrayer had given them a sign, saying, 'The one I shall kiss is the man; seize him.' He came up to Jesus and said, 'Hail, Master!' And he kissed him. Jesus said, 'Friend, why are you here?' Then they came up and laid hands on Jesus and seized him. One of those who were with Jesus drew his sword, and struck the slave of the high priest, and cut off his ear. Jesus said, 'Put your sword back into its place; for all who take the sword will perish by the sword. Do you think that I cannot appeal to my Father, and he will at once send me more than twelve legions of angels? But how then should the scriptures be fulfilled, that it must be so?' At that hour Jesus said to the crowds, 'Have you come out as against a robber, with swords and clubs to capture me? Day after day I sat in the temple teaching, and you did not seize me. But all this has taken place, that the scriptures of the prophets might be fulfilled.' Then all the disciples forsook him and fled.
St Matthew 26.47–56*

RESPONSE 'Thy power and thy righteousness, O God,
reach the high heavens.'

Eternal God, your Son surrendered his freedom so that we might share his divine life – we contemplate this mystery with awe and praise . . .
'The one I shall kiss is the man' – Lord, help us to be honest and truthful in all things . . .
'All who take the sword will perish by the sword' – Lord, inspire the leaders of the nations to follow your ways of justice and peace . . .

INTERCESSIONS *pages 390–393* CLOSING PRAYERS *page 402–403*

17 March (St Patrick) *Jesus is Tried before the High Priest*

OPENING PRAYER Eternal God, you alone are holy and the source of all holiness. Cleanse us from our sins and unite our prayers with the worship of your one Church, in heaven and on earth . . . Glory be . . .

PSALMODY My soul shall rejoice in the Lord,
exulting in his deliverance.
All my bones shall say, 'O Lord, who is like thee,
thou who deliverest the weak?'
Malicious witnesses rise up;
they ask me of things that I know not. Psalm 35.9–11*

SCRIPTURE READINGS

Great and wonderful are thy deeds,
O Lord God the Almighty!
Just and true are thy ways, O King of the ages!
Who shall not fear and glorify thy name, O Lord?
For thou alone art holy.
All nations shall come and worship thee,
for thy judgements have been revealed. Revelation 15.3–4

They led Jesus to Caiaphas the high priest, where the scribes and the elders gathered. Peter followed at a distance, as far as the courtyard of the high priest, and going inside he sat with the guards to see the end. The chief priests and the whole council sought false testimony against Jesus that they might put him to death, but they found none, though many false witnesses came forward. At last two came forward and said, 'This fellow said, "I am able to destroy the temple of God, and to build it in three days."' The high priest said, 'Have you no answer to make? What is it these men testify against you?' Jesus was silent. The high priest said, 'I adjure you by the living God, tell us if you are the Christ, the Son of God.' Jesus said, 'You have said so. I tell you, you will see the Son of Man seated at the right hand of Power, and coming on the clouds of heaven.' The high priest tore his robes, and said, 'He has uttered blasphemy. Why do we still need witnesses? You have heard his blasphemy. What is your judgement?' They answered, 'He deserves death.' St Matthew 26.57–67

RESPONSE 'Christ be with me, Christ within me,
Christ behind me, Christ before me.'

Eternal God, your Son is our Judge – we rejoice with Saint Patrick and all the saints that Christ is also our Redeemer, Friend and Brother . . .
Your Son was tried in secret during the night – may the truth and justice of your Kingdom shine in the Church and be seen in all the world . . .
Your Son was innocent but declared guilty – Lord, grant integrity and compassion to all who administer justice and the law . . .

INTERCESSIONS *pages 390–393* CLOSING PRAYERS *page 402–403*

18 March *Peter's Denial*

OPENING PRAYER Eternal God, you alone are holy and the source of all holiness. Cleanse us from our sins and unite our prayers with the worship of your one Church, in heaven and on earth . . . Glory be . . .

PSALMODY They requite me evil for good; my soul is forlorn.
But I, when they were sick – I wore sackcloth,
I afflicted myself with fasting.
I prayed with head bowed on my bosom,
as though I grieved for my friend or my brother;
I went about as one who laments his mother,
bowed down and in mourning. Psalm 35.12–14

SCRIPTURE READINGS We who are strong ought to bear with the failings of the weak, and not to please ourselves; let each of us please his neighbour for his good, to edify him. For Christ did not please himself; but, as it is written, 'The reproaches of those who reproached thee fell on me.' For whatever was written in former days was written for our instruction, that by steadfastness and by the encouragement of the scriptures we might have hope. May the God of steadfastness and encouragement grant you to live in such harmony with one another, in accord with Christ Jesus, that together you may with one voice glorify the God and Father of our Lord Jesus Christ. Welcome one another, therefore, as Christ has welcomed you, for the glory of God. Romans 15.1–7

Peter was sitting outside in the courtyard. A maid came up to him, and said, 'You also were with Jesus the Galilean.' He denied it, saying, 'I do not know what you mean.' When he went out to the porch, another maid saw him, and she said, 'This man was with Jesus of Nazareth.' Again he denied it with an oath, 'I do not know the man.' After a little while the bystanders came up and said to Peter, 'Certainly you are also one of them, for your accent betrays you.' He began to invoke a curse on himself and to swear, 'I do not know the man.' Immediately the cock crowed. Peter remembered the saying of Jesus, 'Before the cock crows, you will deny me three times.' He went out and wept bitterly. St Matthew 26.69–75*

RESPONSE 'Just as I am, thou wilt receive,
wilt welcome, pardon, cleanse, relieve:
because thy promise I believe, O Lamb of God I come.'

Almighty God, your Son chose to give up his life to reconcile us to yourself – we worship you and we adore your holy name . . .
'I do not know the man' – Lord, when we deny you, look on us as you looked on Peter, with your love and mercy . . .
'You also were with Jesus the Galilean' – kindle the fire of your love in our hearts, so that the world may know that we have been with Jesus . . .

INTERCESSIONS *pages 390–393* CLOSING PRAYERS *page 402–403*

OPENING PRAYER Eternal God, you alone are holy and the source of all holiness. Cleanse us from our sins and unite our prayers with the worship of your one Church, in heaven and on earth . . . Glory be . . .

PSALMODY I will sing of thy steadfast love, O Lord, for ever;
with my mouth I will proclaim thy faithfulness
to all generations.
For thy steadfast love was established for ever,
thy faithfulness is firm as the heavens.
Thou hast said,
'I have made a covenant with my chosen one,
I have sworn to David my servant:
"I will establish your descendants for ever,
and build your throne for all generations."' Psalm 89.1–4

SCRIPTURE READINGS Put on then, as God's chosen ones, holy and beloved, compassion, kindness, lowliness, meekness, and patience. Colossians 3.12

Now the birth of Jesus Christ took place in this way. When his mother Mary had been betrothed to Joseph, before they came together she was found to be with child of the Holy Spirit; and her husband Joseph, being a just man and unwilling to put her to shame, resolved to divorce her quietly. But as he considered this, behold, an angel of the Lord appeared to him in a dream, saying, 'Joseph, son of David, do not fear to take Mary your wife, for that which is conceived in her is of the Holy Spirit; she will bear a son, and you shall call his name Jesus, for he will save his people from their sins.' All this took place to fulfil what the Lord had spoken by the prophet: 'Behold, a virgin shall conceive and bear a son, and his name shall be called Emmanuel' (which means, God with us). When Joseph woke from sleep, he did as the angel of the Lord commanded him; he took his wife, but knew her not until she had borne a son; and he called his name Jesus.
St Matthew 1.18–25

RESPONSE 'Blessed be the Lord, the God of Israel,
who alone does wondrous things.'

Almighty God, you chose Joseph to be the guardian of your Son, and husband of the Blessed Virgin Mary – in union with your universal Church, we celebrate this feast with praise and thanksgiving . . .
Joseph was kind and loving and honourable – Lord, give us grace to follow his example . . .
Your Church is the guardian of your mysteries and revelations – we pray with Saint Joseph that the Church may always be strong in faith and love . . .

INTERCESSIONS *pages 390–393* CLOSING PRAYERS *page 402–403*

20 March *Judas Iscariot Commits Suicide*

OPENING PRAYER Eternal God, you alone are holy and the source of all holiness. Cleanse us from our sins and unite our prayers with the worship of your one Church, in heaven and on earth . . . Glory be . . .

PSALMODY At my stumbling they gathered in glee,
they gathered together against me;
cripples whom I knew not slandered me without ceasing;
they impiously mocked more and more,
gnashing at me with their teeth.
How long, O Lord, wilt thou look on?
Rescue me from their ravages, my life from the lions!
Then I will thank thee in the great congregation;
in the mighty throng I will praise thee. Psalm 35.15–18

SCRIPTURE READINGS 'In this ministry and apostleship from which Judas turned aside to go to his own place.' Acts 1.25

When morning came, all the chief priests and the elders of the people took counsel against Jesus to put him to death; and they bound him and led him away and delivered him to Pilate the governor. When Judas, his betrayer, saw that he was condemned, he repented and brought back the thirty pieces of silver to the chief priests and the elders, saying, 'I have sinned in betraying innocent blood.' They said, 'What is that to us? See to it yourself.' Throwing down the pieces of silver in the temple, he departed; and he went and hanged himself. But the chief priests, taking the pieces of silver, said, 'It is not lawful to put them into the treasury, since they are blood money.' So they took counsel, and bought with them the potter's field, to bury strangers in. Therefore that field has been called the Field of Blood to this day. Then was fulfilled what had been spoken by the prophet Jeremiah, saying, 'And they took the thirty pieces of silver, the price of him on whom a price had been set by some of the sons of Israel, and they gave them for the potter's field, as the Lord directed me.'
St Matthew 27.1–10

RESPONSE 'Thou, O Lord, art my hope,
my trust, O Lord, from my youth.'

Heavenly Father, your Son allowed himself to be led like a lamb to the slaughter – we thank you for his perfect offering at Calvary . . .
Your Son was betrayed for thirty pieces of silver – guard the Church from the love of money and power, and protect it from treachery and evil . . .
Judas realized his mistake too late – give wisdom to Church leaders, and keep us all firm in the faith of the crucified and risen Christ . . .

INTERCESSIONS *pages 390–393* CLOSING PRAYERS *page 402–403*

OPENING PRAYER Eternal God, you alone are holy and the source of all holiness. Cleanse us from our sins and unite our prayers with the worship of your one Church, in heaven and on earth . . . Glory be . . .

PSALMODY Let not those rejoice over me who are wrongfully my foes,
and let not those wink the eye who hate me without cause.
For they do not speak peace,
but against those who are quiet in the land
they conceive words of deceit.
They open wide their mouths against me;
they say, 'Aha, Aha! our eyes have seen it!' Psalm 35.19–21

SCRIPTURE READINGS

Behold, the Lord God helps me;
who will declare me guilty? Isaiah 50.9

Jesus stood before the governor; and the governor asked him, 'Are you the King of the Jews?' Jesus said, 'You have said so.' But when he was accused by the chief priests and elders, he made no answer. Then Pilate said, 'Do you not hear how many things they testify against you?' But he gave no answer, not even to a single charge; so that the governor wondered greatly. Now at the feast the governor was accustomed to release for the crowd any one prisoner whom they wanted. When they had gathered, Pilate said, 'Whom do you want me to release for you, Barabbas or Jesus who is called Christ?' For he knew that it was out of envy that they had delivered him up. His wife sent word to him, 'Have nothing to do with that righteous man, for I have suffered much over him today in a dream.' The governor again said, 'Which of the two do you want me to release for you?' They said, 'Barabbas.' Pilate said to them, 'Then what shall I do with Jesus who is called Christ?' They all said, 'Let him be crucified.' He said, 'Why, what evil has he done?' But they shouted all the more, 'Let him be crucified.' When Pilate saw that he was gaining nothing, but rather that a riot was beginning, he took water and washed his hands, saying, 'I am innocent of this man's blood; see to it yourselves.' The people answered, 'His blood be on us and on our children!' St Matthew 27.11–25*

RESPONSE 'Arise, O God, judge the earth;
for to thee belong all the nations.'

Loving Father in heaven, great is the mystery of your love for us – we sing your praise with joyful hearts . . .
Your Son is King of kings and Lord of lords, and for our sake he allowed himself to be put on trial by earthly rulers – we thank you for the humility and courage of your Son . . .
'What is truth' – lead your Church in the way of truth and love . . .

INTERCESSIONS *pages 390–393* CLOSING PRAYERS *page 402–403*

22 March *Jesus is Mocked*

OPENING PRAYER Eternal God, you alone are holy and the source of all holiness. Cleanse us from our sins and unite our prayers with the worship of your one Church, in heaven and on earth . . . Glory be . . .

PSALMODY Thou hast seen, O Lord; be not silent!
O Lord, be not far from me!
Bestir thyself, and awake for my right,
for my cause, my God and my Lord!
Vindicate me, O Lord, my God,
according to thy righteousness. Psalm 35.22–24*

SCRIPTURE READINGS

He was despised and rejected by men;
a man of sorrows, and acquainted with grief;
and as one from whom men hide their faces
he was despised, and we esteemed him not.
Surely he has borne our griefs
and carried our sorrows;
yet we esteemed him stricken,
smitten by God, and aflicted.
But he was wounded for our transgressions,
he was bruised for our iniquities;
upon him was the chastisement that made us whole,
and with his stripes we are healed.
All we like sheep have gone astray;
we have turned every one to his own way;
and the Lord has laid on him
the iniquity of us all. Isaiah 53.3–6

The soldiers took Jesus into the praetorium, and gathered the whole battalion before him. They stripped him and put a scarlet robe upon him, and plaiting a crown of thorns they put it on his head, and put a reed in his right hand. Kneeling before him they mocked him, saying, 'Hail, King of the Jews!' They spat upon him, and took the reed and struck him on the head. When they had mocked him, they stripped him of the robe, and put his own clothes on him, and led him away to crucify him.

St Matthew 27.27–31*

RESPONSE 'Blessed are the men whose strength is in thee,
in whose heart are the highways to Zion.'

Heavenly Father, your Son endured mockery and false homage for our salvation – help us to offer you true worship through Jesus Christ . . .
Jesus suffered for our salvation – help us to enter his suffering . . .
Our hope and our glory come from the victory of your Son on the Cross – all glory and praise to Christ our Redeemer and Lord . . .

INTERCESSIONS *pages 390–393* CLOSING PRAYERS *page 402–403*

23 March *Jesus is Crucified*

OPENING PRAYER Eternal God, you alone are holy and the source of all holiness. Cleanse us from our sins and unite our prayers with the worship of your one Church, in heaven and on earth . . . Glory be . . .

PSALMODY Transgression speaks to the wicked deep in his heart;
there is no fear of God before his eyes.
For he flatters himself in his own eyes
that his iniquity cannot be found out and hated.
The words of his mouth are mischief and deceit;
he has ceased to act wisely and do good.
He plots mischief while on his bed;
he sets himself in a way that is not good;
he spurns not evil. Psalm 36.1–4

SCRIPTURE READINGS
Thy glory, O Israel, is slain upon thy high places.
How are the mighty fallen. 2 Samuel 1.19

As they went out, they came upon a man of Cyrene, Simon by name; this man they compelled to carry his cross. And when they came to a place called Golgotha (which means the place of a skull), they offered him wine to drink, mingled with gall; but when he had tasted it, he would not drink it. And when they had crucified him, they divided his garments among them by casting lots; then they sat down and kept watch over him there. And over his head they put the charge against him, which read, 'This is Jesus the King of the Jews.' Then two robbers were crucified with him, one on the right and one on the left. And those who passed by derided him, wagging their heads and saying, 'You who would destroy the temple and build it in three days, save yourself! If you are the Son of God, come down from the cross.' So also the chief priests, with the scribes and elders, mocked him, saying, 'He saved others; he cannot save himself. He is the King of Israel; let him come down now from the cross, and we will believe in him. He trusts in God; let God deliver him now, if he desires him; for he said, "I am the Son of God."' And the robbers who were crucified with him also reviled him in the same way. St Matthew 27.32–44

RESPONSE 'Gladden the soul of thy servant,
for to thee, O Lord, do I lift up my soul.'

Heavenly Father, your Son entered glory by way of the Cross – unite our prayers and praises with his perfect sacrifice of love . . .
Your Son died to atone for all sins, and each new sin contributes to his death – have mercy on us and make us holy . . .
Your Son brings joy to the world through his victory on the Cross – we venerate the Cross and rejoice in his glorious resurrection . . .

INTERCESSIONS *pages 390–393* CLOSING PRAYERS *page 402–403*

OPENING PRAYER Eternal God, you alone are holy and the source of all holiness. Cleanse us from our sins and unite our prayers with the worship of your one Church, in heaven and on earth . . . Glory be . . .

PSALMODY How precious is thy steadfast love, O God!
The children of men take refuge in the shadow of thy wings.
They feast on the abundance of thy house,
and thou givest them drink from the river of thy delights.
For with thee is the fountain of life;
in thy light do we see light.
O continue thy steadfast love to those who know thee,
and thy salvation to the upright of heart! Psalm 36.7–10

SCRIPTURE READINGS God shows his love for us in that while we were yet sinners Christ died for us. Romans 5.8

From the sixth hour there was darkness over all the land until the ninth hour. About the ninth hour Jesus cried with a loud voice, 'Eli, Eli, lama sabach-thani?' that is 'My God, my God, why hast thou forsaken me?' Some of the bystanders hearing it said, 'This man is calling Elijah.' One of them at once ran and took a sponge, filled it with vinegar, and put it on a reed, and gave it to him to drink. But the others said, 'Wait, let us see whether Elijah will come to save him.' Jesus cried again with a loud voice and yielded up his spirit. And behold the curtain of the temple was torn in two, from top to bottom; and the earth shook, and the rocks were split; the tombs also were opened, and many bodies of the saints who had fallen asleep were raised, and coming out of the tombs after his resurrection they went into the holy city and appeared to many. When the centurion and those who were with him, keeping watch over Jesus, saw the earthquake and what took place, they were filled with awe, and said, 'Truly, this was the Son of God!' There were many women there, looking on from afar, who had followed Jesus from Galilee, ministering to him; among whom were Mary Magdalene, and Mary the mother of James and Joseph, and the mother of the sons of Zebedee. St Matthew 27.45–56

RESPONSE 'Blessed be the Lord for ever!
Amen and Amen.'

Holy Father, you alone are immortal – we praise you for the self-offering of your beloved Son for our salvation . . .
Your Son redeemed us by his Cross and precious blood – Lord, help us to share the fellowship of his suffering and seek your will in all things . . .
'My God, my God, why hast thou forsaken me?' – Lord, we rejoice that you are always with us, even to the end of time . . .

INTERCESSIONS *pages 390–393* CLOSING PRAYERS *page 402–403*

25 March *The Annunciation of our Lord*

OPENING PRAYER Eternal God, you alone are holy and the source of all holiness. Cleanse us from our sins and unite our prayers with the worship of your one Church, in heaven and on earth . . . Glory be . . .

PSALMODY O Lord, my heart is not lifted up,
my eyes are not raised too high;
I do not occupy myself with things too great
and too marvellous for me.
But I have calmed and quieted my soul,
like a child quieted at its mother's breast;
like a child that is quieted is my soul.
O Israel, hope in the Lord
from this time forth and for evermore. Psalm 131

SCRIPTURE READINGS 'The Lord himself will give you a sign. Behold, a young woman shall conceive and bear a son, and shall call his name Immanuel.' Isaiah 7.14

In the sixth month the angel Gabriel was sent from God to a city of Galilee named Nazareth, to a virgin betrothed to a man whose name was Joseph, of the house of David; and the virgin's name was Mary. He came to her and said, 'Hail, O favoured one, the Lord is with you!' She was greatly troubled at the saying, and considered in her mind what sort of greeting this might be. The angel said, 'Do not be afraid, Mary, for you have found favour with God. Behold, you will conceive in your womb and bear a son, and you shall call his name Jesus. He will be great, and will be called the Son of the Most High; and the Lord God will give to him the throne of his father David, and he will reign over the house of Jacob for ever; and of his kingdom there will be no end.' Mary said, 'How shall this be, since I have no husband?' The angel said, 'The Holy Spirit will come upon you, and the power of the Most High will overshadow you; therefore the child to be born will be called holy, the Son of God.' Mary said, 'Behold, I am the handmaid of the Lord; let it be to me according to your word.' And the angel departed from her. St Luke 1.26–38*

RESPONSE 'Sing to the Lord, bless his name;
tell of his salvation from day to day.'

Eternal God, you gave a unique place to Mary in your plan for our salvation – with joy we celebrate her acceptance of your calling . . .
'The Holy Spirit will come upon you' – we rejoice that Mary is blessed among women in all generations and we rejoice in her Son Jesus . . .
Mary accepted her destiny with perfect faith – Lord, help us by your grace to follow her example . . .

INTERCESSIONS *pages 390–393* CLOSING PRAYERS *page 402–403*

26 March *The Burial of Jesus*

OPENING PRAYER Eternal God, you alone are holy and the source of all holiness. Cleanse us from our sins and unite our prayers with the worship of your one Church, in heaven and on earth . . . Glory be . . .

PSALMODY Fret not yourself because of the wicked,
be not envious of wrongdoers!
For they will soon fade like the grass,
and wither like the green herb.
Trust in the Lord, and do good;
so you will dwell in the land, and enjoy security.
Take delight in the Lord,
and he will give you the desires of your heart. Psalm 37.1–4

SCRIPTURE READINGS Christ died for sins once for all, the righteous for the unrighteous, that he might bring us to God, being put to death in the flesh but made alive in the spirit; in which he went and preached to the spirits in prison, who formerly did not obey. 1 Peter 3.18–20

When it was evening, there came a rich man from Arimathea, named Joseph, who also was a disciple of Jesus. He went to Pilate and asked for the body of Jesus. Then Pilate ordered it to be given to him. And Joseph took the body, and wrapped it in a clean linen shroud, and laid it in his own new tomb, which he had hewn in the rock; and he rolled a great stone to the door of the tomb, and departed. Mary Magdalene and the other Mary were there, sitting opposite the sepulchre. Next day, that is, after the day of Preparation, the chief priests and the Pharisees gathered before Pilate and said, 'Sir, we remember how that imposter said, while he was still alive, "After three days I will rise again." Therefore order the sepulchre to be made secure until the third day, lest his disciples go and steal him away, and tell the people, "He has risen from the dead," and the last fraud will be worse than the first.' Pilate said to them, 'You have a guard of soldiers; go, make it as secure as you can.' So they went and made the sepulchre secure by sealing the stone and setting a guard.
St Matthew 27.57–66

RESPONSE 'How great are thy works, O Lord!
Thy thoughts are very deep.'

Holy Father, your Son finished the cup of suffering and died on the Cross for us – we praise you for the greatness of your redeeming love . . .
'Joseph took the body, and wrapped it in a clean linen shroud' – Lord, free us from fear of death, and keep us steadfast in faith . . .
We have recalled the death and burial of your Son – we praise you and bless you for the promise of eternal life in Jesus Christ . . .

INTERCESSIONS *pages 390–393* CLOSING PRAYERS *page 402–403*

OPENING PRAYER Eternal God, you alone are holy and the source of all holiness. Cleanse us from our sins and unite our prayers with the worship of your one Church, in heaven and on earth . . . Glory be . . .

PSALMODY Commit your way to the Lord;
trust in him, and he will act.
Be still before the Lord, and wait patiently for him.
Refrain from anger, and forsake wrath!
Depart from evil, and do good;
so shall you abide for ever.
For the Lord loves justice;
he will not forsake his saints.
The righteous shall be preserved for ever,
but the children of the wicked shall be cut off.
The salvation of the righteous is from the Lord;
he is their refuge in the time of trouble. Psalm 37.5–39*

SCRIPTURE READINGS
Sing praises to the Lord, for he has done gloriously.
Let this be known in all the earth. Isaiah 12.5

After the sabbath, toward the dawn of the first day of the week, Mary Magdalene and the other Mary went to the sepulchre. There was a great earthquake; for an angel of the Lord descended from heaven and rolled back the stone, and sat upon it. His appearance was like lightning, and his raiment white as snow. For fear of him the guards trembled and became like dead men. But the angel said to the women, 'Do not be afraid; for I know that you seek Jesus who was crucified. He is not here; for he has risen, as he said. See the place where he lay. Go quickly and tell his disciples that he has risen from the dead, and he is going before you to Galilee; there you will see him. Lo, I have told you.' They departed quickly from the tomb with fear and great joy, and ran to tell his disciples. Behold, Jesus met them and said, 'Hail!' They took hold of his feet and worshipped him. Jesus said, 'Do not be afraid; go and tell my brethren to go to Galilee, and there they will see me.' St Matthew 28.1–10

RESPONSE 'O sing to the Lord a new song,
sing to the Lord, all the earth.'

Eternal God, you raised your Son from the grave early on the third day. . .we praise you for raising us to new life and eternal joy in Christ . . .
Your Son was raised with power by the Holy Spirit and unseen by mortal eye – we rejoice that our Redeemer is alive and now intercedes for us . . .
Your Church is the resurrection community and we are the Easter people – we rejoice that Christ is risen and is present in His Church . . .

INTERCESSIONS *pages 390–393* CLOSING PRAYERS *page 402–403*

OPENING PRAYER Eternal God, you alone are holy and the source of all holiness. Cleanse us from our sins and unite our prayers with the worship of your one Church, in heaven and on earth . . . Glory be . . .

PSALMODY O Lord, rebuke me not in thy anger,
nor chasten me in thy wrath!
My wounds grow foul because of my foolishness,
I am utterly bowed down and prostrate;
all the day I go about mourning.
Lord, all my longing is known to thee,
my sighing is not hidden from thee.
Do not forsake me, O Lord!
O my God, be not far from me!
Make haste to help me, O Lord, my salvation! Psalm 38.1–22*

SCRIPTURE READINGS God was in Christ reconciling the world to himself, not counting their trespass against them, and entrusting to us the message of reconciliation. So we are ambassadors for Christ, God making his appeal through us. 2 Corinthians 5.19–20

While they were going, some of the guard went into the city and told the chief priests all that had taken place. When they had assembled with the elders and taken counsel, they gave a sum of money to the soldiers, and said, 'Tell people, "His disciples came by night and stole him away while we were asleep." If this comes to the governor's ears, we will satisfy him and keep you out of trouble.' So they took the money and did as they were directed; and this story has been spread among the Jews to this day. Now the eleven disciples went to Galilee, to the mountain to which Jesus had directed them. When they saw him they worshipped him; but some doubted. Jesus said, 'All authority in heaven and on earth has been given to me. Go therefore and make disciples of all nations, baptizing them in the name of the Father and of the Son and of the Holy Spirit, teaching them to observe all that I have commanded you; and Lo, I am with you always, to the close of the age.' St Matthew 28.11–20

RESPONSE 'Great is the Lord,
and greatly to be praised.'

Almighty God, you call us to share in the mission of your Son – we praise you for gathering faithful witnesses for the Gospel in every age . . .
'Go and make disciples of all nations' – Lord, renew your whole Church, and help us to spread your Gospel of love by our words and actions . . .
'Lo, I am with you always, to the close of the age' – we proclaim your glory and we rejoice in your presence with us always . . .

INTERCESSIONS *pages 390–393* CLOSING PRAYERS *page 402–403*

OPENING PRAYER Eternal God, you alone are holy and the source of all holiness. Cleanse us from our sins and unite our prayers with the worship of your one Church, in heaven and on earth . . . Glory be . . .

PSALMODY I said, 'I will guard my ways,
that I may not sin with my tongue.'
I was dumb and silent, I held my peace to no avail.
As I mused, the fire burned,
then I spoke with my tongue:
'Lord, let me know my end,
let me know how fleeting my life is!
And now, Lord, for what do I wait? My hope is in thee.
Hear my prayer, O Lord, and give ear to my cry;
For I am a passing guest,
a sojourner, like all my fathers.' Psalm 39.1–12*

SCRIPTURE READINGS

The Lord is the everlasting God,
the Creator of the ends of the earth. Isaiah 40.28

The beginning of the gospel of Jesus Christ, the Son of God. As it is written in Isaiah the prophet:

'Behold, I send my messenger before thy face,
who shall prepare thy way;
the voice of one crying in the wilderness:
Prepare the way of the Lord, make his paths straight.'

John the baptizer appeared in the wilderness, preaching a baptism of repentance for the forgiveness of sins. And there went out to him all the country of Judea, and all the people of Jerusalem; and they were baptized by him in the river Jordan, confessing their sins. Now John was clothed with camel's hair, and had a leather girdle around his waist, and ate locusts and wild honey. He preached, saying, 'After me comes he who is mightier than I, the thong of whose sandals I am not worthy to stoop down and untie. I have baptized you with water; but he will baptize you with the Holy Spirit.' St Mark 1.1–8

RESPONSE 'Let thy work be manifest to thy servants,
and the glorious power to their children.'

Eternal God, you raised up John the Baptist to prepare for the mission of your Son – we proclaim your glory and we worship your holy name . . .
You raised up John the Baptist to preach a message of repentance – we praise you for all who repent and turn to Christ in penitence and faith . . .
'I send my messenger before thy face' – Lord, strengthen your Church with your grace to share in the mission of your Son to the world . . .

INTERCESSIONS *pages 390–393* CLOSING PRAYERS *page 402–403*

30 March *The Baptism of Jesus*

OPENING PRAYER Eternal God, you alone are holy and the source of all holiness. Cleanse us from our sins and unite our prayers with the worship of your one Church, in heaven and on earth . . . Glory be . . .

PSALMODY I waited patiently for the Lord;
he inclined to me and heard my cry.
He drew me up from the desolate pit, out of the miry bog,
and set my feet upon a rock, making my steps secure.
He put a new song in my mouth,
a song of praise to our God.
Many will see and fear, and put their trust in the Lord.
Blessed is the man who makes the Lord his trust,
who does not turn to the proud.
Thou hast multiplied, O Lord my God,
thy wonderous deeds and thy thoughts towards us;
none can compare with thee! Psalm 40.1–5*

SCRIPTURE READINGS The Spirit of the Lord God is upon me, because the Lord has anointed me to bring good tidings to the afflicted; he has sent me to bind up the broken-hearted, to proclaim liberty to the captives, and the opening of the prison to those who are bound; to proclaim the year of the Lord's favour, and the day of vengance of our God; to comfort all who mourn; to grant to those who mourn in Zion – to give them a garland instead of ashes, the oil of gladness instead of mourning, the mantle of praise instead of a faint spirit; that they may be called oaks of righteousness, the planting of the Lord, that he may be glorified. Isaiah 61.1–3

In those days Jesus came from Nazareth of Galilee and was baptized by John in the Jordan. And when he came up out of the water, immediately he saw the heavens opened and the Spirit descending upon him like a dove; and a voice came from heaven, 'Thou art my beloved Son; with thee I am well pleased.' The Spirit immediately drove him out into the wilderness. And he was in the wilderness forty days, tempted by Satan; and he was with the wild beasts; and the angels ministered to him. St Mark 1.9–13

RESPONSE 'Let the favour of the Lord our God be upon us,
and establish thou the work of our hands upon us.'

Eternal God, you proclaimed Jesus as your beloved Son at his Baptism –
All glory and praise to the Father, Son and Holy Spirit . . .
'He was tempted by Satan' – Lord, help us by the Spirit to overcome all temptations and to grow into union with Christ . . .
You anointed your Son with power as prophet, priest and king, when the Spirit came upon him – we praise you for your eternal love . . .

INTERCESSIONS *pages 390–393* CLOSING PRAYERS *page 402–403*

31 March *The Call of the First Disciples*

OPENING PRAYER Eternal God, you alone are holy and the source of all holiness. Cleanse us from our sins and unite our prayers with the worship of your one Church, in heaven and on earth . . . Glory be . . .

PSALMODY Then I said, 'Lo, I come;
in the roll of the book it is written of me;
I delight to do thy will, O my God;
thy law is within my heart.'
I have told the glad news of deliverance
in the great congregation;
lo, I have not restrained my lips, as thou knowest, O Lord.
I have not hid thy saving help within my heart,
I have spoken of thy faithfulness and thy salvation.
Psalm 40.6–10

SCRIPTURE READINGS The word of the Lord came to Jonah the second time, saying, 'Arise, go to Nineveh, that great city, and proclaim to it the message that I tell you.' So Jonah arose and went to Nineveh, according to the word of the Lord. And he cried, 'Yet forty days, and Nineveh shall be overthrown!' And the people of Nineveh believed God; they proclaimed a fast, and put on sackcloth. When God saw what they did, how they turned from their evil way, he repented of the evil which he had said he would do to them; and he did not do it. Jonah 3.1–10*

After John was arrested, Jesus came into Galilee, preaching the gospel of God, saying, 'The time is fulfilled, and the Kingdom of God is at hand; repent, and believe the Gospel.' Passing along by the Sea of Galilee, he saw Simon and Andrew the brother of Simon casting a net in the sea; for they were fishermen. Jesus said, 'Follow me and I will make you become fishers of men.' Immediately they left their nets and followed him. And going on a little farther, he saw James the son of Zebedee and John his brother, who were in their boat mending the nets. Immediately he called them; and they left their father Zebedee in the boat with the hired servants, and followed him. St Mark 1.14–20

RESPONSE 'I will sing of thy steadfast love, O Lord, for ever,
with my mouth I will proclaim thy faithfulness to all generations.'

Heavenly Father, your Son gathered his disciples around him – we praise you for his mission to gather disciples in every age . . .
'The time is fulfilled, and the Kingdom of God is at hand' – Lord, help us to regard all our time on earth as a precious gift from you . . .
'Follow me and I will make you become fishers of men' – fill your Church with your graces, and strengthen us for your service . . .

INTERCESSIONS *pages 390–393* CLOSING PRAYERS *page 402–403*

1 April

Teaching with Authority

OPENING PRAYER O come, let us worship and bow down, and kneel before the Lord, our Maker! For you are our God, and we are the people of your pasture, and the sheep of your hand . . . Glory be . . .

PSALMODY Do not thou, O Lord, withhold thy mercy from me,
For evils have encompassed me without number;
my iniquities have overtaken me,
till I cannot see.
Be pleased, O Lord, to deliver me.
O Lord, make haste to help me.
May all who seek thee rejoice and be glad in thee;
may those who love thy salvation say continually,
'Great is the Lord!'
Psalm 40.11–16*

SCRIPTURE READINGS The Lord said to Moses, 'I will raise up a prophet like you from among their brethren; and I will put my words in his mouth, and he shall speak to them all that I command him.'
Deuteronomy 18.17–18*

Jesus and the disciples went into Capernaum; immediately on the sabbath Jesus entered the synagogue and taught. They were astonished at his teaching, for he taught as one who had authority, and not as the scribes. There was in their synagogue a man with an unclean spirit; he cried out, 'What have you to do with us, Jesus of Nazareth? Have you come to destroy us? I know who you are, the Holy One of God.' Jesus rebuked him, saying, 'Be silent, and come out of him!' The unclean spirit, convulsing him and crying with a loud voice, came out of him. They were all amazed, so that they questioned among themselves, saying, 'What is this? A new teaching! With authority he commands even the unclean spirits, and they obey him.' His fame spread throughout the surrounding region of Galilee. Immediately he left the synagogue, and entered the house of Simon and Andrew, with James and John. Now Simon's mother-in-law lay sick with a fever, and immediately they told him of her. He took her by the hand and lifted her up, and the fever left her; and she served them.
St Mark 1.21–31

RESPONSE 'So teach us to number our days,
that we may get a heart of wisdom.'

Heavenly Father, you are the source of authority in the Church – we rejoice that the Church is a sign and sacrament of the Gospel in the world . . .
'He taught them as one who had authority' – Lord, give wisdom and understanding to all who teach and to all who learn the Faith . . .
'Jesus entered the house of Simon and Andrew' – be with us in our homes, at our work and leisure, and help us to reflect your love in our lives . . .

INTERCESSIONS *pages 390–393* CLOSING PRAYERS *page 402–403*

OPENING PRAYER O come, let us worship and bow down, and kneel before the Lord, our Maker! For you are our God, and we are the people of your pasture, and the sheep of your hand . . . Glory be . . .

PSALMODY God is our refuge and strength,
a very present help in trouble.
Therefore we will not fear though the earth should change,
though the mountains shake in the heart of the sea;
though its waters roar and foam,
though the mountains tremble with its tumult.
There is a river whose streams make glad the city of God,
the holy habitation of the Most High.
God is in the midst of her, she shall not be moved;
God will help her right early. Psalm 46.1–5

SCRIPTURE READINGS If I preach the gospel, that gives me no ground for boasting. For necessity is laid upon me. Woe to me if I do not preach the gospel! For if I do this of my own will, I have a reward; but if not of my own will, I am entrusted with a commission. What then is my reward? Just this: that in my preaching I may make the gospel free of charge, not making full use of my right in the gospel. For though I am free from all men, I have made myself a slave to all, that I might win the more. To the weak I became weak, that I might win the weak. I have become all things to all men, that I might by all means save some. I do it all for the sake of the gospel, that I may share in its blessings. 1 Corinthians 9.16–23*

In the morning, a great while before day, Jesus rose and went out to a lonely place, and there he prayed. Simon and those who were with him pursued him, and they found him and said, 'Every one is searching for you.' He said, 'Let us go on to the next towns, that I may preach there also; for that is why I came out.' He went throughout all Galilee, preaching in their synagogues and casting out demons. St Mark 1.35–40

RESPONSE 'Thou art great and doest wonderous things,
thou alone art God.'

Gracious God, your Son gave authority to the Church to preach the Gospel – we praise you for his presence in the Church through the Spirit . . .
Your Son rose early and went to a lonely place to pray – help us to find you in the depths and stillness of our souls . . .
Your Son prayed to you and he gave us an example to follow – Lord, teach us through the Spirit to respond to your love for us in Jesus Christ . . .

INTERCESSIONS *pages 390–393* CLOSING PRAYERS *page 402–403*

OPENING PRAYER O come, let us worship and bow down, and kneel before the Lord, our Maker! For you are our God, and we are the people of your pasture, and the sheep of your hand . . . Glory be . . .

PSALMODY We have thought on thy steadfast love, O God.
As thy name, O God,
so thy praise reaches to the ends of the earth.
Thy right hand is filled with victory.
Let the daughters of Judah rejoice
because of thy judgements!
Walk about Zion, go round about her, number her towers,
that you may tell the next generation that this is God,
our God for ever and ever. Psalm 48.9–14*

SCRIPTURE READINGS As surely as God is faithful, our word to you has not been Yes and No. For the Son of God, Jesus Christ, whom we preached among you, was not Yes and No; but in him it is always Yes. For all the promises of God find their Yes in him. That is why we utter the Amen through him, to the glory of God. 2 Corinthians 1.18–20*

They came, bringing to Jesus a paralytic carried by four men. When they could not get near him because of the crowd, they removed the roof above him; when they had made an opening, they let down the pallet on which the paralytic lay. When Jesus saw their faith, he said, 'My Son, your sins are forgiven.' Some of the scribes were sitting there, questioning in their hearts, 'Why does this man speak thus? It is blasphemy! Who can forgive sins but God alone?' Immediately Jesus, perceiving in his spirit that they questioned within themselves, said, 'Why do you question thus in your hearts? Which is easier, to say to the paralytic, "Your sins are forgiven," or to say, "Rise, take up your pallet and walk"? But that you may know that the Son of Man has authority on earth to forgive sins' – he said to the paralytic – 'I say to you, rise, take up your pallet and go home.' And he rose, and immediately took up the pallet and went out before them all; so that they were all amazed and glorified God. St Mark 2.2–12

RESPONSE 'Ascribe to the Lord the glory due his name,
bring an offering, and come into his courts.'

Heavenly Father, you call us to a new relationship with yourself in Christ – we praise you for all who repent of their sins and believe the Gospel . . .
'They came, bringing to him a paralytic' – Lord, have mercy on all who are disabled, their relatives, and those who care for them . . .
'Your sins are forgiven' – we thank you for the grace of reconciliation and inner healing . . .

INTERCESSIONS *pages 390–393* CLOSING PRAYERS *page 402–403*

OPENING PRAYER O come, let us worship and bow down, and kneel before the Lord, our Maker! For you are our God, and we are the people of your pasture, and the sheep of your hand . . . Glory be . . .

PSALMODY Why should I fear in times of trouble,
when the iniquity of my persecutors surrounds me,
men who trust in their wealth
and boast of the abundance of their riches?
Truly no man can ransom himself,
or give to God the price of his life,
for the ransom of his life is costly, and can never suffice,
that he should continue to live on for ever,
and never see the Pit.
Be not afraid when one becomes rich,
when the glory of his house increases.
For when he dies he will carry nothing away;
his glory will not go down after him.
Man cannot abide in his pomp,
he is like the beasts that perish. Psalm 49.5–20*

SCRIPTURE READINGS
My son, do not despise the Lord's discipline
or be weary of his reproof,
for the Lord reproves him whom he loves,
as a father the son in whom he delights. Proverbs 3.11–12

The crowd gathered about him, and he taught them. He saw Levi the son of Alphaeus sitting at the tax office, and he said, 'Follow me.' He rose and followed him. As he sat at table in his house, many tax collectors and sinners were sitting with Jesus and his disciples; for there were many who followed him. The scribes of the Pharisees, when they saw that he was eating with sinners and tax collectors, said to his disciples, 'Why does he eat with tax collectors and sinners?' And when Jesus heard it, he said, 'Those who are well have no need of a physician, but those who are sick; I came not to call the righteous, but sinners.' St Mark 2.13–17

RESPONSE 'Seek the Lord and his strength,
seek his presence continually.'

Heavenly Father, you called Levi to be a disciple – we praise you for all who respond to your call in every generation . . .
'Follow me' – Lord, help us by your grace to grow into union with your Son Jesus Christ . . .
'I came not to call the righteous, but sinners' – purify our motives and help us to grow in holiness and love . . .

INTERCESSIONS *pages 390–393* CLOSING PRAYERS *page 402–403*

OPENING PRAYER O come, let us worship and bow down, and kneel before the Lord, our Maker! For you are our God, and we are the people of your pasture, and the sheep of your hand . . . Glory be . . .

PSALMODY The Mighty One, God the Lord, speaks and summons the earth
Our God comes, he does not keep silence,
before him is a devouring fire,
round about him a mighty tempest.
The heavens declare his righteousness,
for God himself is judge. Psalm 50.1–6*

SCRIPTURE READINGS

The Lord said to Hosea:
'Behold, I will allure her,
and bring her into the wilderness,
and speak tenderly to her.
And there she shall answer as in the days of her youth,
as at the time when she came out of the land of Egypt.
I will betroth you to me for ever;
I will betroth you to me in righteousness and in justice,
in steadfast love, and in mercy.
I will betroth you to me in faithfulness;
and you shall know the Lord.' Hosea 2.14–20*

John's disciples and the Pharisees were fasting; and people said to Jesus, 'Why do John's disciples and the disciples of the Pharisees fast, but your disciples do not fast?' Jesus said, 'Can the wedding guests fast while the bridegroom is with them? As long as they have the bridegroom, they cannot fast. The days will come, when the bridegroom is taken away from them, and they will fast in that day. No one sews a piece of unshrunk cloth on an old garment; if he does, the patch tears away from it, the new from the old, and a worse tear is made. No one puts new wine into old wineskins; if he does, the wine will burst the skins, and the wine is lost, and so are the skins; but new wine is for fresh skins.' St Mark 2.18–22*

RESPONSE 'Full of honour and majesty is his work,
and his righteousness endures for ever.'

Heavenly Father, you make all things new in Christ – we praise you for the continual presence of the Spirit in the Church . . .
'Your Son is the Bridegroom and the Church is his Bride – Lord, make us worthy to be your guests at the wedding feast of the Lamb . . .
'The days will come, when the bridegroom is taken away from them' – even though we cannot see you, we rejoice that you are with us always . . .

INTERCESSIONS *pages 390–393* CLOSING PRAYERS *page 402–403*

OPENING PRAYER O come, let us worship and bow down, and kneel before the Lord, our Maker! For you are our God, and we are the people of your pasture, and the sheep of your hand . . . Glory be . . .

PSALMODY 'Offer to God a sacrifice of thanksgiving,
and pay your vows to the Most High;
and call upon me in the day of trouble;
I will deliver you, and you shall glorify me.'
But to the wicked, God says:
'What right have you to recite my statutes,
or take my covenant on your lips?
For you hate discipline,
and you cast my words behind you.
These things you have done and I have been silent;
you thought that I was one like yourself.
But now I rebuke you, and lay the charge before you.
He who brings thanksgiving as his sacrifice honours me;
to him who orders his way aright
I will show the salvation of God.' Psalm 50.14–23*

SCRIPTURE READINGS Moses said, 'Observe the sabbath day, to keep it holy, as the Lord your God commanded you. Six days you shall labour, and do all your work; but the seventh day is a sabbath to the Lord your God; in it you shall not do any work.' Deuteronomy 5.12–14

One sabbath Jesus was going through the grainfields; and his disciples began to pluck heads of grain. The Pharisees said, 'Look, why are they doing what is not lawful on the sabbath?' He said, 'Have you never read what David did, when he was in need and was hungry, he and those who were with him: how he entered the house of God, when Abiathar was high priest, and ate the bread of the Presence, which it is not lawful for any but the priests to eat, and also gave it to those who were with him?' And he said to them, 'The sabbath was made for man, not man for the sabbath; so the Son of Man is lord even of the sabbath.' St Mark 2.23–28

RESPONSE 'Thou, O Lord, art enthroned for ever;
thy name endures to all generations.'

Heavenly Father, you created the soil and the corn which grows in the fields – we rejoice that your Spirit renews the face of the earth . . .
'King David entered the House of God and ate the bread of the Presence' – we thank you for feeding us with your Body and Blood in the Eucharist . . .
'The Son of Man is Lord of the Sabbath' – we rejoice that your Son is also Lord of the years and King of all creation . . .

INTERCESSIONS *pages 390–393* CLOSING PRAYERS *page 402–403*

7 April *Healing on the Sabbath*

OPENING PRAYER O come, let us worship and bow down, and kneel before the Lord, our Maker! For you are our God, and we are the people of your pasture, and the sheep of your hand . . . Glory be . . .

PSALMODY Have mercy on me, O God, according to thy steadfast love;
according to thy abundant mercy blot out my transgressions.
Wash me thoroughly from my iniquity,
and cleanse me from my sin!
For I know my transgressions, and my sin is ever before me.
Against thee, thee only, have I sinned,
and done that which is evil in thy sight,
so that thou art justified in thy sentence
and blameless in thy judgement.
Behold, thou desirest truth in the inward being;
therefore teach me widsom in my secret heart.
Purge me with hyssop, and I shall be clean;
wash me, and I shall be whiter than snow.
Fill me with joy and gladness;
Create in me a clean heart, O God,
and put a new and right spirit within me.
Restore to me the joy of thy salvation,
and uphold me with a willing spirit.
Then I will teach transgressors thy ways,
and sinners will return to thee. Psalm 51.1–13*

SCRIPTURE READINGS Jesus entered the synagogue, and a man was there who had a withered hand. They watched him, to see whether he would heal him on the sabbath, so that they might accuse him. He said to the man who had the withered hand, 'Come here.' He said to them, 'Is it lawful on the sabbath to do good or to do harm, to save life or to kill?' But they were silent. He looked around with anger, grieved at their hardness of heart, and said to the man, 'Stretch out your hand.' He stretched it out, and his hand was restored. The Pharisees went out, and immediately held counsel with the Herodians, how to destroy him. St Mark 3.1–6*

RESPONSE 'Let them thank the Lord for his steadfast love,
for his wonderful works to the sons of men.'

Eternal God, you alone are the source of health and healing – we praise you for the compassion and love of your Son . . .
'Stretch out your hand' – Lord, help us to reach out in friendship and compassion, and with your love in our hearts, to all who are ill . . .
'He grieved at their hardness of heart' – help the Church to share your love with all who reject the Gospel of Jesus Christ . . .

INTERCESSIONS *pages 390–393* CLOSING PRAYERS *page 402–403*

8 April *Jesus appoints the Twelve Apostles*

OPENING PRAYER O come, let us worship and bow down, and kneel before the Lord, our Maker! For you are our God, and we are the people of your pasture, and the sheep of your hand . . . Glory be . . .

PSALMODY Why do you boast, O mighty man,
of mischief done against the godly?
Your tongue is like a sharp razor, you worker of treachery.
You love evil more than good,
and lying more than speaking the truth.
I trust in the steadfast love of God for ever and ever.
I will thank thee for ever, because thou hast done it.
I will proclaim thy name, for it is good. Psalm 52.1–9*

SCRIPTURE READINGS
This is the covenant I will make
with the house of Israel after those days,
says the Lord:
I will put my laws into their minds,
and write them on their hearts,
and I will be their God, and they shall be my people.
And they shall not teach every one his fellow
or every one his brother, saying, 'Know the Lord,'
for all shall know me,
from the least to the greatest.
For I will be merciful toward their iniquities,
and I will remember their sins no more. Hebrews 8.10–12

Jesus went up into the hills, and called to him those who he desired; and they came to him. He appointed twelve, to be with him, and to be sent out to preach and have authority to cast out demons: Simon whom he surnamed Peter; James the son of Zebedee and John the brother of James, whom he surnamed Boanerges, that is, sons of thunder; Andrew, and Philip, and Bartholomew, and Matthew, and Thomas, and James the son of Alphaeus, and Thaddaeus, and Simon the Cananaean, and Judas Iscariot, who betrayed him. St Mark 3.13-19*

RESPONSE 'One generation shall laud thy works to another,
and shall declare thy mighty acts.'

Eternal God, you gave your graces to the apostles to witness to your Son – we praise you for transforming their lives by the power of the Spirit . . .
'He called to him those whom he desired' – we thank you for calling us to be a Royal Priesthood, and to share in the mission of your Son . . .
'Jesus sent out the Twelve to preach' – Lord, inspire a true love of souls in your Church, and keep it steadfast to the faith of the apostles . . .

INTERCESSIONS *pages 390–393* CLOSING PRAYERS *page 402–403*

OPENING PRAYER O come, let us worship and bow down, and kneel before the Lord, our Maker! For you are our God, and we are the people of your pasture, and the sheep of your hand . . . Glory be . . .

PSALMODY The fool says in his heart, 'There is no God.'
They are corrupt, doing abominable iniquity.
They have all fallen away;
they are all alike depraved;
there is none that does good, no, not one.
Have those who work evil no understanding?
They will be put to shame,
for God has rejected them.
O that deliverance for Israel would come from Zion!
When God restores the fortunes of his people,
Jacob will rejoice and Israel be glad. Psalm 53.1–6*

SCRIPTURE READINGS The Spirit of the Lord departed from Saul, and an evil spirit from the Lord tormented him. Whenever the evil spirit from God was upon Saul, David took the lyre and played it; so Saul was refreshed, and was well, and the evil spirit departed from him. 1 Samuel 16.14–23*

The crowd came together again, so that they could not even eat. When his family heard it, they went to seize him, for people were saying, 'He is beside himself.' The scribes said, 'He is possessed by Beelzebub, and by the prince of demons he casts out the demons.' He said, 'How can Satan cast out Satan? If a kingdom is divided against itself, that kingdom cannot stand. If a house is divided against itself, that house will not be able to stand. If Satan has risen up against himself and is divided, he cannot stand, but is coming to an end. No one can enter a strong man's house and plunder his goods, unless he first binds the strong man; then he may plunder his house. Truly, I say to you, all sins will be forgiven the sons of men, and whatever blasphemies they utter; but whoever blasphemes against the Holy Spirit never has forgiveness, but is guilty of an eternal sin' – for they had said, 'He has an unclean spirit.' St Mark 3.20–30*

RESPONSE 'Thy kingdom is an everlasting kingdom,
and thy dominion endures throughout all generations.'

Almighty God, you chose the way of perfect love to bring salvation to the world – all praise and glory to your holy name . . .
Your Son conquered sin and evil on the Cross – Lord, give us grace to conquer our sins, and help us to fight against evil . . .
'If a Kingdom is divided against itself' – help us to remove the divisions in the Church, and make us worthy to witness to your love in Christ . . .

INTERCESSIONS *pages 390–393* CLOSING PRAYERS *page 402–403*

10 April *His Father's Will*

OPENING PRAYER O come, let us worship and bow down, and kneel before the Lord, our Maker! For you are our God, and we are the people of your pasture, and the sheep of your hand . . . Glory be . . .

PSALMODY Save me, O God, by thy name,
and vindicate me by thy might.
Hear my prayer, O God.
For insolent men have risen against me,
ruthless men seek my life;
they do not set God before them.
Behold, God is my helper;
the Lord is the upholder of my life.
With a freewill offering I will sacrifice to thee;
I will give thanks to thy name, O Lord, for it is good.
For thou hast delivered me from every trouble. Psalm 54.1–7*

SCRIPTURE READINGS Jesus fell on his face and prayed, 'My Father, if it be possible, let this cup pass from me; nevertheless, not as I will, but as thou wilt.' St Matthew 26.39

Jesus said, 'My food is to do the will of him who sent me, and to accomplish his work.' St John 4.34

'God is at work in you, both to will and to work for his good pleasure.' Philippians 2.13

His mother and his brothers came; and standing outside they sent to him and called him. And a crowd was sitting about him; and they said to him, 'Your mother and your brothers are outside, asking for you.' And he replied, 'Who are my mother and my brothers?' Looking around on those who sat about him, he said, 'Here are my mother and my brothers! Whoever does the will of God is my brother, and sister, and mother.' St Mark 3.31–35

RESPONSE 'Teach me to do thy will,
for thou art my God.'

Loving Father in heaven, the mother of your Son obeyed your will in all things – we praise you for the unique love and obedience of Mary . . .
'Not as I will, but as thou wilt' – Lord, we ask you to guide and direct us so that our wills may be united with your will . . .
'Who are my mother and my brothers?' – we rejoice to be members of your family the Church, together with the Blessed Virgin Mary, the holy apostles, patriarchs and prophets, the saints and martyrs, and all faithful Christians living and departed in the Lord Jesus . . .

INTERCESSIONS *pages 390–393* CLOSING PRAYERS *page 402–403*

OPENING PRAYER O come, let us worship and bow down, and kneel before the Lord, our Maker! For you are our God, and we are the people of your pasture, and the sheep of your hand . . . Glory be . . .

PSALMODY Give ear to my prayer, O God;
and hide not thyself from my supplication!
My heart is in anguish within me,
the terrors of death have fallen upon me.
And I say, 'O that I had wings like a dove!
I would fly away and be at rest;
I would haste to find me a shelter
from the raging wind and tempest.
Cast your burden on the Lord, and he will sustain you;
he will never permit the righteous to be moved.

Psalm 55.1–22*

SCRIPTURE READINGS When Christ had offered for all time a single sacrifice for sins, he sat down at the right hand of God, then to wait until his enemies should be made a stool for his feet. For by a single offering he has perfected for all time those who are sanctified. And the Holy Spirit also bears witness to us; for after saying,

'This is the covenant that I will make with them
after those days, says the Lord:
I will put my laws on their hearts,
and write them on their minds.' Hebrews 10.12–16

Jesus said, 'A sower went out to sow. As he sowed, some seed fell along the path, and the birds came and devoured it. Other seed fell on rocky ground, where it had not much soil, and immediately it sprang up, since it had no depth of soil; and when the sun rose it was scorched, and since it had no root it withered away. Other seed fell among thorns and the thorns grew up and choked it, and it yielded no grain. Other seeds fell into good soil and brought forth grain, growing up and increasing and yielding thirtyfold and sixtyfold and a hundredfold.' He said, 'He who has ears to hear, let him hear.' St Mark 4.2–9*

RESPONSE 'My mouth will speak the praise of the Lord,
and all flesh bless his holy name for ever and ever.'

Eternal God, you give to all who are baptized a share in the priesthood of your Son – we praise you for all your gifts of grace in the Church . . .
'Some seed withered and died' – Lord, give grace to the Church to nurture the faith of all new converts . . .
'Other seeds fell upon good soil and brought forth grain' – bless and prosper the work of all who proclaim the Gospel in the world . . .

INTERCESSIONS *pages 390–393* CLOSING PRAYERS *page 402–403*

OPENING PRAYER O come, let us worship and bow down, and kneel before the Lord, our Maker! For you are our God, and we are the people of your pasture, and the sheep of your hand . . . Glory be . . .

PSALMODY It is not an enemy who taunts me,
then I could bear it;
it is not an adversary who deals insolently with me –
then I could hide from him.
But it is you, my equal,
my companion, my familiar friend.
We used to hold sweet converse together;
within God's house we walked in fellowship.
But I call upon God: and the Lord will save me.

Psalm 55.12–16*

SCRIPTURE READINGS

'Incline your ear, and come to me;
hear, that your soul may live.' Isaiah 55.3

When Jesus was alone, those who were about him with the twelve asked him concerning the parables. He said, 'To you has been given the secret of the Kingdom of God, but for those outside everything is in parables; so that they may indeed see but not perceive, and may indeed hear but not understand; lest they should turn again, and be forgiven.' He said, 'Do you not understand this parable? How then will you understand all the parables? The sower sows the word. These are the ones along the path, where the word is sown; when they hear, Satan immediately comes and takes away the word which is sown in them. These in like manner are the ones sown upon rocky ground, who, when they hear the word, immediately receive it with joy; and they have no root in themselves, but endure for a while; then, when tribulation or persecution arises on account of the word, immediately they fall away. Others are the ones sown among thorns; they are those who hear the word, but the cares of the world, and the delight in riches, and the desire for other things, enter in and choke the word, and it proves unfruitful. But those that were sown upon the good soil are the ones who hear the word and accept it and bear fruit, thirtyfold and sixtyfold and a hundredfold.' St Mark 4.10–20

RESPONSE 'The Lord is near to all who call upon him,
to all who call upon him in truth.'

Gracious God and Father, you plant the gift of faith in our hearts – we praise you for all who have helped us to grow in the faith . . .
'Do not harden your hearts' – help us always to be open to your Word . . .
'To you has been given the secret of the Kingdom of God' – Lord, inspire and equip your Church to work for the growth of your Kingdom . . .

INTERCESSIONS *pages 390–393* CLOSING PRAYERS *page 402–403*

OPENING PRAYER O come, let us worship and bow down, and kneel before the Lord, our Maker! For you are our God, and we are the people of your pasture, and the sheep of your hand . . . Glory be . . .

PSALMODY Be gracious to me, O God, for men trample upon me;
all day long foemen oppress me;
my enemies trample upon me all day long,
for many fight against me proudly.
When I am afraid, I put my trust in thee.
In God, whose word I praise, in God I trust without a fear.
What can flesh do to me? Psalm 56.1–4

SCRIPTURE READINGS God said, 'Let there be light: and there was light.' And God saw that the light was good: and God separated the light from the darkness. God called the light Day, and the darkness he called Night. And there was evening and there was morning, one day Genesis 1.2–5

Yea, thou art my lamp, O Lord,
and my God lightens my darkness. 2 Samuel 22.29

Even if our gospel is veiled, it is veiled only to those who are perishing. In their case the god of this world has blinded the minds of the unbelievers, to keep them from seeing the light of the gospel of the glory of Christ, who is the likeness of God. For what we preach is not ourselves, but Jesus Christ as Lord, with ourselves as your servants for Jesus's sake. For it is the God who said, 'Let light shine out of darkness,' who has shone in our hearts to give the light of the knowledge of the glory of God in the face of Christ.
2 Corinthians 4.3–6

Jesus said, 'Is the lamp brought in to be put under a bushel, or under a bed, and not on a stand? For there is nothing hid, except to be made manifest; nor is anything secret, except to come to light. If any man has ears to hear, let him hear.' St Mark 4.21–23

RESPONSE 'Thy word is a lamp to my feet,
and a light to my path.'

Almighty God, your Son is the eternal light which the darkness has never put out – we praise you for the living flame of faith in the Church . . .
'Let your light shine out of darkness' – Lord, purify us so that the light of Christ may shine in the Church and be seen in the world . . .
'There is nothing hid, except it be made manifest' – Lord, forgive us all our sins, and help us to grow into union with Christ . . .

INTERCESSIONS *pages 390–393* CLOSING PRAYERS *page 402–403*

OPENING PRAYER O come, let us worship and bow down, and kneel before the Lord, our Maker! For you are our God, and we are the people of your pasture, and the sheep of your hand . . . Glory be . . .

PSALMODY All day long they seek to injure my cause.
Thou hast kept count of my tossings;
put thou my tears in thy bottle!
Are they not in thy book?
Then my enemies will be turned back in the day when I call.
This I know, that God is for me.
In God, whose word I praise, in the Lord whose word I praise,
in God I trust without a fear. What can man do to me?
My vows to thee I must perform, O God;
I will render thank offerings to thee.
For thou hast delivered my soul from death,
that I may walk before God in the light of life.

Psalm 56.5–13*

SCRIPTURE READINGS Thus says the Lord God: 'I myself will take a sprig from the lofty top of the cedar, and will set it out; I will break off from the topmost of its young twigs a tender one, and I myself will plant it upon a high and lofty mountain; on the mountain height of Israel will I plant it, that it may bring forth boughs and bear fruit.' Ezekiel 17.22–23

Jesus said, 'The Kingdom of God is as if a man should scatter seed upon the ground, and should sleep and rise night and day, and the seed should sprout and grow, he knows not how. The earth produces of itself, first the blade, then the ear, then the full grain in the ear. But when the grain is ripe, at once he puts in the sickle, because the harvest has come.' And he said, 'With what can we compare the Kingdom of God, or what parable shall we use for it? It is like a grain of mustard seed, which, when sown upon the ground, is the smallest of all the seeds on earth; yet when it is sown it grows up and becomes the greatest of all shrubs, and puts forth large branches, so that the birds of the air can make nests in its shade.'

St Mark 4.26–32

RESPONSE 'Let thy steadfast love come to me, O Lord,
thy salvation according to thy promise.'

God our Father, your Son plants the seeds of faith in our hearts – we praise you for all who respond to your love in Christ . . .
'The seed should sprout and grow' – Lord, we rejoice at the secret growth of your Kingdom in the Church and in our hearts . . .
'When the grain is ripe, he puts in the sickle' – have mercy on us now and at the hour of our death, and bring us to eternal life in Jesus Christ . . .

INTERCESSIONS *pages 390–393* CLOSING PRAYERS *page 402–403*

Fear in the Storm

OPENING PRAYER O come, let us worship and bow down, and kneel before the Lord, our Maker! For you are our God, and we are the people of your pasture, and the sheep of your hand . . . Glory be . . .

PSALMODY Be merciful to me, O God, be merciful to me,
for in thee my soul takes refuge;
in the shadow of thy wings I will take refuge,
till the storms of destruction pass by.
I cry to God Most High, to God who fulfils his purpose for me.
God will send forth his steadfast love and his faithfulness!
Be exalted, O God, above the heavens!
Let thy glory be over all the earth!
I will give thanks to thee, O Lord, among the peoples.
For thy steadfast love is great to the heavens.
Be exalted, O God, above the heavens!
Let thy glory be over all the earth! Psalm 57.1–11*

SCRIPTURE READINGS

The Lord answered Job out of the whirlwind:
'Who shut in the sea with doors,
when it burst forth from the womb;
when I made clouds its garment,
and thick darkness its swaddling band,
and I prescribed bounds for it,
and set bars and doors?' Job 38.8–10

When evening had come, Jesus said, 'Let us go across to the other side.' Leaving the crowd, they took him in the boat, just as he was. Other boats were with him. And a great storm of wind arose, and the waves beat into the boat, so that the boat was already filling. But he was in the stern, asleep on the cushion; and they woke him and said, 'Teacher, do you not care if we perish?' He awoke and rebuked the wind, and said to the sea, 'Peace! Be still!' And the wind ceased, and there was a great calm. He said, 'Why are you afraid? Have you no faith?' They were filled with awe, and said, 'Who is this, that even wind and sea obey him?' St Mark 4.35–41

RESPONSE 'Let thy steadfast love be ready to comfort me
according to thy promise to thy servant.'

Almighty God, you created the oceans and the hills – we rejoice that you are with us always in stormy and peaceful times . . .
'Do you not care if we perish?' – Lord, we praise you for your perfect love on the Cross for our salvation . . .
'Peace! Be still' – Lord, grant your gift of inner peace and joy to all who call on your name with faith and love . . .

INTERCESSIONS *pages 390–393* CLOSING PRAYERS *page 402–403*

16 April *Gadarene Swine*

OPENING PRAYER O come, let us worship and bow down, and kneel before the Lord, our Maker! For you are our God, and we are the people of your pasture, and the sheep of your hand . . . Glory be . . .

PSALMODY I will sing aloud of thy steadfast love in the morning.
O my strength, I will sing praises to thee,
for thou, O God, art my fortress,
the God who shows me steadfast love. Psalm 59.16–17*

SCRIPTURE READINGS We were met by a slave girl who had a spirit of divination and brought her owners much gain by soothsaying. She followed Paul and us, crying, 'These men are servants of the Most High God, who proclaim to you the way of salvation.' Acts 16.16–17

When Jesus had come out of the boat, there met him out of the tombs a man with an unclean spirit, who lived among the tombs; and no one could bind him any more, even with a chain. Night and day among the tombs and on the mountains he was always crying out, and bruising himself with stones. When he saw Jesus from afar, he ran and worshipped him; and crying out, he said, 'What have you to do with me, Jesus, Son of the Most High God? I adjure you by God, do not torment me.' For he had said to him, 'Come out of the man, you unclean spirit!' Jesus asked him, 'What is your name?' He replied, 'My name is Legion; for we are many.' He begged him eagerly not to send them out of the country. Now a great herd of swine was feeding there on the hillside; and they begged him, 'Send us to the swine, let us enter them.' So he gave them leave. The unclean spirits came out, and entered the swine; and the herd, numbering about two thousand, rushed down the steep bank into the sea, and were drowned. The herdsmen fled, and told it in the city and in the country. People came to see what it was that had happened. They began to beg Jesus to depart from their neighbourhood. The man who had been possessed with demons begged him that he might be with him. He refused, and said, 'Go home to your friends, and tell them how much the Lord has done for you, and how he has had mercy on you.' St Mark 5.1–19*

RESPONSE 'The Lord is my strength and my shield;
in him my heart trusts.'

Eternal God, you put the thought of eternity into our hearts – accept our adoration and praise and love . . .
'What have you to do with me, Jesus, Son of the Most High God?' – Lord, we rejoice that your Son is our High Priest and Redeemer and Friend . . .
'Tell them how much the Lord has done for you' – Lord, equip your Church to spread the Good News of the Gospel in the world . . .

INTERCESSIONS *pages 390–393* CLOSING PRAYERS *page 402–403*

OPENING PRAYER O come, let us worship and bow down, and kneel before the Lord, our Maker! For you are our God, and we are the people of your pasture, and the sheep of your hand . . . Glory be . . .

PSALMODY Hear my cry, O God, listen to my prayer;
from the end of the earth I call to thee.
Lead thou me to a rock that is higher than I;
for thou art my refuge,
a strong tower against the enemy. Psalm 61.1–3*

SCRIPTURE READINGS Now as you excel in everything – in faith, in utterance, in knowledge, in all earnestness, and in your love for us – we see that you excel in this gracious work also. Under the test of this service, you will glorify God by your obedience in acknowledging the gospel of Christ, and by the generosity of your contribution for them and for all others; while they long for you and pray for you, because of the surpassing grace of God in you. Thanks be to God for his inexpressible gift!
2 Corinthians 8.7–15*

Then came one of the rulers of the synagogue, Jairus by name; and seeing Jesus, he fell at his feet, saying, 'My little daughter is at the point of death. Come and lay your hands on her, so that she may be made well, and live.' While he was still speaking, there came from the ruler's house some who said, 'Your daughter is dead. Why trouble the Teacher any further?' But ignoring what they said, Jesus said, 'Do not fear, only believe.' He allowed no one to follow him except Peter and James and John. When they came to the house, he saw a tumult, and people weeping and wailing loudly. When he entered, he said, 'Why do you make a tumult and weep? The child is not dead but sleeping.' They laughed at him. But he put them all outside, and took the child's father and mother and those who were with him, and went in where the child was. Taking her by the hand he said, 'Talitha cumi' which means, 'Little girl, I say to you, arise.' Immediately the girl got up and walked (she was twelve years of age), and they were immediately overcome with amazement. St Mark 5.21–43*

RESPONSE 'The Lord is my strength and my song,
he has become my salvation.'

Almighty God, you are the Lord and giver of all life – we bless and praise you for the powerful resurrection of your Son from the dead . . .
You overcame death and opened the gate of eternal life through your Son – we thank you for your redeeming love . . .
Your Son alone brings comfort and hope in our sorrows – Lord, comfort all who mourn, and help them to find the consolation of your love . . .

INTERCESSIONS *pages 390–393* CLOSING PRAYERS *page 402–403*

OPENING PRAYER O come, let us worship and bow down, and kneel before the Lord, our Maker! For you are our God, and we are the people of your pasture, and the sheep of your hand . . . Glory be . . .

PSALMODY Let me dwell in thy tent for ever!
Oh to be safe under the shelter of thy wings!
For thou, O God, hast heard my vows.
Prolong the life of the king.
May he be enthroned for ever before God;
bid steadfast love and faithfulness watch over him!
So will I ever sing praises to thy name,
as I pay my vows day after day. Psalm 61.4–8

SCRIPTURE READINGS Since we are surrounded by so great a cloud of witnesses, let us also lay aside every weight, and sin which clings so closely, and let us run with perseverance the race that is set before us, looking to Jesus the pioneer and perfecter of our faith, who for the joy that was set before him endured the cross, despising the shame, and is seated at the right hand of the throne of God. Hebrews 12.1–2

A great crowd followed him and thronged him. There was a woman who had had a flow of blood for twelve years, and who had suffered much under many physicians, and had spent all that she had, and was no better but rather grew worse. She had heard the reports about Jesus, and came up behind him in the crowd and touched his garment. She said, 'If I touch even his garments, I shall be made well.' Immediately the haemorrhage ceased; and she felt in her body that she was healed of her disease. Jesus, perceiving in himself that power had gone from him, immediately turned about in the crowd, and said, 'Who touched my garments?' His disciples said, 'You see the crowd pressing around you, and yet you say, "Who touched me?"' He looked to see who had done it. The woman, knowing what had been done to her, came in fear and trembling and fell down before him, and told him the whole truth. He said, 'Daughter, your faith has made you well; go in peace, and be healed of your disease.'
St Mark 5.24–34*

RESPONSE 'O give thanks to the Lord, for he is good,
his steadfast love endures for ever.'

Loving Father, the grace of Faith is your gift to us – give us ever thankful hearts to bless you and praise you in glory . . .
You are the source of health and healing – Lord, bless the work of all surgeons, doctors and nurses, and all involved in caring for the sick . . .
Your Son promised to be with us always – Lord, in your mercy, comfort and heal the sick, and make your presence known to them . . .

INTERCESSIONS *pages 390–393* CLOSING PRAYERS *page 402–403*

OPENING PRAYER O come, let us worship and bow down, and kneel before the Lord, our Maker! For you are our God, and we are the people of your pasture, and the sheep of your hand . . . Glory be . . .

PSALMODY For God alone my soul waits in silence,
for my hope is from him.
He only is my rock and my salvation,
my fortress;
I shall not be shaken.
On God rests my deliverance and my honour;
my mighty rock, my refuge is God.
Trust in him at all times, O people;
pour out your heart before him;
God is a refuge for us. Psalm 62.5–8

SCRIPTURE READINGS In him, according to the purpose of him who accomplishes all things according to the counsel of his will, we who first hoped in Christ have been destined and appointed to live for the praise of his glory. In him you also, who have heard the word of truth, the gospel of your salvation, and have believed in him, were sealed with the promised Holy Spirit, which is the guarantee of our inheritance until we acquire possession of it, to the praise of his glory Ephesians 1.11–14

Jesus went about among the villages teaching. And he called to him the twelve, and began to send them out two by two, and gave them authority over the unclean spirits. He charged them to take nothing for their journey except a staff, no bread, no bag, no money in their belts; but to wear sandals and not put on two tunics. He said, 'Where you enter a house, stay there until you leave the place. And if any place will not receive you and they refuse to hear you, when you leave, shake off the dust that is on your feet for a testimony against them.' So they went out and preached that men should repent. They cast out many demons, and anointed with oil many that were sick and healed them. St Mark 6.6–13

RESPONSE 'Great are the works of the Lord,
studied by all who have pleasure in this.'

Eternal God, you created the Church to continue the mission of your Son – we praise you for sharing your eternal love with us in Jesus Christ . . .
You entrusted the Good News of salvation to the Church – Lord, give to all who are baptized the graces needed to share in Christ's mission . . .
'They preached that men should repent' – inspire us by your Holy Spirit to repent of our own sins, and give us grace to overcome them . . .

INTERCESSIONS *pages 390–393* CLOSING PRAYERS *page 402–403*

OPENING PRAYER O come, let us worship and bow down, and kneel before the Lord, our Maker! For you are our God, and we are the people of your pasture, and the sheep of your hand . . . Glory be . . .

PSALMODY Once God has spoken; twice have I heard this:
that power belongs to God; Psalm 62.11

SCRIPTURE READINGS Remember those who are in prison, as though in prison with them; and those who are ill treated, since you also are in the body. Hebrews 13.3

King Herod heard about Jesus. Some said, 'John the baptizer has been raised from the dead; that is why these powers are at work in him.' Others said, 'It is Elijah.' Others said, 'It is a prophet, like one of the prophets of old.' When Herod heard of it he said, 'John, whom I beheaded, has been raised.' For Herod had seized John, and bound him in prison for the sake of Herodias, his brother Philip's wife; because he had married her. For John said to Herod, 'It is not lawful for you to have your brother's wife.' Herodias had a grudge against him, and wanted to kill him. But she could not, for Herod feared John, knowing that he was a righteous and holy man, and kept him safe. When he heard him, he was much perplexed; yet he heard him gladly. An opportunity came when Herod on his birthday gave a banquet for his courtiers and officers and the leading men of Galilee. When Herodias' daughter danced, she pleased Herod and his guests; and the king said, 'Ask me for whatever you wish, and I will grant it.' He vowed to her, 'Whatever you ask me, I will give you, even half of my kingdom.' She went out, and said to her mother, 'What shall I ask?' She said, 'The head of John the baptizer.' She came in with haste to the king, and asked, saying, 'I want you to give me the head of John the Baptist on a platter.' The king was exceedingly sorry; but because of his oaths and his guests he did not want to break his word to her. The king sent a soldier of the guard and gave orders to bring his head. He beheaded him in the prison, and brought his head on a platter, and gave it to the girl; and the girl gave to her mother. St Mark 6.14–28

RESPONSE 'Blessed are those whose way is blameless,
who walk in the way of the Lord.'

Almighty God, you are glorified in the lives of your saints – we praise you for all who bear witness to your saving love in Jesus Christ . . .
The saints are made perfect in suffering – Lord, we pray that we may share their life in Christ . . .
'Herodias had a grudge' – purify all our relationships and lead us in your ways of forgiveness and truth and love . . .

INTERCESSIONS *pages 390–393* CLOSING PRAYERS *page 402–403*

OPENING PRAYER O come, let us worship and bow down, and kneel before the Lord, our Maker! For you are our God, and we are the people of your pasture, and the sheep of your hand . . . Glory be . . .

PSALMODY O God, thou art my God, I seek thee,
my soul thirsts for thee;
my flesh faints for thee,
as in a dry and weary land where no water is.
Because thy steadfast love is better than life,
my lips will praise thee. Psalm 63.1–3*

SCRIPTURE READINGS Through him then let us continually offer up a sacrifice of praise to God, that is, the fruit of lips that acknowledge his name. Do not neglect to do good and to share what you have, for such sacrifices are pleasing to God. Hebrews 13.15–16

Jesus said to the disciples, 'Come away by yourselves to a lonely place, and rest a while.' For many were coming and going, and they had no leisure even to eat. They went in the boat to a lonely place by themselves. As he went ashore, he saw a great throng, and he had compassion on them, because they were like sheep without a shepherd; and he began to teach them many things. His disciples said, 'This is a lonely place, and the hour is now late; send them away, to go into the country and villages round about and buy themselves something to eat.' He answered, 'You give them something to eat.' They said, 'Shall we go and buy two hundred denarii worth of bread, and give it to them to eat?' He said, 'How many loaves have you? Go and see.' When they had found out, they said, 'Five, and two fish.' Then he commanded them all to sit down by companies upon the green grass. So they sat down in groups, by hundreds and by fifties. Taking the five loaves and the two fish he looked up to heaven, and blessed, and broke the loaves, and gave them to the disciples to set before the people; and he divided the two fish among them all. They all ate and were satisfied. And they took up twelve baskets full of broken pieces and of the fish. Those who ate the loaves were five thousand men. St Mark 6.31–43*

RESPONSE 'Accept my offerings of praise, O Lord,
and teach me thy ordinances.'

Heavenly Father, your compassion goes out to all people in every generation – we praise you for your eternal love . . .
'He began to teach them many things' – Lord, help us to learn about your will and to grow in your love . . .
'You give them something to eat' – we pray for all who are hungry, destitute or homeless . . .

INTERCESSIONS *pages 390–393* CLOSING PRAYERS *page 402–403*

OPENING PRAYER O come, let us worship and bow down, and kneel before the Lord, our Maker! For you are our God, and we are the people of your pasture, and the sheep of your hand . . . Glory be . . .

PSALMODY My soul is feasted as with marrow and fat,
and my mouth praises thee with joyful lips,
when I think of thee upon my bed,
and meditate on thee in the watches of the night;
for thou hast been my help,
and in the shadow of thy wings I sing for joy.
My soul clings to thee;
thy right hand upholds me. Psalm 63.5–8

SCRIPTURE READINGS Jesus made his disciples get into the boat and go before him to the other side, to Bethsaida, while he dismissed the crowd. After he had taken leave of them, he went up on the mountain to pray. When evening came, the boat was out on the sea, and he was alone on the land. He saw that they were making headway painfully, for the wind was against them. About the fourth watch of the night he came to them, walking on the sea. He meant to pass by them, but when they saw him walking on the sea they thought it was a ghost, and cried out; for they all saw him, and were terrified. Immediately he spoke to them and said, 'Take heart, it is I; have no fear.' He got into the boat with them and the wind ceased. They were utterly astounded, for they did not understand about the loaves, but their hearts were hardened. When they had crossed over, they came to land at Gennesaret, and moored to the shore. When they got out of the boat, immediately the people recognised him, and ran about the whole neighbourhood and began to bring sick people on their pallets to any place where they heard he was. Wherever he came, in villages, cities, or country, they laid the sick in the market places, and besought him that they might touch even the fringe of his garment; and as many as touched it were made well. St Mark 6.45–56

'Lo, I am with you always, to the close of the age.' St Matthew 28.20

RESPONSE: 'Drop thy still dews of quietness, till all our strivings cease;
take from our souls the strain and stress,
and let our ordered lives confess the beauty of thy peace.'

Eternal Father, you are always present in every part of the universe – we praise you for your power and majesty and love . . .
'Take heart, it is I; have no fear' – Lord, guard us and guide us in all dangers, and fill our hearts with your love and peace . . .
'Their hearts were hardened' – Lord, cleanse us from our sins, and open our hearts to the influence of your Holy Spirit . . .

INTERCESSIONS *pages 390–393* CLOSING PRAYERS *page 402–403*

23 April (St George) *Honour your Father and Mother*

OPENING PRAYER O come, let us worship and bow down, and kneel before the Lord, our Maker! For you are our God, and we are the people of your pasture, and the sheep of your hand . . . Glory be . . .

PSALMODY Hear my voice, O God, in my complaint;
hide me from the secret plots of the wicked.
Because of their tongue he will bring them to ruin.
Then all men will fear;
they will tell what God has wrought.
Let the righteous rejoice in the Lord,
and take refuge in him!
Let all the upright in heart glory! Psalm 64.1–10*

SCRIPTURE READINGS You shall not add to the word which I command you, nor take from it; that you may keep the commandments of the Lord your God which I command you. Deuteronomy 4.2

When the Pharisees gathered together to Jesus with some of the scribes, they saw that some of his disciples ate with hands defiled, that is, unwashed. (For the Pharisees, and all the Jews, do not eat unless they wash their hands, observing the tradition of the elders). The Pharisees and the scribes asked, 'Why do your disciples not live according to the tradition of the elders, but eat with hands defiled?' He said, 'Well did Isaiah prophesy of you hypocrites, as it is written, "This people honours me with their lips, but their heart is far from me; in vain do they worship me, teaching as doctrines the precepts of men." You leave the commandment of God, and hold fast the tradition of men.' He said, 'You have a fine way of rejecting the commandment of God, in order to keep your tradition! Moses said, "Honour your father and your mother"; and, "He who speaks evil of father or mother, let him surely die"; but you say, "If a man tells his father or his mother, What you would have gained from me is Corban" (that is, given to God) – then you no longer permit him to do anything for his father or mother, thus making void the word of God through your tradition.'
St Mark 7.1–13*

RESPONSE 'Thy testimonies are my heritage for ever,
yea, they are the joy of my heart.'

Eternal God, you are unchanging and your love is eternal – we praise you for sharing your love with us in your Son . . .
'This people honours me with their lips, but their heart is far from me' – purify our motives, and help us to honour you in our words and deeds . . .
'Honour your father and mother' – we thank you for our parents who shared in your work of creation, and we thank you for your gift of life . . .

INTERCESSIONS *pages 390–393* CLOSING PRAYERS *page 402–403*

OPENING PRAYER O come, let us worship and bow down, and kneel before the Lord, our Maker! For you are our God, and we are the people of your pasture, and the sheep of your hand . . . Glory be . . .

PSALMODY Praise is due to thee, O God, in Zion;
and to thee shall vows be performed,
O thou who hearest prayer!
To thee shall all flesh come on account of sins.
When our transgressions prevail over us,
thou dost forgive them.
Blessed is he whom thou dost choose and bring near,
to dwell in thy courts! Psalm 65.1–4

SCRIPTURE READING My brethren, show no partiality as you hold the faith of our Lord Jesus Christ, the Lord of glory. For if a man with gold rings and in fine clothing comes into your assembly, and a poor man in shabby clothing also comes in, and you pay attention to the one who wears the fine clothing and say, 'Have a seat here, please,' while you say to the poor man, 'Stand there,' or, 'Sit at my feet,' have you not made distinctions among yourselves, and become judges with evil thoughts? Listen, my beloved brethren. Has not God chosen those who are poor in the world to be rich in faith and heirs of the kingdom which he has promised to those who love him? St James 2.1–5

Jesus went through Sidon to the Sea of Galilee, through the region of the Decapolis. They brought to him a man who was deaf and had an impediment in his speech; and they besought him to lay his hand upon him. Taking him aside from the multitude privately, he put his fingers into his ears, and he spat and touched his tongue; and looking up to heaven, he sighed, and said, 'Ephphatha,' that is, 'Be opened.' His ears were opened, and his tongue was released, and he spoke plainly. He charged them to tell no one; but the more he charged them, the more zealously they proclaimed it. They were astonished beyond measure, 'He has done all things well; he even makes the deaf hear and the dumb speak.' St Mark 7.31–37

RESPONSE 'Deal bountifully with thy servant,
that I may live and observe thy word.'

God of Abraham, Isaac and Jacob, your Son conquered sin and death – we praise you for your healing love in Christ our Lord . . .
Your Son entered Gentile territory – Lord, we rejoice that the Holy Spirit makes effective Christ's redeeming work in all the world . . .
'He has done all things well' – Lord, fill us with your Spirit, and help us to live and work to your praise and glory . . .

INTERCESSIONS *pages 390–393* CLOSING PRAYERS *page 402–403*

OPENING PRAYER O come, let us worship and bow down, and kneel before the Lord, our Maker! For you are our God, and we are the people of your pasture, and the sheep of your hand . . . Glory be . . .

PSALMODY My heart overflows with a goodly theme;
I address my verses to the king;
my tongue is like the pen of a ready scribe.
You are the fairest of the sons of men;
grace is poured upon your lips;
therefore God has blessed you for ever. Psalm 45.1–2

SCRIPTURE READINGS Grace was given to each of us according to the measure of Christ's gift. Therefore it is said, 'When he ascended on high he led a host of captives, and gave gifts to men.' And his gifts were that some should be apostles, some prophets, some evangelists, some pastors and teachers, to equip the saints for the work of ministry, for building up the body of Christ, until we all attain to the unity of the faith and of the knowledge of the Son of God, to mature manhood, to the measure of the stature of the fullness of Christ; so that we may no longer be children, tossed to and fro and carried about with every wind of doctrine, by the cunning of men, by their craftiness in deceitful wiles. Rather, speaking the truth in love, we are to grow up in every way into him who is the head, into Christ, from whom the whole body, joined and knit together by every joint with which it is supplied, when each part is working properly, makes bodily growth and upbuilds itself in love. Ephesians 4.7–16*

Jesus said, 'Go into all the world and preach the gospel to the whole creation. He who believes and is baptized will be saved.' St Mark 16.15–16

I remind you in what terms I preached the gospel, which you received, in which you stand, by which you are saved, if you hold it fast.
1 Corinthians 15.1–2*

RESPONSE 'Hear us, we humbly pray, and where the Gospel day
sheds not its glorious ray, Let there be light.'

Heavenly Father, you raised up Saint Mark to record the Gospel of your Son – we praise you for his inspired writings to enlighten your Church . . .
Christians through the centuries have been strengthened in their faith through the Scriptures – we praise you on this Feast of Saint Mark . . .
'Go into all the world and preach the Gospel' – Lord, we pray with Saint Mark for Christ's continuous mission in the world through the Church . . .

INTERCESSIONS *pages 390–393* CLOSING PRAYERS *page 402–403*

OPENING PRAYER O come, let us worship and bow down, and kneel before the Lord, our Maker! For you are our God, and we are the people of your pasture, and the sheep of your hand . . . Glory be . . .

PSALMODY By dread deeds thou dost answer us with deliverance,
O God of our salvation,
who art the hope of all the ends of the earth;
who by thy strength hast established the mountains,
so that those who dwell at earth's farthest bounds
are afraid at thy signs;
thou makest the outgoings of the morning
and the evening to shout for joy. Psalm 65.5–8

SCRIPTURE READINGS The Lord God called to the man, and said, 'Where are you? He said, 'I heard the sound of thee in the garden, and I was afraid, because I was naked; and I hid myself.' He said, 'Who told you that you were naked? Have you eaten of the tree of which I commanded you not to eat?' The man said, 'The woman whom thou gavest to be with me, she gave me fruit of the tree, and I ate.' The woman said, 'The serpent beguiled me and I ate.' Genesis 3.9–13

When again a great crowd gathered, and they had nothing to eat, Jesus called his disciples, and said, 'I have compassion on the crowd, because they have been with me now three days, and have nothing to eat; and if I send them away hungry to their homes, they will faint on the way; and some of them have come a long way.' His disciples answered, 'How can one feed these men with bread here in the desert?' He asked, 'How many loaves have you?' They said, 'Seven.' He commanded the crowd to sit down on the ground; and he took the seven loaves, and having given thanks be broke them and gave them to his disciples to set before the people; and they set them before the crowd. They had a few small fish; and having blessed them, he commanded that these also should be set before them. And they ate, and were satisfied; and they took up the broken pieces left over, seven baskets full. There were about four thousand people.
St Mark 8.1–9

RESPONSE 'Rejoice in the Lord, O you righteous,
and give thanks to his holy name.'

Ever-living God, all good things come from you – we rejoice and we praise you for your perfect love in Jesus Christ . . .
You provide food for our souls and bodies – give us grateful hearts for all your many blessings . . .
Your Son fed the multitudes – Lord, sanctify your Church, and make it a channel of your love to feed people today . . .

INTERCESSIONS *pages 390–393* CLOSING PRAYERS *page 402–403*

OPENING PRAYER O come, let us worship and bow down, and kneel before the Lord, our Maker! For you are our God, and we are the people of your pasture, and the sheep of your hand . . . Glory be . . .

PSALMODY Thou visitest the earth and waterest it,
thou greatly enrichest it; the river of God is full of water;
thou providest their grain, for so thou hast prepared it.
Thou waterest its furrows abundantly, settling its ridges,
softening it with showers, and blessing its growth.
Psalm 65.9–10

SCRIPTURE READINGS Blessed is the man who endures trial, for when he has stood the test he will receive the crown of life which God has promised to those who love him. Let no one say when he is tempted, 'I am tempted by God'; for God cannot be tempted with evil and he himself tempts no one; but each person is tempted when he is lured and enticed by his own desire. Then desire when it has conceived gives birth to sin; and sin when it is full-grown brings forth death. Do not be deceived, my beloved brethren. Every good endowment and every perfect gift is from above, coming down from the Father of lights with whom there is no variation or shadow due to change. Of his own will he brought us forth by the word of truth that we should be a kind of first fruits of his creatures. James 1.12–18

Getting into the boat, Jesus departed to the other side. Now the disciples had forgotten to bring bread; and they had only one loaf with them in the boat. He cautioned them, saying, 'Take heed, beware of the leaven of the Pharisees and the leaven of Herod.' They discussed it, saying, 'We have no bread.' Being aware of it, Jesus said, 'Why do you discuss the fact that you have no bread? Do you not yet perceive or understand? Are your hearts hardened? Having eyes do you not see, and having ears do you not hear? And do you not remember? When I broke the five loaves for the five thousand, how many baskets full of broken pieces did you take up?' They said, 'Twelve.' 'And the seven for the four thousand, how many baskets full of broken pieces did you take up?' They said, 'Seven.' He said, 'Do you not yet understand?' St Mark 8.14–21

RESPONOSE 'Make me understand the way of thy precepts,
and I will meditate on thy wondrous works.'

Loving Father, your faithfulness and truth endure from age to age – we praise you for all who are growing into union with Christ . . .
'Do you not yet perceive or understand?' – open our minds and help us to understand the mystery of your love for us in Jesus Christ . . .
'Are your hearts hardened?' – Lord, remove from us all hardness of heart, and send your Spirit to sanctify us . . .

INTERCESSIONS *pages 390–393* CLOSING PRAYERS *page 402–403*

OPENING PRAYER O come, let us worship and bow down, and kneel before the Lord, our Maker! For you are our God, and we are the people of your pasture, and the sheep of your hand . . . Glory be . . .

PSALMODY Thou crownest the year with thy bounty;
the hills gird themselves with joy,
the meadows clothe themselves with flocks,
the valleys deck themselves with grain,
they shout and sing together for joy. Psalm 65.11–13*

SCRIPTURE READINGS

I gave my back to the smiters,
and my cheeks to those who pulled out the beard;
I hid not my face from shame and spitting.
For the Lord God helps me;
therefore I have set my face like a flint,
and I know that I shall not be put to shame;
he who vindicates me is near.
Who will contend with me? Let us stand together.
Who is my adversary? Let him come near to me.
Isaiah 50.6–8

Jesus went with his disciples, to the villages of Caesarea Philippi; and on the way he asked his disciples, 'Who do men say that I am?' They told him, 'John the Baptist; and others say, Elijah; and others one of the prophets.' He asked, 'But who do you say that I am?' Peter answered, 'You are the Christ.' And he charged them to tell no one about him. He began to teach them that the Son of Man must suffer many things, and be rejected by the elders and the chief priests and the scribes, and be killed, and after three days rise again. He said this plainly. Peter took him, and began to rebuke him. But turning and seeing his disciples, he rebuked Peter, and said, 'Get behind me, Satan! For you are not on the side of God, but of men.' He called to him the multitude with his disciples, and said, 'If any man would come after me, let him deny himself and take up his cross and follow me. For whoever would save his life will lose it; and whoever loses his life for my sake and the gospel's will save it. St Mark 8.27–35

RESPONSE 'O give thanks to the God of heaven,
for his steadfast love endures for ever.'

Heavenly Father, your Son predicted his suffering and death for our salvation – we praise you for the faith of all who suffer for Christ . . .
'Get thee behind me, Satan' – Lord, help us to overcome all temptation, and give us grace to persevere . . .
'If any man would come after me, let him deny himself and take up his cross and follow me' – give us courage, and also give us peace and joy . . .

INTERCESSIONS *pages 390–393* CLOSING PRAYERS *page 402–403*

OPENING PRAYER O come, let us worship and bow down, and kneel before the Lord, our Maker! For you are our God, and we are the people of your pasture, and the sheep of your hand . . . Glory be . . .

PSALMODY Make a joyful noise to God, all the earth;
sing the glory of his name; give to him glorious praise!
Say to God, 'How terrible are thy deeds!
All the earth worships thee; they sing praises to thee,
sing praises to thy name.' Psalm 66.1–4*

SCRIPTURE READINGS We were eyewitnesses of his majesty. For when we received honour and glory from God the Father and the voice was bourne to him by the Majestic Glory, 'This is my beloved Son, with whom I am well pleased,' we heard this voice borne from heaven, for we were with him on the holy mountain. 2 Peter 1.16–18

After six days Jesus took with him Peter and James and John, and led them up a high mountain apart by themselves; and he was transfigured before them, and his garments became glistening, intensely white, as no fuller on earth could bleach them. There appeared to them Elijah with Moses; and they were talking to Jesus. Peter said to Jesus, 'Master, it is well that we are here; let us make three booths, one for you and one for Moses and one for Elijah.' For he did not know what to say, for they were exceedingly afraid. A cloud overshadowed them, and a voice came out of the cloud. 'This is my beloved Son; listen to him.' Suddenly looking around they no longer saw any one with them but Jesus only. As they were coming down the mountain, he charged them to tell no one what they had seen, until the Son of Man should have risen from the dead. So they kept the matter to themselves, questioning what the rising from the dead meant. They asked, 'Why do the scribes say that first Elijah must come?' He said, 'Elijah does come first to restore all things; and how is it written of the Son of Man, that he should suffer many things and be treated with contempt? I tell you that Elijah has come, and they did to him whatever they pleased, as it is written of him.' St Mark 9.2–13

RESPONSE 'Thy name, O Lord, endures for ever,
thy renown, O Lord, throughout all ages.'

Loving Father, you revealed your glory to Peter, James and John on the mountain – we rejoice that your glory is unchanging and eternal . . .
'Master, it is well that we are here' – Lord, in your mercy, renew us with your gifts of joy and peace and love . . .
'They saw no one with them but only Jesus' – Lord, we rejoice that you are always with us, and we thank you for your love . . .

INTERCESSIONS *pages 390–393* CLOSING PRAYERS *page 402–403*

OPENING PRAYER O come, let us worship and bow down, and kneel before the Lord, our Maker! For you are our God, and we are the people of your pasture, and the sheep of your hand . . . Glory be . . .

PSALMODY Bless our God, O peoples,
let the sound of his praise be heard,
who has kept us among the living,
and has not let our feet slip. Psalm 66.8–9

SCRIPTURE READINGS The wisdom from above is first pure, then peaceable, gentle, open to reason, full of mercy and good fruits, without uncertainty or insincerity. And the harvest of righteousness is sown in peace by those who make peace. James 4.16–17

When they came to the disciples, they saw a great crowd, and scribes arguing with them. Jesus asked, 'What are you discussing with them?' One of the crowd answered, 'Teacher, I brought my son to you, for he has a dumb spirit; and wherever it seizes him, it dashes him down; and he foams and grinds his teeth and becomes rigid; and I asked your disciples to cast it out, and they were not able.' He answered, 'O faithless generation, how long am I to be with you? How long am I to bear with you? Bring him to me.' They brought the boy to him; and when the spirit saw him, immediately it convulsed the boy, and he fell on the ground and rolled about, foaming at the mouth. Jesus asked his father, 'How long has he had this?' He said, 'From childhood. It has often cast him into the fire and into the water, to destroy him; but if you can do anything, have pity on us and help us.' Jesus said, 'If you can! All things are possible to him who believes.' The father said, 'I believe; help my unbelief!' Jesus rebuked the unclean spirit, saying, 'You dumb and deaf spirit, I command you, come out of him, and never enter him again.' After crying out and convulsing him terribly, it came out, and the boy was like a corpse; most of them said, 'He is dead.' Jesus took him by the hand and lifted him up, and he arose. His disciples asked him privately, 'Why could not we cast it out?' He said, 'This kind cannot be driven out by anything but prayer.'

St Mark 9.14–19*

RESPONSE 'Let my prayer be counted as the incense before thee,
and the lifting up of my hands as an evening sacrifice.'

Lord of all power and might, you are the source of all life and health and goodness – we praise you for your perfect love revealed in your Son . . .
Your Son always found time to help people with a problem – fill your Church with the same love and compassion today . . .
'Why could not we cast it out?' – purify your Church, and teach us how to pray . . .

INTERCESSIONS *pages 390–393* CLOSING PRAYERS *page 402–403*

1 May *Saint Philip and Saint James*

OPENING PRAYER Eternal God, your power and glory are unchanging and last for ever. You are closer than breathing, and nearer than hands and feet. Help us to draw near with faith in this time of prayer . . . Glory be . . .

PSALMODY Rejoice in the Lord, O you righteous!
Praise befits the upright.
Praise the Lord with the lyre,
make melody to him with the harp of ten strings!
Sing to him a new song,
play skilfully on the strings, with loud shouts.
For the word of the Lord is upright;
and all his work is done in faithfulness. Psalm 33.1–4

SCRIPTURE READINGS O people in Zion who dwell at Jerusalem; you shall weep no more. He will surely be gracious to you at the sound of your cry; when he hears it, he will answer you. And though the Lord give you the bread of adversity and the water of affliction, yet your Teacher will not hide himself any more, but your eyes shall see your Teacher. Your ears shall hear a word behind you, saying, 'This is the way, walk in it,' when you turn to the right or when you turn to the left. Isaiah 30.19–21

Philip said to Jesus, 'Lord, show us the Father, and we shall be satisfied.' Jesus said, 'Have I been with you so long, and yet you do not know me, Philip? He who has seen me has seen the Father; how can you say, "Show us the Father"? Do you not believe that I am in the Father and the Father in me? The words that I say to you I do not speak on my own authority; but the Father who dwells in me does his works. Believe me that I am in the Father and the Father in me; or else believe me for the sake of the works themselves. Truly, truly, I say to you, he who believes in me will also do the works that I do; and greater works than these will he do, because I go to the Father. Whatever you ask in my name, I will do it, that the Father may be glorified in the Son; if you ask anything in my name, I will do it.'
St John 14.8–14

RESPONSE 'We will bless the Lord
from this time forth and for evermore.'

Almighty God, your Son chose Philip and James to be apostles in his Church – on this day we honour the apostles and we praise you for your love . . .
The bishops of the Church are the successors of the apostles – Lord, bless all bishops, and especially our bishop in this diocese . . .
'Whatever you ask in my name, I will do it' – united in the one Spirit, we pray with James and John for the growth of your Church . . .

INTERCESSIONS *pages 390–393* CLOSING PRAYERS *page 402–403*

OPENING PRAYER Eternal God, your power and glory are unchanging and last for ever. You are closer than breathing, and nearer than hands and feet. Help us to draw near with faith in this time of prayer . . . Glory be . . .

PSALMODY Blessed be God, because he has not rejected my prayer
or removed his steadfast love from me. Psalm 66.20

SCRIPTURE READINGS

Then Job answered the Lord:
'I know that thou canst do all things,
and that no purpose of thine can be thwarted.
"Who is this that hides counsel without knowledge?"
Therefore I have uttered what I did not understand,
things too wonderful for me, which I did not know.
I had heard of thee by the hearing of the ear,
but now my eyes see thee;
therefore I despise myself,
and repent in dust and ashes.' Job 42.1–6*

They came to Capernaum, and Jesus asked the disciples, 'What were you discussing on the way?' But they were silent, for on the way they had discussed with one another who was the greatest. He said, 'If any one would be first, he must be last of all and servant of all.' And he took a child, and put him in the midst of them; and taking him in his arms, he said, 'Whoever receives one such child in my name receives me; and whoever receives me, receives not me but him who sent me.' John said, 'Teacher, we saw a man casting out demons in your name, and we forbade him, because he was not following us.' Jesus said, 'Do not forbid him; for no one who does a mighty work in my name will be able soon after to speak evil of me. For he that is not against us is for us. For truly, I say to you, whoever gives you a cup of water to drink because you bear the name of Christ, will by no means lose his reward. Whoever causes one of these little ones who believe in me to sin, it would be better for him if a great millstone were hung round his neck and he were thrown into the sea.'

St Mark 9.33–42*

RESPONSE 'Be pleased, O God, to deliver me!
O Lord, make haste to help me.'

Eternal God, the fullness of Godhead dwells in your Son – we praise you that Christ emptied himself of his glory for our salvation . . .
'If any would be first, he must be last of all and servant of all' – Lord, inspire your Church with the graces of humility and love . . .
'Blessed are the pure in heart, for they shall see God' – Lord, purify your Church from all earthly ambition and power, and make it holy . . .

INTERCESSIONS *pages 390–393* CLOSING PRAYERS *page 402–403*

OPENING PRAYER Eternal God, your power and glory are unchanging and last for ever. You are closer than breathing, and nearer than hands and feet. Help us to draw near with faith in this time of prayer . . . Glory be . . .

PSALMODY May God be gracious to us and bless us,
that thy way may be known upon earth,
thy saving power among all nations. Psalm 67.1–3*

SCRIPTURE READINGS We see Jesus, who for a little while was made lower than the angels, crowned with glory and honour because of the suffering of death, so that by the grace of God he might taste death for every one. For it was fitting that he, for whom and by whom all things exist, in bringing many sons to glory, should make the pioneer of their salvation perfect through suffering. For he who sanctifies and those who are sanctified have all one origin. Hebrews 2.9–11

Pharisees in order to test Jesus asked, 'Is it lawful for a man to divorce his wife?' He answered, 'What did Moses command you?' They said, 'Moses allowed a man to write a certificate of divorce, and to put her away.' Jesus said, 'For your hardness of heart he wrote you this commandment. But from the beginning of creation, "God made them male and female." "For this reason a man shall leave his father and mother and be joined in his wife, and the two shall become one flesh." So they are no longer two but one flesh. What therefore God has joined together, let not man put asunder.' In the house the disciples asked him about this. He said, 'Whoever divorces his wife and marries another, commits adultery against her; and if she divorces her husband and marries another, she commits adultery.' And they were bringing children to him, that he might touch them; and the disciples rebuked them. When Jesus saw it he was indignant, and said, 'Let the children come to me, do not hinder them; for to such belongs the Kingdom of God. Whoever does not receive the Kingdom of God like a child shall not enter it.' He took them in his arms and blessed them.
St Mark 10.2–16*

RESPONSE 'Blessed be the Lord, who daily bears us up;
God is our salvation.'

Eternal Father, your love for us is far greater than we can imagine or deserve – we praise you for your gift of perfect love in your Son . . .
Your Son shared the life of a human home at Nazareth – Lord, bless all who are married, and help them to grow together in your love . . .
You love all people – bless all who are divorced or separated, children from broken homes, single parent families, and all who live alone . . .
'All have sinned and all fall short of the glory of God' – Lord, bring your healing to all our relationships, and guide us in all things . . .

INTERCESSIONS *pages 390–393* CLOSING PRAYERS *page 402–403*

OPENING PRAYER Eternal God, your power and glory are unchanging and last for ever. You are closer than breathing, and nearer than hands and feet. Help us to draw near with faith in this time of prayer . . . Glory be . . .

PSALMODY Let the peoples praise thee, O God;
let all the peoples praise thee!
The earth has yielded its increase;
God, our God, has blessed us.
God has blessed us;
Let all the ends of the earth fear him! Psalm 67.5–7

SCRIPTURE READINGS Those who desire to be rich fall into temptation, into a snare, into many senseless and hurtful desires that plunge men into ruin and destruction. For the love of money is the root of all evils.
1 Timothy 6.9–10

A man ran up and asked Jesus, 'Good Teacher, what must I do to inherit eternal life?' And Jesus said, 'Why do you call me good? No one is good but God alone. You know the commandments: "Do not kill, Do not commit adultery, Do not steal, Do not bear false witness, Do not defraud, Honour your father and mother."' And he said, 'Teacher, all these I have observed from my youth.' And Jesus looking upon him loved him, and said to him, 'You lack one thing; go, sell what you have, and give to the poor, and you will have treasure in heaven; and come, follow me.' At that saying his countenance fell, and he went away sorrowful; for he had great possessions. And Jesus looked around and said to his disciples, 'How hard it will be for those who have riches to enter the Kingdom of God!' The disciples were amazed at his words. But Jesus said to them again, 'Children, how hard it is to enter the Kingdom of God! It is easier for a camel to go through the eye of a needle than for a rich man to enter the Kingdom of God.' And they were exceedingly astonished, and said to him, 'Then who can be saved?' Jesus said, 'With men it is impossible, but not with God; for all things are possible with God.' St Mark 10.17–27*

RESPONSE 'In thee, O Lord, do I take refuge;
let me never be put to shame.'

Eternal God, your Son was rich in glory but born in poverty for our salvation – we worship you, one God, Father, Son and Holy Spirit . . .
'How hard it will be for those who have riches to enter the Kingdom of God' – bless rich and poor, and help us to seek the riches of your grace . . .
Your Kingdom cannot be bought or earned – thank you for accepting us as we are, and help us to work for the justice of your Kingdom . . .

INTERCESSIONS *pages 390–393* CLOSING PRAYERS *page 402–403*

OPENING PRAYER Eternal God, your power and glory are unchanging and last for ever. You are closer than breathing, and nearer than hands and feet. Help us to draw near with faith in this time of prayer . . . Glory be . . .

PSALMODY Let God arise, let his enemies be scattered.
But let the righteous be joyful.
Sing to God, sing praises to his name.
Father of the fatherless and protector of widows
is God in his holy habitation. Psalm 68.1–5*

SCRIPTURE READINGS Since we have a great high priest who has passed through the heavens, Jesus, the Son of God, let us hold fast our confession. For we have not a high priest who is unable to sympathize with our weaknesses, but one who in every respect has been tempted as we are, yet without sinning. Let us then with confidence draw near to the throne of grace, that we may receive mercy and find grace to help in time of need.
Hebrews 4.14–16

James and John came forward, and said, 'Teacher, we want you to do for us whatever we ask of you.' He said, 'What do you want me to do for you?' They said, 'Grant us to sit, one at your right hand and one at your left, in your glory.' Jesus said, 'You do not know what you are asking. Are you able to drink the cup that I drink, or to be baptized with the baptism with which I am baptized?' They said, 'We are able.' Jesus said, 'The cup that I drink you will drink; and with the baptism with which I am baptized, you will be baptized; but to sit at my right hand or at my left is not mine to grant, but it is for those for whom it has been prepared.' When the ten heard it, they began to be indignant at James and John. Jesus called them to him and said, 'You know that those who are supposed to rule over the Gentiles lord it over them, and their great men exercise authority over them. But it shall not be so among you; but whoever would be great among you must be your servant, and whoever would be first among you must be slave of all. The Son of Man also came not to be served but to serve, and to give his life as a ransom for many.' St Mark 10.32–45*

RESPONSE 'Sing to God, O kingdoms of the earth;
sing praises to the Lord.'

Gracious God, your Son is both the Suffering Servant and our great High Priest – we praise you and thank you for the mystery of your love . . .
'What do you want me to do for you?' – Lord, guide us through our earthly pilgrimage, and in your mercy, bring us to your eternal Kingdom . . .
'After three days, he will rise' – we rejoice in the blessed hope of eternal life through the glorious resurrection of your Son . . .

INTERCESSIONS *pages 390–393* CLOSING PRAYERS *page 402–403*

6 May *Blind Bartimaeus*

OPENING PRAYER Eternal God, your power and glory are unchanging and last for ever. You are closer than breathing, and nearer than hands and feet. Help us to draw near with faith in this time of prayer . . . Glory be . . .

PSALMODY O God, when thou didst go forth before thy people,
when thou didst march through the wilderness,
the earth quaked, the heavens poured down rain,
The Lord gives the command;
great is the host of those who bore the tidings.
Blessed be the Lord, who daily bears us up;
God is our salvation. Our God is a God of salvation;
and to God, the Lord, belongs escape from death.

Psalm 68.7–20*

SCRIPTURE READINGS

Sing aloud with gladness for Jacob,
and raise shouts for the chief of the nations;
proclaim, give praise, and say,
'The Lord has saved his people,
the remnant of Israel.'
Behold, I will bring them from the north country,
and gather them from the farthest parts of the earth,
among them the blind and the lame,
the woman with child and her who is in travail;
a great company, they shall return here. Isaiah 31.7–8

As Jesus was leaving Jericho, Bartimaeus, a blind beggar, was sitting by the roadside. When he heard that it was Jesus, he began to cry out and say, 'Jesus, Son of David, have mercy on me!' Many rebuked him, telling him to be silent; but he cried out all the more, 'Son of David, have mercy on me!' Jesus stopped and said, 'Call him.' And they called the blind man, saying, 'Take heart; rise, he is calling you.' Throwing off his mantle he sprang up and came to Jesus. Jesus said, 'What do you want me to do for you?' The blind man said, 'Master, let me receive my sight.' Jesus said, 'Go your way; your faith has made you well.' Immediately he received his sight and followed him on the way. St Mark 10.46–52*

RESPONSE 'May God be gracious to us and bless us,
and make his face to shine upon us.'

Eternal God, you created the Church to continue the work of your Son – we praise you for the light of faith in the Church in every generation . . . You are pure light and there is no darkness in you – Lord, we thank you for your wonderful gift of sight and for the beauty of your creation . . . Father of light, you live in unapproachable light – have mercy on all who are blind, and one day, bring us all to your everlasting light . . .

INTERCESSIONS *pages 390–393* CLOSING PRAYERS *page 402–403*

OPENING PRAYER Eternal God, your power and glory are unchanging and last for ever. You are closer than breathing, and nearer than hands and feet. Help us to draw near with faith in this time of prayer . . . Glory be . . .

PSALMODY Thy solemn processions are seen, O God,
the processions of my God, my King, in the sanctuary –
the singers in front, the minstrels last,
'Bless God in the great congregation,
the Lord, O you who are of Israel's fountain!'
Sing to God, O kingdoms of the earth;
Ascribe power to God, whose majesty is over Israel.
Blessed be God. Psalm 68.24–36*

SCRIPTURE READINGS Being found in human form he humbled himself and became obedient unto death, even death on a cross. Therefore God has exalted him and bestowed on him the name which is above every name, that at the name of Jesus every knee should bow, in heaven and on earth and under the earth, and every tongue confess that Jesus Christ is Lord, to the glory of God the Father. Philippians 2.8–11

When they drew near to Jerusalem, to Bethphage and Bethany, at the Mount of Olives, Jesus sent two of his disciples, and said, 'Go into the village opposite you, and immediately as you enter it you will find a colt tied, on which no one has ever sat, untie it and bring it. If any one says, "Why are you doing this?" say, "The Lord has need of it and will send it back here immediately."' They found a colt tied at the door out in the open street; and they untied it. Those who stood there said, 'What are you doing, untying the colt?' They told them what Jesus had said; and they let them go. They brought the colt to Jesus, and threw their garments on it; and he sat upon it. Many spread their garments on the road, and others spread leafy branches which they had cut from the fields. Those who went before and those who followed cried out, 'Hosanna! Blessed is he who comes in the name of the Lord! Blessed is the kingdom of our father David that is coming! Hosanna in the highest!' St Mark 11.1–10

RESPONSE 'Make a joyful noise to God, all the earth;
sing the glory of his name; give to him glorious praise.'

Heavenly Father, you ordained that your Son should enter the glory of his Kingdom through suffering – we worship and adore your holy name . . .
Your Son made his last appeal of love, but they wanted a political leader and not a King of Love – help us to discover your love in all things . . .
The people cried 'Hosanna' and then they shouted 'Crucify' a few days later – help us to be steadfast and faithful followers of Christ . . .

INTERCESSIONS *pages 390–393* CLOSING PRAYERS *page 402–403*

OPENING PRAYER Eternal God, your power and glory are unchanging and last for ever. You are closer than breathing, and nearer than hands and feet. Help us to draw near with faith in this time of prayer . . . Glory be . . .

PSALMODY Save me, O God! For the waters have come up to my neck.
I sink in deep mire, where there is no foothold;
I am weary with my crying; my throat is parched.
My eyes grow dim with waiting for my God.
Zeal for thy house has consumed me,
and the insults of those who insult thee have fallen on me.
But as for me, my prayer is to thee, O Lord. Psalm 69.1–13*

SCRIPTURE READINGS Jesus entered the temple and began to drive out those who sold and those who bought in the temple, and he overturned the tables of the money-changers and the seats of those who sold pigeons; and he would not allow any one to carry anything through the temple. He said, 'Is it not written, "My house shall be called a house of prayer for all the nations"? But you have made it a den of robbers.' The chief priests and the scribes heard it and sought a way to destroy him. St Mark 11.15–18*

And I saw no temple in the city, for its temple is the Lord God the Almighty and the Lamb. And the city has no need of sun or moon to shine upon it, for the glory of God is its light, and its lamp is the Lamb. By its light shall the nations walk; and the kings of the earth shall bring their glory into it, and its gates shall never be shut by day – and there shall be no night there; they shall bring into it the glory and the honour of the nations. But nothing unclean shall enter it, nor any one who practises abomination or falsehood, but only those who are written in the Lamb's book of life.
Revelation 21.22–27

Jacob said, 'Surely the Lord is in his place; and I did not know it.' He was afraid, and said, 'How awesome is this place! This is none other than the house of God, and this is the gate of heaven.' Genesis 28.16–17

RESPONSE 'This is the gate of the Lord;
the righteous shall enter through it.'

Heavenly Father, your Son cleansed the temple – cleanse the Church by the fire of your Spirit, and unite our praises with the worship of heaven . . .
'This is none other than the house of God' – we thank you for the opportunities you provide for us to grow into union with Christ . . .
'This is the gate of heaven' – Lord, we praise you for those who loved and served you in former times, and are now in your nearer presence . . .

INTERCESSIONS *pages 390–393* CLOSING PRAYERS *page 402–403*

OPENING PRAYER Eternal God, your power and glory are unchanging and last for ever. You are closer than breathing, and nearer than hands and feet. Help us to draw near with faith in this time of prayer . . . Glory be . . .

PSALMODY In thee, O Lord, do I take refuge.
Incline thy ear to me, and save me!
Upon thee I have leaned from my birth;
thou art he who took me from my mother's womb.
Do not cast me off in the time of old age;
forsake me not when my strength is spent.
O God, from my youth thou hast taught me,
and I still proclaim thy wondrous deeds.
So even to old age and grey hairs, O God, do not forsake me,
till I proclaim thy might to all the generations to come.
My lips will shout for joy, when I sing praises to thee;
my soul also, which thou hast rescued. Psalm 71.1–24*

SCRIPTURE READINGS The end of all things is at hand; therefore keep sane and sober for your prayers. Above all hold unfailing your love for one another, since love covers a multitude of sins. Practise hospitality ungrudgingly to one another. As each has received a gift, employ it for one another, as good stewards of God's varied grace: whoever speaks, as one who utters oracles of God; whoever renders service, as one who renders it by the strength which God supplies; in order that in everything God may be glorified through Jesus Christ. To him belong glory and dominion for ever and ever. Amen. 1 Peter 4.7–11

Jesus said, 'Have faith in God. Truly, I say to you, whoever says to this mountain, "Be taken up and cast into the sea," and does not doubt in his heart, but believes that what he says will come to pass, it will be done for him. Therefore I tell you, whatever you ask in prayer, believe that you have received it, and it will be yours. Whenever you stand praying, forgive, if you have anything against any one; so that your Father also who is in heaven may forgive you your trespasses.' St Mark 11.22–26

RESPONSE 'Thou art my God, and I will give thanks to thee;
thou art my God, I will extol thee.'

Eternal God, you create us to worship you and to reflect your likeness – Lord, let our praises rise before you like incense to heaven . . .
'Whatever you ask in prayer' – help us to make all our prayers according to your will and in the name of your only Son, Jesus Christ our Lord . . .
'Have faith in God' – bless us with a strong and constant faith and help us to make our lives an extension of our prayers . . .

INTERCESSIONS *pages 390–393* CLOSING PRAYERS *page 402–403*

10 May *By what Authority*

OPENING PRAYER Eternal God, your power and glory are unchanging and last for ever. You are closer than breathing, and nearer than hands and feet. Help us to draw near with faith in this time of prayer . . . Glory be . . .

PSALMODY Give the king thy justice, O God,
and thy righteousness to the royal son!
May he judge thy people with righteousness,
and thy poor with justice!
May he defend the cause of the poor of the people,
give deliverance to the needy, and crush the oppressor!
May he have dominion from sea to sea.
May his name endure for ever,
his fame continue as long as the sun!
May men bless themselves by him, all nations call him blessed!
Blessed be his glorious name for ever. Psalm 72.1–19*

SCRIPTURE READINGS You must remember, beloved, the predictions of the apostles of our Lord Jesus Christ; they said to you, 'In the last time there will be scoffers, following their own ungodly passions. It is these who set up divisions, worldly people, devoid of the Spirit. But you, beloved, build yourselves up on your most holy faith; pray in the Holy Spirit; keep yourselves in the love of God; wait for the mercy of our Lord Jesus Christ unto eternal life. Jude 17–21

As Jesus was walking in the temple, the chief priests and the scribes and the elders came to him, and said, 'By what authority are you doing these things, or who gave you this authority to do them?' Jesus said, 'I will ask you a question; answer me, and I will tell you by what authority I do these things. Was the baptism of John from heaven or from men? Answer me.' They argued with one another. 'If we say, "From heaven," he will say, "Why then did you not believe him?" But shall we say, "From men"?' – they were afraid of the people, for all held that John was a real prophet. They answered Jesus, 'We do not know.' Jesus said, 'Neither will I tell you by what authority I do these things.' St Mark 11.27–33*

RESPONSE 'Great peace have those who love thy law;
nothing can make them stumble.'

Heavenly Father, you gave all authority in heaven and on earth to your Son – bless us with the fullness of your love, and accept our praises . . .
'Who gave you this authority?' – bless the bishops and help them to fulfil the office and work of an apostle given to them by your Son . . .
'Was the baptism of John from heaven?' – we praise you for the ministry of John the Baptist, and we thank you for our own baptism into Christ . . .

INTERCESSIONS *pages 390–393* CLOSING PRAYERS *page 402–403*

OPENING PRAYER Eternal God, your power and glory are unchanging and last for ever. You are closer than breathing, and nearer than hands and feet. Help us to draw near with faith in this time of prayer . . . Glory be . . .

PSALMODY Truly God is good to the upright,
to those who are pure in heart.
But as for me, my feet had almost stumbled.
For I was envious of the arrogant,
when I saw the prosperity of the wicked.
But when I thought how to understand this,
it seemed to me a wearisome task,
until I went into the sanctuary of God;
then I perceived their end. Psalm 73.1–17*

SCRIPTURE READINGS Make every effort to supplement your faith with virtue, and virtue with knowledge, and knowledge with self-control, and self-control with steadfastness, and steadfastness with godliness, and godliness with brotherly affection, and brotherly affection with love.
2 Peter 1.5–7

Jesus said, 'A man planted a vineyard, and set a hedge around it, and dug a pit for the wine press, and built a tower, and let it out to tenants, and went into another country. When the time came, he sent a servant to the tenants, to get from them some of the fruit of the vineyard. They took him and beat him, and sent him away empty-handed. He sent to them another servant, and they wounded him in the head, and treated him shamefully. He sent another, and him they killed; and so with many others, some they beat and some they killed. He had still one other, a beloved son; finally he sent him, saying, "They will respect my son." But those tenants said, "This is the heir; come, let us kill him, and the inheritance will be ours." They took him and killed him, and cast him out of the vineyard. What will the owner of the vineyard do? He will come and destroy the tenants, and give the vineyard to others. Have you not read this scripture: "The very stone which the builders rejected has become the head of the corner; this is the Lord's doing, and it is marvellous in our eyes"?' St Mark 12.1–12*

RESPONSE 'My help comes from the Lord,
who made heaven and earth.'

Loving Father, you planted a vine long ago in Israel – we thank you for the prayer and praise offered in your name under the old Covenant . . .
You created for yourself a universal Church through the death and resurrection of your Son – help us by your grace to fulfil your will . . .
'This is the Lord's doing and it is wonderful in our eyes' – Lord, we praise you for all the benefits which were won for us on the Cross . . .

INTERCESSIONS *pages 390–393* CLOSING PRAYERS *page 402–403*

OPENING PRAYER Eternal God, your power and glory are unchanging and last for ever. You are closer than breathing, and nearer than hands and feet. Help us to draw near with faith in this time of prayer . . . Glory be . . .

PSALMODY We give thanks to thee, O God; we give thanks;
we call on thy name and recount thy wondrous deeds.
At the set time which I appoint I will judge with equity.
When the earth totters, and all its inhabitants,
it is I who keep steady its pillars.
I say to the boastful, 'Do not boast,'
and to the wicked, 'Do not lift up your horn;
or speak with insolent neck.'
For in the hand of the Lord there is a cup,
with foaming wine, well mixed;
and he will pour a draught from it,
and all the wicked of the earth
shall drain it down to the dregs.
But I will rejoice for ever,
I will sing praises to the God of Jacob. Psalm 75.1–9*

SCRIPTURE READINGS God spoke, saying, 'I am the Lord your God, who brought you out of the land of Egypt, out of the house of bondage. You shall have no other gods before me. You shall not make yourself a graven image. You shall not take the name of the Lord your God in vain.'
Exodus 20.1–7*

Some of the Pharisees and some of Herodians came and said to Jesus, 'Teacher, we know that you are true, and fear no man; for you do not regard the position of men, but truly teach the way of God. Is it lawful to pay taxes to Caesar, or not? Should we pay them, or should we not?' But knowing their hypocrisy, he said, 'Why put me to the test? Bring me a coin, and let me look at it.' And they brought one. He said, 'Whose likeness and inscription is this?' They said, 'Caesar's.' Jesus said, 'Render to Caesar the things that are Caesar's, and to God the things that are God's.' And they were amazed at him. St Mark 12.13–17*

RESPONSE 'The Lord is the strength of his people,
he is the saving refuge of his anointed.'

Eternal God, you are King of Kings and Lord or Lords – we praise you for the humility and love of your Son for our salvation . . .
'Render to Caesar the things that are Caesar's' – Lord, inspire all who are baptized to be responsible members of society . . .
'Render to God the things that are God's' – Lord, help us by your grace to worship you with all our heart and mind and soul and strength . . .

INTERCESSIONS *pages 390–393* CLOSING PRAYERS *page 402–403*

Like Angels in Heaven

OPENING PRAYER Eternal God, your power and glory are unchanging and last for ever. You are closer than breathing, and nearer than hands and feet. Help us to draw near with faith in this time of prayer . . . Glory be . . .

PSALMODY In Judah God is known,
his name is great in Israel.
Glorious art thou,
more majestic than the everlasting mountains.
The earth feared and was still,
when God arose to establish judgement
to save all the oppressed of the earth.
Make your vows to the Lord your God, and perform them;
let all around him bring gifts
to him who is to be feared. Psalm 76.1–11*

SCRIPTURE READINGS So it is with the resurrection of the dead. What is sown is perishable, what is raised is imperishable. It is sown in dishonour, it is raised in glory. It is sown in weakness, it is raised in power. It is sown a physical body, it is raised a spiritual body. 1 Corinthians 15.42–44

The Sadducees, who say there is no resurrection, asked Jesus a question, saying, 'Teacher, Moses wrote that if a man's brother dies and leaves a wife, but no child, the man must take the wife, and raise up children for his brother. There were seven brothers; the first took a wife, and when he died left no children; the second took her, and died, leaving no children; the third likewise; and the seven left no children. Last of all the woman died. In the resurrection whose wife will she be? For the seven had her as wife.' Jesus said, 'Is not this why you are wrong, that you know neither the scriptures nor the power of God? When they rise from the dead, they neither marry nor are given in marriage, but are like angels in heaven. As for the dead being raised, have you not read in the book of Moses, in the passage about the burning bush, how God said, "I am the God of Abraham, and the God of Isaac, and the God of Jacob"? He is not God of the dead, but of the living; you are quite wrong.' St Mark 12.18–27

RESPONSE 'Let thy face shine on thy servant;
save me in thy steadfast love.'

Ever-living God, you have given us the hope of eternal life through the resurrection of your Son – we praise and exalt your holy name . . .
'You know neither the Scriptures nor the power of God' – Lord, enlighten our minds to understand your living Word in the Scriptures . . .
'Eye has not seen nor ear heard what good things you have prepared for those who love you' – we thank you for the blessed hope of heaven . . .

INTERCESSIONS *pages 390–393* CLOSING PRAYERS *page 402–403*

14 May *Saint Matthias the Apostle*

OPENING PRAYER Eternal God, your power and glory are unchanging and last for ever. You are closer than breathing, and nearer than hands and feet. Help us to draw near with faith in this time of prayer . . . Glory be . . .

PSALMODY Preserve me, O God, for in thee I take refuge.
As for the saints in the land, they are the noble,
in whom is all my delight
The Lord is my chosen portion and my cup;
thou holdest my lot.
The lines have fallen for me in pleasant places;
yea, I have a goodly heritage. Psalm 16.1–6*

SCRIPTURE READINGS I chose him to be my priest, to go up to my altar, to burn incense, to wear an ephod before me. Those who despise me shall be lightly esteemed. Behold, the days are coming when I will cut off your strength and the strength of your father's house. And I will raise up for myself a faithful priest, who shall do according to what is in my heart and in my mind. 1 Samuel 2.28–35*

Peter said, 'Brethren, the scripture had to be fulfilled, which the Holy Spirit spoke beforehand by the mouth of David, concerning Judas who was guide to those who arrested Jesus. For he was numbered among us, and was allotted his share in this ministry. For it is written in the Book of Psalms, "Let his habitation become desolate, and let there be no one to live in it"; and "His office let another take." One of the men who have accompanied us during all the time that the Lord Jesus went in and out among us, beginning from the baptism of John until the day when he was taken up from us – one of these men must become with us a witness to his resurrection.' They put forward two, Joseph called Barsabbas, who was surnamed Justus, and Matthias. They prayed and said, 'Lord, who knowest the hearts of all men, show which one of these two thou hast chosen to take the place in his ministry and apostleship from which Judas turned aside, to go to his own place.' They cast lots for them, and the lot fell on Matthias; and he was enrolled with the eleven apostles. Acts 1.15–26*

RESPONSE 'Sing praises to the Lord, O you his saints,
and give thanks to his holy name.'

Almighty God, you are glorified in the lives of the holy apostles – we bless and praise you as we celebrate this Feast of Saint Matthias . . .
Matthias made up the number of the Twelve – we pray with Saint Matthias for the protection of your Church against treachery and evil . . .
The bishops are the successors of the apostles and guardians of the Faith – protect the bishops of your Church and fill them with your love . . .

INTERCESSIONS *pages 390–393* CLOSING PRAYERS *page 402–403*

15 May *The Greatest Commandment*

OPENING PRAYER Eternal God, your power and glory are unchanging and last for ever. You are closer than breathing, and nearer than hands and feet. Help us to draw near with faith in this time of prayer . . . Glory be . . .

PSALMODY I consider the days of old, I remember the years long ago.
I meditate and search my spirit:
'Has his steadfast love for ever ceased?
Are his promises at an end for all time?'
I will call to mind the deeds of the Lord,
yea, I will remember thy wonders of old. Psalm 77.5–11*

SCRIPTURE READINGS It was not because you were more in number than any other people that the Lord set his love upon you and chose you; but it is because the Lord loves you, that the Lord has brought you out with a mighty hand, and redeemed you from the house of bondage, from the hand of Pharaoh king of Egypt. Deuteronomy 7.7–8*

If anyone says, 'I love God,' and hates his brother, he is a liar; for he who does not love his brother whom he has seen, cannot love God whom he has not seen. This commandment we have from him, that he who loves God should love his brother also. 1 John 4.20–21

One of the scribes asked, 'Which commandment is the first of all?' Jesus answered, 'The first is, "Hear, O Israel: The Lord our God, the Lord is one; and you shall love the Lord your God with all your heart, and with all your soul, and with all your mind, and with all your strength." The second is this, "You shall love your neighbour as yourself." There is no other commandment greater than these.' The scribe said, 'You are right, Teacher; you have truly said that he is one, and there is no other but he; and to love him with all the heart, and with all the understanding, and with all the strength, and to love one's neighbour as oneself, is much more than all whole burnt offerings and sacrifices.' When Jesus saw that he answered wisely, he said, 'You are not far from the Kingdom of God.'
St Mark 12.28–34

RESPONSE 'Love divine, all loves excelling,
joy of heaven to earth come down.'

Heavenly Father, you have given us a new commandment to love other people – we praise you for your eternal love in Jesus Christ . . .
You are the source of all love – kindle the fire of your perfect love in the hearts of all who are baptized into Christ's body the Church . . .
You are worthy of greater love than we can give you – we pray that the power of your love may fulfil its work of salvation through the Church . . .

INTERCESSIONS *pages 390–393* CLOSING PRAYERS *page 402–403*

OPENING PRAYER Eternal God, your power and glory are unchanging and last for ever. You are closer than breathing, and nearer than hands and feet. Help us to draw near with faith in this time of prayer . . . Glory be . . .

PSALMODY I will meditate on all thy work, and muse on thy mighty deeds.
Thy way, O God, is holy. What god is great like our God?
Thou art the God who workest wonders,
who hast manifested thy might among the peoples.
Thou didst with thy arm redeem thy people,
the sons of Jacob and Joseph. Psalm 77.12–15

SCRIPTURE READINGS Christ has entered, not into a sanctuary made with hands, a copy of the true one, but into heaven itself, now to appear in the presence of God on our behalf. Nor was it to offer himself repeatedly, as the high priest enters the Holy Place yearly with blood not his own; for then he would have had to suffer repeatedly since the foundation of the world. But as it is, he has appeared once for all at the end of the age to put away sin by the sacrifice of himself. And just as it is appointed for men to die once, and after that comes the judgement, so Christ, having been offered once to bear the sins of many, will appear a second time, not to deal with sin but to save those who are eagerly waiting for him.

Hebrews 9.24–28

Jesus said, 'Beware of the scribes, who like to go about in long robes, and to have salutations in the market places and the best seats in the synagogues and the places of honour at feasts, who devour widow's houses and for a pretence make long prayers. They will receive the greater condemnation.' He sat down opposite the treasury, and watched the multitude putting money into the treasury. Many rich people put in large sums. A poor widow came, and put in two copper coins, which make a penny. He called his disciples and said, 'Truly, I say to you, this poor widow has put in more than all those who are contributing to the treasury. For they all contributed out of their abundance; but she out of her poverty has put in everything she had, her whole living.' St Mark 12.38–44

RESPONSE 'My vows to thee I perform, O God;
I will render thank offerings to thee.'

Heavenly Father, your Son gave his life on the Cross for our salvation – help us to respond to his total offering with praise and thanksgiving . . .
Your Son gave everything on the Cross for us – Lord, teach us about sacrifical giving from his perfect offering . . .
'They contributed out of their abundance' – inspire us to support the work of your Church in a responsible way with our money and time . . .

INTERCESSIONS *pages 390–393* CLOSING PRAYERS *page 402–403*

17 May *What Wonderful Buildings*

OPENING PRAYER Eternal God, your power and glory are unchanging and last for ever. You are closer than breathing, and nearer than hands and feet. Help us to draw near with faith in this time of prayer . . . Glory be . . .

PSALMODY When the waters saw thee, O God,
when the waters saw thee, they were afraid,
yea, the deep trembled.
The clouds poured out water; the skies gave forth thunder;
thy arrows flashed on every side.
The crash of thy thunder was in the whirlwind;
the lightnings lighted up the world;
the earth trembled and shook.
Thy way was through the sea, thy path through the great waters;
yet thy footprints were unseen.
Thou didst lead thy people like a flock,
by the hand of Moses and Aaron. Psalm 77. 16–20

SCRIPTURE READINGS 'Will God indeed dwell on the earth? Behold, heaven and the highest heaven cannot contain thee; how much less this house which I have built!' 1 Kings 8.27

As he came out of the temple, one of his disciples said, 'Look, Teacher, what wonderful stones and what wonderful buildings!' Jesus said, 'Do you see these great buildings? There will not be left here one stone upon another, that will not be thrown down.' And as he sat on the Mount of Olives opposite the temple, Peter and James and John and Andrew asked him privately, 'Tell us, when will this be, and what will be the sign when these things are all to be accomplished?' And Jesus began to say to them, 'Take heed that no one leads you astray. Many will come in my name, saying, "I am he!" and they will lead many astray. When you hear of wars and rumours of wars, do not be alarmed; this must take place, but the end is not yet. For nation will rise against nation, and kingdom against kingdom; there will be earthquakes in various places, there will be famines; this is but the beginning of the birth pangs. St Mark 13.1–8

RESPONSE 'O my strength, I will sing praises to thee,
for thou, O God, art my fortress.'

Almighty God, you created the universe and you are not limited by time and space – to you the hosts of heaven sing hymns of joyful praise . . .
'Take heed that no one leads you astray' – Lord, strengthen the Church in the faith of the apostles, and guard it from error and false teaching . . .
'Will God indeed dwell on earth?' – we thank you for taking flesh in the womb of Mary, and we thank you for your presence with us always . . .

INTERCESSIONS *pages 390–393* CLOSING PRAYERS *page 402–403*

OPENING PRAYER Eternal God, your power and glory are unchanging and last for ever. You are closer than breathing, and nearer than hands and feet. Help us to draw near with faith in this time of prayer . . . Glory be . . .

PSALMODY Give ear, O my people, to my teaching,
incline your ears to the words of my mouth!
I will open my mouth in a parable;
I will utter dark sayings from of old,
things that we have heard and know,
that our fathers have told us.
We will not hide them from their children,
but tell to the coming generation
the glorious deeds of the Lord, and of his might,
and the wonder which he has wrought. Psalm 78.1–4*

SCRIPTURE READINGS
The Lord will judge the ends of the earth;
he will give strength to his king,
and exalt the power of his anointed. 1 Samuel 2.10

It was two days before the Passover and the feast of Unleavened Bread. The chief priests and the scribes were seeking how to arrest Jesus by stealth, and kill him; for they said, 'Not during the feast, lest there be a tumult of the people.' While he was at Bethany in the house of Simon the leper, as he sat at table, a woman came with an alabaster flask of ointment of pure nard, very costly, and she broke the flask and poured it over his head. There were some who said to themselves indignantly, 'Why was the ointment thus wasted? For this ointment might have been sold for more than three hundred denarii, and given to the poor.' And they reproached her. But Jesus said, 'Let her alone; why do you trouble her? She has done a beautiful thing to me. For you always have the poor with you, and whenever you will, you can do good to them; but you will not always have me. She has done what she could; she has anointed my body beforehand for burying. Truly, I say to you, wherever the gospel is preached in the whole world, what she has done will he told in memory of her.'
St Mark 14.1–9

RESPONSE 'Steadfast love and faithfulness will meet,
righteousness and peace will kiss each other.'

Heavenly Father, you anointed your Son with the Holy Spirit and with power to bring us the joys of your Kingdom – we praise you and bless you . . .
'You always have the poor with you' – inspire the Church to help the poor and to work for the justice of your Kingdom . . .
'Judas went to the chief priests to betray him' – Lord, help us to be steadfast and faithful to your Son all the days of our life . . .

INTERCESSIONS *pages 390–393* CLOSING PRAYERS *page 402–403*

OPENING PRAYER Eternal God, your power and glory are unchanging and last for ever. You are closer than breathing, and nearer than hands and feet. Help us to draw near with faith in this time of prayer . . . Glory be . . .

PSALMODY He established a testimony in Jacob,
and appointed a law in Israel,
which he commanded our fathers to teach to their children;
that the next generation might know them,
the children yet unborn,
and arise and tell them to their children,
so that they should set their hope in God. Psalm 78.5–7

SCRIPTURE READINGS On the first day of Unleavened Bread, when they sacrificed the passover lamb, the disciples said to Jesus, 'Where will you have us go and prepare for you to eat the passover?' He sent two disciples, and said to them, 'Go into the city, and a man carrying a jar of water will meet you; follow him, and wherever he enters, say to the householder, "The Teacher says, Where is my guest room, where I am to eat the passover with my disciples?" He will show you a large upper room furnished and ready; there prepare for us.' The disciples went to the city, and found it as he had told them; and they prepared the passover. When it was evening he came with the twelve. As they were at table eating, Jesus said, 'Truly, I say to you, one of you will betray me, one who is eating with me.' They began to be sorrowful, and to say to him one after another, 'Is it I?' He said, 'It is one of the twelve, one who is dipping bread into the dish with me. For the Son of Man goes as it is written of him, but woe to that man by whom the Son of Man is betrayed! It would have been better for that man if he had not been born.' As they were eating, he took bread, and blessed, and broke it, and gave it to them, and said, 'Take; this is my body.' And he took a cup, and when he had given thanks he gave it to them, and they all drank of it. He said, 'This is my blood of the covenant, which is poured out for many. Truly, I say to you, I shall not drink again of the fruit of the vine until that day when I drink it new in the Kingdom of God.' When they had sung a hymn, they went out to the Mount of Olives. St Mark 14.12–26*

RESPONSE 'O Lord my God,
I will give thanks to thee for ever.'

Eternal God, you delivered the Israelites from slavery in Egypt – we praise you for freeing us from the slavery of sin and death . . .
You entrusted the Eucharist to the Church – Lord, we thank you for giving us the benefits won by your Son on the Cross through the Eucharist . . .
You give yourself to us in the Eucharist – we thank you for your love . . .

INTERCESSIONS *pages 390–393* CLOSING PRAYERS *page 402–403*

OPENING PRAYER Eternal God, your power and glory are unchanging and last for ever. You are closer than breathing, and nearer than hands and feet. Help us to draw near with faith in this time of prayer . . . Glory be . . .

PSALMODY They did not keep God's covenant,
but refused to walk according to his law.
They forgot what he had done,
and the miracles that he had shown them. Psalm 78.10–11

SCRIPTURE READINGS

Rejoice not over me, O my enemy;
when I fall, I shall rise. Micah 7.8

Jesus said, 'You will all fall away; for it is written, "I will strike the shepherd, and the sheep will be scattered." But after I am raised up, I will go before you to Galilee.' Peter said, 'Even though they all fall away, I will not.' Jesus said, 'Truly, I say to you, this very night, before the cock crows twice, you will deny me three times.' But he said vehemently, 'If I must die with you, I will not deny you.' And they all said the same. And they went to a place which was called Gethsemane; and he said, 'Sit here, while I pray.' He took with him Peter and James and John, and began to be greatly distressed and troubled. He said, 'My soul is very sorrowful, even to death; remain here, and watch.' And going a little further, he fell on the ground and prayed that, if it were possible, the hour might pass from him. He said, 'Abba, Father, all things are possible to thee; remove this cup from me; yet not what I will, but what thou wilt.' He came and found them sleeping, and he said to Peter, 'Simon, are you asleep? Could you not watch one hour? Watch and pray that you may not enter into temptation; the spirit indeed is willing, but the flesh is weak.' And again he went away and prayed, saying the same words. And again he came and found them sleeping, for their eyes were very heavy; and they did not know what to answer him. He came the third time, and said, 'Are you still sleeping and taking your rest? It is enough; the hour has come; the Son of Man is betrayed into the hands of sinners. Rise, let us be going; see my betrayer is at hand.' St Mark 14.27–42

RESPONSE 'Be strong, and let your heart take courage,
all who wait for the Lord.'

O Lord, your Son prayed to you in his agony in the Garden – we thank you for always hearing our prayers offered through your Son . . .
'Could you not watch one hour?' – Lord, give us grace to watch with Christ in his passion and to share the fellowship of his suffering . . .
'Not my will, but thine, be done' – give us grace to seek and to do your will . . .

INTERCESSIONS *pages 390–393* CLOSING PRAYERS *page 402–403*

OPENING PRAYER Eternal God, your power and glory are unchanging and last for ever. You are closer than breathing, and nearer than hands and feet. Help us to draw near with faith in this time of prayer . . . Glory be . . .

PSALMODY He divided the sea and let them pass through it.
In the daytime he led them with a cloud,
and all the night with a fiery light.
He made streams come out of the rock.
Yet they sinned still more against him.
They spoke against God, saying,
'Can he also give bread, or provide meat for his people?'
Therefore, when the Lord heard, he was full of wrath;
because they had no faith in God.
Yet he commanded the skies above,
and opened the doors of heaven;
and he rained down upon them manna to eat.
In spite of all this they still sinned;
despite his wonders they did not believe. Psalm 78.13–32*

SCRIPTURE READINGS Did not one come out from you, who plotted evil against the Lord, and counselled villainy? Nahum 1.11

While Jesus was still speaking, Judas came, and with him a crowd with swords and clubs, from the chief priests and the scribes and elders. The betrayer had given them a sign, saying, 'The one I shall kiss is the man; seize him and lead him away under guard.' When he came, he went up to him at once, and said, 'Master!' He kissed him. They laid hands on him and seized him. One of those who stood by drew his sword, and struck the slave of the high priest and cut off his ear. Jesus said, 'Have you come out as against a robber, with swords and clubs to capture me? Day after day I was with you in the temple teaching, and you did not seize me. But let the scriptures be fulfilled.' They all forsook him, and fled. A young man followed him, with nothing but a linen cloth about his body; they seized him, but he left the linen cloth and ran away naked. St Mark 14.43–52*

RESPONSE 'Let thy steadfast love, O Lord, be upon us,
even as we hope in thee.'

Lord God, your Son was willing to be arrested for our salvation – we thank you for the greatness of his self-offering and eternal love . . .
'They laid hands on him and seized him' – Lord, inspire us to surrender more of our freedom for use in your service . . .
'Let the scriptures be fulfilled' – open our hearts and minds so that we may respond to your living Word and fulfil your purposes in our lives . . .

INTERCESSIONS *pages 390–393* CLOSING PRAYERS *page 402–403*

OPENING PRAYER Eternal God, your power and glory are unchanging and last for ever. You are closer than breathing, and nearer than hands and feet. Help us to draw near with faith in this time of prayer . . . Glory be . . .

PSALMODY O God, the heathen have come into thy inheritance;
they have defiled thy holy temple. Psalm 79.1

SCRIPTURE READINGS If you really fulfil the royal law, according to the scripture, 'You shall love your neighbour as yourself,' you do well. But if you show partiality, you commit sin, and are convicted by the law as transgressors. For whoever keeps the whole law but fails in one point has become guilty of all of it. So speak and so act as those who are to be judged under the law of liberty. For the judgement is without mercy to one who has shown no mercy; yet mercy triumphs over judgement. James 2.8–13*

They led Jesus to the high priest; and all the chief priests and the elders and the scribes were assembled. Peter had followed at a distance, right into the courtyard of the high priest; and he was sitting with the guards, and warming himself at the fire. Now the chief priests and the whole council sought testimony against Jesus to put him to death; but they found none. Many bore false witness against him, and their witness did not agree. Some stood up and bore false witness against him, saying, 'We heard him say, "I will destroy this temple that is made with hands, and in three days I will build another, not made with hands."' Yet not even so did their testimony agree. The high priest stood up, and asked Jesus, 'Have you no answer to make? What is it that these men testify against you?' But he was silent and made no answer. Again the high priest asked, 'Are you the Christ, the Son of the Blessed?' Jesus said, 'I am; and you will see the Son of Man seated at the right hand of Power, and coming with the clouds of heaven.' The high priest tore his garments, and said, 'Why do we still need witnesses? You have heard his blasphemy. What is your decision?' They all condemned him as deserving death. Some began to spit on him, and to cover his face, and to strike him, saying to him 'Prophesy!' And the guards received him with blows. St Mark 14.53–65

RESPONSE 'The word of the Lord is upright,
and all his work is done in faithfulness.'

Everlasting Father, you brought salvation to the world through your Son – make us one in heart and mind, and accept our sacrifice of praise . . .
'The chief priests and the whole council sought testimony' – Lord, give integrity to all who administer the law, and protect the innocent . . .
'Are you the Christ, the Son of the Blessed?' – we rejoice and acclaim your Son as Lord and God and Saviour . . .

INTERCESSIONS *pages 390–393* CLOSING PRAYERS *page 402–403*

OPENING PRAYER Eternal God, your power and glory are unchanging and last for ever. You are closer than breathing, and nearer than hands and feet. Help us to draw near with faith in this time of prayer . . . Glory be . . .

PSALMODY Do not remember against us
the iniquities of our forefathers;
let thy compassion come speedily to meet us,
for we are brought very low.
Help us, O God of our salvation, for the glory of thy name;
deliver us, and forgive our sins, for thy name's sake!
Why should the nations say, 'Where is their God?'
Psalm 79.8–10

SCRIPTURE READINGS
The Lord God helps me;
therefore I have not been confounded;
therefore I have set my face like a flint,
and I know that I shall not be put to shame;
he who vindicates me is near.
Who will contend with me? Let us stand up together.
Who is my adversary? Let him come near to me.
Behold, the Lord God helps me;
who will declare me guilty? Isaiah 50.7–9

As Peter was below in the courtyard, one of the maids of the high priest came; and seeing Peter warming himself, she looked at him, and said, 'You also were with the Nazarene, Jesus.' But he denied it, saying, 'I neither know nor understand what you mean.' He went out into the gateway. And the maid saw him, and began again to say to the bystanders, 'This man is one of them.' But again he denied it. After a little while again the bystanders said to Peter, 'Certainly you are one of them; for you are a Galilean.' But he began to invoke a curse on himself and to swear, 'I do not know this man of whom you speak.' Immediately the cock crowed a second time. Peter remembered how Jesus had said, 'Before the cock crows twice, you will deny me three times.' And he broke down and wept. St Mark 14.66–72

RESPONSE 'God of all grace, we come to thee with broken contrite hearts;
give, which thine eye delights to see, truth in the inward parts.'

Merciful Father, your gift of forgiveness is more than we deserve – we praise you for forgiving all who are truly sorry for their sins . . .
With great courage, Peter entered the courtyard – give us courage to acknowledge Jesus as Lord and Friend and Redeemer . . .
We have all sinned and fallen short of the glory of God – Lord, we thank you for your forgiveness many times and for accepting us as we are . . .

INTERCESSIONS *pages 390–393* CLOSING PRAYERS *page 402–403*

OPENING PRAYER Eternal God, your power and glory are unchanging and last for ever. You are closer than breathing, and nearer than hands and feet. Help us to draw near with faith in this time of prayer . . . Glory be . . .

PSALMODY Let the groans of the prisoners come before thee;
according to thy great power preserve those doomed to die!
Then we thy people, the flock of thy pasture,
will give thanks to thee for ever. Psalm 79.11

SCRIPTURE READINGS

Destruction and violence are before me;
strife and contention arise.
So the law is slacked and justice never goes forth.
For the wicked surround the righteous,
so justice goes forth perverted. Habakkuk 1.3–4

As soon as it was morning the chief priests, with the elders and scribes, and the whole council held a consultation; and they bound Jesus and led him away and delivered him to Pilate. And Pilate asked, 'Are you the King of the Jews?' And he answered, 'You have said so.' The chief priests accused him of many things. And Pilate again asked, 'Have you no answer to make? See how many charges they bring against you.' But Jesus made no further answer, so that Pilate wondered. Now at the feast he used to release for them one prisoner for whom they asked. And among the rebels in prison, who had committed murder in the insurrection, there was a man called Barabbas. And the crowd came up and began to ask Pilate to do as he was wont to do for them. And he answered them, 'Do you want me to release for you the King of the Jews?' For he perceived that it was out of envy that the chief priests had delivered him up. But the chief priests stirred up the crowd to have him release for them Barabbas instead. Pilate again said, 'Then what shall I do with the man whom you call the King of the Jews?' They cried out again, 'Crucify him.' Pilate said, 'Why, what evil has he done?' But they shouted all the more, 'Crucify him.' So Pilate, wishing to satisfy the crowds, released Barabbas; and having scourged Jesus, he delivered him to be crucified. St Mark 15.1–15*

RESPONSE 'Give us a pure and lowly heart,
a temple meet for thee.'

Eternal God, you are the source of justice and truth – we rejoice in your love, and we praise you for the perfect justice of your Kingdom . . .
Your Son was unjustly condemned by earthly rulers – Lord, strengthen the Church to work for justice and truth in all things . . .
'Are you the King of the Jews?' – You are the King of glory and Lord of all creation. You are our God and King, and we praise and adore you . . .

INTERCESSIONS *pages 390–393* CLOSING PRAYERS *page 402–403*

OPENING PRAYER Eternal God, your power and glory are unchanging and last for ever. You are closer than breathing, and nearer than hands and feet. Help us to draw near with faith in this time of prayer . . . Glory be . . .

PSALMODY Give ear, O Shepherd of Israel.
Thou who art enthroned upon the cherubim, shine forth.
Stir up thy might, and come to save us!
Restore us, O God;
let thy face shine, that we may be saved! Psalm 80.1–3*

SCRIPTURE READINGS
He gathers for himself all nations,
and collects as his own all peoples. Habakkuk 2.5

The soldiers led Jesus away inside the palace (that is, the praetorium); and they called together the whole battalion. They clothed him in a purple cloak, and plaiting a crown of thorns they put it on him. They began to salute him, 'Hail, King of the Jews!' They struck his head with a reed, and spat upon him, and knelt down in homage to him. When they had mocked him, they stripped him of the purple cloak, and put his own clothes on him. They led him out to crucify him. They compelled a passer-by, Simon of Cyrene, who was coming in from the country, the father of Alexander and Rufus, to carry his cross. They brought him to a place called Golgotha (which means the place of a skull). They offered him wine mingled with myrrh; but he did not take it. They crucified him, and divided his garments among them, casting lots for them, to decide what each should take. It was the third hour, when they crucified him. The inscription of the charge against him read, 'The King of the Jews.' With him they crucified two robbers, one on his right and one on his left. Those who passed by derided him, wagging their heads, saying, 'Aha! You who would destroy the temple and build it in three days, save yourself, and come down from the cross!' Also the chief priests mocked him, saying, 'He saved others; he cannot save himself. Let the Christ, the King of Israel, come down from the cross, that we may see and believe.' Those who were crucified with him also reviled him. St Mark 15.16–32

RESPONSE 'Awake, my soul, and sing of him who died for thee,
and hail him as thy matchless King through all eternity.'

Eternal God, you sent your Son to reconcile us to yourself and to make all things new – have mercy on us and make us worthy of your love . . .
Your Son was scourged and mocked, and led away with his Cross to die – help us by the Spirit to die to our sins which were the cause of his passion, and to grow into union with Christ . . .
Jesus died for our salvation – Risen Lord, we thank you for your love . . .

INTERCESSIONS *pages 390–393* CLOSING PRAYERS *page 402–403*

OPENING PRAYER Eternal God, your power and glory are unchanging and last for ever. You are closer than breathing, and nearer than hands and feet. Help us to draw near with faith in this time of prayer . . . Glory be . . .

PSALMODY Thou didst bring a vine out of Egypt;
thou didst drive out the nations and plant it.
Thou didst clear the ground for it;
it took deep root and filled the land.
Why then hast thou broken down its walls,
so that all who pass along the way pluck its fruit?
Look down from heaven, and see;
have regard for this vine,
the stock which thy right hand planted.
They have burned it with fire, they have cut it down.
But let thy hand be upon the man of thy right hand,
the son of man whom thou hast made strong for thyself!
Give us life, and we will call on thy name!
Restore us, O Lord God of Hosts!
let thy face shine, that we may be saved! Psalm 80.8–19*

SCRIPTURE READINGS
He was numbered with the transgressors;
yet he bore the sin of many,
and made intercession for the transgressors. Isaiah 53.12

When the sixth hour had come, there was darkness over the whole land until the ninth hour. And at the ninth hour Jesus cried with a loud voice, 'Elo-i, Elo-i, lama sabachthani?' which means 'My God, my God, why hast thou forsaken me?' Some bystanders hearing it said, 'Behold, he is calling Elijah.' One ran and, filling a sponge full of vinegar, put it on a reed and gave it to him to drink, saying, 'Wait, let us see whether Elijah will come to take him down.' And Jesus uttered a loud cry, and breathed his last. And the curtain of the temple was torn in two, from top to bottom. And when the centurion, who stood facing him, saw that he thus breathed his last, he said, 'Truly this man was the Son of God!' St Mark 15.33–40*

RESPONSE 'All wreaths of empire meet upon his brow,
and our hearts confess him, King of glory now.'

Heavenly Father, your Son paid the ransom to free us from the bondage of sin and death – we thank you for his perfect love on the Cross . . .
'My God, my God, why hast thou forsaken me?' – Lord, we rejoice that not even death itself can separate us from your love in Jesus Christ . . .
'This man was the Son of God' – we pray that more people will come to acknowledge Jesus as Lord through the mission and work of your Church . . .

INTERCESSIONS *pages 390–393* CLOSING PRAYERS *page 402–403*

OPENING PRAYER Eternal God, your power and glory are unchanging and last for ever. You are closer than breathing, and nearer than hands and feet. Help us to draw near with faith in this time of prayer . . . Glory be . . .

PSALMODY Whither shall I go from thy Spirit?
Or whither shall I flee from thy presence?
If I ascend to heaven, thou art there!
If I make my bed in Sheol, thou art there!
If I take the wings of the morning
and dwell in the uttermost parts of the sea,
even there thy hand shall lead me.
If I say, 'Let only darkness cover me,
and the light about me be night,'
the night is bright as the day;
for darkness is as light with thee. Psalm 139.7–12*

SCRIPTURE READINGS
If a man die, shall he live again?
All the days of my service I would wait,
till my release should come. Job 14.14

There were women looking from afar, among them were Mary Magdalene, Mary the mother of James the younger and of Joses, and Salome, who, when he was in Galilee, followed him, and ministered to him; and many other women who came up with him to Jerusalem. When evening had come, since it was the day of Preparation, that is, the day before the sabbath, Joseph of Arimathea, a respected member of the council, who was also himself looking for the Kingdom of God, took courage and went to Pilate, and asked for the body of Jesus. Pilate wondered if he were already dead; summoning the centurion, he asked him whether he was already dead. When he learned from the centurion that he was dead, he granted the body to Joseph. And he bought a linen shroud, and taking him down, wrapped him in the linen shroud, and laid him in a tomb which had been hewn out of the rock; and he rolled a stone against the door of the tomb. Mary Magdalene and Mary the mother of Joses saw where he was laid.
St Mark 15.40–47*

RESPONSE 'Salvation's giver, Christ the only Son,
by that his Cross and Blood the victory won.'

Almighty God, your Son poured out his life on the Cross to redeem the world – we praise you for his perfect offering of love . . .
Joseph of Arimathea 'was looking for the Kingdom of God' – Lord, may the death and resurrection of your Son draw all people to your Kingdom . . .
Your Son conquered the power of death and opened the gate of eternal life – we praise and adore the sacred name of Jesus . . .

INTERCESSIONS *pages 390–393* CLOSING PRAYERS *page 402–403*

OPENING PRAYER Eternal God, your power and glory are unchanging and last for ever. You are closer than breathing, and nearer than hands and feet. Help us to draw near with faith in this time of prayer . . . Glory be . . .

PSALMODY Sing aloud to God our strength;
shout for joy to the God of Jacob!
Blow the trumpet at the new moon,
at the full moon, on our feast day.
For it is a statute for Israel,
an ordinance of the God of Jacob.
He made it a decree in Joseph,
when he went out over the land of Egypt.
'There shall be no strange god among you;
you shall not bow down to a foreign god.
I am the Lord your God,
who brought you up out of the land of Egypt.
Open your mouth wide, and I will fill it.' Psalm 81.1–10*

SCRIPTURE READINGS
The Lord God is my strength and my song,
and he has become my salvation. Isaiah 12.2

When the sabbath was past, Mary Magdalene, Mary the mother of James, and Salome, bought spices, so that they might go and anoint Jesus. Very early on the first day of the week they went to the tomb when the sun had risen. They were saying to one another, 'Who will roll away the stone for us from the door of the tomb?' Looking up, they saw that the stone was rolled back – it was very large. Entering the tomb, they saw a young man sitting on the right side, dressed in a white robe; and they were amazed. He said, 'Do not be amazed; you seek Jesus of Nazareth, who was crucified.' He has risen, he is not here; see the place where they laid him. But go, tell his disciples and Peter that he is going before you to Galilee; there you will see him, as he told you.' They went out and fled from the tomb; for trembling and astonishment had come upon them; they said nothing to any one, for they were afraid. St Mark 16.1–8

RESPONSE 'Sing to God a hymn of gladness,
sing to God a hymn of praise.'

Ever-living God and Father, you raised your Beloved Son on the third day – we acclaim your glory and we worship and adore your holy name . . .
'The Lord is risen' – Lord, help us to enter more fully into the new life which flows from the death and resurrection of your Son . . .
Your Son was raised on the third day – we rejoice in your love . . .

INTERCESSIONS *pages 390–393* CLOSING PRAYERS *page 402–403*

OPENING PRAYER Eternal God, your power and glory are unchanging and last for ever. You are closer than breathing, and nearer than hands and feet. Help us to draw near with faith in this time of prayer . . . Glory be . . .

PSALMODY I heard a voice I had not known;
'I relieved your shoulder of the burden,
your hands were freed from the basket.
O that my people would listen to me,
that Israel would walk in my ways!
I would feed you with the finest of the wheat,
and with honey from the rock I would satisfy you.'

Psalm 81.5–16

SCRIPTURE READINGS

The Lord is my strength and my song,
and he has become my salvation;
this is my God and I will praise him. Exodus 15.2

When Jesus rose early on the first day of the week, he appeared first to Mary Magdalene, from whom he had cast out seven demons. She went out and told those who had been with him, as they mourned and wept. When they heard that he was alive and had been seen by her, they would not believe it. After this he appeared in another form to two of them, as they were walking into the country. They went back and told the rest, but they did not believe them. Afterward he appeared to the eleven themselves as they sat at table; and he upbraided them for their unbelief and hardness of heart because they had not believed those who saw him after he had risen. He said, 'Go into all the world and preach the gospel to the whole creation. He who believes and is baptized will be saved; but he who does not believe will be condemned. And these signs will accompany those who believe: in my name they will cast out demons; they will speak in new tongues; they will pick up serpents, and if they drink any deadly thing, it will not hurt them; they will lay their hands on the sick, and they will recover.'

St Mark 16.9–18

RESPONSE 'Let all things seen and unseen, their notes of gladness blend,
For Christ the Lord hath risen, our joy that hath no end.'

Heavenly Father, a new age dawned with the resurrection of your Son – we praise you for the gift of new life in Christ . . .
The resurrection was a new beginning for the apostles in their journey of faith – Lord, assist us in our journey into union with Christ . . .
'Go into all the world and preach the Gospel' – Lord, equip your Church to share the Good News of the risen Christ . . .

INTERCESSIONS *pages 390–393* CLOSING PRAYERS *page 402–403*

30 May *Jesus was taken up into Heaven*

OPENING PRAYER Eternal God, your power and glory are unchanging and last for ever. You are closer than breathing, and nearer than hands and feet. Help us to draw near with faith in this time of prayer . . . . Glory be . . .

PSALMODY God has taken his place in the divine council;
in the midst of the gods he holds judgement.
'How long will you judge unjustly
and show partiality to the wicked?'
Give justice to the weak and the fatherless;
maintain the right of the afflicted and destitute.
Rescue the weak and the needy;
deliver them from the hand of the wicked.'
I say, 'You are gods,
sons of the Most High, all of you;
nevertheless, you shall die like men,
and fall like any prince.'
Arise, O God, judge the earth;
for to thee belong all the nations! Psalm 82.1–8*

SCRIPTURE READINGS So then the Lord Jesus, after he had spoken to them, was taken up into heaven, and sat down at the right hand of God. And they went forth and preached everywhere, while the Lord worked with them and confirmed the message by the signs that attended it. Amen.
Mark 16.19–20

I saw in the night visions,
and behold, with the clouds of heaven
there came one like a son of man,
and he came to the Ancient of Days
and was presented before him.
And to him was given dominion and glory and kingdom,
that all peoples, nations, and languages should serve him;
his dominion is an everlasting dominion,
which shall not pass away,
and his kingdom one that shall not be destroyed.
Daniel 7.13–14

RESPONSE 'The King of kings and Lord of lords,
and heaven's eternal Light.'

Eternal God, your Son ascended to your right hand in heaven – we praise you for opening the Kingdom of Heaven to all believers . . .
Your Son is our great High Priest who lives to make intercessions for us in heaven – we rejoice in your eternal love . . .
The Ascension of your Son is our hope – Lord, guide us in all things, and in your mercy, bring us one day to the joys of your eternal Kingdom . . .

INTERCESSIONS *pages 390–393* CLOSING PRAYERS *page 402–403*

31 May *The Visitation of the Blessed Virgin Mary*

OPENING PRAYER Eternal God, your power and glory are unchanging and last for ever. You are closer than breathing, and nearer than hands and feet. Help us to draw near with faith in this time of prayer . . . Glory be . . .

PSALMODY O Lord, my heart is not lifted up,
my eyes are not raised too high;
I do not occupy myself with things too great
and too marvellous for me.
But I have calmed and quieted my soul,
like a child quieted at its mother's breast;
like a child that is quieted is my soul.
O Israel, hope in the Lord
from this time forth and for evermore. Psalm 131

SCRIPTURE READINGS In those days Mary arose and went with haste into the hill country, to a city of Judah, and she entered the house of Zechariah and greeted Elizabeth. And when Elizabeth heard the greeting of Mary, the babe leaped in her womb; and Elizabeth was filled with the Holy Spirit and she exclaimed with a loud cry, 'Blessed are you among women, and blessed is the fruit of your womb! And why is this granted me, that the mother of my Lord should come to me? For behold, when the voice of your greeting came to my ears, the babe in my womb leaped for joy. And blessed is she who believed that there would be a fulfilment of what was spoked to her from the Lord.' And Mary said,

'My soul magnifies the Lord,
and my spirit rejoices in God my Saviour,
for he has regarded the low estate of his handmaiden.
For behold, henceforth all generations will call me blessed.
St Luke 2.39–48

How beautiful upon the mountains
are the feet of him who brings good tidings,
who publishes salvation,
who says to Zion, 'Your God reigns.' Isaiah 52.7

RESPONSE 'O magnify the Lord with me,
and let us exalt his name together.'

Eternal Father, it was by your grace that Elizabeth rejoiced and greeted Mary as Mother of the Lord – we praise and bless your holy name . . .
'My soul magnifies the Lord' – give us grace to rejoice with Mary and all the saints at the greatness of our salvation through Mary's son . . .
'Blessed are you among women and blessed is the fruit of your womb' – all glory to you, Eternal Lord, for exalting the humble and meek, when you chose Mary to be the mother of our Saviour, Jesus Christ . . .

INTERCESSIONS *pages 390–393* CLOSING PRAYERS *page 402–403*

1 June *Why Saint Luke wrote the Gospel*

OPENING PRAYER Eternal God, it is only your Son who offers you perfect praise. Lift up our hearts into your presence, and help us to become one with his offering to you . . . Glory be . . .

PSALMODY Thou hast multiplied, O Lord my God,
thy wondrous deeds and thy thoughts toward us;
none can compare with thee!
Were I to proclaim and tell of them,
they would be more than can be numbered.
Then I said, 'Lo, I come;
in the roll of the book it is written of me;
I delight to do thy will, O my God;
thy law is within my heart.'
I have told the glad news of deliverance
in the great congregation;
lo, I have not restrained my lips,
as thou knowest, O Lord.
Be pleased, O Lord, to deliver me
O Lord, make haste to help me! Psalm 40.5–13*

SCRIPTURE READINGS All scripture is inspired by God and profitable for teaching, for reproof, for correction, and for training in righteousness, that the man of God may be complete, equipped for every good work.
2 Timothy 3.16–17

Inasmuch as many have undertaken to compile a narrative of the things which have been accomplished among us, just as they were delivered to us by those who from the beginning were eyewitnesses and ministers of the word, it seemed good to me also, having followed all things closely for some time past, to write an orderly account for you, most excellent Theophilus, that you may know the truth concerning the things of which you have been informed. St Luke 1.1–4

RESPONSE 'Let my cry come before thee, O Lord,
give me understanding according to thy Word.'

Heavenly Father, you inspired Saint Luke to write an orderly account of the Gospel of your Son – we give thanks for your living Word in the Scriptures . . .
Your Son is the Way, the Truth and the Life – Lord, enlighten our minds and guide your Church in the way of life eternal . . .
Luke wrote down the greatest story in the world – help us to discover and re-discover the living Christ in the Scriptures and in our lives . . .

INTERCESSIONS *pages 390–393* CLOSING PRAYERS *page 402–403*

2 June *Zechariah in the Temple*

OPENING PRAYER Eternal God, it is only your Son who offers you perfect praise. Lift up our hearts into your presence, and help us to become one with his offering to you . . . Glory be . . .

PSALMODY How lovely is thy dwelling place, O Lord of hosts!
My soul longs, yea, faints for the courts of the Lord;
my heart and flesh sing for joy to the living God.
Even the sparrow finds a home,
at thy altars, O Lord of hosts, my King and my God.
Blessed are those who dwell in thy house,
ever singing thy praise! Psalm 84.1–4*

SCRIPTURE READINGS The angel said, 'You shall conceive and bear a son. He shall begin to deliver Israel from the hand of the Philistines.' The woman bore a son, and called his name Samson; and the boy grew, and the Lord blessed him. The Spirit of the Lord began to stir in him.
Judges 13.3–25*

In the days of Herod, king of Judea, there was a priest named Zechariah. According to the custom of the priesthood, it fell to him by lot to enter the temple and burn incense. The people were praying outside at the hour of incense. There appeared an angel of the Lord standing on the right side of the altar of incense. Zechariah was troubled, and fear fell upon him. The angel said, 'Do no be afraid, Zechariah, for your prayer is heard, and your wife Elizabeth will bear you a son, and you shall call his name John. You will have joy and gladness, and many will rejoice at his birth; for he will be great before the Lord, and he shall drink no wine nor strong drink, and he will be filled with the Holy Spirit, even from his mother's womb. He will turn many of the sons of Israel to the Lord their God, and he will go before him in the spirit and power of Elijah, to turn the hearts of the fathers to the children, and the disobedient to the widsom of the just, to make ready for the Lord a people prepared.' When his time of service was ended, he went to his home. His wife Elizabeth conceived, and for five months she hid herself, saying, 'Thus the Lord has done to me, to take away my reproach among men.' St Luke 1.5–25*

RESPONSE 'Blessed be the Lord!
for he has heard the voice of my supplications.'

Eternal God, you alone are worthy of praise – we worship you, Father, Son and Holy Spirit, one God, to be adored and glorified for ever . . .
'It fell to Zechariah to enter the temple and burn incense' – we praise you in union with the worship of the whole Church, on earth and in heaven . . .
'He will turn many of the sons of Israel to the Lord their God' – Lord, we pray that the Jewish people may be led into the fullness of your truth . . .

INTERCESSIONS *pages 390–393* CLOSING PRAYERS *page 402–403*

OPENING PRAYER Eternal God, it is only your Son who offers you perfect praise. Lift up our hearts into your presence, and help us to become one with his offering to you . . . Glory be . . .

PSALMODY Blessed are the men whose strength is in thee,
in whose heart are the highways to Zion.
They go from strength to strength;
the God of gods will be seen in Zion.
O Lord God of hosts, hear my prayer;
give ear, O God of Jacob!
Behold our shield, O God;
look upon the face of thine anointed. Psalm 84.5–9*

SCRIPTURE READINGS
How beautiful upon the mountains
are the feet of him who brings good tidings,
who publishes peace, who brings good tidings of good,
who publishes salvation,
who says to Zion, 'Your God reigns.'
Hark, your watchmen lift up their voice,
together they sing for joy;
Break forth together into singing,
for the Lord has comforted his people,
The Lord has bared his holy arm
and all the ends of the earth shall see
the salvation of our God. Isaiah 52.7–10

The angel Gabriel said to Mary, 'Hail, O favoured one, the Lord is with you! Do not be afraid, Mary, for you have found favour with God. And behold, you will conceive in your womb and bear a son, and you shall call his name Jesus. He will be great, and will be called the Son of the Most High; and the Lord God will give to him the throne of his father David, and he will reign over the house of Jacob for ever; and of his kingdom there will be no end.' St Luke 1.28–33*

RESPONSE 'Be glad in the Lord, O righteous,
and shout for joy, all you upright in heart.'

Heavenly Father, you sent to Mary a message of hope and joy to the world – we praise you for your tender and unchanging love . . .
'The child to be born will be called holy, the Son of God' – sanctify our bodies and souls, and help us to grow in holiness and love . . .
'All the ends of the earth shall see the salvation of our God' – equip your Church to share in your Son's work of salvation in the world . . .

INTERCESSIONS *pages 390–393* CLOSING PRAYERS *page 402–403*

OPENING PRAYER Eternal God, it is only your Son who offers you perfect praise. Lift up our hearts into your presence, and help us to become one with his offering to you . . . Glory be . . .

PSALMODY Look upon the face of thine anointed!
A day in thy courts is better than a thousand elsewhere.
I would rather be a doorkeeper in the house of my God
than dwell in the tents of wickedness.
For the Lord God is a sun and shield;
he bestows favour and honour.
No good thing does the Lord withhold
from those who walk uprightly.
Blessed is the man who trusts in thee! Psalm 84.9–12*

SCRIPTURE READINGS He showed me the river of the water of life, bright as crystal, flowing from the throne of God and of the Lamb.
Revelation 22.1

Mary said, 'My soul magnifies the Lord,
and my spirit rejoices in God my Saviour,
for he has regarded the low estate of his handmaiden.
For behold, henceforth all generations will call me blessed;
for he who is mighty has done great things for me,
and holy is his name.
And his mercy is on those who fear him
from generation to generation.
He has shown strength with his arm,
he has scattered the proud in the imagination of their hearts
he has put down the mighty from their thrones,
and exalted those of low degree;
he has filled the hungry with good things,
and the rich he has sent empty away.
He has helped his servant Israel,
in remembrance of his mercy, as he spoke to our fathers,
to Abraham and to his posterity for ever.' St Luke 1.46–55

RESPONSE 'Be exalted, O God, above the heavens!
Let thy glory be over all the earth.'

Gracious God, you started a new age of love with the birth of your Son – we rejoice with Mary and all the company of saints, and we praise you . . .
'He has scattered the proud in the imagination of their hearts' – Lord, scatter evil thoughts from our minds and guard us from all sin . . .
'He has filled the hungry with good things' – help your Church to feed the hungry with spiritual and physical food . . .

INTERCESSIONS *pages 390–393* CLOSING PRAYERS *page 402–403*

5 June *His name is John*

OPENING PRAYER Eternal God, it is only your Son who offers you perfect praise. Lift up our hearts into your presence, and help us to become one with his offering to you . . . Glory be . . .

PSALMODY Lord, thou wast favourable to thy land;
thou didst restore the fortunes of Jacob.
Thou didst pardon all their sin.
Restore us again, O God of our salvation,
Show us thy steadfast love, O Lord,
and grant us thy salvation. Psalm 85.1–7*

SCRIPTURE READINGS
The Lord called me from the womb,
from the body of my mother he named my name.
And he said to me, 'You are my servant,
Israel, in whom I will be glorified.' Isaiah 49.1–3*

The angel said, 'Do not be afraid, Zechariah, for your prayer is heard, and your wife Elizabeth will bear you a son, and you shall call his name John. You will have joy and gladness, and many will rejoice at his birth.' Zechariah said, 'How shall I know this? For I am an old man, and my wife is advanced in years.' The angel answered, 'I am Gabriel, who stand in the presence of God; and I was sent to bring you this good news. Behold, you will be silent and unable to speak until the day that these things come to pass, because you did not believe my words, which will be fulfilled in their time.' After these days his wife Elizabeth conceived. Now the time came for Elizabeth to be delivered, and she gave birth to a son. Her neighbours and kinsfold heard that the Lord had shown great mercy to her, and they rejoiced with her. On the eighth day they came to circumcise the child; and they would have named him Zechariah after his father, but his mother said, 'Not so; he shall be called John.' They said, 'None of your kindred is called by this name.' They made signs to his father, inquiring what he would have him called. He asked for a writing tablet, and wrote, 'His name is John.' They all marvelled. Immediately his mouth was opened and his tongue loosed, and he spoke, blessing God. St Luke 1.13–64*

RESPONSE 'I will bless the Lord at all times;
his praise shall continually be in my mouth.'

Eternal God, you gave joy to the world with the birth of your Son – accept our joyful song of praise and thanksgiving . . .
'Many will rejoice at his birth' – we praise you for John the Baptist, and for all your faithful servants in every generation . . .
'His mouth was opened and his tongue loosed' – open our lips that we may tell of your love in Christ, and sing praises to your holy name . . .

INTERCESSIONS *pages 390–393* CLOSING PRAYERS *page 402–403*

OPENING PRAYER Eternal God, it is only your Son who offers you perfect praise. Lift up our hearts into your presence, and help us to become one with his offering to you . . . Glory be . . .

PSALMODY Let me hear what God the Lord will speak,
for he will speak peace to his people,
to his saints, to those who turn to him in their hearts.
Surely his salvation is at hand for those who fear him,
that glory may dwell in our land. Psalm 85.8–9

SCRIPTURE READINGS John's father Zechariah was filled with the Holy Spirit, and prophesied, saying,

Blessed be the Lord God of Israel,
for he has visited and redeemed his people,
and has raised up a horn of salvation for us
in the house of his servant David,
as he spoke by the mouth of his holy prophets from of old,
that we should be saved from our enemies,
and from the hand of all who hate us;
to perform the mercy promised to our fathers,
and to remember his holy covenant,
the oath which he swore to our father Abraham, to grant us
that we, being delivered from the hand of our enemies,
might serve him without fear,
in holiness and righteousness before him all the days of our life.
And you, child, will be called the prophet of the Most High;
for you will go before the Lord to prepare his ways,
to give knowledge of salvation to his people
in the forgiveness of their sins,
through the tender mercy of our God,
when the day shall dawn upon us from on high
to give light to those who sit in darkness
and in the shadow of death,
to guide our feet in the way of peace.' St Luke 1.67–79

RESPONSE 'Let the peoples praise thee, O God;
let all the peoples praise thee.'

Lord God of Israel, you have raised up a Saviour for all people on earth – blessed be the sacred name of Jesus, for time and for eternity . . .
'He has visited and redeemed his people' – Lord, we thank you for the birth of your Son to bring us into union with yourself . . .
'To give knowledge of salvation' – Lord, we thank you for your gift of forgiveness to all who are truly sorry for their sins, and turn to you . . .

INTERCESSIONS *pages 390–393* CLOSING PRAYERS *page 402–403*

OPENING PRAYER Eternal God, it is only your Son who offers you perfect praise. Lift up our hearts into your presence, and help us to become one with his offering to you . . . Glory be . . .

PSALMODY Steadfast love and faithfulness will meet;
righteousness and peace will kiss each other.
Yea, the Lord will give what is good.
Righteousness will go before him,
and make his footsteps a way. Psalm 85.10–13*

SCRIPTURE READINGS When the goodness and loving kindness of God our Saviour appeared, he saved us, not because of deeds done by us in righteousness, but in virtue of his own mercy, by the washing of regeneration and renewal in the Holy Spirit, which he poured out upon us richly through Jesus Christ our Saviour. Titus 3.4–6

In those days a decree went out from Caesar Augustus that all the world should be enrolled. This was the first enrolment, when Quirinius was governor of Syria. All went to be enrolled, each to his own city. Joseph went from Galilee, to the city of David, which is called Bethlehem, because he was of the house and lineage of David, to be enrolled with Mary, his betrothed, who was with child. And while they were there, the time came for her to be delivered. She gave birth to her first-born and wrapped him in swaddling cloths, and laid him in a manger, because there was no place for them in the inn. And in that region there were shepherds out in the field, keeping watch over their flock by night. An angel appeared to them, and the glory of the Lord shone around them, and they were filled with fear. The angel said, 'Be not afraid; for behold, I bring you good news of a great joy which will come to all the people; for to you is born this day in the city of David a Saviour, who is Christ the Lord. This will be a sign: you will find a babe wrapped in swaddling cloths and lying in a manger.' Suddenly there was with the angel a multitude of the heavenly host praising God and saying, 'Glory to God in the highest, and on earth peace among men with whom he is pleased! St Luke 2.1–14*

RESPONSE 'Rise to adore the mystery of love,
which hosts of angels chanted from above.'

Eternal God, it is your will to reconcile the whole of creation to yourself through your Son – we praise you for your creative love . . .
'Mary gave birth to her first-born' – we thank you for taking flesh in the womb of Mary, that we may share your nature and reflect your glory . . .
'I bring you news of great joy' – we thank you for the greatest honour and blessing you give to us in the birth of your Son . . .

INTERCESSIONS *pages 390–393* CLOSING PRAYERS *page 402–403*

OPENING PRAYER Eternal God, it is only your Son who offers you perfect praise. Lift up our hearts into your presence, and help us to become one with his offering to you . . . Glory be . . .

PSALMODY Incline thy ear, O Lord, and answer me,
for I am poor and needy.
Preserve my life, for I am godly;
save thy servant who trusts in thee.
Thou art my God; be gracious to me, O Lord,
for to thee do I cry all the day. Psalm 86.1–3*

SCRIPTURE READINGS May you be strengthened with all power, according to his glorious might, for all endurance and patience with joy, giving thanks to the Father, who has qualified us to share in the inheritance of the saints in light. He has delivered us from the dominion of darkness and transferred us to the kingdom of his beloved Son, in whom we have redemption, the forgiveness of our sins. Colossians 1.11–14

Now his parents went to Jerusalem every year at the feast of the Passover. When he was twelve years old, they went up according to custom; and when the feast was ended, as they were returning, the boy Jesus stayed behind in Jerusalem. His parents did not know it, but supposing him to be in the company they went a day's journey, and they sought him among their kinsfolk and acquaintances; and when they did not find him, they returned to Jerusalem, seeking him. After three days, they found him in the temple, sitting among the teachers, listening to them and asking them questions; and all who heard him were amazed at his understanding and his answers. When they saw him they were astonished; and his mother said to him, 'Son, why have you treated us so? Your father and I have been looking for you anxiously.' He said, 'How is it that you sought me? Did you not know that I must be in my Father's house?' They did not understand the saying which he spoke to them. He went with them to Nazareth, and was obedient to them; and his mother kept all these things in her heart. And Jesus increased in wisdom and in stature, and in favour with God and man. St Luke 2.41–52

RESPONSE 'O Lord, our Lord, how majestic is thy name in all the earth.'

Heavenly Father, your Son humbly sat with the teachers in the temple – we praise you for all who help us to grow in the Faith . . .
'How is it that you sought me?' – we seek you because you first seek us, and you are our Creator and Redeemer and Friend . . .
'Jesus increased in wisdom and in stature' – give us a deeper understanding of your ways, and help us to grow into union with your Son . . .

INTERCESSIONS *pages 390–393* CLOSING PRAYERS *page 402–403*

OPENING PRAYER Eternal God, it is only your Son who offers you perfect praise. Lift up our hearts into your presence, and help us to become one with his offering to you . . . Glory be . . .

PSALMODY Gladden the soul of thy servant,
for to thee, O Lord, do I lift up my soul.
For thou, O Lord, art good and forgiving,
abounding in steadfast love
to all who call on thee. Psalm 86.4–5

SCRIPTURE READINGS Moses said, 'If I have found favour in thy sight, O Lord, let the Lord go in the midst of us, although it is a stiff-necked people; pardon our iniquity and sin, and take us for thy inheritance.' Exodus 34.9

The word of God came to John the son of Zechariah in the wilderness; and he went into all the region about the Jordan, preaching a baptism of repentance for the forgiveness of sins. As it is written in the book of the words of Isaiah the prophet,

'The voice of one crying in the wilderness:
Prepare the way of the Lord, make his paths straight.
The rough ways shall be made smooth;
and all flesh shall see the salvation of our God.'

He said to the multitudes that came to be baptized, 'You brood of vipers! Who warned you to flee from the wrath to come? Bear fruits that befit repentance, and do not begin to say to yourselves, "We have Abraham as our father"; for I tell you, God is able from these stones to raise up children to Abraham. Even now the axe is laid to the root of the trees; every tree therefore that does not bear good fruit is cut down and thrown into the fire.' The multitudes asked, 'What then shall we do?' He answered, 'He who has two coats, let him share with him who has none; and he who has food, let him do likewise.' Tax collectors said, 'Teacher what shall we do?' He said, 'Collect no more than is appointed you.' Soldiers also asked, 'And we, what shall we do?' He said, 'Rob no one by violence or by false accusation, and be content with your wages.' St Luke 3.2–14*

RESPONSE 'I cry to God Most High;
God will send forth his steadfast love and his faithfulness.'

Gracious God, your servant John the Baptist prepared for a new era of grace – we thank you for fulfilling all your promises in your Son . . .
'Bear fruit that befits repentance' – give us both an inward change of heart, and lead us to outward changes in our daily lives . . .
John the Baptist stands at the boundary between the Old and New Covenants – we praise you for your gift of new life in Jesus Christ . . .

INTERCESSIONS *pages 390–393* CLOSING PRAYERS *page 402–403*

10 June *Jesus is Baptized by John*

OPENING PRAYER Eternal God, it is only your Son who offers you perfect praise. Lift up our hearts into your presence, and help us to become one with his offering to you . . . Glory be . . .

PSALMODY Give ear, O Lord, to my prayer.
In the day of my trouble I call on thee,
for thou dost answer me.
There is none like thee among the gods, O Lord,
nor are there any works like thine. Psalm 86.6–8*

SCRIPTURE READINGS Jesse made seven of his sons pass before Samuel. Samuel said, 'Are all your sons here?' He said, 'There remains yet the youngest, but behold, he is keeping the sheep.' Samuel said, 'Send and fetch him; for we will not sit down till he comes here.' He sent, and brought him in. Now he was ruddy, and had beautiful eyes, and was handsome. The Lord said, 'Arise, anoint him; for this is he.' Then Samuel took the horn of oil, and anointed him in the midst of his brothers; and the Spirit of the Lord came mightily upon David from that day forward.
1 Samuel 16.11–13

As the people were in expectation, and all men questioned in their hearts concerning John, whether perhaps he were the Christ, John answered, 'I baptize you with water; but he who is mightier than I is coming, the thong of whose sandals I am not worthy to untie; he will baptize you with the Holy Spirit and with fire. His winnowing fork is in his hand, to clear his threshing floor, and to gather the wheat into his granary, but the chaff he will burn with unquenchable fire.' But Herod the tetrarch, who had been reproved by him for Herodias, his brother's wife, and for all the evil things that Herod had done, added this to them all, that he shut up John in prison. Now when all the people were baptized, and when Jesus also had been baptized and was praying, the heaven was opened, and the Holy Spirit descended upon him in bodily form, as a dove, and a voice came from heaven, 'Thou art my beloved Son; with thee I am well pleased.'
St Luke 3.15–22

RESPONSE 'Hail to the Lord's Anointed, great David's greater Son.
Hail in the time appointed, his reign on earth begun.'

Eternal God, the Baptism of your Son is a sign of his role as servant and his acceptance of the Cross – we praise you for your eternal love . . .
'Thou art my Beloved Son; with thee I am well pleased' – we praise you for anointing Jesus as Messiah and Lord of all creation at his Baptism . . .
Your Son began his public ministry at his Baptism – Lord, inspire us to surrender more of our lives to your service . . .

INTERCESSIONS *pages 390–393* CLOSING PRAYERS *page 402–403*

11 June *Saint Barnabas the Apostle*

OPENING PRAYER Eternal God, it is only your Son who offers you perfect praise. Lift up our hearts into your presence, and help us to become one with his offering to you . . . Glory be . . .

PSALMODY All thy works shall give thanks to thee, O Lord,
and all thy saints shall bless thee!
They shall speak of the glory of thy kingdom,
and tell of thy power,
to make known to the sons of men thy mighty deeds,
and the glorious splendour of thy kingdom.
Thy kingdom is an everlasting kingdom,
and thy dominion endures through all generations.
The Lord is faithful in all his words,
and gracious in all his deeds. Psalm 145.10–13

SCRIPTURE READINGS Jesus said, 'You did not choose me, but I chose you and appointed you that you should go and bear fruit and that your fruit should abide. St John 15.16

Those who were scattered because of the persecution that arose over Stephen travelled as far as Phoenicia and Cyprus and Antioch, speaking the word to none except Jews. But there were some of them, men of Cyprus and Cyrene, who on coming to Antioch spoke to the Greeks also, preaching the Lord Jesus. The hand of the Lord was with them, and a great number that believed turned to the Lord. News of this came to the ears of the church in Jerusalem, and they sent Barnabas to Antioch. When he came and saw the grace of God, he was glad; and he exhorted them all to remain faithful to the Lord with steadfast purpose; for he was a good man, full of the Holy Spirit and of faith. A large company was added to the Lord. So Barnabas went to Tarsus to look for Saul; and when he had found him, he brought him to Antioch. For a whole year they met with the church, and taught a large company of people; and in Antioch the disciples were for the first time called Christians. Acts 11.19–26

RESPONSE 'May all who seek thee
rejoice and be glad in thee.'

God our Father, you chose the Apostles to be pillars of your Church – on this day, we praise you for the faith and love of Saint Barnabas . . .
The secret at the heart of the Church is the mysterious presence of the risen Christ – strengthen the Church and build it up in faith and love . . .
'The hand of the Lord was with him' – in union with Saint Barnabas, we pray for the work and mission of your Church throughout the world . . .

INTERCESSIONS *pages 390–393* CLOSING PRAYERS *page 402–403*

OPENING PRAYER Eternal God, it is only your Son who offers you perfect praise. Lift up our hearts into your presence, and help us to become one with his offering to you . . . Glory be . . .

PSALMODY On the holy mount stands the city he founded;
the Lord loves the gates of Zion
more than all the dwelling places of Jacob.
Glorious things are spoken of you, O city of God.
Psalm 87.1–3

SCRIPTURE READINGS The word of God is living and active, sharper than any two-edged sword, piercing to the division of soul and spirit, of joints and marrow, and discerning the thoughts and intentions of the heart. And before him no creature is hidden, but all are open and laid bare to the eyes of him with whom we have to do. Hebrews 4.12–13

Jesus, full of the Holy Spirit, returned from the Jordan, and was led by the Spirit for forty days in the wilderness, tempted by the devil. He ate nothing in those days; and when they were ended, he was hungry. The devil said to him, 'If you are the Son of God, command this stone to become bread.' Jesus answered him, 'It is written, "Man shall not live by bread alone."' And the devil took him up, and showed him all the kingdoms of the world in a moment of time, and said, 'To you I will give all this authority and their glory; for it has been delivered to me, and I give it to whom I will. If you, then, will worship me, it shall all be yours.' Jesus answered, 'It is written, "You shall worship the Lord your God, and him only shall you serve."' And he took him to Jerusalem, and set him on the pinnacle of the temple, and said, 'If you are the Son of God, throw yourself down from here; for it is written, "He will give his angels charge of you, to guard you," and "On their hands they will bear you up, lest you strike your foot against a stone."' Jesus answered, 'It is said, "You shall not tempt the Lord your God."' When the devil had ended every temptation, he departed from him until an opportune time. St Luke 4.1–13

RESPONSE 'O God, be not far from me;
O my God, make haste to help me.'

Heavenly Father, your Son heard the voice of temptation in the silent wilderness – we praise you for the faithfulness of your Son . . .
Your Son overcame all temptation – help us by the Spirit to know what is wrong in our lives, and give us grace to overcome all our sins . . .
'You shall worship the Lord your God and him only shall you serve' – purify our worship and send us out to love and serve you in the world . . .

INTERCESSIONS *pages 390–393* CLOSING PRAYERS *page 402–403*

13 June *A Prophet without Honour*

OPENING PRAYER Eternal God, it is only your Son who offers you perfect praise. Lift up our hearts into your presence, and help us to become one with his offering to you . . . Glory be . . .

PSALMODY O Lord, my God, I call for help by day;
I cry out in the night before thee.
Let my prayer come before thee,
incline thy ear to my cry! Psalm 88.1–2

SCRIPTURE READINGS Ezra the priest brought the law before the assembly. He read from it facing the square before the Water Gate from early morning until mid day. Ezra blessed the Lord, the great God; and all the people answered, 'Amen, Amen,' and they worshipped the Lord.
Nehemiah 8.2–7*

Jesus came to Nazareth; he went to the synagogue, as his custom was, on the sabbath day. He stood up to read. He found the place where it was written, 'The Spirit of the Lord is upon me, because he has anointed me to preach good news to the poor. He has sent me to proclaim release to the captives and recovering of sight to the blind, to set at liberty those who are oppressed, to proclaim the acceptable year of the Lord.' He began, 'Today this scripture has been fulfilled in your hearing.' All spoke well of him, and wondered at the gracious words which proceeded out of his mouth; they said, 'Is not this Joseph's son?' He said, 'Doubtless you will quote this proverb, "Physician, heal yourself; what we have heard you did at Capernaum, do here in your own country."' He said, 'No prophet is acceptable in his own country. There were many widows in the days of Elijah, when the heaven was shut up three years and six months, when there came a great famine; and Elijah was sent to none of them but only to Zarephath, in the land of Sidon, to a woman who was a widow. There were many lepers in Israel in the time of the prophet Elisah; and none of them was cleansed, but only Naaman the Syrian.' When they heard this, all were filled with wrath. They led him to the brow of the hill on which their city was built, that they might throw him down headlong. But passing through the midst of them he went away. St Luke 4.16–30*

RESPONSE 'Jesus is worthy to receive honour and power divine;
and blessings more than we can give, be, Lord, for ever thine.'

Eternal God, you rule the universe with goodness and perfect love – all praise and glory to you, Father, Son and Holy Spirit, one God for ever . . .
'He has anointed me to preach the good news to the poor' – teach us more about the nature of your Kingdom of justice and love . . .
'Passing through the midst of them he went away' – cleanse us from the sins which separate us from you, and enfold us in your love . . .

INTERCESSIONS *pages 390–393* CLOSING PRAYERS *page 402–403*

14 June *Jesus heals the Sick*

OPENING PRAYER Eternal God, it is only your Son who offers you perfect praise. Lift up our hearts into your presence, and help us to become one with his offering to you . . . Glory be . . .

PSALMODY I will sing of thy steadfast love,
O Lord, for ever. Psalm 89.1

SCRIPTURE READINGS On the first day of the week, when we were gathered together to break bread, Paul talked with them; and he prolonged his speech until midnight. A young man named Eutychus was sitting in the window. He sank into a deep sleep as Paul talked still longer; and being overcome by sleep, he fell down from the third story and was taken up dead. But Paul went down and bent over him, and embracing him said, 'Do not be alarmed, for his life is in him.' And they took the lad away alive, and were not a little comforted. Acts 20.7–12*

Jesus went to Capernaum. He was teaching them on the sabbath; and they were astonished at his teaching; for his word was with authority. In the synagogue there was a man who had the spirit of an unclean demon; and he cried out with a loud voice, 'Ah! What have you to do with us, Jesus of Nazareth? Have you come to destroy us? I know who you are, the Holy One of God.' Jesus rebuked him, saying, 'Be silent, and come out of him!' When the demon had thrown him down in the midst, he came out of him, having done him no harm. They were all amazed and said to one another, 'What is this word? For with authority and power he commands the unclean spirits, and they come out.' Reports of him went out into every place in the surrounding region. He left the synagogue, and entered Simon's house. Now Simon's mother-in-law was ill with a high fever, and they besought him for her. He stood over her and rebuked the fever, and it left her; immediately she rose and served them. When the sun was setting all who had any that were sick with various diseases brought them to him; and he laid his hands on every one of them and healed them. Demons came out of many, crying, 'You are the Son of God!' He rebuked them, and would not allow them to speak, because they knew he was the Christ.
St Luke 4.31–42*

RESPONSE 'Just as I am, thou wilt receive,
wilt welcome, pardon, cleanse, relieve.'

O God our merciful Father, you are worthy of praise from every mouth, and glory from every tongue – we adore you, Father, Son and Eternal Spirit . . .
'What have you to do with us, Jesus of Nazareth?' – Lord, you have everything to do with us, and we thank you for your gift of life and love . . .
'I know who you are, the Holy One of God' – Lord, help us and all people to know you as Lord and Redeemer and Friend . . .

INTERCESSIONS *pages 390–393* CLOSING PRAYERS *page 402–403*

15 June *A Great Shoal of Fish*

OPENING PRAYER Eternal God, it is only your Son who offers you perfect praise. Lift up our hearts into your presence, and help us to become one with his offering to you . . . Glory be . . .

PSALMODY Thou hast said, 'I have made a covenant with my chosen one,
I have sworn to David my servant:
"I will establish your descendants for ever,
and build your throne for all generations."'
Let the heavens praise thy wonders, O Lord,
thy faithfulness in the assembly of the holy ones!
For who in the skies can be compared to the Lord?
Who among the heavenly beings is like the Lord?

Psalm 89.3–6

SCRIPTURE READINGS I write this to you who believe in the name of the Son of God, that you may know that you have eternal life. And this is the confidence which we have in him, that if we ask anything according to his will, he hears us.
1 John 5.13–14

While the people pressed upon Jesus to hear the word of God, he was standing by the lake of Gennesaret. He saw two boats; but the fishermen had gone out of them and were washing their nets. Getting into one of the boats, which was Simon's, he asked him to put out a little from the land. He sat down and taught the people from the boat. When he had ceased speaking, he said to Simon, 'Put out into the deep and let down your nets for a catch.' Simon answered, 'Master, we toiled all night and took nothing! But at your word I will let down the nets.' When they had done this, they enclosed a great shoal of fish; and as their nets were breaking, they beckoned to their partners in the other boat to come and help them. They filled both the boats, so that they began to sink. When Simon Peter saw it, he fell down at Jesus' knees, saying, 'Depart from me, for I am a sinful man, O Lord.' Jesus said to Simon, 'Do not be afraid; henceforth you will be catching men.' When they had brought their boats to land, they left everything and followed him.
St Luke 5.1–11

RESPONSE 'Ye servants of God, your Master proclaim,
and publish abroad his wonderful name.'

Eternal God, in the mystery of your love, you created us to share in your divine life – we praise you for uniting us in the fellowship of your love . . .
'Master, we toiled all night and took nothing!' – encourage your Church and give us grace to share in the continuous mission of your Son . . .
'They enclosed a great shoal of fish' – we thank you for gathering us into the glorious community of those who have been baptized into Christ. . .

INTERCESSIONS *pages 390–393* CLOSING PRAYERS *page 402–403*

Through a Hole in the Roof

OPENING PRAYER Eternal God, it is only your Son who offers you perfect praise. Lift up our hearts into your presence, and help us to become one with his offering to you . . . Glory be . . .

PSALMODY O Lord God of hosts, who is mighty as thou art, O Lord,
with thy faithfulness round about thee?
Thou dost rule the raging of the sea;
when its waves rise, thou stillest them.
Thou didst scatter thy enemies with thy mighty arm.
The heavens are thine, the earth also is thine;
the world and all that is in it, thou hast founded them.
Psalm 89.8–11*

SCRIPTURE READINGS No inhabitant will say, 'I am sick'; the people who dwell there will be forgiven their iniquity. Isaiah 33.24

As Jesus was teaching, there were Pharisees and teachers of the law sitting by, who had come from every village of Galilee and Judea and from Jerusalem; and the power of the Lord was with him to heal. Behold, men were bringing on a bed a man who was paralysed, and they sought to bring him in and lay him before Jesus; but finding no way to bring him in, because of the crowd, they went up on the roof and let him down with his bed through the tiles into the midst before Jesus. When he saw their faith he said, 'Man, your sins are forgiven you.' The scribes and the Pharisees began to question, saying, 'Who is this that speaks blasphemies? Who can forgive sins but God only?' When Jesus perceived their questionings, he answered, 'Why do you question in your hearts? Which is easier, to say, "Your sins are forgiven you," or to say, "Rise and walk"? But that you may know that the Son of Man has authority on earth to forgive sins' – he said to the man who was paralysed – 'I say to you, rise, take up your bed and go home.' Immediately he rose before them, and took up that on which he lay, and went home, glorifying God. Amazement seized them all, and they glorified God and were filled with awe. St Luke 5.17–26*

RESPONSE 'Thou of life the fountain art; freely let me take of thee;
spring thou up within my heart, rise to all eternity.'

Almighty God, all that we are and all that we have is your gift to us – we thank you and bless you and praise you for your goodness and love . . .
'Your sins are forgiven you' – forgive us for not using the opportunities you have given to us to share in the mission of your Son . . .
'They were filled with awe' – we tremble with wonder and holy fear at the greatness of your patience and love, and we praise you . . .

INTERCESSIONS *pages 390–393* CLOSING PRAYERS *page 402–403*

Follow Me

OPENING PRAYER Eternal God, it is only your Son who offers you perfect praise. Lift up our hearts into your presence, and help us to become one with his offering to you . . . Glory be . . .

PSALMODY Blessed are the people who know the festal shout.
who walk, O Lord, in the light of thy countenance,
who exult in thy name all the day. Psalm 89.15–16

SCRIPTURE READINGS Beloved, it is a loyal thing you do when you render any service to the brethren, especially to strangers, who have testified to your love before the Church. You will do well to send them on their journey as befits God's service. For they have set out for his sake, and have accepted nothing from the heathen. So we ought to support such men, that we may be fellow workers in the truth. 3 John 1.5–8

Jesus saw a tax collector, named Levi, sitting at the tax office; and he said, 'Follow me.' He left everything and followed him. Levi made him a great feast in his house; and there was a large company of tax collectors and others sitting at table. The Pharisees and their scribes murmured against his disciples, saying, 'Why do you eat and drink with tax collectors and sinners?' Jesus answered, 'Those who are well have no need of a physician, but those who are sick; I have not come to call the righteous, but sinners to repentance.' They said, 'The disciples of John fast often and offer prayers, and so do the disciples of the Pharisees, but yours eat and drink.' Jesus said, 'Can you make wedding guests fast while the bridegroom is with them? The days will come, when the bridegroom is taken away from them, and then they will fast in those days.' He told them a parable: 'No one tears a piece from a new garment and puts it upon an old garment; if he does, he will tear the new, and the piece from the new will not match the old. No one puts new wine into old wine-skins; if he does, the new wine will burst the skins and it will be spilled, and the skins will be destroyed. New wine must be put into fresh wineskins. No one after drinking old wine desires new; for he says, "The old is good."' St Luke 5.27–39*

RESPONSE 'Lord, it is my chief complaint that my love is weak and faint;
yet I love thee, and adore; O for grace to love thee more.'

Eternal God, our vocation to be Christians is one of your great gifts to us – we rejoice in the fellowship of all who respond to your love . . .
'Follow me' – cleanse us and make us worthy to be called followers of your Son, our Lord and Saviour Jesus Christ . . .
'I have not come to call the righteous, but sinners to repentance' – help us by the Spirit to be aware of our sins, and fill us with your love . . .

INTERCESSIONS *pages 390–393* CLOSING PRAYERS *page 402–403*

18 June *Lord of the Sabbath*

OPENING PRAYER Eternal God, it is only your Son who offers you perfect praise. Lift up our hearts into your presence, and help us to become one with his offering to you . . . Glory be . . .

PSALMODY Of old thou didst speak in a vision to thy faithful one,
and say: 'I have set a crown upon one who is mighty,
I have exalted one chosen from the people.
I have found David, my servant;
with my holy oil I have anointed him.' Psalm 89.19–20

SCRIPTURE READINGS You, who once were estranged and hostile in mind, doing evil deeds, he has now reconciled in his body of flesh by his death, in order to present you holy and blameless and irreproachable before him, provided that you continue in the faith, stable and steadfast, not shifting from the hope of the gospel which you heard. Colossians 1.21–23

On a sabbath, while Jesus was going through the grainfields, his disciples plucked and ate some ears of grain, rubbing them in their hands. Some Pharisees said, 'Why are you doing what is not lawful to do on the sabbath?' Jesus answered, 'Have you not read what David did when he was hungry, he and those who were with thim: how he entered the house of God, and took and ate the bread of the Presence, which it is not lawful for any but the priests to eat, and also gave it to those with him?' He said, 'The Son of Man is Lord of the sabbath.' On another sabbath, when he entered the synagogue and taught, a man was there whose right hand was withered. The scribes and the Pharisees watched him, to see whether he would heal on the sabbath, so that they might find an accusation against him. But he knew their thoughts, and he said to the man who had the withered hand, 'Come and stand here.' He rose and stood there. Jesus said, 'I ask you, is it lawful on the sabbath to do good or to do harm, to save life or to destroy it?' He looked around on them all, and said, 'Stretch out your hand.' He did so, and his hand was restored. They were filled with fury and discussed what they might do to Jesus. St Luke 6.1–11*

RESPONSE 'Lord of our life, and God of our salvation,
hear and receive thy Church's supplication.'

Eternal God, you created the corn of the fields and all that exists out of nothing – we praise you for your powerful energy and eternal love . . .
'David entered the house of God, and ate the bread of the Presence' – we praise you for feeding us with your Son in the Eucharist . . .
'The Son of Man is Lord of the Sabbath' – Lord, rule in our hearts on Sunday and all the days of the week . . .

INTERCESSIONS *pages 390–393* CLOSING PRAYERS *page 402–403*

OPENING PRAYER Eternal God, it is only your Son who offers you perfect praise. Lift up our hearts into your presence, and help us to become one with his offering to you . . . Glory be . . .

PSALMODY My faithfulness and my steadfast love shall be with him,
and in my name shall his horn be exalted. Psalm 89.24

SCRIPTURE READINGS If then you have been raised with Christ, seek the things that are above, where Christ is, seated at the right hand of God. Set your minds on things that are above, not on things that are on earth. For you have died, and your life is hid with Christ in God. When Christ who is our life appears, then you also will appear with him in glory. Put on then, as God's chosen ones, holy and beloved, compassion, kindness, lowliness, meekness, and patience, forbearing one another and, if one has a complaint against another, forgiving each other; as the Lord has forgiven you, so you also must forgive. Above all these put on love, which binds all together in perfect harmony. Colossians 3.1–14*

Jesus stood on a level place. He lifted up his eyes on his disciples, and said: 'Blessed are you poor, for yours is the kingdom of God. Blessed are you that hunger now, for you shall be satisfied. Blessed are you that weep now, for you shall laugh. Blessed are you when men hate you, and when they exclude you and revile you, and cast out your name as evil, on account of the Son of Man! Rejoice in that day, and leap for joy, for behold, your reward is great in heaven; for so their fathers did to the prophets. But woe to you that are rich, for you have received your consolation. Woe to you that are full now, for you shall hunger. Woe to you that laugh now, for you shall mourn and weep. Woe to you, when all men speak well of you, for so their fathers did to the false prophets. But I say to you that hear, Love your enemies, do good to those who hate you, bless those who curse you, pray for those who abuse you. To him who strikes you on the cheek, offer the other also; and from him who takes away your coat do not withhold even your shirt. Give to every one who begs from you; and of him who takes away your goods do not ask them again. And as you wish that men would do to you, do so to them.' St Luke 6.17–31*

RESPONSE 'Where is thy reign of peace and purity and love?
When shall all hatred cease, as in the realm above?'

Heavenly Father, your love is pure and holy and without limit – we thank you and praise you for calling us to share your life in your Son . . .
'Blessed are the poor' – help us to work for your justice in the world . . .
Your love is so great that it includes both saints and sinners – draw all people to yourself by the love of Jesus on the Cross . . .

INTERCESSIONS *pages 390–393* CLOSING PRAYERS *page 402–403*

OPENING PRAYER Eternal God, it is only your Son who offers you perfect praise. Lift up our hearts into your presence, and help us to become one with his offering to you . . . Glory be . . .

PSALMODY He shall cry to me, 'Thou art my Father,
my God, and the Rock of my salvation.' Psalm 89.26

SCRIPTURE READINGS I thank him who has given me strength for this, Christ Jesus our Lord, because he judged me faithful by appointing me to his service, though I formerly blasphemed and persecuted and insulted him; but I received mercy because I had acted ignorantly in unbelief, and the grace of our Lord overflowed for me with the faith and love that are in Christ Jesus. 1 Timothy 1.12–14

Jesus said, 'If you love those who love you, what credit is that to you? Even sinners love those who love them. Even sinners lend to sinners, to receive as much again. Love your enemies, and do good, and lend, expecting nothing in return; and your reward will be great, and you will be sons of the Most High; for he is kind to the ungrateful and the selfish. Be merciful, even as your Father is merciful. Judge not, and you will not be judged; condemn not, and you will not be condemned; forgive, and you will be forgiven; give, and it will be given to you; good measure, pressed down, shaken together, running over, will be put into your lap. For the measure you give will be the measure you get back.' He told them a parable: 'Can a blind man lead a blind man? Will they not both fall into a pit? A disciple is not above his teacher, but every one when he is fully taught will be like his teacher. Why do you see the speck that is in your brother's eye, but do not notice the log that is in your own eye? Or how can you say to your brother, "Brother, let me take out the speck that is in your eye," when you yourself do not see the log that is in your own eye? You hypocrite, first take the log out of your own eye, and then you will see clearly to take out the speck that is in your brother's eye.' St Luke 6.32–42*

RESPONSE 'Lord Jesus, give us grace on earth to love thee more,
in heaven, to see thy face, and with thy saints adore.'

Eternal God, your Son taught us to love our enemies – we praise you for the greatness and wonder of your love . . .
'Love your enemies' – Lord, help us to obey this command, and to understand more about the nature of your love . . .
'Forgive, and you will be forgiven' – give us grace to forgive others, and to accept that you love our enemies as you love us . . .

INTERCESSIONS *pages 390–393* CLOSING PRAYERS *page 402–403*

21 June *The House on the Rock*

OPENING PRAYER Eternal God, it is only your Son who offers you perfect praise. Lift up our hearts into your presence, and help us to become one with his offering to you . . . Glory be . . .

PSALMODY 'My steadfast love I will keep for him for ever,
and my covenant will stand firm for him.
I will establish his line for ever
and his throne as the days of the heavens.
If his children forsake my law
then I will punish their transgression with the rod
and their iniquity with scourges;
but I will not remove from him my steadfast love,
or be false to my faithfulness.' Psalm 89.28–33*

SCRIPTURE READINGS The saying is sure and worthy of full acceptance, that Christ Jesus came into the world to save sinners. And I am the foremost of sinners; but I received mercy for this reason, that in me, as the foremost, Jesus Christ might display his perfect patience for an example to those who were to believe in him for eternal life. 1 Timothy 1.15–16

Jesus said, 'No good tree bears bad fruit, nor again does a bad tree bear good fruit; for each tree is known by its own fruit. For figs are not gathered from thorns, nor are grapes picked from a bramble bush. The good man out of the good treasures of his heart produces good, and the evil man out of his evil treasure produces evil; for out of the abundance of the heart his mouth speaks. Why do you call me, "Lord, Lord," and not do what I tell you? Every one who comes to me and hears my words and does them, I will show you what he is like: he is like a man building a house, who dug deep, and laid the foundation upon rock; and when a flood arose, the stream broke against that house, and could not shake it, because it had been well built. But he who hears and does not do them is like a man who built a house on the ground without a foundation; against which the stream broke, and immediately it fell, and the ruin of that house was great.'
St Luke 6.43–49

RESPONSE 'Christ is our corner-stone,
on him alone we build.'

Almighty God, it is through the Spirit that the fruits of redemption are ripened – we praise you for freeing us from the slavery of sin . . .
'Each tree is known by its fruit' – give your Church the grace needed to proclaim the Gospel, and to be active in good works . . .
'Why do you call me, "Lord, Lord" but do not do what I tell you?' – inspire us to praise you with our lips, and serve you in our lives . . .

INTERCESSIONS *pages 390–393* CLOSING PRAYERS *page 402–403*

22 June *The Roman Centurion*

OPENING PRAYER Eternal God, it is only your Son who offers you perfect praise. Lift up our hearts into your presence, and help us to become one with his offering to you . . . Glory be . . .

PSALMODY 'I will not violate my covenant,
or alter the word that went forth from my lips.
Once for all I have sworn by my holiness;
I will not lie to David.
His line shall endure for ever,
his throne as long as the sun before me.
Like the moon it shall be established for ever.
it shall stand firm while the skies endure.' Psalm 89.34–37

SCRIPTURE READINGS I urge that supplications, prayers, intercessions, and thanksgiving be made for all men, for kings and all who are in high positions, that we may lead a quiet and peaceable life, godly and respectful in every way. This is good and acceptable in the sight of God our Saviour. 1 Timothy 2.1–3

Jesus entered Capernaum. Now a centurion had a slave who was dear to him, who was sick and at the point of death. When he heard of Jesus, he sent to him elders of the Jews, asking him to come and heal his slave. When they came to Jesus, they besought him earnestly, saying, 'He is worthy to have you do this for him, for he loves our nation, and he built us our synagogue.' And Jesus went with them. When he was not far from the house, the centurion sent friends to him, saying, 'Lord, do not trouble yourself, for I am not worthy to have you come under my roof; therefore I did not presume to come to you. But say the word, and let my servant be healed. For I am a man set under authority, with soldiers under me: and I say to one, "Go", and he goes; and to another, "Come", and he comes; and to my slave, "Do this", and he does it.' When Jesus heard this he marvelled at him, and turned and said to the multitude that followed him, 'I tell you, not even in Israel have I found such faith.' When those who had been sent returned to the house, they found the slave well. St Luke 7.1–10*

RESPONSE 'Onward Christian soldiers, marching as to war,
with the Cross of Jesus going on before.'

Almighty and Eternal God, you alone are supreme Ruler of the universe – we praise you for your awesome power and timeless love . . .
You give your grace to all people – we praise you for the growth and existence of your Kingdom outside the Church . . .
'I am a man set under authority' – give wisdom and compassion to all in authority, and help them to seek the justice and peace of our Kingdom . . .

INTERCESSIONS *pages 390–393* CLOSING PRAYERS *page 402–403*

23 June

The Widow of Nain

OPENING PRAYER Eternal God, it is only your Son who offers you perfect praise. Lift up our hearts into your presence, and help us to become one with his offering to you . . . Glory be . . .

PSALMODY Remember, O Lord, what the measure of life is,
for what vanity thou hast created all the sons of men!
What man can live and never see death?
Who can deliver his soul from the power of Sheol?

Psalm 89.47–48

SCRIPTURE READINGS Jesus went to a city called Nain, and his disciples and a great crowd went with him. As he drew near to the gate of the city, behold, a man who had died was being carried out, the only son of his mother, and she was a widow; and a large crowd from the city was with her. When the Lord saw her, he had compassion on her and said, 'Do not weep.' He came and touched the bier, and the bearers stood still. And he said, 'Young man, I say to you, arise.' And the dead man sat up, and began to speak. He gave him to his mother. Fear seized them all; and they glorified God, saying, 'A great prophet has arisen among us!' and 'God has visited his people!' This report concerning him spread through the whole of Judea and all the surrounding country. St Luke 7.11–17*

The steadfast love of the Lord never ceases,
his mercies never come to an end;
they are new every morning;
great is thy faithfulness. Lamentations 3.22–23

Christ has been raised from the dead, the first fruits of those who have fallen asleep. For as by a man came death, by a man has come also the resurrection of the dead. For as in Adam all die, so also in Christ shall all be made alive. But each in his own order: Christ the first fruits, then at his coming those who belong to Christ. Then comes the end, when he delivers the kingdom to God the Father after destroying every rule and every authority and power. For he must reign until he has put all his enemies under his feet. The last enemy to be destroyed is death.

1 Corinthians 15.20–26

RESPONSE 'Jesus lives, our hearts know well
naught from us his love shall sever.'

Loving Father in heaven, you raised your Son from the grave by the power of the Spirit – we praise you for your gift of eternal life in Christ . . .
'He had compassion on her' – give grace to your Church to share in your Son's compassion with the bereaved and dying . . .
'In Christ shall all be made alive' – grant rest and peace to those who have died in faith, and raise them on the last day . . .

INTERCESSIONS *pages 390–393* CLOSING PRAYERS *page 402–403*

OPENING PRAYER Eternal God, it is only your Son who offers you perfect praise. Lift up our hearts into your presence, and help us to become one with his offering to you . . . Glory be . . .

PSALMODY O Lord God of hosts,
how long wilt thou be angry with thy people's prayers?
Thou hast fed them with the bread of tears,
and given them tears to drink in full measure.
Thou dost make us the scorn of our neighbours,
and our enemies laugh among themselves.
Restore us, O God of hosts;
let thy face shine, that we may be saved! Psalm 80.4–7

SCRIPTURE READINGS Paul said, 'God has brought to Israel a Saviour, Jesus, as he promised. Before his coming John had preached a baptism of repentance to all the people of Israel. As John was finishing his course, he said, "What do you suppose that I am? I am not he. No, but after me one is coming, the sandals of whose feet I am not worthy to untie." Brethren, sons of the family of Abraham, and those among you that fear God, to us has been sent the message of this salvation.' Acts 13.23–26

Zechariah said,
'And you, child, will be called the prophet of the Most High,
for you will go before the Lord to prepare his ways,
to give knowledge of salvation to his people
in the forgiveness of their sins,
through the tender mercy of our God,
when the day shall dawn upon us from on high
to give light to those who sit in darkness and in the shadow of death,
to guide our feet into the way of peace.' St Luke 1. 76–79

There was a man sent from God, whose name was John. He came to bear witness to the light, that all might believe through him. He was not the light, but came to bear witness to the light. St John 1. 6–8*

RESPONSE 'It is good to give thanks to the Lord,
to sing praises to thy name, O Most High.'

Eternal God, you called John the Baptist to fulfil your purpose – on this feast of his birth, we praise you for John's preparations for Christ . . .
You gave a special task to Saint John – give your Church the grace needed to share in the mission of your Son in the world today . . .
'The sandals of whose feet I am not worthy to untie' – make us more worthy followers of your Son, and fill us with your love . . .

INTERCESSIONS *pages 390–393* CLOSING PRAYERS *page 402–403*

25 June

Are you the one who is to come?

OPENING PRAYER Eternal God, it is only your Son who offers you perfect praise. Lift up our hearts into your presence, and help us to become one with his offering to you . . . Glory be . . .

PSALMODY Lord, where is thy steadfast love of old?
Remember, O Lord, how thy servant is scorned;
how I bear in my bosom the insults of the peoples,
with which they mock the footsteps of thy anointed.
Blessed be the Lord for ever! Amen and Amen.

Psalm 89.49–52

SCRIPTURE READINGS

Should this be said, O house of Jacob?
Is the Spirit of the Lord impatient?
Are these his doings?
Do not my words do good to him who walks uprightly?

Micah 2.7

The disciples of John told him of all these things. John, calling to him two of his disciples, sent them to the Lord. When the men had come to him, they said, 'John the Baptist has sent us to you, saying, "Are you he who is to come, or shall we look for another?"' In that hour he cured many of diseases and plagues and evil spirits, and on many that were blind he bestowed sight. He answered, 'Go and tell John what you have seen and heard: the blind receive their sight, the lame walk, lepers are cleansed, and the deaf hear, the dead are raised up, the poor have good news preached to them. And blessed is he who takes no offence at me.' When the messengers had gone, he began to speak concerning John: 'What did you go out into the wilderness to behold! A reed shaken by the wind? What then did you go out to see? A man clothed in soft clothing? Behold, those who are gorgeously apparelled and live in luxury are in kings' courts. What then did you go out to see? A prophet? Yes, I tell you, and more than a prophet. This is he of whom it is written, "Behold, I send my messenger before thy face, who shall prepare thy way before thee." I tell you, among those born of women none is greater than John; yet he who is least in the Kingdom of God is greater than he.'

St Luke 7.18–28*

RESPONSE 'Watch! 'tis your Lord's command,
and while we speak, he's near.'

Almighty God, you sent your Son to be the long expected Messiah – to you be the glory, Father, Son and Holy Spirit, for time and for eternity . . .
'Blessed is he who takes no offence at me' – Lord, we pray that all people may find the way of life and salvation in the Cross . . .
You showed the completion of your purposes in your Son – give the Church the grace needed to continue his work in the world . . .

INTERCESSIONS *pages 390–393* CLOSING PRAYERS *page 402–403*

26 June *Jesus is Anointed*

OPENING PRAYER Eternal God, it is only your Son who offers you perfect praise. Lift up our hearts into your presence, and help us to become one with his offering to you . . . Glory be . . .

PSALMODY Before the mountains were brought forth,
from everlasting to everlasting thou art God. Psalm 90.1–2*

SCRIPTURE READINGS Set the believers an example in speech and conduct, in love, in faith, in purity. 1 Timothy 4.12

One of the Pharisees asked Jesus to eat with him, and he went into the Pharisees's house, and took his place at table. A woman of the city, who was a sinner, when she learned that he was at table in the Pharisees's house, brought an alabaster flask of ointment, and standing behind him at his feet, weeping, she began to wet his feet with her tears, and wiped them with the hair of her head, and kissed his feet, and anointed them with the ointment. When the Pharisee who invited him saw it, he said to himself, 'If this man were a prophet, he would have known who and what sort of woman this is who is touching him, for she is a sinner.' Jesus answering said, 'Simon, I have something to say to you.' He answered, 'What is it, Teacher?' 'A certain creditor had two debtors; one owed five hundred denarii, and the other fifty. When they could not pay, he forgave them both. Which of them will love him more?' Simon answered, 'The one, I suppose, to whom he forgave more.' He said, 'You have judged rightly.' Turning toward the woman he said to Simon, 'Do you see this woman? I entered your house, you gave me no water for my feet, but she has wet my feet with her tears and wiped them with her hair. You gave me no kiss, but from the time I came in she has not ceased to kiss my feet. You did not anoint my head with oil, but she has anointed my feet with ointment. I tell you, her sins, which are many, are forgiven, for she loved much; but he who is forgiven little, loves little.' He said to her, 'Your sins are forgiven.' Those at table with him began to say among themselves, 'Who is this, who even forgives sins?' He said to the woman, 'Your faith has saved you; go in peace.'
St Luke 7.36–50*

RESPONSE 'I will sing to the Lord as long as I live;
I will sing praise to my God while I have my being.'

Almighty God, it is good for us to confess our sins and to sing praises to your glory – accept our sacrifice of praise and love . . .
'I have something to say to you' – Lord, open our minds and help us to understand and accept your living Word in the Scriptures . . .
'Your sins are forgiven' – we thank you for your gift of forgiveness through the redeeming love of Christ on the Cross . . .

INTERCESSIONS *pages 390–393* CLOSING PRAYERS *page 402–403*

27 June *The Parable of the Sower*

OPENING PRAYER Eternal God, it is only your Son who offers you perfect praise. Lift up our hearts into your presence, and help us to become one with his offering to you . . . Glory be . . .

PSALMODY Thou turnest man back to the dust,
and sayest, 'Turn back, O children of men!'
For a thousand years in thy sight
are but as yesterday when it is past,
or as a watch in the night. Psalm 90.3–4

SCRIPTURE READINGS In the presence of God who gives life to all things, I charge you to keep the commandments unstained and free from reproach until the appearing of our Lord Jesus Christ. 1 Timothy 6.13–14*

Jesus said in a parable: 'A sower went out to sow his seed; and as he sowed, some fell along the path, and was trodden under foot, and the birds of the air devoured it. Some fell on the rock; and as it grew up, it withered away, because it had no moisture. Some fell among thorns; and the thorns grew with it and choked it. Some fell into good soil and grew, and yielded a hundredfold.' He called out, 'He who has ears to hear, let him hear.' When his disciples asked what this parable meant, he said, 'To you it has been given to know the secrets of the Kingdom of God; but for others they are in parables, so that seeing they may not see, and hearing they may not understand. Now the parable is this: The seed is the word of God. The ones along the path are those who have heard; then the devil comes and takes away the word from their hearts, that they may not believe and be saved. The ones on the rock are those who, when they hear the word, receive it with joy; but these have no root, they believe for a while and in time of temptation fall away. As for what fell among the thorns, they are those who hear, but as they go on their way they are choked by the cares and riches and pleasures of life, and their fruit does not mature. As for that in the good soil, they are those who, hearing the word, hold it fast in an honest and good heart, and bring forth fruit with patience.'
St Luke 8.4–15*

RESPONSE 'My gracious Master and my God, assist me to proclaim
and spread through all the earth abroad the honours of thy name.'

Eternal God, you created the Church to share in the work of your Son – we rejoice that you gather a holy people to yourself from age to age . . .
'A sower went out to sow his seed' – empower your Church with the Holy Spirit to proclaim the Good News to all creation . . .
'Some fell into good soil, and grew and yielded a hundredfold' – bless the mission of the Church and gather all people into the unity of your love . . .

INTERCESSIONS *pages 390–393* CLOSING PRAYERS *page 402–403*

28 June

The Gadarene Swine

OPENING PRAYER Eternal God, it is only your Son who offers you perfect praise. Lift up our hearts into your presence, and help us to become one with his offering to you . . . Glory be . . .

PSALMODY Thou hast set our iniquities before thee,
our secret sins in the light of thy countenance.
So teach us to number our days
that we may get a heart of wisdom. Psalm 90.8–12

SCRIPTURE READINGS
Behold, the Lord is coming forth out of his place,
and will come down
and tread upon the high places of the earth.
And the mountains will melt under him. Micah 1.3

As Jesus stepped out on land, there met him a man who had demons; for a long time he had worn no clothes, and he lived not in a house but among the tombs. When he saw Jesus, he fell down before him, and said with a loud voice, 'What have you to do with me, Jesus, Son of the Most High God? I beseech you, do not torment me.' For he had commanded the unclean spirit to come out of the man. (For many a time it had seized him; and was kept under guard, and bound with chains and fetters, but he broke the bonds and was driven by the demon into the desert.) Jesus asked, 'What is your name?' He said, 'Legion'; for many demons had entered him. They begged him not to command them to depart into the abyss. Now a large herd of swine was feeding on the hillside; and they begged him to let them enter these. So he gave them leave. The demons came out of the man and entered the swine, and the herd rushed down the steep bank into the lake and were drowned. When the herdsmen saw what had happened, they fled, and told it in the city and in the country. People went out, and found the man from whom the demons had gone, sitting at the feet of Jesus, clothed and in his right mind; and they were afraid. Those who had seen it told them how he was healed. All the people asked him to depart. The man from whom the demons had gone begged that he might be with him; but he said, 'Return to your home, and declare how much God has done for you.' St Luke 8.26–39*

RESPONSE 'Peace, perfect peace, by thronging duties pressed?
to do the will of Jesus, this is rest.'

Ever-living God, you are our protector and guide – we praise you with awe and wonder for your great love for us in Jesus Christ . . .
'They were afraid' – drive away all fear from our hearts, and fill us with your perfect love . . .
'Declare how much God has done for you' – give your Church the courage to tell people about your goodness and love for us and for all people . . .

INTERCESSIONS *pages 390–393* CLOSING PRAYERS *page 402–403*

St Peter & St Paul – Apostles

OPENING PRAYER Eternal God, it is only your Son who can offer you perfect praise. Lift up our hearts into your presence, and help us to become one with his offering to you . . . Glory be . . .

PSALMODY Praise the Lord! Sing to the Lord a new song,
his praise in the assembly of the faithful!
Let Israel be glad in his Maker,
let the sons of Zion rejoice in their King!
For the Lord takes pleasure in his people;
he adorns the humble with victory. Psalm 149.1–4*

SCRIPTURE READINGS Rejoice in so far as you share in Christ's sufferings, that you may also rejoice and be glad when his glory is revealed. If you are reproached for the name of Christ, you are blessed, because the spirit of glory and of God rests upon you. 1 Peter 4. 13–14

I am already on the point of being sacrificed; the time of my departure has come. I have fought the good fight, I have finished the race, I have kept the faith. Henceforth there is laid up for me the crown of righteousness, which the Lord, the righteous judge, will award to me on that day, and not only to me but also to all who have loved his appearing. 2 Timothy 4.6–8

When Jesus came into the district of Caesarea Philippi, he asked his disciples, 'Who do men say that the Son of Man is?' They said, 'Some say John the Baptist, others say Elijah, and others Jeremiah or one of the prophets.' He said, 'But who do you say that I am?' Simon Peter replied, 'You are the Christ, the Son of the living God.' Jesus answered, 'Blessed are you, Simon Bar-Jona! For flesh and blood has not revealed this to you, but my Father who is in heaven. I tell you, you are Peter, and on this rock I will build my Church, and the powers of death shall not prevail against it. I will give you the keys of the Kingdom of Heaven, and whatever you bind on earth shall be bound in heaven, and whatever you loose on earth shall be loosed in heaven.' St Matthew 16.13–20

RESPONSE 'Captains of the saintly band, lights who lighten every land,
Princes who with Jesus dwell, Judges of his Israel.'

Almighty God, you chose Peter and Paul to be Apostles in your Church – we praise and glorify you, Father, Son and Holy Spirit, one God for ever . . .

'You are Peter, and on this rock I will build my Church' – we praise you for your Church which spans the centuries and encircles the world . . .

In life and in death, Peter and Paul glorified your holy name – we pray with Peter and Paul for the building up and growth of the Church today . . .

INTERCESSIONS *pages 390–393* CLOSING PRAYERS *page 402–403*

30 June *(Petertide Ember Day)*

OPENING PRAYER Eternal God, it is only your Son who can offer you perfect praise. Lift up our hearts into your presence, and help us to become one with his offering to you . . . Glory be . . .

PSALMODY Return, O Lord! How long?
Have pity on thy servants!
Satisfy us in the morning with thy steadfast love,
that we may rejoice and be glad all our days.
Make us glad as many days as thou hast afflicted us.
Let thy work be manifest to thy servants,
and thy glorious power to their children.
Let the favour of the Lord our God be upon us,
and establish thou the work of our hands upon us,
yea, the work of our hands establish thou it. Psalm 90.13–17*

SCRIPTURE READINGS Moses said to the Lord, 'Let the Lord, the God of the spirits of all flesh, appoint a man over the congregation, who shall go out before them and come in before them, who shall lead them out and bring them in; that the congregation of the Lord may not be as sheep which have no shepherd.' The Lord said to Moses, 'Take Joshua the son of Nun, a man in whom is the spirit, and lay your hand upon him; cause him to stand before Eleazar the priest and all the congregation, and you shall commission him in their sight. You shall invest him with some of your authority, that all the congregation of the people of Israel may obey.
Numbers 27.15–20

Jesus called the twelve together and gave them power and authority over all demons and to cure diseases, and he sent them out to preach the Kingdom of God and to heal. He said, 'Take nothing for your journey, no staff, nor bag, nor bread, nor money; and do not have two tunics. Whatever house you enter, stay there, and from there depart. Wherever they do not receive you, when you leave that town shake off the dust from your feet as a testimony against them.' They departed and went through the villages, preaching the gospel and healing everywhere. St Luke 9.1–6

RESPONSE 'His twelve apostles first he made his ministers of grace;
and they their hands on others laid, to fill in turn their place.'

Eternal God, you continue the priestly work of your Son through the Sacred Ministry of the Church – we praise you and we acclaim your glory . . .
'Jesus called the Twelve' – inspire those whom you are calling to offer themselves for the work of the Sacred Ministry . . .
'Jesus gave them power and authority' – pour out your Spirit on all to be ordained at this season, and on the bishops who will ordain them . . .

INTERCESSIONS *pages 390–393* CLOSING PRAYERS *page 402–403*

1 July *Feeding the Multitudes*

OPENING PRAYER Eternal God, to you alone belong honour and glory and power. In your mercy, assist us in these prayers and praises, offered to you through our Lord and Saviour Jesus Christ . . . Glory be . . .

PSALMODY He who dwells in the shelter of the Most High,
who abides in the shadow of the Almighty,
will say to the Lord, 'My refuge and my fortress;
my God, in whom I trust.'
For he will deliver you from the snare of the fowler
and from the deadly pestilence;
he will cover you with his pinions,
and under his wings you will find refuge;
his faithfulness is a shield and buckler. Psalm 91.1–4

SCRIPTURE READINGS My God will supply every need of yours according to his riches in glory in Christ Jesus. To our God and Father be glory for ever and ever. Amen. Philippians 4.19–20

Jesus took the disciples and withdrew apart to a city called Bethsaida. When the crowds learned it, they followed him; and he welcomed them and spoke to them of the Kingdom of God, and cured those who had need of healing. Now the day began to wear away; and the twelve came and said to him, 'Send the crowd away, to go into the villages and country round about, to lodge and get provisions; for we are here in a lonely place.' He said, 'You give them something to eat.' They said, 'We have no more than five loaves and two fish – unless we are to go and buy food for all these people.' For there were about five thousand men. He said to his disciples, 'Make them sit down in companies, about fifty each.' They did so, and made them all sit down. Taking the five loaves and the two fish he looked up to heaven, and blessed and broke them, and gave them to the disciples to set before the crowd. All ate and were satisfied. They took up what was left over, twelve baskets of broken pieces. St Luke 9.10–17*

RESPONSE 'Bread of heaven, on thee we feed, for thy flesh is meat indeed;
ever may our souls be fed with this true and living bread.'

Eternal God, you provide for all our needs in your Son – we praise you for your perfect love from generation to generation . . .
You created a world with enough food for everyone – Lord, give us generous hearts, and make us willing to share with the needy . . .
'He blessed and broke them, and gave them to the disciples' – we rejoice that you still nourish us with your Son in the Eucharist today . . .

INTERCESSIONS *pages 390–393* CLOSING PRAYERS *page 402–403*

2 July *Jesus predicts His death*

OPENING PRAYER Eternal God, to you alone belong honour and glory and power. In your mercy, assist us in these prayers and praises, offered to you through our Lord and Saviour Jesus Christ . . . Glory be . . .

PSALMODY You will not fear the terror of the night,
nor the arrow that flies by day,
nor the pestilence that stalks in darkness,
nor the destruction that wastes at noonday.
A thousand may fall at your side,
ten thousand at your right hand;
but it will not come near you. Psalm 91.5–8

SCRIPTURE READINGS 'Who is left among you that saw this house in its former glory? Once again, in a little while, I will shake the heavens and the earth and the sea and the dry land; and I will shake all nations, so that the treasures of all nations shall come in, and I will fill this house with splendour. The latter glory of this house shall be greater than the former, says the Lord of hosts.' Haggai 2.3–9*

Jesus asked the disciples, 'Who do the people say that I am?' They answered, 'John the Baptist; but others say, Elijah; and others, that one of the old prophets has arisen.' He said, 'But who do you say that I am?' Peter answered, 'The Christ of God.' He commanded them to tell this to no one, saying, 'The Son of Man must suffer many things, and be rejected by the elders and chief priests and scribes, and be killed, and on the third day be raised.' And he said to all, 'If any man would come after me, let him deny himself and take up his cross daily and follow me. For whoever would save his life will lose it; and whoever loses his life for my sake, he will save it. For what does it profit a man if he gains the whole world and loses or forfeits himself? For whoever is ashamed of me and of my words, of him will the Son of Man be ashamed when he comes in his glory and the glory of the Father and of the holy angels. But I tell you truly, there are some standing here who will not taste death before they see the Kingdom of God.' St Luke 9.18–27*

RESPONSE 'Inscribed upon the Cross we see in shining letters, "God is love;"
he bears our sins upon the Tree; he brings us mercy from above.'

Heavenly Father, your Son predicted that he would be killed and raised on the third day – we praise you for his perfect obedience and love . . .
'If any man would come after me, let him deny himself and take up his cross daily and follow me' – give us grace to be better disciples . . .
'Whoever loses his life for my sake, he will save it' – help us to be faithful and loyal to Christ, and lead us to eternal life . . .

INTERCESSIONS *pages 390–393* CLOSING PRAYERS *page 402–403*

OPENING PRAYERS Eternal God, to you alone belong honour and glory and power. In your mercy, assist us in these prayers and praises, offered to you through our Lord and Saviour Jesus Christ . . . Glory be . . .

PSALMODY Look to him, and be radiant;
so your faces shall never be ashamed.
The angel of the Lord encamps around those who fear him,
and delivers them.
O taste and see that the Lord is good!
Happy is the man who takes refuge in him!
O fear the Lord, you his saints,
for those who fear him have no want! Psalm 34.5–9*

SCRIPTURE READINGS Thomas, one of the twelve, called the Twin, was not with them when Jesus came. The other disciples told him, 'We have seen the Lord.' He said, 'Unless I see in his hands the print of the nails, and place my finger in the mark of the nails, and place my hands in his side, I will not believe.' Eight days later, his disciples were again in the house, and Thomas was with them. The doors were shut, but Jesus came and stood among them, and said, 'Peace be with you.' Then he said to Thomas, 'Put your finger here, and see my hands, and put out your hand, and place it in my side; do not be faithless, but believing.' Thomas answered, 'My Lord and my God!' Jesus said, 'Have you believed because you have seen me? Blessed are those who have not seen and yet believe.' St John 20.24–29

Do not throw away your confidence, which has a great reward. You have need of endurance, so that you may do the will of God and receive what is promised. 'For yet a little while, and the coming one shall come and shall not tarry; but my righteous one shall live by faith, and if he shrinks back, my soul has no pleasure in him.' We are not of those who shrink back and are destroyed, but of those who have faith and keep their souls. Faith is the assurance of things hoped for, the conviction of things not seen.
Hebrews 10.35–11,1

RESPONSE 'Hail the Lord of earth and heaven! Praise to thee by both be given:
Thee we greet triumphant now; Hail, the Resurrection thou!'

Eternal Father, our faith is a gift from you and your Son acting together – we praise you for your gift of faith on this feast of Saint Thomas . . .
'How can we know the way?' – we rejoice that you have guided your Apostolic Church through the centuries, and thank you for your love . . .
'Blessed are those who have not seen and yet believe' – united in the one Spirit, we pray with Saint Thomas for the work of the Church in India . . .

INTERCESSIONS *pages 390–393* CLOSING PRAYERS *page 402–403*

The Mission of the Seventy

OPENING PRAYER Eternal God, to you alone belong honour and glory and power. In your mercy, assist us in these prayers and praises, offered to you through our Lord and Saviour Jesus Christ . . . Glory be . . .

PSALMODY Because you have made the Lord your refuge,
the Most High your habitation,
no evil shall befall you,
no scourge come near your tent. Psalm 91.9–10

SCRIPTURE READINGS The Lord appointed seventy others, and sent them on ahead of him two by two. He said, 'The harvest is plentiful, but the labourers are few; pray therefore the Lord of the harvest to send out labourers into his harvest. Go your way; behold, I send you out as lambs in the midst of wolves. Carry no purse, no bag, no sandals; and salute no one on the road. Whatever house you enter, first say, "Peace be to this house!" If a son of peace is there, your peace shall rest upon him; but if not, it shall return to you. Remain in the same house, eating and drinking what they provide, for the labourer deserves his wages; do not go from house to house. Whenever you enter a town and they receive you, eat what is set before you; heal the sick in it and say to them, "The Kingdom of God has come near to you." But whenever you enter a town and they do not receive you, go into its streets and say, "Even the dust of your town that clings to our feet, we wipe off against you; nevertheless know this, that the Kingdom of God has come near." I tell you, it shall be more tolerable on that day for Sodom than for that town.' The seventy returned with joy, saying, 'Lord, even the demons are subject to us in your name!' He said. 'I saw Satan fall like lightning from heaven.' Turning to the disciples he said privately, 'Blessed are the eyes which see what you see! For I tell you that many prophets and kings desired to see what you see, and did not see it, and to hear what you hear, and did not hear it.' St Luke 10.1–24*

Far be it from me to glory except in the cross of our Lord Jesus Christ, by which the world has been crucified to me, and I to the world.
Galatians 6.14

RESPONSE 'What can we do to work God's work, to prosper and increase the brotherhood of all mankind, the reign of the Prince of Peace?'

Almighty God, you call the Church to proclaim the Gospel in all the world – we praise you for your faithful servants in every country . . .
'The harvest is plentiful but the labourers are few' – Lord, forgive us for our past failures to do your work, and renew us for your service . . .
'Many prophets and kings desired to see what you see' – give us ever-grateful hearts for all the blessings we so richly enjoy in Christ . . .

INTERCESSIONS *pages 390–393* CLOSING PRAYERS *page 402–403*

OPENING PRAYER Eternal God, to you alone belong honour and glory and power. In your mercy, assist us in these prayers and praises, offered to you through our Lord and Saviour Jesus Christ . . . Glory be . . .

PSALMODY He will give his angels charge of you
to guard you in all your ways.
On their hands they will bear you up
lest you dash your foot against a stone.
You will tread on the lion and the adder,
the young lion and the serpent you will trample under foot.
Psalm 91.11–13

SCRIPTURE READINGS Love does no wrong to a neighbour; therefore love is the fulfilling of the law. Romans 13.10

A lawyer put Jesus to the test, saying, 'Teacher, what shall I do to inherit eternal life?' He said, 'What is written in the law? How do you read?' He answered, 'You shall love the Lord your God with all your heart, and with all your soul, and with all your strength, and with all your mind; and your neighbour as yourself.' He said, 'You have answered right; do this, and you will live.' But he, desiring to justify himself, said, 'And who is my neighbour?' Jesus replied, 'A man was going down from Jerusalem to Jericho, and he fell among robbers, who stripped him and beat him, and departed, leaving him half dead. By chance a priest was going down that road; when he saw him he passed by on the other side. So likewise a Levite, when he came to the place and saw him, passed by on the other side. But a Samaritan, as he journeyed, came to where he was; and when he saw him, he had compassion, and went to him and bound up his wounds, pouring on oil and wine; then he set him on his own beast and brought him to an inn, and took care of him. The next day he took out two denarii and gave them to the innkeeper, saying, "Take care of him; whatever more you spend, I will repay you when I come back." Which of these three, do you think, proved neighbour to the man who fell among the robbers?' He said, 'The one who showed mercy on him.' Jesus said, 'Go and do likewise.'
St Luke 10.25–37*

RESPONSE 'In our wanderings be our guide,
through endeavour, failure, danger,
Father, be thou at our side.'

Almighty God, you call us through your Son to love other people with your endless love – we praise you for the divine compassion revealed in Christ . . .
'You shall love the Lord your God' – help us to respond to your love with all our heart, and soul, and mind and strength, and to give you thanks . . .
'Go and do likewise' – Lord, fill us with the fire of your love, and help us to love you by serving the needs of our neighbours . . .

INTERCESSIONS *pages 390–393* CLOSING PRAYERS *page 402–403*

6 July *Martha and Mary*

OPENING PRAYER Eternal God, to you alone belong honour and glory and power. In your mercy, assist us in these prayers and praises, offered to you through our Lord and Saviour Jesus Christ . . . Glory be . . .

PSALMODY Because he cleaves to me in love, I will deliver him;
I will protect him, because he knows my name.
When he calls to me, I will answer him;
I will be with him in trouble.
I will rescue him and honour him.
With long life I will satisfy him,
and show him my salvation. Psalm 91.14–16

SCRIPTURE READINGS Now as they went on their way, he entered a village. A woman named Martha received him into her house. She had a sister called Mary, who sat at the Lord's feet and listened to his teaching. But Martha was distracted with much serving; and she went to him and said, 'Lord, do you not care that my sister has left me to serve alone? Tell her to help me.' The Lord answered her, 'Martha, Martha, you are anxious and troubled about many things; one thing is needful. Mary has chosen the good portion, which shall not be taken away from her.' St Luke 10.38–42

Now I rejoice in my sufferings for your sake, and in my flesh I complete what is lacking in Christ's afflictions for the sake of his body, that is, the church, of which I became a minister according to the divine office which was given to me for you, to make the word of God fully known, the mystery hidden for ages and generations but now made manifest to his saints. To them God chose to make known how great among the Gentiles are the riches of the glory of this mystery, which is Christ in you, the hope of glory. Him we proclaim, warning every man and teaching every man in all wisdom, that we may present every man mature in Christ.
Colossians 1.24–28

RESPONSE 'Lord, it is my chief complaint that my love is weak and faint; yet I love thee, and adore; O for grace to love the more.'

God our Father, you love us all, even though we forget you, and we are all unworthy of your love – help us to model our lives on Jesus . . .
'Mary sat at the feet of Jesus and listened to his teaching' – help us by the Spirit to understand and to receive Christ's teaching in the scriptures . . .
'You are anxious and troubled about many things' – give us the blessing of your gift of peace in our hearts . . .

INTERCESSIONS *pages 390–393* CLOSING PRAYERS *page 402–403*

OPENING PRAYER Eternal God, to you alone belong honour and glory and power. In your mercy, assist us in these prayers and praises, offered to you through our Lord and Saviour Jesus Christ . .. Glory be . . .

PSALMODY It is good to give thanks to the Lord,
to sing praises to thy name, O Most High;
to declare thy steadfast love in the morning,
and thy faithfulness by night,
to the music of the lute and the harp.
For thou, O Lord, hast made me glad by thy work;
at the works of thy hands I sing for joy. Psalm 92.1–4*

SCRIPTURE READINGS Paul an apostle – not from men nor through man, but through Jesus Christ and God the Father, who raised him from the dead – and all the brethren who are with me, To the Churches of Galatia: Grace to you and peace from God the Father and our Lord Jesus Christ, who gave himself for our sins to deliver us from the present evil age, according to the will of our God and Father, to whom be the glory for ever and ever. Amen. Galatians 1.1–5

Jesus said, 'Which of you who has a friend will go to him at midnight and say, "Friend, lend me three loaves; for a friend of mine has arrived on a journey, and I have nothing to set before him"; and he will answer from within, "Do not bother me; the door is now shut, and my children are with me in bed; I cannot get up and give you anything"? Though he will not get up and give him anything because he is his friend, yet because of his importunity he will rise and give him whatever he needs. I tell you, ask, and it will be given you; seek, and you will find; knock, and it will be opened to you, For every one who asks receives, and he who seeks finds, and to him who knocks it will be opened. What father among you, if his son asks for a fish, will instead of a fish give him a serpent; or if he asks for an egg, will give him a scorpion? If you then, who are evil, know how to give good advice to your children, how much more will the Heavenly Father give the Holy Spirit to those who ask him!' St Luke 11.5–13

RESPONSE 'Hear the prayer we offer, not for ease that prayer should be,
but for strength that we may ever live our lives courageously.'

God our Father in heaven, you are always ready to hear our prayers – may your name be praised on earth as it is in heaven . . .
'Ask and it will be given to you' – Lord, teach us to seek only those things which are pleasing to your will . . .
'How much more will the heavenly Father give the Holy Spirit to those who ask him' – renew your gift of the Spirit in all who are baptized . . .

INTERCESSIONS *pages 390–393* CLOSING PRAYERS *page 402–403*

OPENING PRAYER Eternal God, to you alone belong honour and glory and power. In your mercy, assist us in these prayers and praises, offered to you through our Lord and Saviour Jesus Christ . . . Glory be . . .

PSALMODY How great are thy works, O Lord!
Thy thoughts are very deep! Psalm 92.5

SCRIPTURE READINGS Christ redeemed us from the curse of the law, having become a curse for us – for it is written, 'Cursed be every one who hangs on a tree' – that in Christ Jesus the blessing of Abraham might come upon the Gentiles, that we might receive the promise of the Spirit through faith. Galatians 3.13–14

Jesus was casting out a demon that was dumb; when the demon had gone out, the dumb man spoke, and the people marvelled. Some said, 'He casts out demons by Beelzebub, the prince of demons'; while others, to test him, sought from him a sign from heaven. But he, knowing their thoughts, said, 'Every kingdom divided against itself is laid waste, and a divided household falls. If Satan is divided against himself, how will his kingdom stand? For you say that I cast out demons by Beelzebub. If I cast out demons by Beelzebub, by whom do your sons cast them out? Therefore they shall be your judges. But if it is by the finger of God that I cast out demons, then the Kingdom of God has come upon you. When a strong man, fully armed, guards his own palace, his goods are in peace; but when one stronger than he overcomes him, he takes away his armour wherein he trusted, and divides his spoil. He who is not with me is against me, and he who does not gather with me scatters. When the unclean spirit has gone out of a man, he passes through waterless places seeking rest; and finding none he says, "I will return to my house from which I came." When he comes he finds it swept and put in order. Then he goes and brings seven other spirits more evil than himself, and they enter and dwell there; and the last state of that man becomes worse than the first.' A woman in the crowd said, 'Blessed is the womb that bore you, and the breasts that you sucked!' He said, 'Blessed rather are those who hear the word of God and keep it.' St Luke 11.14–28*

RESPONSE Fight the good fight with all thy might.
Christ is thy strength, and Christ thy right.'

Merciful Father, you established your Kingdom of peace and love through your Son – we praise you for his victory over sin and death on the Cross . . .

'Every kingdom divided against itself is laid waste' – draw all Christians into unity to work for the victory of your love in the world . . .

'He who is not with me is against me' – Lord, stir up the wills of all who are baptized, and help us to witness to your love in Jesus Christ . . .

INTERCESSIONS *pages 390–393* CLOSING PRAYERS *page 402–403*

The Holy Spirit will Teach You

OPENING PRAYER Eternal God, to you alone belong honour and glory and power. In your mercy, assist us in these prayers and praises, offered to you through our Lord and Saviour Jesus Christ . . . Glory be . . .

PSALMODY The righteous flourish like the palm tree,
and grow like a cedar in Lebanon.
They are planted in the house of the Lord,
they flourish in the courts of our God.
They still bring forth fruit in old age,
they are ever full of sap and green,
to show that the Lord is upright; Psalm 92.12–15

SCRIPTURE READINGS Jesus said, 'Beware of the leaven of the Pharisees, which is hypocrisy. Nothing is covered up that will not be revealed, or hidden that will not be known. Therefore whatever you have said in the dark shall be heard in the light, and whatever you have whispered in private rooms shall be proclaimed upon the housetops. I tell you, my friends, do not fear those who kill the body, and after that have no more that they can do. But I will warn you whom to fear: fear him who, after he has killed, has power to cast into hell; yes, I tell you, fear him! Are not five sparrows sold for two pennies? And not one of them is forgotten before God. Why, even the hairs of your head are all numbered. Fear not; you are of more value than many sparrows. And I tell you, every one who acknowledges me before men, the Son of Man also will acknowledge before the angels of God; but he who denies me before men will be denied before the angels of God. Everyone who speaks a word against the Son of Man will be forgiven, but he who blasphemes against the Holy Spirit will not be forgiven. When they bring you before the synagogues and the rulers and the authorities, do not be anxious how or what you are to answer or what you are to say; for the Holy Spirit will teach you in that very hour what you ought to say.'
St Luke 12.1–12*

Blessed are those whose iniquities are forgiven, and whose sins are covered.
Romans 4.7

RESPONSE 'Life with its way before us lies;
Christ is the path, and Christ the prize.'

Eternal God, your Son will come again to judge the living and the dead – lead us by the Spirit to repent of our sins and bring us to eternal life . . .
'Nothing is covered that will not be revealed' – strengthen our faith and help us to follow your Son who is the Way, the Truth and the Life . . .
'Do not be anxious' – give us your peace in our hearts, and fill us with your love . . .

INTERCESSIONS *pages 390–393* CLOSING PRAYERS *page 402–403*

10 July *The Lilies*

OPENING PRAYER Eternal God, to you alone belong honour and glory and power. In your mercy, assist us in these prayers and praises, offered to you through our Lord and Saviour Jesus Christ . . . Glory be . . .

PSALMODY The Lord reigns; he is robed in majesty;
thou art from everlasting. Psalm 93.1–2*

SCRIPTURE READINGS
Behold, I create new heavens and a new earth;
and the former things shall not be remembered.
But be glad and rejoice for ever,
in that which I create. Isaiah 65.17–18*

Jesus told them a parable, saying, 'The land of a rich man brought forth plentifully; and he thought to himself, "What shall I do, for I have nowhere to store my crops?" He said, "I will do this: I will pull down my barns, and build larger ones; and there I will store all my grain and my goods. I will say to my soul, Soul, you have ample goods laid up for many years; take your ease, eat, drink, be merry." But God said, "Fool! This night your soul is required of you; and the things you have prepared, whose will they be?" So is he who lays up treasure for himself, and is not rich toward God.' He said to his disciples, 'Therefore I tell you, do not be anxious about your life, what you shall eat, nor about your body, what you shall put on. For life is more than food, and the body more than clothing. Consider the ravens: they neither sow nor reap, they have neither storehouse nor barn, and yet God feeds them. Of how much more value are you than the birds! Which of you by being anxious can add a cubit to his span of life? If then you are not able to do as small a thing as that, why are you anxious about the rest? Consider the lilies, how they grow; they neither toil nor spin; yet I tell you, even Solomon in all his glory was not arrayed like one of these. If God so clothes the grass which is alive in the field today and tomorrow is thrown into the oven, how much more will he clothe you, O men of little faith! Do not seek what you are to eat and what you are to drink, nor be of anxious mind. Instead, seek first his Kingdom, and these things shall be yours as well.' St Luke 12.16–31*

RESPONSE 'In the beauty of the lilies Christ was born across the sea,
with a glory in his bosom that transfigures you and me.'

God of eternal goodness, in your love you create all that exists – we praise you and rejoice in the beauty of your holiness and love . . .
'Fool! This night your soul is required of you' – Lord, help us to prepare for that day when you will call us to yourself . . .
'Seek ye first the Kingdom, and these things shall be yours as well' – give us grace to seek your perfect will in all things . . .

INTERCESSIONS *pages 390–393* CLOSING PRAYERS *page 402–403*

OPENING PRAYER Eternal God, to you alone belong honour and glory and power. In your mercy, assist us in these prayers and praises, offered to you through our Lord and Saviour Jesus Christ . . . Glory be . . .

PSALMODY The Lord on high is mighty! Thy decrees are very sure;
holiness befits thy house, O Lord, for evermore. Psalm 93.4–5

SCRIPTURE READINGS Faith is the assurance of things hoped for, the conviction of things not seen. Hebrews 11.1

Jesus said, 'Let your loins be girded and your lamps burning, and be like men who are waiting for their master to come home from the marriage feast, so that they may open to him at once when he comes and knocks. Blessed are those servants whom the master finds awake when he comes; he will gird himself and have them sit at table, and he will come and serve them. If he comes in the second watch, or in the third, and finds them so, blessed are those servants! But know this, that if the householder had known at what hour the thief was coming, he would not have left his house. You must be ready for the Son of Man is coming at an unexpected hour.' Peter said, 'Lord, are you telling this parable for us or for all?' The Lord said, 'Who then is the faithful and wise steward, whom his master will set over his household, to give them their portion of food at the proper time? Blessed is that servant whom his master when he comes will find so doing. He will set him over all his possessions. But if that servant says to himself, "My master is delayed in coming," and begins to beat the menservants and the maidservants, and to eat and drink and get drunk, the master of that servant will come on a day when he does not expect him and at an hour he does not know, and will punish him, and put him with the unfaithful. And that servant who knew his master's will, but did not make ready or act according to his will, shall receive a severe beating. But he who did not know, and did what deserved a beating, shall receive a light beating. Every one to whom much is given, of him will much be required; and of him to whom men commit much they will demand the more.' St Luke 12.35–48

RESPONSE 'Take my life, and let it be consecrated, Lord, to thee;
take my moments and my days,
let them flow in ceaseless praise.'

Lord God Almighty, you reign in endless glory – we praise you for your promise of eternal life to all who put their trust in you . . .
'Who then is a faithful and wise steward' – give us wisdom and grace to fulfil the work which you have committed to us to do . . .
'Every one to whom much is given, of him much will be expected' – inspire us to be good stewards of the Gospel of Christ . . .

INTERCESSIONS *pages 390–393* CLOSING PRAYERS *page 402–403*

OPENING PRAYER Eternal God, to you alone belong honour and glory and power. In your mercy, assist us in these prayers and praises, offered to you through our Lord and Saviour Jesus Christ . . . Glory be . . .

PSALMODY Rise up, O judge of the earth;
render to the proud their deserts!
O Lord, how long shall the wicked,
how long shall the wicked exult?
They pour out their arrogant words,
they boast, all the evildoers.
And they say, 'The Lord does not see,
the God of Jacob does not perceive.' Psalm 94.2–7*

SCRIPTURE READINGS You did not receive the spirit of slavery to fall back into fear, but you have received the spirit of sonship. When we cry, 'Abba! Father!' it is the Spirit himself bearing witness with our spirit that we are children of God, and if children, then heirs, heirs of God and fellow heirs with Christ, provided we suffer with him in order that we may also be glorified with him. Romans 8.15–17

Jesus was teaching in the synagogue on the sabbath. There was a woman who had had a spirit of infirmity for eighteen years; she was bent over and could not fully straighten herself. When Jesus saw her, he said, 'Woman, you are freed from your infirmity.' He laid his hands upon her, and immediately she was made straight, and she praised God. The ruler of the synagogue, indignant because Jesus had healed on the sabbath, said to the people, 'There are six days on which work ought to be done; come on those days and be healed, and not on the sabbath day.' The Lord answered, 'You hypocrites! Does not each of you on the sabbath untie his ox or ass and lead it away to water it? Ought not this woman, a daughter of Abraham whom Satan bound for eighteen years, be loosed from this bond on the sabbath day?' His adversaries were put to shame; and the people rejoiced at the glorious things that were done by him. St Luke 13.10–18*

RESPONSE 'Rejoice in the Lord, O you righteous!
Praise befits the upright.'

Everliving God, you are the strength and salvation of all who put their trust in you – we praise you for your goodness and infinite love . . .
'She praised God' – we praise you and we thank you for all the blessings and benefits won for us by your Beloved Son on the Cross . . .
'The people rejoiced' – we too rejoice and we join our prayers and praises with the endless worship of the saints in heaven . . .

INTERCESSIONS *pages 390–393* CLOSING PRAYERS *page 402–403*

OPENING PRAYER Eternal God, to you alone belong honour and glory and power. In your mercy, assist us in these prayers and praises, offered to you through our Lord and Saviour Jesus Christ . . . Glory be . . .

PSALMODY Understand, O dullest of the people!
Fools, when will you be wise?
He who planted the ear, does he not hear?
He who formed the eye, does he not see?
He who chastens the nations, does he not chastise?
He who teaches men knowledge,
the Lord, knows the thoughts of men,
that they are but a breath. Psalm 94.8–11

SCRIPTURE READINGS 'I know their works and their thoughts, and I am coming to gather all nations and tongues; and they shall see my glory, and I will set a sign among them. From them I will send survivors to the nations, and they shall declare my glory among the nations.'
Isaiah 66.18–19*

For the moment all discipline seems painful rather than pleasant; later it yields the peaceful fruit of righteousness to those who have been trained by it.
Hebrews 12.11

Someone said, 'Lord, will those who are saved be few?' He said, 'Strive to enter by the narrow door; for many, I tell you, will seek to enter and will not be able. When once the householder has shut the door, you will begin to stand outside and knock at the door, saying, "Lord, open to us." He will answer, "I do not know where you come from." Then you will say, "We ate and drank in your presence, and you taught in our streets." But he will say, "I tell you, I do not know where you come from; depart from me, all you workers of iniquity!" You will weep and gnash your teeth, when you see Abraham and Isaac and Jacob and all the prophets in the Kingdom of God and yourselves thrust out. Men will come from east and west, and from north and south, and sit at table in the Kingdom of God. Some are last who will be first, and some are first who will be last.'
St Luke 13.23–30*

RESPONSE 'Run the straight race through God's good grace,
lift up thine eyes and seek his face.'

Loving Father, it is your will for all people to be saved – we rejoice that your Spirit works in and through the Church and also in the world . . .
'Will those who are saved be few?' – fill your Church with all the grace needed to share in the mission of your Son to the world . . .
Your Kingdom exists where people accept your will in their lives – we pray for the extension of your Kingdom in our hearts and in the world . . .

INTERCESSIONS *pages 390–393* CLOSING PRAYERS *page 402–403*

Friend, Go Up Higher

OPENING PRAYER Eternal God, to you alone belong honour and glory and power. In your mercy, assist us in these prayers and praises, offered to you through our Lord and Saviour Jesus Christ . . . Glory be . . .

PSALMODY Blessed is the man whom thou dost chasten, O Lord,
and whom thou dost teach out of thy law
to give him respite from days of trouble.
For the Lord will not forsake his people;
he will not abandon his heritage;
for justice will return to the righteous,
and all the upright in heart will follow it. Psalm 94.12–15*

SCRIPTURE READINGS It is my prayer that your love may abound more and more, with knowledge and all discernment, so that you may approve what is excellent, and may be pure and blameless for the day of Christ, filled with the fruits of righteousness which come through Jesus Christ, to the glory and praise of God. Philippians 1.9–11

One sabbath when he went to dine at the house of a ruler who belonged to the Pharisees, they were watching him. There was a man before him who had dropsy. Jesus spoke to the lawyers and Pharisees, saying, 'Is it lawful to heal on the sabbath, or not?' But they were silent. Then he took him and healed him, and let him go. He said, 'Which of you, having a son or an ox that has fallen into a well, will not immediately pull him out on a sabbath day?' And they could not reply. Now he told a parable, when he marked how they chose the places of honour, saying, 'When you are invited by any one to a marriage feast, do not sit down in a place of honour, lest a more eminent man than you be invited by him; and he who invited you will come and say, "Give place to this man," and you will begin with shame to take the lowest place. When you are invited, go and sit in the lowest place, so that when your host comes he may say to you, "Friend, go up higher"; then you will be honoured in the presence of all who sit at table with you. For every one who exalts himself will be humbled, and he who humbles himself will be exalted.' St Luke 14.1–11*

RESPONSE 'Still to the lowly soul he doth himself impart,
and for his dwelling and his throne chooseth the pure in heart.'

Heavenly Father, you are the God of our salvation – we praise you and thank you for accepting us as we are with all our failings . . .
'Friend, go up higher' – Lord, grant us advancement in the faith and spiritual understanding, that we may worship you in spirit and in truth . . .
Every one who exalts himself will be humbled' – Lord, free us from the sin of pride, and help us to grow in the likeness of Christ . . .

INTERCESSIONS *pages 390–393* CLOSING PRAYERS *page 402–403*

The King's Banquet

OPENING PRAYER Eternal God, to you alone belong honour and glory and power. In your mercy, assist us in these prayers and praises, offered to you through our Lord and Saviour Jesus Christ . . . Glory be . . .

PSALMODY Who rises up for me against the wicked?
Who stands up for me against evil doers?
If the Lord had not been my help,
my soul would soon have dwelt in the land of silence.
When I thought, 'My foot slips,'
thy steadfast love, O Lord, held me up.
When the cares of my heart are many,
thy consolations cheer my soul.

Psalm 94.16–19

SCRIPTURE READINGS Day by day, attending the temple together and breaking bread in their homes, they partook of food with glad and generous hearts, praising God and having favour with all the people. And the Lord added to their number day by day those who were being saved.

Acts 2.46–47

One of those who sat at table with Jesus said, 'Blessed is he who shall eat bread in the Kingdom of God!' Jesus said, 'A man once gave a great banquet, and invited many; and at the time for the banquet he sent his servant to say to those who had been invited, "Come; for all is now ready." But they all alike began to make excuses. The first said, "I have bought a field, and I must go out and see it; I pray you, have me excused." Another said, "I have bought five yoke of oxen, and I go to examine them; I pray you, have me excused." Another said, "I have married a wife, and therefore I cannot come." So the servant reported this to his master. Then the householder in anger said to his servant, "Go out quickly to the streets and lanes of the city, and bring in the poor and the maimed and blind and lame." The servant said, "Sir, what you commanded has been done, and still there is room." The master said, "Go out to the highways and hedges, and compel people to come in, that my house may be filled. For I tell you, none of those men who were invited shall taste my banquet."'

St Luke 14.15–24

RESPONSE 'Lord of our life, and God of our salvation,
hear and receive thy Church's supplication.'

Heavenly Father, you are the fountain of all goodness and love – we praise you for inviting all people to your heavenly banquet . . .
'Come; for all is now ready' – Lord, we praise you for the sacrifice of Christ, who is both Priest and victim on the altar of the Cross . . .
'They all alike began to make excuses' – purify our motives, and help us to be faithful disciples of Christ throughout our lives . . .

INTERCESSIONS *pages 390–393* CLOSING PRAYERS *page 402–403*

16 July *The Lost Sheep*

OPENING PRAYER Eternal God, to you alone belong honour and glory and power. In your mercy, assist us in these prayers and praises, offered to you through our Lord and Saviour Jesus Christ . . . Glory be . . .

PSALMODY O come, let us sing to the Lord;
let us make a joyful noise
to the rock of our salvation!
For the Lord is a great God,
and a great King above all gods.
In his hand are the depths of the earth;
the heights of the mountains are his also.
The sea is his, for he made it;
for his hands formed the dry land. Psalm 95.1–5*

SCRIPTURE READINGS It is God who establishes us with you in Christ, and has commissioned us; he has put his seal upon us and given us his Spirit in our hearts as a guarantee. 2 Corinthians 1.21–22

Tax collectors and sinners were drawing near to hear Jesus. The Pharisees and scribes murmured, saying, 'This man receives sinners and eats with them.' So he told them this parable: 'What man of you, having a hundred sheep, if he has lost one of them, does not leave the ninety-nine in the wilderness, and go after the one which is lost, until he finds it? When he has found it, he lays it on his shoulders, rejoicing. When he comes home, he calls together his friends and neighbours, saying, "Rejoice with me, for I have found my sheep which was lost." Just so, there will be more joy in heaven over one sinner who repents than over ninety-nine righteous persons who need no repentance. Or what woman, having ten silver coins, if she loses one coin, does not light a lamp and sweep the house and seek diligently until she finds it? When she has found it, she calls together her friends and neighbours, saying, "Rejoice with me, for I have found the coin which I had lost." Just so, I tell you, there is joy before the angels of God over one sinner who repents.' St Luke 15.1–10*

RESPONSE 'Angels of Jesus, angels of light,
singing to welcome the pilgrim of the night.'

Eternal God, you are merciful and you seek us when we are lost in sin – we praise you for your forgiveness to restore us to union with yourself . . .
'I have found my sheep which was lost' – strengthen your Church to share in the mission of your Son to those who do not know our love . . .
'Rejoice with me' – with joy in our hearts, we praise your holy name . . .

INTERCESSIONS *pages 390–393* CLOSING PRAYERS *page 402–403*

17 July *The Prodigal Son*

OPENING PRAYER Eternal God, to you alone belong honour and glory and power. In your mercy, assist us in these prayers and praises, offered to you through our Lord and Saviour Jesus Christ . . . Glory be . . .

PSALMODY O come, let us worship and bow down,
let us kneel before the Lord, our Maker!
For he is our God, and we are the people of his pasture,
and the sheep of his hand. Psalm 95.6–7a

SCRIPTURE READINGS Jesus said, 'There was a man who had two sons; and the younger of them said to his father, "Father give me the share of property that falls to me." He divided his living between them. Not many days later, the younger son gathered all he had and took his journey into a far country, and he squandered his property in loose living. When he came to himself he said, "How many of my father's hired servants have bread enough and to spare, but I perish here with hunger! I will arise and go to my father, and I will say, 'Father, I have sinned against heaven and before you; I am no longer worthy to be called your son; treat me as one of your hired servants.'" He arose and came to his father. While he was yet at a distance, his father saw him and had compassion, and ran and embraced him and kissed him. The father said to his servants, "Bring quickly the best robe, and put it on him; and put a ring on his hand, and shoes on his feet; and bring the fatted calf and kill it, and let us eat and make merry; for this my son was dead; and is alive again; he was lost, and is found." And they began to make merry. Now his elder son was in the field; as he drew near to the house, he heard music and dancing. He was angry and refused to go in. His father said, "Son, you are always with me, and all that is mine is yours! It was fitting to make merry and be glad, for your brother was dead, and is alive, he was lost, and is found."' St Luke 15.11–32*

Put on then, as God's chosen ones, holy and beloved, compassion, kindness, lowliness, meekness, and patience, forbearing one another and, if one has a complaint against another, forgiving each other; as the Lord has forgiven you, so you also must forgive. Colossians 3.12–13

RESPONSE 'Love divine, all loves excelling, joy of heaven to earth come down,
fix in us thy humble dwelling, all thy faithful mercies crown.'

Loving Father, you are the source of all mercy and compassion – we praise you for your perfect love and forgiveness in your Son Jesus Christ . . .
Your forgiveness and reconciliation are gifts we do not earn or deserve – Lord, help us to forgive other people as you forgive us . . .
You continue to call us to yourself, even when we turn away in sin – strengthen our faith and bring us into closer union with your Son . . .

INTERCESSIONS *pages 390–393* CLOSING PRAYERS *page 402–403*

The Dishonest Steward

OPENING PRAYER Eternal God, to you alone belong honour and glory and power. In your mercy, assist us in these prayers and praises, offered to you through our Lord and Saviour Jesus Christ . . . Glory be . . .

PSALMODY O that today you would hearken to his voice!
Harden not your hearts, as at Meribah,
when your fathers tested me,
and put me to the proof, though they had seen my work.
For forty years I loathed that generation and said,
'They are a people who err in heart,
and they do not regard my ways.' Psalm 95.8–10

SCRIPTURE READINGS In Christ Jesus, I have reason to be proud of my work for God. I will not venture to speak of anything except what Christ has wrought through me to win obedience from the Gentiles.
Romans 15.17–18

Jesus said, 'There was a rich man who had a steward, and charges were brought to him that this man was wasting his goods. He called him and said, "What is this that I hear about you? Turn in the account of your stewardship, for you can no longer be steward." The steward said to himself, "What shall I do, since my master is taking the stewardship away from me? I am not strong enough to dig, and I am ashamed to beg. I have decided what to do, so that people may receive me into their houses when I am put out of the stewardship." So, summoning his master's debtors one by one, he said to the first, "How much do you owe my master?" He said, "A hundred measures of oil." He said, "Take your bill, and sit down quickly and write fifty." He said to another, "How much do you owe?" He said, "A hundred measures of wheat." He said, "Take your bill, and write eighty." The master commended the dishonest steward for his shrewdness, for the sons of this world are more shrewd in dealing with their own generation than the sons of light. I tell you, make friends for yourselves by means of unrighteous mammon, so that when it fails they may receive you into the eternal habitations.' St Luke 16.1–9*

RESPONSE 'Do thou, O Lord, keep watch within,
and save my soul from wrong.'

We sing praises to you, Heavenly Father, for you are the source of all purity and truth and goodness – to you be praise and endless glory . . .
'The sons of this world are more shrewd in dealing with their own generation than the sons of light' – help us to use the skills you have given to us to help the work of your Church . . .
'Turn in the account of your stewardship' – have mercy on us, and make us responsible stewards of all that you have entrusted to us . . .

INTERCESSIONS *pages 390–393* CLOSING PRAYERS *page 402–403*

19 July *No Servant Can Serve Two Masters*

OPENING PRAYER Eternal God, to you alone belong honour and glory and power. In your mercy, assist us in these prayers and praises, offered to you through our Lord and Saviour Jesus Christ . . . Glory be . . .

PSALMODY O sing to the Lord a new song;
sing to the Lord, all the earth!
Tell of his salvation from day to day.
Declare his glory among the nations,
his marvellous works among all the peoples!
For great is the Lord, and greatly to be praised.
Honour and majesty are before him;
strength and beauty are in his sanctuary. Psalm 96.1–6*

SCRIPTURE READINGS To him who is able to strengthen you according to my gospel and the preaching of Jesus Christ, according to the revelation of the mystery kept secret for long ages but is now disclosed and through the prophetic writings is made known to all nations, according to the command of the eternal God, to bring about obedience to the faith – to the only wise God be glory for evermore through Jesus Christ! Amen.

Romans 16.25–27*

Jesus said, 'He who is faithful in a very little is faithful also in much; and he who is dishonest in a very little is dishonest also in much. If then you have not been faithful in the unrighteous mammon, who will entrust to you the true riches? And if you have not been faithful in that which is another's, who will give you that which is your own? No servant can serve two masters; for either he will hate the one and love the other, or he will be devoted to the one and despise the other. You cannot serve God and mammon.' The Pharisees, who were lovers of money, heard all this, and scoffed at him. But he said, 'You are those who justify yourselves before men, but God knows your hearts; for what is exalted among men is an abomination in the sight of God. The law and the prophets were until John; since then the good news of the Kingdom of God is preached, and every one enters it violently. But it is easier for heaven and earth to pass away, than for one dot of the law to become void.' St Luke 16.10–17*

RESPONSE 'Take my life and let it be consecrated, Lord, to thee;
take my moments and my days, let them flow in ceaseless praise.'

Heavenly Father, you are the God of justice and truth – accept our praise, offered to you through Jesus, our great High Priest . . .
'He who is faithful in a very little is faithful also in much' – help us to be faithful and honest in all things, great and small alike . . .
'No one can serve two masters' – guard your Church against the temptations of earthly wealth and power and glory, and help us to follow Christ . . .

INTERCESSIONS *pages 390–393* CLOSING PRAYERS *page 402–403*

Dives and Lazarus

OPENING PRAYER Eternal God, to you alone belong honour and glory and power. In your mercy, assist us in these prayers and praises, offered to you through our Lord and Saviour Jesus Christ . . . Glory be . . .

PSALMODY Ascribe to the Lord the glory due his name;
bring an offering, and come into his courts!
Worship the Lord in holy array;
tremble before him, all the earth! Psalm 96.8–9

SCRIPTURE READINGS
You will be sated with contempt instead of glory.
The cup in the Lord's right hand
will come around to you,
and shame will come upon your glory! Habakkuk 2.16*

Jesus said, 'There was a rich man, who was clothed in purple and fine linen and who feasted sumptuously every day. At his gate lay a poor man named Lazarus, full of sores, who desired to be fed with what fell from the rich man's table; the dogs came and licked his sores. The poor man died and was carried by the angels to Abraham's bosom. The rich man also died and was buried, and in Hades, being in torment, he lifted up his eyes, and saw Abraham far off and Lazarus in his bosom. He called out, "Father Abraham, have mercy upon me, and send Lazarus to dip the end of his finger in water and cool my tongue; for I am in anguish in this flame." Abraham said, "Son, remember that you in your lifetime received your good things, and Lazarus in like manner evil things; but now he is comforted here, and you are in anguish. Besides all this, between us and you a great chasm has been fixed, in order that those who would pass from here to you may not be able, and none may cross from there to us." He said, "Then I beg you, father, to send him to my father's house, for I have five brothers, so that he may warn them, lest they also come into this place of torment." Abraham said, "They have Moses and the prophets; let them hear them." He said, "No, father Abraham; but if some one goes to them from the dead, they will repent." He said, "If they do not hear Moses and the prophets, neither will they be convinced if some one should rise from the dead."' St Luke 16.19–31

RESPONSE 'Just as I am, without one plea,
but that thy blood was shed for me, O Lamb of God I come.'

Eternal Father, you pour the riches of your grace on all who truly turn to Christ – we praise you for your mercy and love . . .
'There was a rich man who was clothed in purple' – inspire us to set our hearts on spiritual treasures, and make us rich in faith and love . . .
'At his gate lay a poor man named Lazarus' – fill your Church with compassion, and inspire us to work for the justice of your Kingdom . . .

INTERCESSIONS *pages 390–393* CLOSING PRAYERS *page 402–403*

OPENING PRAYER Eternal God, to you alone belong honour and glory and power. In your mercy, assist us in these prayers and praises, offered to you through our Lord and Saviour Jesus Christ . . . Glory be . . .

PSALMODY Say among the nations, 'The Lord reigns!
Yea, the world is established, it shall never be moved;
he will judge the peoples with equity.'
Let the heavens be glad, and let the earth rejoice;
let the sea roar, and all that fills it;
let the field exult, and everything in it!
Then shall all the trees of the wood sing for joy
before the Lord, for he comes,
for he comes to judge the earth.
He will judge the world with righteousness,
and the peoples with his truth. Psalm 96.10–13

SCRIPTURE READINGS Samuel said, 'Thus says the Lord, the God of Israel, "I brought up Israel out of Egypt, and I delivered you from the hand of the Egyptians and from the hand of all the kingdoms that were oppressing you." But you have this day rejected your God. 1 Samuel 10.17–19*

As Jesus entered a village, he was met by ten lepers, who stood at a distance, and lifted up their voices and said, 'Jesus, Master, have mercy on us.' When he saw them he said to them, 'Go and show yourselves to the priests.' And as they went they were cleansed. Then one of them, when he saw that he was healed, turned back, praising God with a loud voice, and he fell on his face at Jesus' feet, giving him thanks. Now he was a Samaritan. Then said Jesus, 'Were not ten cleansed? Where are the nine? Was no one found to return and give praise to God except this foreigner?' And he said to him, 'Rise and go your way; your faith has made you well.' Being asked by the Pharisees when the Kingdom of God was coming, he answered them, 'The Kingdom of God is not coming with signs to be observed; nor will they say, "Lo, here it is!" or "There!" for behold, the Kingdom of God is in the midst of you.' St Luke 17.12–21

RESPONSE 'Let us, with a gladsome mind, praise the Lord for he is kind,
for his mercies ay endure, ever faithful, ever sure.'

Bless the Lord, O my soul, and forget not all his benefits – we thank you for your gift of life and for your goodness and love . . .
'Was there no one found to return and give praise to God except this foreigner?' – give us ever-grateful hearts for all your blessings . . .
'The Kingdom of God is in the midst of you' – Lord, purify the Church and help us by the Spirit to work and pray for the coming of your Kingdom . . .

INTERCESSIONS *pages 390–393* CLOSING PRAYERS *page 402–403*

OPENING PRAYER Eternal God, to you alone belong honour and glory and power. In your mercy, assist us in these prayers and praises, offered to you through our Lord and Saviour Jesus Christ . . . Glory be . . .

PSALMODY O Lord my God, I cried to thee for help,
and thou hast healed me.
O Lord, thou hast brought up my soul from Sheol,
restored me to life from among those gone down to the Pit.
Sing praises to the Lord, O you his saints,
and give thanks to his holy name. Psalm 30.2–4

SCRIPTURE READINGS

Sing aloud, O daughter of Zion; shout, O Israel!
Rejoice and exult with all your heart,
O daughter of Jerusalem!
The Lord has taken away the judgements against you.
The King of Israel, the Lord, is in your midst;
you shall fear evil no more. Zephaniah 3.14–15*

If any one is in Christ, he is a new creation; the old has passed away, behold, the new has come. 2 Corinthians 5.17

Mary stood weeping outside the tomb, and as she wept she stooped to look into the tomb; and she saw two angels in white, sitting where the body of Jesus had lain, one at the head and one at the feet. They said, 'Woman, why are you weeping?' She said, 'Because they have taken away my Lord, and I do not know where they have laid him.' Saying this, she turned round and saw Jesus standing, but she did not know that it was Jesus. Jesus said, 'Woman, why are you weeping? Whom do you seek?' Supposing him to be the gardener, she said, 'Sir, if you have carried him away, tell me where you have laid him, and I will take him away.' Jesus said, 'Mary.' She turned and said in Hebrew, 'Rabboni' (which means Teacher). Jesus said, 'Do not hold me, for I have not yet ascended to the Father; but go to my brethren and say to them, I am ascending to my Father and your Father, to my God and your God.' Mary Magdalene went and said to the disciples, 'I have seen the Lord'; and she told them that he had said these things to her. St John 20.11–18*

RESPONSE 'Soldiers, who are Christ's below, strong in faith resist the foe,
boundless is the pledged reward unto them who serve the Lord.'

Loving Father, you chose Mary Magdalene to be the first witness of your Son's resurrection – we celebrate this feast with joy and thanksgiving . . .
'Her many sins are forgiven, because she loved much' – forgive us as you forgave Mary Magdalene, and help us to respond to your love in Jesus . . .
'I have seen the Lord' – we pray with Saint Mary Magdalene for the conversion of all who reject your love in Jesus Christ . . .

INTERCESSIONS *pages 390–393* CLOSING PRAYERS *page 402–403*

23 July

The Unjust Judge

OPENING PRAYER Eternal God, to you alone belong honour and glory and power. In your mercy, assist us in these prayers and praises, offered to you through our Lord and Saviour Jesus Christ . . . Glory be . . .

PSALMODY The Lord reigns; let the earth rejoice;
let the many coastlands be glad!
Clouds and thick darkness are round about him;
righteousness and justice are the foundation of his throne.
Fire goes before him,
and burns up his adversaries round about.
His lightnings lighten the world;
the earth sees and trembles.
The mountains melt like wax before the Lord,
before the Lord of all the earth.
Psalm 97.1–5

SCRIPTURE READINGS Samuel said to all Israel, 'Here I am; testify against me before the Lord and before his anointed. Whose ox have I taken? Or whose ass have I taken? Or whom have I defrauded? Whom have I oppressed? Or from whose hand have I taken a bribe to blind my eyes with it? Testify against me and I will restore it to you.' They said, 'You have not defrauded us or oppressed us or taken anything from any man's hand.'
1 Samuel 12.3–5

Jesus told them a parable, to the effect that they ought always to pray and not lose heart. He said, 'In a certain city there was a judge who neither feared God nor regarded man; and there was a widow in that city who kept coming to him and saying, "Vindicate me against my adversary." For a while he refused; but afterward he said to himself, "Though I neither fear God nor regard man, yet because this widow bothers me, I will vindicate her, or she will wear me out by her continual coming."' And the Lord said, 'Hear what the unrighteous judge says. And will not God vindicate his elect, who cry to him day and night? Will he delay long over them? I tell you, he will vindicate them speedily. Nevertheless, when the Son of Man comes, will he find faith on earth?'
St Luke 18.1–8

RESPONSE 'There's a wideness of God's mercy like the wideness of the sea;
there's a kindness in his justice which is more than liberty.'

Heavenly Father, your Son is our redeemer and friend, and also our judge – in your mercy, help us to grow into union with Christ . . .
'There was a judge who neither feared God nor regarded man' – Lord, give wisdom and integrity to all who administer and uphold the law . . .
'When the Son of Man comes, will he find faith on earth?' – increase in us your gift of faith, and keep us steadfast in your love . . .

INTERCESSIONS *pages 390–393* CLOSING PRAYERS *page 402–403*

The Pharisee and the Tax Collector

OPENING PRAYER Eternal God, to you alone belong honour and glory and power. In your mercy, assist us in these prayers and praises, offered to you through our Lord and Saviour Jesus Christ . . . Glory be . . .

PSALMODY The mountains melt like wax before the Lord.
The heavens proclaim his righteousness;
and all the peoples behold his glory.
Zion hears and is glad,
and the daughters of Judah rejoice,
because of thy judgements, O God. Psalm 97.5–8*

SCRIPTURE READINGS I am already on the point of being sacrificed; the time of my departure has come. I have fought the good fight, I have finished the race, I have kept the faith. Henceforth there is laid up for me the crown of righteousness, which the Lord, the righteous judge, will award to me on that Day, and not only to me but also to all who have loved his appearing. At my first defence no one took my part; all deserted me. May it not be charged against them! But the Lord stood by me and gave me strength to proclaim the word fully, that all the Gentiles might hear it. So I was rescued from the lion's mouth. The Lord will rescue me from every evil and save me for his heavenly kingdom. To him be the glory for ever and ever. Amen. 2 Timothy 4.6–18*

Jesus told this parable to some who trusted in themselves that they were righteous and despised others: 'Two men went up into the temple to pray, one a Pharisee and the other a tax collector. The Pharisee stood and prayed thus with himself, "God, I thank thee that I am not like other men, extortioners, unjust, adulterers, or even like this tax collector. I fast twice a week, I give tithes of all that I get." But the tax collector, standing far off, would not even lift up his eyes to heaven, but beat his breast, saying, "God be merciful to me a sinner!" I tell you, this man went down to his house justified rather than the other; for every one who exalts himself will be humbled, but he who humbles himself will be exalted.' St Luke 18.9–14

RESPONSE 'Saviour, breathe forgiveness o'er us,
all our weakness thou dost know.'

To God be the glory for ever and ever – Blessing and honour and glory and praise belong to the Lord our God for time and for eternity . . .
'God be merciful to me a sinner' – Lord, have mercy on us all . . .
To pray is an act of faith in Jesus Christ – Lord, help your Church to be faithful in prayer, and to grow in holiness and love . . .

INTERCESSIONS *pages 390–393* CLOSING PRAYERS *page 402–403*

Saint James the Apostle

OPENING PRAYER Eternal God, to you alone belong honour and glory and power. In your mercy, assist us in these prayers and praises, offered to you through our Lord and Saviour Jesus Christ . . . Glory be . . .

PSALMODY It is God who executes judgement,
putting down one and lifting up another.
For in the hand of the Lord there is a cup,
with foaming wine, well mixed;
and he will pour a draught from it,
and all the wicked of the earth
shall drain it down to the dregs.
But I will rejoice for ever,
I will sing praises to the God of Jacob. Psalm 75.7–9

SCRIPTURE READINGS Herod the king laid violent hands upon some who belonged to the Church. He killed James the brother of John with the sword.
Acts 12.1–2

James and John, the sons of Zebedee, came to Jesus, and said, 'Teacher, we want you to do for us whatever we ask of you.' He said, 'What do you want me to do for you?' They said, 'Grant us to sit, one at your right hand and one at your left, in your glory.' Jesus said, 'You do not know what you are asking. Are you able to drink the cup that I drink, or to be baptized with the baptism with which I am baptized?' They said, 'We are able.' Jesus said, 'The cup that I drink you will drink; and with the baptism with which I am baptized, you will be baptized; but to sit at my right hand or at my left is not mine to grant, but it is for those for whom it has been prepared.' When the ten heard it, they began to be indignant at James and John. Jesus called them and said, 'You know that those who are supposed to rule over the Gentiles lord it over them, and their great men exercise authority over them. But it shall not be so among you; but whoever would be great among you must be your servant, and whoever would be first among you must be slave of all. For the Son of Man came not to be served but to serve, and to give his life as a ransom for many.'
St Mark 10.35–45*

RESPONSE 'The salvation of the righteous is from the Lord;
he is their refuge in the time of trouble.'

Eternal God, you called the apostles to govern and lead your Church – we praise you as we celebrate this feast of Saint James . . .
Your Son called James and John, and they immediately left their father and their boats – Lord, help us to be always ready to obey your call . . .
'The Son of Man came not to be served but to serve' – united in the one Spirit, we pray with Saint James for the work of your whole Church . . .

INTERCESSIONS *pages 390–393*

CLOSING PRAYERS *page 402–403*

26 July *Through the Eye of a Needle*

OPENING PRAYER Eternal God, to you alone belong honour and glory and power. In your mercy, assist us in these prayers and praises, offered to you through our Lord and Saviour Jesus Christ . . . Glory be . . .

PSALMODY Thou, O Lord, art most high over all the earth.
The Lord loves those who hate evil;
he preserves the lives of his saints.
Light dawns for the righteous,
and joy for the upright in heart.
Rejoice in the Lord, O you righteous,
and give thanks to his holy name! Psalm 97.9–12*

SCRIPTURE READINGS Samuel said to Saul, 'You have done foolishly; you have not kept the commandment of the Lord your God. Now your Kingdom shall not continue; the Lord has sought out a man after his own heart; and the Lord has appointed him to be prince over his people.'
1 Samuel 13.13–14*

They were bringing even infants to Jesus that he might touch them; when the disciples saw it, they rebuked them. But Jesus called them to him, saying, 'Let the children come to me, and do not hinder them; for to such belongs the Kingdom of God. Truly, I say to you, whoever does not receive the Kingdom of God like a child shall not enter it.' And a ruler asked him, 'Good Teacher, what shall I do to inherit eternal life?' Jesus said, 'Why do you call me good? No one is good but God alone. You know the commandments. "Do not commit adultery, Do not kill, Do not steal, Do not bear false witness, Honour your father and mother."' And he said, 'All these I have observed from my youth.' When Jesus heard it, he said, 'One thing you still lack. Sell all that you have and distribute to the poor, and you will have treasure in heaven; and come, follow me.' When he heard this he became sad, for he was very rich. Jesus said, 'How hard it is for those who have riches to enter the Kingdom of God! For it is easier for a camel to go through the eye of a needle than for a rich man to enter the Kingdom of God.' Those who heard it said, 'Then who can be saved?' But he said, 'What is impossible with men is possible with God.'
St Luke 18.15–27*

RESPONSE 'Thine for ever! thou our Guide, all our wants by thee supplied, all our sins by thee forgiven, lead us, Lord, from earth to heaven.'

Almighty God, you assure us of everlasting life through your son – we praise you with the eternal fellowship of Christians through the ages . . .
'What shall I do to inherit eternal life?' – help us to grow into union with your Son, and in your mercy, bring us to life eternal . . .
'How hard it is for those who have riches to enter the Kingdom of God' – Lord, help us to set our hearts where lasting joys are to be found . . .

INTERCESSIONS *pages 390–393* CLOSING PRAYERS *page 402–403*

27 July

Receive your Sight

OPENING PRAYER Eternal God, to you alone belong honour and glory and power. In your mercy, assist us in these prayers and praises, offered to you through our Lord and Saviour Jesus Christ . . . Glory be . . .

PSALMODY O sing to the Lord a new song,
for he has done marvellous things!
His right hand and his holy arm
have gotten him the victory.
The Lord has made known his victory,
he has revealed his vindication
in the sight of the nations.
He has remembered his steadfast love
and faithfulness to the house of Israel.
All the ends of the earth
have seen the victory of our God. Psalm 98.1–3

SCRIPTURE READINGS The revelation of Jesus Christ, which God gave him to show to his servants what must soon take place; and he made it known by sending his angel to his servant John, who bore witness to the word of God and to the testimony of Jesus Christ, even to all that he saw. Blessed is he who reads aloud the words of the prophecy, and blessed are those who hear, and who keep what is written therein; for the time is near.
Revelation 1.1–4

As Jesus drew near to Jericho, a blind man was sitting by the roadside begging; and hearing a multitude going by, he inquired what this meant. They told him, 'Jesus of Nazareth is passing by.' He cried, 'Jesus, Son of David, have mercy on me!' Those in front rebuked him; but he cried out all the more, 'Son of David, have mercy on me!' Jesus stopped, and commanded him to be brought to him; and when he came near, he asked, 'What do you want me to do for you?' He said, 'Lord, let me receive my sight.' Jesus said, 'Receive your sight; your faith has made you well.' Immediately he received his sight and followed him, glorifying God; all the people, when they saw it, gave praise to God. St Luke 18.35–43*

RESPONSE 'We trust to find thee when the night is past,
and daylight breaks across the morning sky.'

Heavenly Father, you were in Christ Jesus reconciling the world to yourself – we praise you for making us inheritors of your Kingdom . . .
'They will scourge him and kill him' – help us to be more aware of the suffering of Christ, caused by our sins today . . .
Your Son has a special love for those who are handicapped – bless them, and strengthen them with an awareness of your presence and love . . .

INTERCESSIONS *pages 390–393* CLOSING PRAYERS *page 402–403*

OPENING PRAYER Eternal God, to you alone belong honour and glory and power. In your mercy, assist us in these prayers and praises, offered to you through our Lord and Saviour Jesus Christ . . . Glory be . . .

PSALMODY Make a joyful noise to the Lord, all the earth;
break forth into joyous song and sing praises!
Sing praises to the Lord with the lyre,
with the lyre and the sound of melody!
With trumpets and the sound of the horn
make a joyful noise before the King, the Lord!
Let the sea roar, and all that fills it;
the world and those who dwell in it.
He will judge the world with righteousness,
and the peoples with equity. Psalm 98.4–9*

SCRIPTURE READINGS To this end we always pray for you, that our God may make you worthy of his call, and may fulfil every good resolve and work of faith by his power, so that the name of our Lord Jesus may be glorified in you, and you in him, according to the grace of our God and the Lord Jesus Christ. 2 Thessalonians 1.11–12

He entered Jericho and was passing through. There was a man named Zacchaeus; he was a chief tax collector, and rich. He sought to see who Jesus was, but could not, on account of the crowd, because he was small of stature. So he ran on ahead and climbed up into a sycamore tree to see him, for he was to pass that way. When Jesus came to the place, he looked up and said, 'Zacchaeus, make haste and come down; for I must stay at your house today.' So he made haste and came down, and received him joyfully. When they saw it they all murmured, 'He has gone in to be the guest of a man who is a sinner.' Zacchaeus stood and said to the Lord, 'Behold, Lord, the half of my goods I give to the poor; and if I have defrauded any one of anything, I restore it fourfold.' Jesus said, 'Today salvation has come to this house, since he also is a son of Abraham. For the Son of Man came to seek and to save the lost.' St Luke 19.1–10

RESPONSE 'Jesus, confirm my heart's desire,
to work, and speak and think for thee.'

Lord God of our salvation, you grant us forgiveness when we repent and turn to you – we praise you for your Son's redeeming love . . .
'Zacchaeus received him joyfully' – come, Holy Spirit, and fill us with your love and joy and peace . . .
'The Son of Man came to seek and to save the lost' – equip us to share in your Son's continuous mission to all who do not know your love . . .

INTERCESSIONS *pages 390–393* CLOSING PRAYERS *page 402–403*

OPENING PRAYER Eternal God, to you alone belong honour and glory and power. In your mercy, assist us in these prayers and praises, offered to you through our Lord and Saviour Jesus Christ . . . Glory be . . .

PSALMODY Let the sea roar, and all that fills it;
let the hills sing for joy together before the Lord,
for he comes to judge the earth. Psalm 98.7–9*

SCRIPTURE READINGS The twenty four elders fall down before him who is seated on the throne and worship him, singing, 'Worthy art thou, our Lord and God, to receive glory and honour and power, for thou didst create all things, and by thy will they existed and were created.' Revelation 4.2–11*

Jesus said, 'A nobleman went into a far country to receive kingly power and then return. Calling ten of his servants, he gave them ten pounds, and said, 'Trade with these till I come.' But his citizens hated him and sent an embassy after him, saying, "We do not want this man to reign over us." When he returned, having received the kingly power, he commanded these servants to be called to him, that he might know what they had gained by trading. The first came, saying, "Lord, your pound has made ten pounds more." He said, "Well done, good servant! Because you have been faithful in a very little, you shall have authority over ten cities." The second came, saying, "Lord, your pound has made five pounds." He said, "And you are to be over five cities." Then another came, saying, "Lord, here is your pound, which I kept laid away in a napkin; for I was afraid of you, because you are a severe man; you take up what you did not lay down, and reap what you did not sow." He said, "I will condemn you out of your own mouth, you wicked servant! You knew that I was a severe man, taking up what I did not lay down and reaping what I did not sow! Why then did you not put my money into the bank, and at my coming I should have collected it with interest?" He said, "Take the pound from him, and give it to him who has the ten pounds." I tell you, that to everyone who has will more be given; but from him who has not, even what he has will be taken away.' St Luke 19.12–26*

RESPONSE 'Ye servants of God, your Master proclaim,
and publish abroad his wonderful name.'

Eternal God, you are the giver of all good gifts – we praise you for your love which surpasses all our desires and understanding . . .
'Trade with these till I come' – help us to use our time and skills in a responsible way, and for the benefit of your Church and Kingdom . . .
'We do not want this man to reign over us' – Lord, help us to seek and to accept your will with joy in all areas of our lives . . .

INTERCESSIONS *pages 390–393* CLOSING PRAYERS *page 402–403*

OPENING PRAYER Eternal God, to you alone belong honour and glory and power. In your mercy, assist us in these prayers and praises, offered to you through our Lord and Saviour Jesus Christ . . . Glory be . . .

PSALMODY The Lord reigns; let the peoples tremble!
He sits enthroned upon the cherubin; let the earth quake!
The Lord is great in Zion; he is exalted over all the peoples.
Let them praise thy great and terrible name! Holy is he!
Mighty King, lover of justice, thou has established equity;
thou has executed justice and righteousness in Jacob.
Extol the Lord our God; worship at his footstool!
Holy is he! Psalm 99.1–5

SCRIPTURE READINGS

Rejoice greatly, O daughter of Zion!
Lo, your king comes to you;
triumphant and victorious is he,
humble and riding on an ass. Zechariah 9.9*

When Jesus drew near to Bethphage and Bethany, at the mount that is called Olivet, he sent two disciples, saying, 'Go into the village opposite, where on entering you will find a colt tied, on which no one has ever yet sat: untie it and bring it here. If any one asks you, "Why are you untying it?" you shall say this, "The Lord has need of it."' So those who were sent went away and found it as he had told them. As they were untying the colt, its owners said, 'Why are you untying the colt?' They said, 'The Lord has need of it.' They brought it to Jesus, and throwing their garments on the colt they set Jesus upon it. As he rode along, they spread their garments on the road. As he was now drawing near, at the descent of the Mount of Olives, the whole multitude of the disciples began to rejoice and praise God with a loud voice for all the mighty works that they had seen, saying, 'Blessed is the King who comes in the name of the Lord! Peace in heaven and glory in the highest!' Some Pharisees said, 'Teacher, rebuke your disciples.' He answered, 'I tell you, if these were silent, the very stones would cry out.' St Luke 19.29–40*

RESPONSE 'Thou art the King of Israel, thou David's royal Son,
who in the Lord's name comest, the King and blessed one.'

Heavenly Father, you call us to live for the praise of your glory. . .we rejoice to acclaim your Son as Messiah and King . . .
Your Son showed great courage by riding into Jerusalem in triumph – Lord, strengthen your Church, and give us courage to do your will . . .
'The whole multitude of the disciples began to rejoice and praise God' – receive our praises offered through the perfect praise of your Son . . .

INTERCESSIONS *pages 390–393* CLOSING PRAYERS *page 402–403*

OPENING PRAYER Eternal God, to you alone belong honour and glory and power. In your mercy, assist us in these prayers and praises, offered to you through our Lord and Saviour Jesus Christ . . . Glory be . . .

PSALMODY Moses and Aaron were among his priests,
Samuel also was among those who called on his name.
They cried to the Lord, and he answered them.
O Lord our God, thou didst answer them;
thou wast a forgiving God to them,
but an avenger of their wrongdoings.
Extol the Lord our God,
and worship at his holy mountain;
for the Lord our God is holy. Psalm 99.6–9

SCRIPTURE READINGS Examine yourselves, to see whether you are holding to your faith. Test yourselves. Do you not realize that Jesus Christ is in you? – unless indeed you fail to meet the test! I hope you will find out that we have not failed. But we pray God that you may not do wrong – not that we may appear to have met the test, but that you may do what is right, though we may seem to have failed. For we cannot do anything against the truth, but only for the truth. 2 Corinthians 13.5–8

One day, as Jesus was teaching the people in the temple and preaching the gospel, the chief priests and the scribes with the elders came up and said, 'Tell us by what authority you do these things, or who it is that gave you this authority.' He answered, 'I also will ask you a question; now tell me, Was the baptism of John from heaven or from men?' They discussed it with one another, saying, 'If we say "From heaven," he will say, "Why did you not believe him?" But if we say, "From men," all the people will stone us; for they are convinced that John was a prophet.' So they answered that they did not know whence it was. Jesus said, 'Neither will I tell you by what authority I do these things.' St Luke 20.1–8*

RESPONSE 'All hail the power of Jesus's name; let angels prostrate fall.
Bring forth the royal diadem, and crown him Lord of all.'

Eternal God, you gave all authority in heaven and on earth to your Son – we praise you for the mystery of your power and love in the Church . . .
'Was the baptism of John from heaven or from men?' – we thank you for our baptism into the death and resurrection of Christ, and we praise you . . .
'They were convinced that John was a prophet' – Lord, we pray that all people will come to accept your Son as Lord and Saviour . . .

INTERCESSIONS *pages 390–393* CLOSING PRAYERS *page 402–403*

1 August *The Parable of the Vineyard*

OPENING PRAYER O come, let us sing to the Lord; let us make a joyful noise to the God of our salvation. Let us come into his presence with thanksgiving. Let us offer to him our songs of praise . . . Glory be . . .

PSALMODY Give thanks to him, bless his name!
For the Lord is good;
his steadfast love endures for ever,
and his faithfulness to all generations. Psalm 100.4–5

SCRIPTURE READINGS Isaac said to Abraham, 'Behold, the fire and the wood; but where is the lamb for a burnt offering?' Abraham said, 'God will provide himself the lamb for a burnt offering, my son.' When they came to the place of which God had told him, Abraham built an altar, and laid the wood in order, and bound Isaac his son, and laid him on the altar. Abraham took the knife to slay his son. The angel of the Lord called, 'Do not lay your hand on the lad; for now I know that you fear God, seeing you have not withheld your son, your only son, from me.' Abraham lifted up his eyes, and behind him was a ram, caught in a thicket; and Abraham offered it as a burnt offering instead of his son. Genesis 22.7–14*

Jesus told this parable: 'A man planted a vineyard, and let it out to tenants, and went into another country. When the time came, he sent a servant to the tenants, that they should give him some of the fruit of the vineyard; but the tenants beat him, and sent him away empty-handed. He sent another servant; him they beat and treated shamefully, and sent him away empty-handed. He sent a third; this one they wounded and cast out. Then the owner of the vineyard said, "What shall I do? I will send my beloved son; it may be they will respect him." When the tenants saw him, they said, "This is the heir; let us kill him, that the inheritance may be ours." They cast him out of the vineyard and killed him. What then will the owner of the vineyard do? He will come and destroy those tenants, and give the vineyard to others.' When they heard this, they said, 'God forbid!' He said, 'What then is this that is written: "The very stone which the builders rejected has become the head of the corner"?' St Luke 20.9–17*

RESPONSE 'There is a green hill far away, without a city wall,
where the dear Lord was crucified, who died to save us all.'

Eternal God, you chose to reveal your will to the Israelites – we rejoice that our salvation is of the Jews, and we praise you for your love in Jesus Christ . . .
'A man planted a vineyard, and let it out to tenants' – we pray for the Jews, and we rejoice that they are still your chosen people . . .
'I will send my Beloved Son' – Lord, we thank you for the death and resurrection of your Son, and for the Church which he created . . .

INTERCESSIONS *pages 390–393* CLOSING PRAYERS *page 402–403*

2 August *God and Caesar*

OPENING PRAYER O come, let us sing to the Lord; let us make a joyful noise to the God of our salvation. Let us come into his presence with thanksgiving. Let us offer to him our songs of praise . . . Glory be . . .

PSALMODY I will sing of loyalty and of justice;
to thee, O Lord, I will sing.
I will give heed to the way that is blameless.
Oh when wilt thou come to me?
I will walk with integrity of heart within my house.

Psalm 101.1–2

SCRIPTURE READINGS David said to the Philistine, 'You come to me with a sword and with a spear and with a javelin; but I come to you in the name of the Lord of hosts, the God of the armies of Israel, whom you have defied. This day the Lord will deliver you into my hand, and I will strike you down; that all the earth may know that there is a God in Israel, and that all this assembly may know that the Lord saves not with sword and spear; for the battle is the Lord's and he will give you into our hand.' So David prevailed over the Philistine with a sling and with a stone.

1 Samuel 17.45–50*

The scribes and the chief priests tried to lay hands on Jesus at that very hour, but they feared the people; for they perceived that he had told this parable against them. So they watched him, and sent spies, who pretended to be sincere, that they might take hold of what he said, so as to deliver him up to the authority and jurisdiction of the governor. They asked him, 'Teacher, we know that you speak and teach rightly, and show no partiality, but truly teach the way of God. Is it lawful for us to give tribute to Caesar, or not?' But he perceived their craftiness, and said to them, 'Show me a coin. Whose likeness and inscription has it?' They said, 'Caesar's.' He said, 'Then render to Caesar the things that are Caesar's, and to God the things that are God's.' They were not able in the presence of the people to catch him by what he said; but marvelling at his answer they were silent.

St Luke 20.19–26

RESPONSE 'The Lord reigns; he is robed in majesty;
the Lord is robed, he is girded with strength.'

Eternal God, you are enthroned on high and rule in majesty and power – all praise and glory to you, Father, Son and Holy Spirit, one God for ever . . .
'Render to Caesar the things that are Caesar's' – inspire all Christians to be responsible members of their local community . . .
'Render to God the things that are God's' – purify our lives, and help us to worship you with all our heart and mind and soul and strength . . .

INTERCESSIONS *pages 390–393* CLOSING PRAYERS *page 402–403*

OPENING PRAYER O come, let us sing to the Lord; let us make a joyful noise to the God of our salvation. Let us come into his presence with thanksgiving. Let us offer to him our songs of praise . . . Glory be . . .

PSALMODY I will look with favour on the faithful in the land,
that they may dwell with me;
he who walks in the way that is blameless shall minister to me.
No man who practises deceit shall dwell in my house;
no man who utters lies shall continue in my presence.
Psalm 101.6–8

SCRIPTURE READINGS Now may our Lord Jesus Christ himself, and God our Father, who loved us and gave us eternal comfort and good hope through grace, comfort your hearts and establish them in every good work and word. 2 Thessalonians 2.16–17

Some Sadducees, who say that there is no resurrection, asked Jesus a question, saying, 'Teacher, Moses wrote for us that if a man's brother dies, having a wife but no children, the man must take the wife and raise up children for his brother. Now there were seven brothers; the first took a wife, and died without children; and the second and the third took her, and likewise all seven left no children and died. Afterward the woman also died. In the resurrection, therefore, whose wife will the woman be? For the seven had her as wife.' Jesus said, 'The sons of this age marry and are given in marriage; but those who are accounted worthy to attain to that age and to the resurrection from the dead neither marry nor are given in marriage, for they cannot die any more; because they are equal to angels and are sons of God, being sons of the resurrection. But that the dead are raised, even Moses showed, in the passage about the bush, where he calls the Lord the God of Abraham and the God of Isaac and the God of Jacob. Now he is not God of the dead, but of the living; for all live to him.' Some of the scribes answered, 'Teacher, you have spoken well.' St Luke 20.27–40

RESPONSE 'Father of Jesus, love's reward, what rapture will it be
prostrate before thy throne to lie, and gaze and gaze on thee.'

Eternal Father, you are the God of Abraham, Isaac and Jacob – we praise you for the glorious hope of eternal life in your Son . . .
'The sons of this age marry and are given in marriage' – bless all who are married and all who live alone, and purify all our relationships . . .
'He is not God of the dead, but of the living' – we praise you with the Blessed Virgin Mary, the prophets, apostles and the saints of heaven . . .

INTERCESSIONS *pages 390–393* CLOSING PRAYERS *page 402–403*

OPENING PRAYER O come, let us sing to the Lord; let us make a joyful noise to the God of our salvation. Let us come into his presence with thanksgiving. Let us offer to him our songs of praise . . . Glory be . . .

PSALMODY Hear my prayer, O Lord; let my cry come to thee!
Do not hide thy face from me in the day of my distress!
Incline thy ear to me;
answer me speedily in the day when I call!
For my days pass away like smoke,
and my bones burn like a furnace.
My days are like an evening shadow.
But thou, O Lord, art enthroned for ever;
thy name endures to all generations.
Thou wilt arise and have pity on Zion;
it is the time to favour her;
the appointed time has come. Psalm 102.1–13*

SCRIPTURE READINGS Another angel came out of the temple, calling with a loud voice to him who sat upon the cloud, 'Put in the sickle, and reap, for the hour to reap has come, for the harvest of the earth is fully ripe.'
Revelation 14.15

Jesus saw the rich putting their gifts into the treasury; and he saw a poor widow put in two copper coins. He said, 'Truly I tell you, this poor widow has put in more than all of them; for they all contributed out of their abundance, but she out of her poverty put in all the living that she had.' And as some spoke of the temple, how it was adorned with noble stones and offerings, he said, 'As for these things which you see, the days will come when there shall not be left here one stone upon another that will not be thrown down.' They asked, 'Teacher, when will this be, and what will be the sign when this is about to take place?' He said, 'Take heed that you are not led astray; for many will come in my name, saying, "I am he!" and, "The time is at hand!" Do not go after them. When you hear of wars and tumults, do not be terrified; for this must first take place, but the end will not be at once.' St Luke 21.1–9

RESPONSE 'On God rests my deliverance and my honour;
my mighty rock, my refuge is God.'

Heavenly Father, you give yourself to us in your Son – we offer praise to you in union with the perfect praise of your Son . . .
'She out of her poverty put in all the living she had' – inspire your Church to reflect on the sacrificial giving of your Son . . .
'The time is at hand' – Lord, help us to use all our time wisely . . .

INTERCESSIONS *pages 390–393* CLOSING PRAYERS *page 402–403*

OPENING PRAYER O come, let us sing to the Lord; let us make a joyful noise to the God of our salvation. Let us come into his presence with thanksgiving. Let us offer to him our songs of praise . . . Glory be . . .

PSALMODY The nations will fear the name of the Lord,
and all the kings of the earth thy glory.
For the Lord will build up Zion,
he will appear in his glory;
he will regard the prayer of the destitute,
and will not despise their supplication. Psalm 102.15–17

SCRIPTURE READINGS 'It is the Lord's Passover. For I will pass through the land of Egypt that night, and I will smite all the first-born in the land of Egypt, both man and beast; and on all the gods of Egypt I will execute judgements: I am the Lord. The blood shall be a sign for you, upon the houses where you are; and when I see the blood, I will pass over you, and no plague shall fall upon you to destroy you, when I smite the land of Egypt. This day shall be for you a memorial day, and you shall keep it as a feast to the Lord.' Exodus 12.11–14

Then came the day of Unleavened Bread, on which the passover lamb had to be sacrificed. So Jesus sent Peter and John, saying, 'Go and prepare the passover for us, that we may eat it.' They said to him, 'Where will you have us prepare it?' He said to them, 'Behold, when you have entered the city, a man carrying a jar of water will meet you; follow him into the house which he enters, and tell the householder, "The Teacher says to you, Where is the guest room, where I am to eat the passover with my disciples?" And he will show you a large upper room furnished; there make ready.' And they went, and found it as he had told them; and they prepared the passover. St Luke 22.7–13

RESPONSE 'My God, and is thy Table spread,
and does thy Cup with love o'erflow?'

Eternal God, you made a new and everlasting Covenant with us through the self-offering of your Son – we rejoice in the hope of sharing his glory . . .
'Go and prepare the Passover for us' – Lord, help us to prepare ourselves properly to receive the Body and Blood of Christ in the Eucharist . . .
'We are the Body of Christ' – feed us with the Body of Christ at the altar and strengthen us to serve you as His Body in the world . . .

INTERCESSIONS *pages 390–393* CLOSING PRAYERS *page 402–403*

OPENING PRAYER O come, let us sing to the Lord; let us make a joyful noise to the God of our salvation. Let us come into his presence with thanksgiving. Let us offer to him our songs of praise . . . Glory be . . .

PSALMODY How lovely is thy dwelling place, O Lord of hosts!
My soul longs, yea, faints for the courts of the Lord;
my heart and flesh sing for joy to the living God.
Even the sparrow finds a home,
and the swallow a nest for herself,
where she may lay her young,
at thy altars, O Lord of hosts,
my King and my God.
Blessed are those who dwell in thy house,
ever singing thy praise! Psalm 84.1–4

SCRIPTURE READINGS It is the God who said, 'Let light shine out of darkness,' who has shone in our hearts to give the light of the knowledge of the glory of God in the face of Christ. 2 Corinthians 4.6

Jesus took with him Peter and John and James, and went up on the mountain to pray. As he was praying, the appearance of his countenance was altered, and his raiment became dazzling white. And behold, two men talked with him, Moses and Elijah, who appeared in glory and spoke of his departure, which he was to accomplish at Jerusalem. Peter and those who were with him were heavy with sleep, and when they wakened they saw his glory and the two men who stood with him. As the men were parting from him, Peter said to Jesus, 'Master, it is well that we are here; let us make three booths, one for you and one for Moses and one for Elijah' – not knowing what he said. As he said this a cloud came and overshadowed them; and they were afraid as they entered the cloud. A voice came out of the cloud, saying, 'This is my Son, my Chosen; listen to him!' When the voice had spoken, Jesus was found alone. They kept silence and told no one in those days anything of what they had seen. St Luke 9.28–36

RESPONSE 'Praise to the holiest in the height, and in the depth be praise,
in all his words most wonderful, most sure in all his ways.'

God of Eternal Glory, you revealed the glory of your Son before he suffered on the Cross – we celebrate this Feast of the Transfiguration in union with your holy Church throughout the world . . .
Your son was revealed in glory – Lord, open our eyes and give us a new vision of your glory in the world . . .
The Transfiguration gave your approval for your Son to set out for Jerusalem and the Cross – we praise you for his redeeming love . . .

INTERCESSIONS *pages 390–393* CLOSING PRAYERS *page 402–403*

OPENING PRAYER O come, let us sing to the Lord; let us make a joyful noise to the God of our salvation. Let us come into his presence with thanksgiving. Let us offer to him our songs of praise . . . Glory be . . .

PSALMODY Let this be recorded for a generation to come,
so that a people yet unborn may praise the Lord:
that men may declare in Zion the name of the Lord,
and in Jerusalem his praise,
when peoples gather together,
and kingdoms, to worship the Lord. Psalm 102.18–22*

SCRIPTURE READINGS You shall observe this rite as an ordinance for you and for your sons for ever. When you come to the land which the Lord will give you, as he has promised, you shall keep this service. And when your children say to you, "What do you mean by this service?" you shall say, "It is the sacrifice of the Lord's passover, for he passed over the houses of the people of Israel in Egypt, when he slew the Egyptians but spared our houses."' Exodus 12.24–27

When the hour came, Jesus sat at table, and the apostles with him. He said, 'I have earnestly desired to eat this passover with you before I suffer; for I tell you I shall not eat it until it is fulfilled in the Kingdom of God.' And he took a cup, and when he had given thanks he said, 'Take this, and divide it among yourselves; for I tell you that from now on I shall not drink of the fruit of the vine until the Kingdom of God comes.' And he took bread, and when he had given thanks he broke it and gave it to them, saying, 'This is my body which is given for you. Do this in remembrance of me.' And likewise the cup after supper, saying, 'This cup which is poured out for you is the new covenant in my blood. But behold the hand of him who betrays me is with me on the table. For the Son of Man goes as it has been determined; but woe to that man by whom he is betrayed!' And they began to question one another, which of them it was that would do this. A dispute also arose among them, which of them was to be regarded as the greatest.
St Luke 22.14–24

RESPONSE 'Hail, sacred feast which Jesus makes,
rich banquet of his flesh and blood.'

Almighty God, in the Eucharist, you give us the benefits won by your Son at Calvary – we praise you for uniting us in your love . . .
Your Son builds up the Church by the Holy Spirit in the Eucharist – we rejoice that we are in communion with Jesus and with each other . . .
'This is my Body' – help us to look back to our last Eucharist with thanksgiving, and to look forward to the next in hope . . .

INTERCESSIONS *pages 390–393* CLOSING PRAYERS *page 402–403*

8 August *Faith*

OPENING PRAYER O come, let us sing to the Lord; let us make a joyful noise to the God of our salvation. Let us come into his presence with thanksgiving. Let us offer to him our songs of praise . . . Glory be . . .

PSALMODY He has broken my strength in mid-course;
he has shortened my days.
'Oh my God,' I say, 'take me not hence
in the midst of my days,
thou whose years endure
through all generations!' Psalm 102.23–24

SCRIPTURE READINGS We see Jesus, who for a little while was made lower than the angels, crowned with glory and honour because of the suffering of death, so that by the grace of God he might taste death for every one. For it was fitting that he, for whom and by whom all things exist, in bringing many sons to glory, should make the pioneer of their salvation perfect through suffering. For he who sanctifies and those who are sanctified have all one origin. Hebrews 2.9–11

Jesus said, 'You are those who have continued with me in my trials; and I assign to you, as my Father assigned to me, a kingdom, that you may eat and drink at my table in my kingdom, and sit on thrones judging the twelve tribes of Israel. Simon, Simon, behold, Satan demanded to have you, that he might sift you like wheat, but I have prayed for you that your faith may not fail; and when you have turned again, strengthen your brethren.' He said to him, 'Lord, I am ready to go with you to prison and to death.' He said, 'I tell you, Peter, the cock will not crow this day, until you three times deny that you know me.' He said, 'When I sent you out with no purse or bag or sandals, did you lack anything?' They said, 'Nothing.' He said, 'But now, let him who has a purse take it, and likewise a bag. Let him who has no sword sell his mantle and buy one. For I tell you that this scripture must be fulfilled in me, "And he was reckoned with transgressors"; for what is written about me has its fulfilment.' They said, 'Look, Lord, here are two swords.' And he said, 'It is enough.' St Luke 22.28–38

RESPONSE 'Be pleased, O Lord, to deliver me!
O Lord, make haste to help me.'

Heavenly Father, you reach out to us in love through your Son – help us by the Spirit to respond with praise and thanksgiving and love . . .
'I have prayed for you that your faith may not fail' – forgive us when we fail you, and strengthen your gift of faith in our hearts . . .
'The cock will not crow this day, until you three times deny that you know me' – when we fail, look on us with mercy, and restore us to yourself . . .

INTERCESSIONS *pages 390–393* CLOSING PRAYERS *page 402–403*

9 August *Jesus is Arrested*

OPENING PRAYER O come, let us sing to the Lord; let us make a joyful noise to the God of our salvation. Let us come into his presence with thanksgiving. Let us offer to him our songs of praise . . . Glory be . . .

PSALMODY Of old thou didst lay the foundation of the earth,
and the heavens are the work of thy hands.
They will perish, but thou dost endure;
they will all wear out like a garment.
Thou changest them like raiment, and they pass away;
but thou art the same, and thy years have no end.
The children of thy servants shall dwell secure;
their posterity shall be established before thee.
Psalm 102.25–28

SCRIPTURE READINGS Every high priest is appointed to offer gifts and sacrifices; hence it is necessary for this priest also to have something to offer. Hebrews 8.3

Jesus went to the Mount of Olives; and the disciples followed him. He said, 'Pray that you may not enter into temptation.' He withdrew from them about a stone's throw, and knelt down and prayed, 'Father, if thou art willing, remove this cup from me; nevertheless not my will, but thine, be done.' When he rose from prayer, he came to the disciples and found them sleeping for sorrow, and he said, 'Why do you sleep? Rise and pray that you may not enter into temptation.' While he was still speaking, there came a crowd, and the man called Judas, one of the twelve, was leading them. He drew near to Jesus to kiss him; but Jesus said, 'Judas, would you betray the Son of Man with a kiss?' When those who were about him saw what would follow, they said, 'Lord, shall we strike with the sword?' One of them struck the slave of the high priest and cut off his right ear. Jesus said, 'No more of this!' He touched his ear and healed him. Jesus said, 'Have you come out as against a robber, with swords and clubs? When I was with you day after day in the temple, you did not lay hands on me. But this is your hour, and the power of darkness.' They seized him and led him away. St Luke 22.39–54

RESPONSE 'In your hearts enthrone him; there let him subdue
all that is not holy, all that is not true.'

All-powerful and eternal God, your Son allowed himself to be arrested for our salvation – we praise you for his faith and courage . . .
'Pray that you may not enter into temptation' – help us to avoid all occasions which may lead to sin, and keep us firm in the faith . . .
'Not my will, but thine, be done' – help us to seek and do your will . . .

INTERCESSIONS *pages 390–393* CLOSING PRAYERS *page 402–403*

10 August *Peter's Denial*

OPENING PRAYER O come, let us sing to the Lord; let us make a joyful noise to the God of our salvation. Let us come into his presence with thanksgiving. Let us offer to him our songs of praise . . . Glory be . . .

PSALMODY Bless the Lord, O my soul;
and all that is within me, bless his holy name!
Bless the Lord, O my soul,
and forget not all his benefits. Psalm 103.1–2

SCRIPTURE READINGS Christ has obtained a ministry which is as much more excellent than the old as the covenant he mediates is better, since it is enacted on better promises. Hebrews 8.6

Peter followed at a distance; when they had kindled a fire in the middle of the courtyard and sat down together, Peter sat among them. Then a maid said, 'This man also was with him.' He denied it, saying, 'Woman, I do not know him.' A little later some one else saw him and said, 'You also are one of them.' But Peter said, 'Man, I am not.' After an interval of about an hour still another insisted, saying, 'Certainly this man also was with him; for he is a Galilean.' Peter said, 'Man, I do not know what you are saying.' Immediately, while he was still speaking, the cock crowed. The Lord turned and looked at Peter. Peter remembered the word of the Lord, how he had said, 'Before the cock crows today, you will deny me three times.' He went out and wept bitterly. The men who were holding Jesus mocked him and beat him; they blindfolded him and asked, 'Prophesy! Who is it that struck you?' They spoke many other words against him, reviling him. When day came, the assembly of the elders of the people gathered together, both chief priests and scribes; and they led him away to their council, and they said, 'If you are the Christ, tell us.' He said, 'If I tell you, you will not believe, and if I ask you, you will not answer. But from now on the Son of Man shall be seated at the right hand of the power of God.' They all said, 'Are you the Son of God, then?' He said, 'You say that I am.' They said, 'What further testimony do we need? We have heard it ourselves from his own lips.' St Luke 22.54–71*

RESPONSE 'Saviour, breathe forgiveness o'er us,
all our weakness thou dost know.'

Heavenly Father, you sent your Son to redeem us – we praise you for the love and obedience of Jesus, even to death on the Cross . . .
'This man also was with him' – grant that we may be with you, and you with us, now and always . . .
'Before the cock crows, you will deny me three times' – Lord, forgive us when we fail you, and help us to grow in faith and love . . .

INTERCESSIONS *pages 390–393* CLOSING PRAYERS *page 402–403*

11 August *Trial Before Pilate and King Herod*

OPENING PRAYER O come, let us sing to the Lord; let us make a joyful noise to the God of our salvation. Let us come into his presence with thanksgiving. Let us offer to him our songs of praise . . . Glory be . . .

PSALMODY The Lord works vindication and justice for all who are oppressed.
He made known his ways to Moses,
his acts to the people of Israel.
The Lord is merciful and gracious,
slow to anger and abounding in steadfast love.
He will not always chide, nor will he keep his anger for ever.
He does not deal with us according to our sins.
For as the heavens are high above the earth,
so great is his steadfast love toward those who fear him.
Psalm 103.6–11*

SCRIPTURE READINGS One is approved if, mindful of God, he endures pain while suffering unjustly. 1 Peter 2.19

Then the whole company of them arose, and brought Jesus before Pilate. They began to accuse him, saying, 'We found this man perverting our nation, and forbidding us to give tribute to Caesar, and saying that he himself is Christ a king.' Pilate asked him, 'Are you the King of the Jews?' He answered, 'You have said so.' Pilate said to the chief priests and the multitudes, 'I find no crime in this man.' But they were urgent, saying, 'He stirs up the people, teaching throughout all Judea, from Galilee even to this place.' When Pilate heard this, he asked whether the man was a Galilean,. When he learned that he belonged to Herod's jurisdiction, he sent him over to Herod, who was himself in Jerusalem at that time. When Herod saw Jesus, he was very glad, for he had long desired to see him, because he had heard about him, and he was hoping to see some sign done by him. He questioned him at some length; but he made no answer. The chief priests and the scribes stood by, vehemently accusing him. Herod with his soldiers treated him with contempt and mocked him; then, arraying him in gorgeous apparel, he sent him back to Pilate. Herod and Pilate became friends with each other that very day, for before this they had been at enmity with each other. St Luke 23.1–12*

RESPONSE 'Jesus, the Saviour reigns, the God of truth and love;
when he had purged our stains, he took his seat above.'

Eternal Lord God, your son will come again to judge the living and the dead – have mercy and forgive us all our sins that we might praise you . . . 'Are you the King of the Jews?' – we worship you, King of all creation . . . 'He stirs up the people' – Lord, stir up our hearts and inspire your Church to work and pray for the coming of your Kingdom . . .

INTERCESSIONS *pages 390–393* CLOSING PRAYERS *page 402–403*

12 August *Delivered up to their Will*

OPENING PRAYER O come, let us sing to the Lord; let us make a joyful noise to the God of our salvation. Let us come into his presence with thanksgiving. Let us offer to him our songs of praise . . . Glory be . . .

PSALMODY As a father pities his children,
so the Lord pities those who fear him.
For he knows our frame;
he remembers that we are but dust.
As for man, his days are like grass;
he flourishes like a flower of the field;
for the wind passes over it, and it is gone.
But the steadfast love of the Lord
is from everlasting to everlasting
upon those who fear him,
and his righteousness to children's children.

Psalm 103.13–17*

SCRIPTURE READINGS He committed no sin; no guile was found on his lips. When he was reviled, he did not revile in return; when he suffered, he did not threaten; but he trusted in him who judges justly. 1 Peter 2.22–23

Pilate called together the chief priests and the rulers and the people, and said, 'You brought me this man as one who was perverting the people; after examining him before you, behold, I did not find this man guilty of any of your charges against him; neither did Herod, for he sent him back to us. Behold, nothing deserving death has been done by him; I will chastise him and release him.' They all cried out, 'Away with this man, and release to us Barabbas' – a man who had been thrown into prison for an insurrection started in the city, and for murder. Pilate addressed them once more, desiring to release Jesus; but they shouted out, 'Crucify, crucify him!' A third time he said, 'Why, what evil has he done? I have found in him no crime deserving death; I will chastise him and release him.' They were urgent, demanding that he should be crucified. Their voices prevailed. So Pilate gave sentence that their demand should be granted. He released the man who had been thrown into prison for insurrection and murder; but Jesus he delivered up to their will. St Luke23.13–25*

RESPONSE 'Be merciful to me, O God, be merciful to me,
for in thee my soul takes refuge.'

Eternal God, you alone are full of compassion and love for all people – to you be the praise, Father, Son and Holy Spirit, one God for ever . . .
'I did not find this man guilty of any of your charges' – in your mercy, wipe away our guilt, and fill us with your love . . .
'They were urgent' – inspire in us a sense of urgency to do your work . . .

INTERCESSIONS *pages 390–393* CLOSING PRAYERS *page 402–403*

OPENING PRAYER O come, let us sing to the Lord; let us make a joyful noise to the God of our salvation. Let us come into his presence with thanksgiving. Let us offer to him our songs of praise . . . Glory be . . .

PSALMODY The Lord has established his throne in the heavens,
and his kingdom rules over all.
Bless the Lord, O you his angels,
you mighty ones who do his word,
Bless the Lord, all his hosts, his ministers that do his will!
Bless the Lord, all his works, in all places of his dominion.
Bless the Lord, O my soul. Psalm 103.19–22*

SCRIPTURE READINGS He himself bore our sins in his body on the tree, that we might die to sin and live to righteousness. By his wounds you have been healed. 1 Peter 2.24

As they led Jesus away, they seized one Simon of Cyrene, who was coming in from the country, and laid on him the cross, to carry it behind Jesus. There followed him a great multitude of the people, and of women who bewailed and lamented him. Jesus turning to them said, 'Daughters of Jerusalem, do not weep for me, but weep for yourselves and for your children. For behold, the days are coming when they will say, "Blessed are the barren, and the wombs that never bore, and the breasts that never gave suck!" Then they will begin to say to the mountains, "Fall on us"; and to the hills, "Cover us." For if they do this when the wood is green, what will happen when it is dry?' Two others also, who were criminals, were led away to be put to death with him. When they came to the place which is called The Skull, there they crucified him, and the criminals, one on the right and one on the left. Jesus said, 'Father, forgive them; for they know not what they do.' They cast lots to divide his garments. The people stood by, watching; but the rulers scoffed at him, saying, "He saved others; let him save himself, if he is the Christ of God, his Chosen One!' The soldiers also mocked him, coming up and offering him vinegar, and saying, 'If you are the King of the Jews, save yourself!' There was an inscription over him, 'This is the King of the Jews.' St Luke 23.26–38

RESPONSE 'We may not know, we cannot tell, what pains he had to bear;
but we believe it was for us he hung and suffered there.'

Merciful Father, your Son accepted death on the Cross for our salvation – we praise you and worship you for your goodness and love . . .
'Father, forgive them, for they know not what they do' – Lord, teach us how to forgive others, as you forgive us . . .
'He saved others; let him save himself' – we thank you for the self-offering of your Son as Priest and Victim on the Cross for us . . .

INTERCESSIONS *pages 390–393* CLOSING PRAYERS *page 402–403*

14 August

Jesus Dies on the Cross

OPENING PRAYER O come, let us sing to the Lord; let us make a joyful noise to the God of our salvation. Let us come into his presence with thanksgiving. Let us offer to him our songs of praise . . . Glory be . . .

PSALMODY Hear my prayer, O Lord; give ear to my supplications!
For the enemy has pursued me;
Let me hear in the morning of thy steadfast love,
for in thee I put my trust. Psalm 143.1–8*

SCRIPTURE READINGS When Christ had offered for all time a single sacrifice for sins, he sat down at the right hand of God, then to wait until his enemies should be made a stool for his feet. Hebrews 10.12–13

One of the criminals who were hanged railed at him, saying, 'Are you not the Christ? Save yourself and us!' But the other rebuked him, saying, 'Do you not fear God, since you are under the same sentence of condemnation? And we indeed justly; for we are receiving the due reward of our deeds; but this man has done nothing wrong.' He said, 'Jesus, remember me when you come into your kingdom.' He said, 'Truly, I say to you, today you will be with me in Paradise.' It was now the sixth hour, and there was darkness over the whole land until the ninth hour, while the sun's light failed; and the curtain of the temple was torn in two. Then Jesus, crying with a loud voice, said, 'Father, into thy hands I commit my spirit!' Having said this he breathed his last. When the centurion saw what had taken place, he praised God, and said, 'Certainly this man was innocent!' The multitudes who assembled to see the sight, when they saw what had taken place, returned home beating their breasts. All his acquaintances and the women who had followed him from Galilee stood at a distance and saw these things. Now there was a man named Joseph from Arimathea. He was a member of the council, a good and righteous man, who had not consented to their purpose and deed, and he was looking for the Kingdom of God. This man went to Pilate and asked for the body of Jesus. He took it down and wrapped it in a linen shroud, and laid him in a rock-hewn tomb, where no one had ever yet been laid. St Luke 23.39–53*

RESPONSE 'O dearly, dearly has he loved, and we must love him too,
and trust in his redeeming Blood, and try his works to do.'

Ever-living God, your Son endured the Cross for our salvation – we praise you and thank you for his eternal victory over sin and death . . .
'The Good Shepherd lays down his life for the sheep' – Lord, draw all people to yourself through the power of the sacred Cross . . .
'Father, into thy hands I commit my spirit' – grant rest and peace to all who have died in the faith of Christ, and raise them on the last day . . .

INTERCESSIONS *pages 390–393* CLOSING PRAYERS *page 402–403*

15 August *Saint Mary the Virgin*

OPENING PRAYER O come, let us sing to the Lord; let us make a joyful noise to the God of our salvation. Let us come into his presence with thanksgiving. Let us offer to him our songs of praise . . . Glory be . . .

PSALMODY Daughters of kings are among your ladies of honour;
at your right hand stands the queen in gold of Ophir.
Hear, O daughter, consider, and incline your ear;
and the king will desire your beauty.
Since he is your lord, bow to him.
With joy and gladness they are led along
as they enter the palace of the king. Psalm 45.8–15*

SCRIPTURE READINGS
You, O Bethlehem Ephrathah,
who are little to be among the clans of Judah,
from you shall come forth for me
one who is to be ruler in Israel,
whose origin is from of old, from ancient days.
Therefore he shall give them up until the time
when she who is in travail has brought forth;
then the rest of his brethren shall return
to the people of Israel.
And he shall stand and feed his flock
in the strength of the Lord,
in the majesty of the name of the Lord his God.
And they shall dwell secure, for now he shall be great
to the ends of the earth. Micah 5.2–4

It is impossible that the blood of bulls and goats should take away sins. Consequently, when Christ came into the world, he said,
'Sacrifices and offerings thou hast not desired,
but a body hast thou prepared for me.
Then I said, "Lo, I have come to do thy will, O God."'
And by that will we have been sanctified through the offering of the body of Jesus Christ once for all. Hebrews 10.4–10*

RESPONSE 'My mouth is filled with thy praise,
and with thy glory all the day.'

Eternal God, you took flesh in the womb of Mary to restore your divine life in fallen humanity – we praise you for the love of Mary . . .
'Blessed are those who hear the Word of God and keep it' – help us to follow the example of Mary in doing your will . . .
You chose Mary to be the mother of our Saviour – in your mercy, bring us to share in the glory of your kingdom with Mary and all the saints . . .

INTERCESSIONS *pages 390–393* CLOSING PRAYERS *page 402–403*

OPENING PRAYER O come, let us sing to the Lord; let us make a joyful noise to the God of our salvation. Let us come into his presence with thanksgiving. Let us offer to him our songs of praise . . . Glory be . . .

PSALMODY Bless the Lord, O my soul!
O Lord my God, thou art very great!
Thou art clothed with honour and majesty,
who coverest thyself with light as with a garment,
who hast stretched out the heavens like a tent,
who hast laid the beams of thy chambers on the waters,
who makest the clouds thy chariot,
who ridest on the wings of the wind,
who makest the winds thy messengers,
fire and flame thy ministers.
Bless the Lord, O my soul! Praise the Lord.

Psalm 104.1–35*

SCRIPTURE READINGS 'Fear not, I am the first and the last, and the living one; I died, and behold I am alive for evermore, and I have the keys of Death and Hades.' Revelation 1.18

On the sabbath day the women from Galilee rested according to the commandment. But on the first day of the week, at early dawn, they went to the tomb, taking the spices which they had prepared. They found the stone rolled away from the tomb, but when they went in they did not find the body. While they were perplexed about this, behold, two men stood by them in dazzling apparel; as they were frightened and bowed their faces to the ground, the men said, 'Why do you seek the living among the dead? Remember how he told you, while he was still in Galilee, that the Son of Man must be delivered into the hands of sinful men, and be crucified, and on the third day rise.' And they remembered his words, and returning from the tomb they told this to the eleven and to all the rest. Now it was Mary Magdalene and Joanna and Mary, the mother of James and the other women with them who told this to the apostles; but these words seemed to them an idle tale, and they did not believe them. St Luke 23.56–24,12

RESPONSE 'Let heaven and earth praise him,
the seas and everything that moves therein.'

Eternal God, on the third day you raised your Son from the grave – with joyful hearts we praise you for the glorious resurrection of your Son . . .
'They found the stone rolled away from the tomb' – we rejoice that Christ, our Paschal Lamb, has been raised from the dead . . .
'They did not find the body' – we give thanks that Christ is alive and reigns with you and the Holy Spirit, one God, for time and eternity . . .

INTERCESSIONS *pages 390–393* CLOSING PRAYERS *page 402–403*

17 August *On the Road to Emmaus*

OPENING PRAYER O come, let us sing to the Lord; let us make a joyful noise to the God of our salvation. Let us come into his presence with thanksgiving. Let us offer to him our songs of praise . . . Glory be . . .

PSALMODY May the glory of the Lord endure for ever,
may the Lord rejoice in his works.
I will sing to the Lord as long as I live. Psalm 104.31–32

SCRIPTURE READINGS You know that you were ransomed from the futile ways inherited from your fathers, not with perishable things such as silver or gold, but with the precious blood of Christ. 1 Peter 1.18–19

That very day two of the disciples were going to a village named Emmaus, about seven miles from Jerusalem, and talking with each other about all these things that had happened. While they were talking, Jesus himself drew near and went with them. But their eyes were kept from recognising him. He said, 'What is this conversation which you are holding with each other as you walk?' One of them, named Cleopas, answered, 'Are you the only visitor to Jerusalem who does not know the things that have happened there in these days?' And he said, 'What things?' They said, 'Concerning Jesus of Nazareth, who was a prophet mighty in deed and word before God and all the people, and how our chief priests and rulers delivered him up to be condemned to death, and crucified him. But we had hoped that he was the one to redeem Israel. Yes, and besides all this, it is now the third day since this happened. Moreover, some women of our company amazed us. They were at the tomb early in the morning and did not find his body; and they came back saying that they had even seen a vision of angels, who said that he was alive. Some of those who were with us went to the tomb, and found it just as the women had said; but him they did not see.' He said, 'O foolish men, and slow of heart to believe all that the prophets have spoken! Was it not necessary that the Christ should suffer these things and enter into his glory?' Beginning with Moses and all the prophets, he interpreted to them in all the scriptures the things concerning himself.
St Luke 24.13–27*

RESPONSE 'Triumphant in his glory now, to him all power is given,
to him in one communion bow all saints in earth and heaven.'

Eternal God, your risen Son walked to Emmaus with the two disciples – we praise you and we rejoice that he is with us always . . .
'We had hoped that he was the one to redeem Israel' – Lord, we rejoice that your Son came to redeem all people in every generation . . .
You raised your Son with power on the third day – we praise you for making us members of the resurrection community through baptism . . .

INTERCESSIONS *pages 390–393* CLOSING PRAYERS *page 402–403*

18 August *The Two Men Returned to Jerusalem*

OPENING PRAYER O come, let us sing to the Lord; let us make a joyful noise to the God of our salvation. Let us come into his presence with thanksgiving. Let us offer to him our songs of praise . . . Glory be . . .

PSALMODY O give thanks to the Lord, call on his name,
make known his deeds among the peoples!
Tell of all his wonderful works! Glory in his holy name;
let the hearts of those who seek the Lord rejoice!
Seek the Lord and his strength,
Seek his presence continually! Psalm 105.1–4*

SCRIPTURE READINGS To them he presented himself alive after his passion by many proofs, appearing to them during the forty days, and speaking of the Kingdom of God. Acts 1.3

Jesus and the two disciples drew near to the village to which they were going. He appeared to be going further, but they constrained him, saying, 'Stay with us, for it is toward evening and the day is now far spent.' So he went in to stay with them. When he was at table with them, he took the bread and blessed, and broke it, and gave it to them. And their eyes were opened and they recognised him; and he vanished out of their sight. They said, 'Did not our hearts burn within us while he talked to us on the road, while he opened to us the scriptures?' They rose and returned to Jerusalem; and they found the eleven gathered together and those who were with them, who said, 'The Lord has risen indeed, and has appeared to Simon!' Then they told what had happened on the road, and how he was known to them in the breaking of the bread. As they were saying this, Jesus himself stood among them. But they were startled and frightened, and supposed that they saw a spirit. He said, 'Why are you troubled, and why do questionings rise in your hearts? See my hands and my feet, that it is I myself; handle me, and see; for a spirit has not flesh and bones as you see that I have.' While they still disbelieved for joy, and wondered, he said, 'Have you anything to eat?' They gave him a piece of broiled fish, and he took it and ate before them. St Luke 24.28–43*

RESPONSE 'Hymns of praise then let us sing, Alleluia!
unto Christ, our heavenly King, Alleluia!'

Eternal God, you reveal your plans for us in the Scriptures – we praise you for the presence of the risen Christ with us always . . .
'Did not our hearts burn within us?' – make our hearts burn with the fire of your love as we meditate on your holy Word in the Scriptures . . .
'He took the bread and blessed, and broke it, and gave it to them' – we thank you for the gift of yourself to us in the Eucharist . . .

INTERCESSIONS *pages 390–393* CLOSING PRAYERS *page 402–403*

You are Witnesses

OPENING PRAYER O come, let us sing to the Lord; let us make a joyful noise to the God of our salvation. Let us come into his presence with thanksgiving. Let us offer to him our songs of praise . . . Glory be . . .

PSALMODY Seek the Lord and his strength!
Remember the wonderful works that he has done,
his miracles, and the judgements he uttered.
He is the Lord our God;
his judgements are in all the earth.
He is mindful of his covenant for ever,
of the word that he commanded, for a thousand generations,
the covenant which he made with Abraham,
his sworn promise to Isaac,
which he confirmed to Jacob as a statute,
to Israel as an everlasting covenant,
saying, 'To you I will give the land of Canaan
as your portion for an inheritance.' Psalm 105.4–11*

SCRIPTURE READINGS 'You shall receive power when the Holy Spirit has come upon you; and you shall be my witnesses in Jerusalem and in all Judea and Samaria and to the end of the earth.' Acts 1.8

Jesus said, 'These are my words which I spoke to you, while I was still with you, that everything written about me in the law of Moses and the prophets and psalms must be fulfilled.' He opened their minds to understand the scriptures, and said, 'It is written, that the Christ should suffer and on the third day rise from the dead, and that repentance and forgiveness of sins should be preached in his name to all nations, beginning from Jerusalem. You are witnesses of these things. Behold, I send the promise of my Father upon you; but stay in the city, until you are clothed with power from on high.' Then he led them out as far as Bethany, and lifting up his hands he blessed them. While he blessed them, he parted from them, and was carried up into heaven. They returned to Jerusalem with great joy, and were continually in the temple blessing God. St Luke 24.44–53

RESPONSE 'Lift high the Cross, the love of Christ proclaim,
till all the world adore his sacred name.'

Eternal God, you call us to witness to your risen Son – we praise you for his continuous presence in the Church . . .
'He opened their minds to understand the Scriptures' – Lord, enlighten our minds with a fuller understanding of your living Word . . .
'Repentance and forgiveness of sins should be preached in his name' – give grace to all who proclaim the Gospel of Christ's redeeming love . . .

INTERCESSIONS *pages 390–393* CLOSING PRAYERS *page 402–403*

OPENING PRAYER O come, let us sing to the Lord; let us make a joyful noise to the God of our salvation. Let us come into his presence with thanksgiving. Let us offer to him our songs of praise . . . Glory be . . .

PSALMODY Praise the Lord!
O give thanks to the Lord, for he is good.
for his steadfast love endures for ever! Psalm 106.1

SCRIPTURE READINGS In the beginning God created the heavens and the earth.
Genesis 1.1

He is the image of the invisible God, the first-born of all creation; for in him all things were created, in heaven and on earth, visible and invisible, whether thrones or dominions or principalities or authorities – all things were created through him and for him. He is before all things, and in him all things hold together. He is the head of the body, the Church; he is the beginning.
Colossians 1.15–18

In the beginning was the Word, and the Word was with God, and the Word was God. He was in the beginning with God; all things were made through him, and without him was not anything made that was made. In him was life, and the life was the light of men. The light shines in the darkness, and the darkness has not overcome it. The true light that enlightens every man was coming into the world. He was in the world and the world was made through him, yet the world knew him not. But to all who received him, who believed in his name, he gave power to become children of God; who were born, not of blood nor of the will of the flesh nor of the will of man, but of God. The Word became flesh and dwelt among us, full of grace and truth; we have beheld his glory, glory as of the only Son from the Father. And from his fullness have we all received, grace upon grace. For the law was given through Moses; grace and truth came through Jesus Christ. No one has ever seen God; the only Son, who is in the bosom of the Father, he has made him known. St John 1.1–18*

RESPONSE 'Veiled in flesh the Godhead see! Hail, incarnate Deity!
Pleased as Man with man to dwell, Jesus, our Emmanuel.'

Eternal God, your Son is both human and divine – we praise you for revealing the richness of your self-giving love in Jesus Christ . . .
Your Son entered our ordinary human life with the energy of your creative love – we rejoice that the universe belongs to you and we praise you . . .
It was out of pure love that you created the world through your living Word – we rejoice that all you have made is good, and we thank you . . .

INTERCESSIONS *pages 390–393* CLOSING PRAYERS *page 402–403*

OPENING PRAYER O come, let us sing to the Lord; let us make a joyful noise to the God of our salvation. Let us come into his presence with thanksgiving. Let us offer to him our songs of praise . . . Glory be . . .

PSALMODY Remember me, O Lord,
when thou showest favour to thy people;
help me when thou deliverest them;
that I may see the prosperity of thy chosen ones,
that I may rejoice in the gladness of thy nation,
that I may glory with thy heritage. Psalm 106.4–5

SCRIPTURE READINGS He who confesses the Son has the Father also. Let what you heard from the beginning abide in you. 1 John 2.23–24

This is the testimony of John, when the Jews sent priests and Levites from Jerusalem to ask him, 'Who are you?' He confessed, he did not deny, but confessed, 'I am not the Christ.' And they asked him, 'What then? Are you Elijah?' He said, 'I am not.' 'Are you the prophet?' He answered, 'No.' They said, 'Who are you? Let us have an answer for those who sent us. What do you say about yourself?' He said, 'I am the voice of one crying in the wilderness, "Make straight the way of the Lord," as the prophet Isaiah said.' Now they had been sent from the Pharisees. They asked, 'Then why are you baptizing, if you are neither the Christ, nor Elijah, nor the prophet?' John answered, 'I baptize with water; but among you stands one whom you do not know, even he who comes after me, the thong of whose sandal I am not worthy to untie.' The next day he saw Jesus coming toward him, and said, 'Behold, the Lamb of God, who takes away the sin of the world!' This is he of whom I said, "After me comes a man who ranks before me, for he was before me." I myself did not know him; but for this I came baptizing with water, that he might be revealed to Israel.' John bore witness, 'I saw the Spirit descend as a dove from heaven, and it remained on him. I myself did not know him; but he who sent me to baptize with water said to me, "He on whom you see the Spirit descend and remain, this is he who baptizes with the Holy Spirit." I have seen and have borne witness that this is the Son of God.' St John 1.19–34*

RESPONSE '"Worthy the Lamb that died", they cry, "to be exalted thus;"
"Worthy the Lamb," our lips reply, "for he was slain for us."'

Eternal God, you sent John the Baptist to herald the advent of your Son – we praise you for all faithful witnesses of Christ in every generation . . .
'This is the testimony of John' – strengthen the Church through the power of the Spirit to bear witness to the Gospel in the world . . .
'This is he who baptizes with the Holy Spirit' – Lord, give us a deeper understanding of our baptism into Christ's death and resurrection . . .

INTERCESSIONS *pages 390–393* CLOSING PRAYERS *page 402–403*

OPENING PRAYER O come, let us sing to the Lord; let us make a joyful noise to the God of our salvation. Let us come into his presence with thanksgiving. Let us offer to him our songs of praise . . . Glory be . . .

PSALMODY O give thanks to the Lord, for he is good;
for his steadfast love endures for ever!
Let them thank the Lord for his steadfast love. Psalm 107.1–8*

SCRIPTURE READINGS Take heed to yourselves and to all the flock, in which the Holy Spirit has made you guardians, to feed the church of the Lord which he obtained with his own blood. Acts 20.28

John was standing with two of his disciples; and he looked at Jesus and said, 'Behold, the Lamb of God!' The two disciples heard him, and they followed Jesus. Jesus said, 'What do you seek?' They said, 'Rabbi' (which means Teacher), 'where are you staying?' He said, 'Come and see.' They stayed with him that day, for it was about the tenth hour. One of the two was Andrew, Simon Peter's brother. He first found his brother Simon, and said, 'We have found the Messiah' (which means Christ). He brought him to Jesus. Jesus said, 'So you are Simon the son of John? You shall be called Cephas' (which means Peter). The next day Jesus decided to go to Galilee. He found Philip and said, 'Follow me.' Philip was from Bethsaida, the city of Andrew and Peter. Philip found Nathanael, and said, 'We have found him of whom Moses in the law and also the prophets wrote, Jesus of Nazareth, the son of Joseph.' Nathanael said, 'Can anything good come out of Nazareth?' Philip said, 'Come and see.' Jesus saw Nathanael coming to him, and said, 'Behold, an Israelite indeed, in whom is no guile!' Nathanael said, 'How do you know me?' Jesus answered, 'Before Philip called you, when you were under the fig tree, I saw you.' Nathanael answered, 'Rabbi, you are the Son of God! You are the King of Israel!' Jesus answered, 'Because I said to you, I saw you under the fig tree, do you believe? You shall see greater things than these.' He said, 'Truly, truly, I say to you, you will see heaven opened, and the angels of God ascending and descending upon the Son of Man.' St John 1.35–51*

RESPONSE 'Jesus calls us! by thy mercies, Saviour make us hear thy call.
Give our hearts to thine obedience, serve and love thee best of all.'

Eternal God, it is by your grace that you call us and accept us – we rejoice that love is at the heart of your relationship with us . . .
'John was standing with two of his disciples' – help us to use the opportunities in daily life to advance your Kingdom . . .
'Andrew found his brother Simon, and brought him to Jesus' – Lord, make us channels of your grace, and help us to bring other people to Christ . . .

INTERCESSIONS *pages 390–393* CLOSING PRAYERS *page 402–403*

OPENING PRAYER O come, let us sing to the Lord; let us make a joyful noise to the God of our salvation. Let us come into his presence with thanksgiving. Let us offer to him our songs of praise . . . Glory be . . .

PSALMODY My heart is steadfast, O God, my heart is steadfast!
I will sing and make melody! Awake my soul!
I will give thanks to thee, O Lord, among the peoples,
I will sing praises to thee among the nations.
For thy steadfast love is great above the heavens,
thy faithfulness reaches to the clouds.
Be exalted, thyself, O God, above the heavens!
Let thy glory be over all the earth!
That thy beloved may be delivered,
give help by thy right hand, and answer me! Psalm 108.1–6

SCRIPTURE READINGS We know that in everything God works for good with those who love him, who are called according to his purpose.
Romans 8.28

There was a marriage at Cana in Galilee, and the mother of Jesus was there; Jesus was invited to the marriage, with his disciples. When the wine gave out, the mother of Jesus said to him, 'They have no wine.' Jesus said, 'O woman, what have you to do with me? My hour has not yet come.' His mother said to the servants, 'Do whatever he tells you.' Now six stone jars were standing there, for the Jewish rites of purification, each holding twenty or thirty gallons. Jesus said, 'Fill the jars with water.' They filled them up to the brim. He said, 'Now draw some out, and take it to the steward of the feast.' So they took it. When the steward of the feast tasted the water now become wine, and did not know where it came from, he called the bridegroom and said, 'Every man serves the good wine first; and when men have drunk freely, then the poor wine; but you have kept the good wine until now.' This, the first of his signs, Jesus did at Cana in Galilee, and manifested his glory; and his disciples believed in him.
St John 2.1–11*

RESPONSE 'O perfect Love, all human thought transcending,
lowly we kneel in prayer before thy throne.'

Gracious God and Father, your Son showed great love and compassion in his earthly ministry – we rejoice in that same love today and we praise you . . .
'Do whatever he tells you' – send the Holy Spirit and assist us to order our lives in accordance with your will . . .
'Six stone jars were standing there, for the Jewish rites of purification' – purify our hearts and help us to grow in your love . . .

INTERCESSIONS *pages 390–393* CLOSING PRAYERS *page 402–403*

OPENING PRAYER O come, let us sing to the Lord; let us make a joyful noise to the God of our salvation. Let us come into his presence with thanksgiving. Let us offer to him our songs of praise . . . Glory be . . .

PSALMODY The Lord loves those who hate evil;
he preserves the lives of his saints;
he delivers them from the hand of the wicked.
Light dawns for the righteous,
and joy for the upright in heart.
Rejoice in the Lord, O you righteous,
and give thanks to his holy name! Psalm 97.10–12

SCRIPTURE READINGS Now many signs and wonders were done among the people by the hands of the apostles. And more than ever believers were added to the Lord, multitudes both of men and women. Acts 5.12–14*

We are ambassadors for Christ, God making his appeal through us. We beseech you on behalf of Christ, be reconciled to God.
2 Corinthians 5.20

You are those who have continued with me in my trials; and I assign to you, as my Father assigned to me, a kingdom, that you may eat and drink at my table in my kingdom, and sit on thrones judging the twelve tribes of Israel. St Luke 22.28–30

Jesus called to him his twelve disciples and gave them authority over unclean spirits, to cast them out, and to heal every disease and every infirmity. The names of the twelve apostles are these: first, Simon, who is called Peter, and Andrew his brother; James the son of Zebedee, and John his brother; Philip and Bartholomew; Thomas and Matthew the tax collector; James the Son of Alphaeus, and Thaddaeus; Simon the Cananean, and Judas Iscariot, who betrayed him. St Matthew 10.1–4

RESPONSE 'O blest communion, fellowship divine, we feebly struggle, they in glory shine; yet all are one in thee, for all are thine.'

Heavenly Father, in your divine providence you raised up Bartholomew to be an apostle of your Son – we celebrate this feast with joy and praise . . .
'Jesus called to him his twelve disciples and gave them authority' – Lord, bless all the bishops of your Church, and especially in this diocese . . .
'We are ambassadors for Christ' – united in the one spirit, we pray with Saint Bartholomew for the mission and unity of your Church . . .

INTERCESSIONS *pages 390–393* CLOSING PRAYERS *page 402–403*

25 August *Cleansing the Temple*

OPENING PRAYER O come, let us sing to the Lord; let us make a joyful noise to the God of our salvation. Let us come into his presence with thanksgiving. Let us offer to him our songs of praise . . . Glory be . . .

PSALMODY The Lord says to my lord: 'Sit at my right hand,
till I make your enemies your footstool.'
The Lord sends forth from Zion your mighty sceptre.
Rule in the midst of your foes!
Your people will offer themselves freely
on the day you lead your host upon the holy mountains.
The Lord is at your right hand;
he will shatter kings on the day of his wrath. Psalm 110.1–5*

SCRIPTURE READINGS

These I will bring to my holy mountain,
and make them joyful in my house of prayer;
their burnt offerings and their sacrifices
will be accepted on my altar;
for my house shall be called a house of prayer
for all peoples. Isaiah 56.7

The Passover of the Jews was at hand, and Jesus went up to Jerusalem. In the temple he found those who were selling oxen and sheep and pigeons, and the money-changers at their business. Making a whip of cords, he drove them all, with the sheep and oxen, out of the temple; and he poured out the coins of the money-changers and overturned their tables. He told those who sold the pigeons, 'Take these things away; you shall not make my Father's house a house of trade.' His disciples remembered that it was written, 'Zeal for thy house will consume me.' The Jews said, 'What sign have you to show us for doing this?' Jesus answered, 'Destroy this temple, and in three days I will raise it up.' The Jews then said, 'It has taken forty-six years to build this temple, and will you raise it up in three days?' But he spoke of the temple of his body. When he was raised from the dead, his disciples remembered that he had said this; and they believed the scripture and the word which Jesus had spoken. St John 2.13–22

RESPONSE 'We love the place, O God, wherein thine honour dwells;
the joy of thine abode, all earthly joy excels.'

Eternal God, your Son cleansed the Temple before the offering of the Passover sacrifice – cleanse your Church and make us holy . . .
You send the Holy Spirit to sanctify the Church – Lord, we praise you for the continuous activity and presence of the Spirit in the Church . . .
You are the source of holiness – make the Church a living temple to your glory, and unite our prayers with the perfect worship of your Son . . .

INTERCESSIONS *pages 390–393* CLOSING PRAYERS *page 402–403*

26 August *He came by Night*

OPENING PRAYER O come, let us sing to the Lord; let us make a joyful noise to the God of our salvation. Let us come into his presence with thanksgiving. Let us offer to him our songs of praise . . . Glory be . . .

PSALMODY I will give thanks to the Lord with my whole heart,
in the company of the upright, in the congregation.
Great are the works of the Lord,
studied by all who have pleasure in them. Psalm 111.1–2

SCRIPTURE READINGS 'My people are foolish, they know me not; they have no understanding.' Jeremiah 4.22*

There was a man of the Pharisees, named Nicodemus, a ruler of the Jews. This man came to Jesus by night and said, 'Rabbi, we know that you are a teacher come from God; for no one can do these signs that you do, unless God is with him.' Jesus answered, 'Truly, truly, I say to you, unless one is born anew, he cannot see the Kingdom of God.' Nicodemus said, 'How can a man be born when he is old? Can he enter a second time into his mother's womb and be born?' Jesus answered, 'Truly, truly, I say to you, unless one is born of water and the Spirit, he cannot enter the Kingdom of God. That which is born of the flesh is flesh, and that which is born of the Spirit is spirit. Do not marvel that I said to you, "You must be born anew." The wind blows where it wills, and you hear the sound of it, but you do not know whence it comes or whither it goes; so it is with everyone who is born of the Spirit.' Nicodemus said, 'How can this be?' Jesus answered, 'Are you a teacher of Israel, and yet you do not understand this? Truly, truly, I say to you, we speak of what we know, and bear witness to what we have seen; but you do not receive our testimony. If I have told you earthly things and you do not believe, how can you believe if I tell you heavenly things? No one has ascended into heaven but he who descended from heaven, the Son of Man. As Moses lifted up the serpent in the wilderness, so must the Son of Man be lifted up, that whoever believes in him may have eternal life. God so loved the world that he gave his only Son, that whoever believes in him should not perish but have eternal life.'
St John 3.1–16

RESPONSE 'O loving wisdom of our God! When all was sin and shame,
a second Adam to the fight and to the rescue came.'

Almighty God, your Holy Spirit is the Lord and giver of life – we praise you for the presence and power of your Spirit in the Church . . .
'So it is with everyone who is born of the Spirit' – Lord, renew your gift of the Spirit in all who have been baptized into Christ . . .
'God so loved the world that he gave his only Son' – we praise you and we bless you and we thank you for the wonderful gift of your Son . . .

INTERCESSIONS *pages 390–393* CLOSING PRAYERS *page 402–403*

27 August *The Woman at the Well of Samaria*

OPENING PRAYER O come, let us sing to the Lord; let us make a joyful noise to the God of our salvation. Let us come into his presence with thanksgiving. Let us offer to him our songs of praise . . . Glory be . . .

PSALMODY The Lord is gracious and merciful.
He is ever mindful of his covenant. Psalm 111.4–5*

SCRIPTURE READINGS Manoah said to the angel of the Lord, 'Pray, let us prepare a kid for you.' The angel said, 'I will not eat of your food; but if you make ready a burnt offering, then offer it to the Lord.' So Manoah took the kid, and offered it upon the rock to the Lord. Judges 13.15–19*

Jesus sat down beside the well. There came a woman of Samaria to draw water. Jesus said, 'Give me a drink.' The woman said, 'How is it that you, a Jew, ask a drink of me, a woman of Samaria?' Jesus answered, 'If you knew the gift of God, and who it is that is saying to you, "Give me a drink," you would have asked him, and he would have given you living water.' The woman said, 'Sir, you have nothing to draw with, and the well is deep; where do you get that living water?' Jesus said, 'Everyone who drinks of this water will thirst again, but whoever drinks of the water that I shall give him will never thirst; the water that I shall give him will become in him a spring of water welling up to eternal life.' The woman said, 'Sir, give me this water that I may not thirst, nor come here to draw.' Jesus said, 'Go, call your husband, and come here.' The woman answered, 'I have no husband.' Jesus said, 'You are right is saying, "I have no husband"; for you have had five husbands, and he whom you now have is not your husband.' The woman said, 'Sir, I perceive you are a prophet. Our fathers worshipped on this mountain; and you say that in Jerusalem is the place where men ought to worship.' Jesus said, 'Woman, the hour is coming, and now is, when the true worshippers will worship the Father in Spirit and truth, for such the Father seeks to worship him. God is spirit and those who worship him must worship him in spirit and truth.' The woman said, 'I know that Messiah is coming; when he comes, he will show us all things.' Jesus said, 'I who speak to you am he.' St John 4.7–26*

RESPONSE 'O worship the Lord in the beauty of holiness!
Bow down before him, his glory proclaim.'

Eternal God, you give us grace to acknowledge your glory and to worship you in spirit and in truth – accept our praise through Christ our Lord . . .
'Salvation is of the Jews' – Lord, we rejoice in Abraham and in the spiritual heritage you give to us in the Old Covenant . . .
'God is spirit and those who worship him must worship him in spirit and truth' – we join our praises with the ceaseless worship of heaven . . .

INTERCESSIONS *pages 390–393* CLOSING PRAYERS *page 402–403*

OPENING PRAYER O come, let us sing to the Lord; let us make a joyful noise to the God of our salvation. Let us come into his presence with thanksgiving. Let us offer to him our songs of praise . . . Glory be . . .

PSALMODY He has shown his people the power of his works,
in giving them the heritage of the nations.
The works of his hands are faithful and just;
all his precepts are trustworthy.
They are established for ever and ever,
to be performed with faithfulness and uprightness.
Psalm 111.6–8

SCRIPTURE READINGS Water was issuing from below the threshold of the temple toward the east. Wherever the river goes every living creature which swarms will live. Ezekiel 47.1–9*

There is in Jerusalem by the Sheep Gate a pool, which has five porticoes. In these lay a multitude of invalids, blind, lame, paralyzed. One man was there, who had been ill for thirty-eight years. When Jesus saw him, he said, 'Do you want to be healed?' The sick man answered, 'Sir, I have no man to put me into the pool when the water is troubled, and while I am going, another steps down before me.' Jesus said, 'Rise, take up your pallet, and walk.' At once the man was healed, and he took up his pallet and walked. That day was the sabbath. So the Jews said to the man who was cured, 'It is the sabbath, it is not lawful for you to carry your pallet.' He answered, 'The man who healed me said, "Take up your pallet, and walk."' They asked, 'Who is the man who said to you, "Take up your pallet, and walk."' Now the man who had been healed did not know who it was, for Jesus had withdrawn, as there was a crowd in the place. Afterward, Jesus found him in the temple, and said, 'See, you are well! Sin no more, that nothing worse befall you.' The man went away and told the Jews that it was Jesus who had healed him. This was why the Jews persecuted Jesus, because he did this on the sabbath. Jesus answered, 'My Father is working still, and I am working.' This was why the Jews sought all the more to kill him, because he not only broke the sabbath but also called God his own Father, thus making himself equal with God. St John 5.2–18*

RESPONSE 'God is working his purpose out as year succeeds to year,
God is working his purpose out and the time is drawing near.'

Gracious God, great is the mystery of your power and compassion – we praise you for your redeeming love in your Son Jesus Christ . . .
'Sin no more, and nothing worse will befall you' – have mercy on us . . .
'Jesus called God his Father, thus making himself equal with God' – all praise to the blessed and eternal Trinity, Father, Son and Holy Spirit . . .

INTERCESSIONS *pages 390–393* CLOSING PRAYERS *page 402–403*

OPENING PRAYER O come, let us sing to the Lord; let us make a joyful noise to the God of our salvation. Let us come into his presence with thanksgiving. Let us offer to him our songs of praise . . . Glory be . . .

PSALMODY Praise the Lord.
Blessed is the man who fears the Lord.
The Lord is gracious, merciful, and righteous.
It is well with the man who deals generously and lends,
who conducts his affairs with justice.
For the righteous will never be moved;
he will be remembered for ever.
He is not afraid of evil tidings;
his heart is firm, trusting in the Lord. Psalm 112.1–7*

SCRIPTURE READINGS He humbled you; that he might make you know that man does not live by bread alone, but that man lives by everything that proceeds out of the mouth of the Lord. Deuteronomy 8.3*

Jesus went up on the mountain, and there sat down with his disciples. Now the Passover, the feast of the Jews, was at hand. Lifting up his eyes, and seeing that a multitude was coming to him, Jesus said to Philip, 'How are we to buy bread, so that these people may eat?' This he said to test him, for he himself knew what he would do. Philip answered, 'Two hundred denarii would not buy enough bread for each of them to get a little.' One of his disciples, Andrew, Simon Peter's brother, said, 'There is a lad here who has five barley loaves and two fish; but what are they among so many?' Jesus said, 'Make the people sit down.' Now there was much grass in the place; so the men sat down, in number about five thousand. Jesus took the loaves, and when he had given thanks, he distributed them to those who were seated; so also the fish, as much as they wanted. When they had eaten their fill, he told his disciples, 'Gather up the fragments left over, that nothing may be lost.' So they gathered them up and filled twelve baskets with fragments from the five barley loaves, left by those who had eaten.
St John 6.1–13

RESPONSE 'All good gifts around us are sent from heaven above:
then thank the Lord, O thank the Lord, for all his love.'

Eternal God, you alone satisfy our spiritual and physical hunger – we praise you and acclaim your goodness and love for all people . . .
'How are we to buy bread?' – Lord, we humbly thank you for your free gift of yourself to us in the Eucharist, which money cannot buy . . .
'Jesus took the loaves' – we thank you for entrusting the Sacrament of the Eucharist to the church for the benefit of your people . . .

INTERCESSIONS *pages 390–393* CLOSING PRAYERS *page 402–403*

OPENING PRAYER O come, let us sing to the Lord; let us make a joyful noise to the God of our salvation. Let us come into his presence with thanksgiving. Let us offer to him our songs of praise . . . Glory be . . .

PSALMODY Praise the Lord. Praise, O servants of the Lord,
praise the name of the Lord.
Blessed be the name of the Lord
from this time forth and for evermore!
From the rising of the sun to its setting,
the name of the Lord is to be praised! Psalm 113.1–3

SCRIPTURE READING Jesus said, 'I am the bread of life; he who comes to me shall not hunger, and he who believes in me shall never thirst. But I said to you that you have seen me and yet do not believe. All that the Father gives me will come to me; and him who comes to me I will not cast out. For I have come down from heaven, not to do my own will, but the will of him who sent me; and this is the will of him who sent me, that I should lose nothing of all that he has given me, but raise it up at the last day. For this is the will of my Father, that everyone who sees the Son and believes in him should have eternal life; and I will raise him up at the last day. Truly, truly, I say to you, he who believes has eternal life. I am the bread of life. Your fathers ate the manna in the wilderness, and they died. This is the bread which comes down from heaven, that a man may eat of it and not die. I am the living bread which came down from heaven; if any one eats of this bread, he will live forever; and the bread which I shall give for the life of the world is my flesh.' St John 6.37–51*

This perishable nature must put on the imperishable, and this mortal nature must put on immortality. 1 Corinthians 15.53

As often as you eat this bread and drink the cup, you proclaim the Lord's death until he comes. 1 Corinthians 11.26

RESPONSE 'Let us with a gladsome mind, praise the Lord for he is kind,
for his mercies ay endure, ever faithful, ever sure.'

Gracious God, you are the guardian of the Church from age to age – we rejoice that Christ is head over the Church and we praise you . . .
'I am the bread of life' – Lord, we praise you and thank you for sharing your life with us in the wonderful sacrament of the altar . . .
'If anyone eats of this bread, he will live for ever' – we rejoice that your Son has opened for us the gate of everlasting life . . .

INTERCESSIONS *pages 390–393* CLOSING PRAYERS *page 402–403*

OPENING PRAYER O come, let us sing to the Lord; let us make a joyful noise to the God of our salvation. Let us come into his presence with thanksgiving. Let us offer to him our songs of praise . . . Glory be . . .

PSALMODY Blessed is the name of the Lord
from this time forth and for evermore!
From the rising of the sun to its setting
the name of the Lord is to be praised! Psalm 113.2–3*

SCRIPTURE READINGS
The Lord made it known to me and I knew;
then thou didst show me their evil deeds.
But he was like a gentle lamb led to the slaughter.
'Let us destroy the tree with its fruit,
let us cut him off from the land of the living,
that his name be remembered no more.' Jeremiah 11.18–19*

On the last day of the feast, the great day, Jesus proclaimed, 'If any one thirst, let him come to me and drink. He who believes in me, as the scripture has said, "Out of his heart shall flow rivers of living water."' This he said about the Spirit, which those who believed in him were to receive; for as yet the Spirit had not been given, because Jesus was not yet glorified. Some said, 'This is really the prophet.' Others said, 'This is the Christ.' But some said, 'Is the Christ to come from Galilee? Has not scripture said that the Christ is descended from David, and comes from Bethlehem, the village where David was?' There was a division. Some wanted to arrest him, but no one laid hands on him. The officers went back to the chief priests and Pharisees, who said, 'Why did you not bring him?' The officers answered, 'No man ever spoke like this man!' The Pharisees answered, 'Are you led astray, you also? Have any of the authorities or of the Pharisees believed in him? But this crowd, who do not know the law, are accursed.' Nicodemus, who had gone to him before, and who was one of them, said, 'Does our law judge a man without first giving him a hearing and learning what he does?' They replied, 'Are you from Galilee too? Search and you will see that no prophet is to rise from Galilee.'
St John 7.37–53*

RESPONSE 'Lord, thy wounds our healing give, to thy Cross we look and live:
Jesus, may we ever be grafted, rooted, built in thee.'

Almighty God, in the fullness of time you sent your Son to be our Redeemer – we raise our voices to acclaim your praise and eternal glory . . .
'If anyone thirst, let him come to me and drink' – we thank you for inviting us to come to you, and we thank you for all your blessings . . .
'No man ever spoke like this man' – Lord, give us grace to hear what you are saying to us, and help us to respond to your living Word . . .

INTERCESSIONS *pages 390–393* CLOSING PRAYERS *page 402–403*

1 September *Go, and Do Not Sin Again*

OPENING PRAYER Eternal Father, you invite us to share in your life. Help us by the Spirit to draw near to the throne of your grace, and to offer our praise to you with the perfect praise of your Son . . . Glory be . . .

PSALMODY The Lord is high above all nations,
and his glory above the heavens!
Who is like the Lord our God,
who is seated on high,
who looks far down upon the heavens and the earth?
He raises the poor from the dust,
and lifts the needy from the ash heap,
to make them sit with princes,
with the princes of his people. Psalm 113.4–8

SCRIPTURE READINGS 'I have no pleasure in the death of any one, says the Lord God; so turn, and live.' Ezekiel 18.32

Do you not know that your body is a temple of the Holy Spirit within you which you have from God. 1 Corinthians 6.19

Early in the morning Jesus came to the temple. The scribes and the Pharisees brought a woman who had been caught in adultery, and placing her in the midst they said to him, 'Teacher, this woman has been caught in the act of adultery. Now in the law Moses commanded us to stone such. What do you say about her?' This they said to test him, that they might have some charge to bring against him. Jesus bent down and wrote with his finger on the ground. As they continued to ask him, he stood up and said, 'Let him who is without sin among you be the first to throw a stone at her.' Once more he bent down and wrote with his finger on the ground. When they heard it, they went away, one by one, beginning with the eldest, and Jesus was left alone with the woman standing before him. Jesus looked up and said to her, 'Woman, where are they? Has no one condemned you?' She said, 'No one, Lord.' And Jesus said, 'Neither do I condemn you; go, and do not sin again.' St John 8.1–11

RESPONSE 'Lord, thou canst save when deadly sin assaileth;
Lord, o'er thy Church nor death nor hell prevaileth.'

Eternal Father, in your goodness you create us in your own image – we praise you for making our bodies a dwelling place for your Holy Spirit . . .
'Let him who is without sin be the first to throw a stone at her' – when we want to condemn others, help us to remember our own sins and our own need of your forgiveness . . .
'Go, and do not sin again' – give us grace to overcome all our sins . . .

INTERCESSIONS *pages 390–393* CLOSING PRAYERS *page 402–403*

2 September *I am the Light of the World*

OPENING PRAYER Eternal Father, you invite us to share in your life. Help us by the Spirit to draw near to the throne of your grace, and to offer our praise to you with the perfect praise of your Son . . . Glory be . . .

PSALMODY When Israel went forth from Egypt,
the house of Jacob from a people of strange language,
Judah became his sanctuary, Israel his dominion.
Tremble, O earth, at the presence of the Lord,
who turns the rocks into a pool of water,
the flint into a spring of water. Psalm 114.1–8*

SCRIPTURE READINGS The Lord will be your everlasting light,
and your God will be your glory. Isaiah 60.19

Jesus said, 'I am the light of the world; he who follows me will not walk in darkness, but will have the light of life.' The Pharisees said, 'You are bearing witness to yourself; your testimony is not true.' Jesus answered, 'Even if I do bear witness to myself, my testimony is true, for I know whence I have come and whither I am going, but you do not know whence I come or whither I am going. You judge according to the flesh, I judge no one. Yet even if I do judge, my judgement is true, for it is not I alone that judge, but I and he who sent me. In your law it is written that the testimony of two men is true; I bear witness to myself, and the Father who sent me bears witness to me.' They said, 'Where is your Father?' Jesus answered, 'You know neither me nor my Father; if you knew me, you would know my Father also.' These words he spoke in the treasury, as he taught in the temple; but no one arrested him, because his hour had not yet come. Jesus said, 'When you have lifted up the Son of Man, then you will know that I am he, and that I do nothing on my own authority but speak thus as the Father taught me. He who sent me is with me; he has not left me alone, for I always do what is pleasing to him.' As he spoke thus, many believed in him. Jesus said to the Jews who had believed in him, 'If you continue in my word, you are truly my disciples, and you will know the truth, and the truth will make you free.' St John 8.12–32*

RESPONSE 'O my Saviour lifted from the earth for me,
draw me, in thy mercy, nearer unto thee.'

Heavenly Father, you give us a great light to shine in the darkness with the birth of your Son – we adore you for your eternal love . . .
'I am the light of the world' – may the light of your truth and love shine brightly in the Church and be seen in the world . . .
'I always do what is pleasing to him' – Lord, help us by the Spirit to unite our wills with your perfect will . . .

INTERCESSIONS *pages 390–393* CLOSING PRAYERS *page 402–403*

3 September *A Man Born Blind*

OPENING PRAYER Eternal Father, you invite us to share in your life. Help us by the Spirit to draw near to the throne of your grace, and to offer our praise to you with the perfect praise of your Son . . . Glory be . . .

PSALMODY Not to us, O Lord, not to us,
but to thy name give the glory.
Our God is in the heavens;
he does whatever he pleases.
The Lord has been mindful of us;
he will bless those who fear the Lord,
both small and great. Psalm 115.1–13*

SCRIPTURE READINGS
Where then is my hope?
Who will see my hope? Job 17.15

Jesus saw a man blind from his birth. His disciples asked, 'Rabbi, who sinned, this man or his parents, that he was born blind?' Jesus answered, 'It was not that this man sinned, or his parents, but that the works of God might be made manifest in him. We must work the works of him who sent me, while it is day; night comes, when no one can work. As long as I am in the world, I am the light of the world.' He spat on the ground and made clay of the spittle and anointed the man's eyes with the clay, saying, 'Go, wash in the pool of Siloam' (which means Sent). He went and washed and came back seeing. The neighbours who had seen him before as a beggar, said, 'Is not this the man who used to sit and beg?' Some said, 'It is he'; others said, 'No, but he is like him.' He said, 'I am the man.' They said, 'How were your eyes opened?' He answered, 'The man called Jesus made clay and anointed my eyes and said, "Go to Siloam and wash"; so I went and washed and received my sight.' They said, 'Where is he?' He said, 'I do not know.' It was a sabbath day when Jesus made the clay and opened his eyes. The Pharisees again asked him how he had received his sight. He said, 'He put clay on my eyes, and I washed, and I see.' Some Pharisees said, 'This man is not from God, for he does not keep the sabbath.' Others said, 'How can a man who is a sinner do such signs?' St John 9.1–16*

RESPONSE 'Divine instructor, gracious Lord, be thou for ever near;
teach me to love thy sacred word, and view my Saviour here.'

Heavenly Father, your Son is the true Light of the world – we rejoice that Christ gives light and hope and salvation to the world . . .
Spiritual blindness is caused by sin – Lord, cleanse us from our sins, and open our eyes to see the light of your truth . . .
'How were your eyes opened?' – Lord, we thank you for those who brought us to baptism, and those who taught us to trust and believe in your Son . . .

INTERCESSIONS *pages 390–393* CLOSING PRAYERS *page 402–403*

OPENING PRAYER Eternal Father, you invite us to share in your life. Help us by the Spirit to draw near to the throne of your grace, and to offer our praise to you with the perfect praise of your Son . . . Glory be . . .

PSALMODY He chose David his servant,
and took him from the sheepfolds;
from tending the ewes that had young he brought him
to be the shepherd of Jacob his people
and of Israel his inheritance.
With upright heart he tended them,
and guided them with skilful hand. Psalm 78.70–72

SCRIPTURE READINGS 'Thus says the Lord God: Behold, I myself will search for my sheep, and will seek them out. As a shepherd seeks out his flock when some of his sheep have been scattered abroad, so will I seek out my sheep; I will rescue them from all places where they have been scattered on a day of clouds and thick darkness. I will bring them out from the peoples, and gather them from the countries, and will bring them into their own land; and I will feed them on the mountains of Israel.'

Ezekiel 34.11–13

Jesus said, 'Truly, truly, I say to you, I am the door of the sheep. All who came before me are thieves and robbers; but the sheep did not heed them. I am the door; if any one enters by me, he will be saved, and will go in and out and find pasture. The thief comes only to steal and kill and destroy; I came that they may have life, and have it abundantly. I am the good shepherd. The good shepherd lays down his life for the sheep. He who is a hireling and not a shepherd, whose own the sheep are not, sees the wolf coming and leaves the sheep and flees; and the wolf snatches them and scatters them. He flees because he is a hireling and cares nothing for the sheep. I am the good shepherd; I know my own and my own know me, as the Father knows me and I know the Father; and I lay down my life for the sheep. I have other sheep, that are not of this fold; I must bring them also, and they will heed my voice. So there shall be one flock, one shepherd.'

St John 10.7–16

RESPONSE 'The King of love my shepherd is, whose goodness faileth never,
I nothing lack if I am his and he is mine for ever.'

Loving Father, you gave your Son to be the perfect priest in his earthly ministry – we praise you for Christ our great High Priest in heaven . . .
'I lay down my life for the sheep' – Lord, inspire your Church to a deeper love and devotion to our Lord for his sacrificial love for us . . .
'I am the Good Shepherd' – renew your gift of the Spirit in the Bishops and clergy of your Church, and make them holy . . .

INTERCESSIONS *pages 390–393* CLOSING PRAYERS *page 402–403*

5 September *I am the Resurrection and the Life*

OPENING PRAYER Eternal Father, you invite us to share in your life. Help us by the Spirit to draw near to the throne of your grace, and to offer our praise to you with the perfect praise of your Son . . . Glory be . . .

PSALMODY The dead do not praise the Lord
nor do any that go down into silence.
But we will bless the Lord,
from this time forth and for evermore. Psalm 115.17–18

SCRIPTURE READINGS 'Eye has not seen, nor ear heard, nor the heart of man conceived, what God has prepared for those who love him.'
1 Corinthians 2.9

A certain man was ill, Lazarus of Bethany, the village of Mary and her sister Martha. It was Mary who anointed the Lord with ointment and wiped his feet with her hair, whose brother Lazarus was ill. When Martha heard that Jesus was coming, she went and met him, while Mary sat in the house. Martha said, 'Lord, if you had been here, my brother would not have died. Even now I know that whatever you ask from God, God will give you.' Jesus said, 'Your brother will rise again.' Martha said, 'I know that he will rise again in the resurrection at the last day.' Jesus said, 'I am the resurrection and the life; he who believes in me, though he die, yet shall he live, and whoever lives and believes in me shall never die. Do you believe this?' She said, 'Yes, Lord; I believe that you are the Christ, the Son of God, he who is coming into the world.' Jesus came to the tomb; it was a cave, and a stone lay upon it. Jesus said, 'Take away the stone.' Martha, the sister of the dead man, said, 'Lord, by this time there will be an odour, for he has been dead four days.' Jesus said, 'Did I not tell you that if you would believe you would see the glory of God?' So they took away the stone. Jesus lifted up his eyes and said, 'Father, I thank thee that thou hast heard me. I knew that thou hearest me always, but I have said this on account of the people standing by, that they may believe that thou didst send me.' When he had said this, he cried with a loud voice, 'Lazarus, come out.' The dead man came out, his hands and feet bound with bandages, and his face wrapped with a cloth. Jesus said, 'Unbind him, and let him go.'
St John 11.1–44*

RESPONSE 'Jesus lives! to him the throne over all the world is given:
May we go where he is gone, rest and reign with him in heaven.'

Eternal God, you give us the strength of new life in your risen Son – we rejoice and blend our prayers with the praise of all creation . . .
'I am the resurrection and the life' – all glory to our risen Redeemer . . .
'He will rise again on the last day' – grant eternal rest to all who have died in the faith, and bring us all to the glory of the resurrection . . .

INTERCESSIONS *pages 390–393* CLOSING PRAYERS *page 402–403*

6 September *Jesus is Anointed at Bethany*

OPENING PRAYER Eternal Father, you invite us to share in your life. Help us by the Spirit to draw near to the throne of your grace, and to offer our praise to you with the perfect praise of your Son . . . Glory be . . .

PSALMODY I love the Lord,
because he has heard my voice and my supplications.
The snares of death encompassed me;
the pangs of Sheol laid hold on me;
I suffered distress and anguish.
Then I called on the name of the Lord;
'O Lord, I beseech thee, save my life!'
Gracious is the Lord, and righteous;
our God is merciful.
What shall I render to the Lord for all his bounty to me?
I will pay my vows to the Lord
in the presence of all his people,
in the courts of the house of the Lord,
in your midst, O Jerusalem. Praise the Lord.

Psalm 116.1–19*

SCRIPTURE READINGS 'Keep your voice from weeping, and your eyes from tears; for your work shall be rewarded, says the Lord.' Jeremiah 31.16

Six days before the Passover, Jesus came to Bethany, where Lazarus was, whom Jesus had raised from the dead. There they made him a supper; Martha served, and Lazarus was one of those at table with him. Mary took a pound of costly ointment of pure nard and anointed the feet of Jesus and wiped his feet with her hair; and the house was filled with the fragrance of the ointment. But Judas Iscariot, one of his disciples (he who was to betray him), said, 'Why was this ointment not sold for three hundred denarii and given to the poor?' This he said, not that he cared for the poor but because he was a thief, and as he had the money box he used to take what was put into it. Jesus said, 'Let her alone, let her keep it for the day of my burial. The poor you always have with you, but you do not always have me.'

St John 12.1–8

RESPONSE 'Let the righteous rejoice in the Lord,
and take refuge in him.'

Gracious God and Father, your creative Spirit penetrates the whole of our lives – help us to live to your praise and glory . . .
'Mary took a pound of costly ointment' – Lord, inspire us to follow her example of extravagant love and adoration . . .
'The house was filled with the fragrance of the ointment' – fill the Church with the fragrance of your love, and give us ever-grateful hearts . . .

INTERCESSIONS *pages 390–393* CLOSING PRAYERS *page 402–403*

7 September *Jesus Enters Jerusalem in Triumph*

OPENING PRAYER Eternal Father, you invite us to share in your life. Help us by the Spirit to draw near to the throne of your grace, and to offer our praise to you with the perfect praise of your Son . . . Glory be . . .

PSALMODY Precious in the sight of the Lord is the death of his saints.
O Lord, I am thy servant;
I am thy servant, the son of thy handmaid.
Thou hast loosed my bonds.
I will offer to thee the sacrifice of thanksgiving
and call on the name of the Lord. Psalm 116.15–17

SCRIPTURE READINGS This is the covenant which I will make with the house of Israel after those days, says the Lord: I will put my law within them, and I will write it upon their hearts; and I will be their God and they shall be my people. Jeremiah 31.33

A great crowd who had come to the feast heard that Jesus was coming to Jerusalem. So they took branches of palm trees and went out to meet him, crying, 'Hosanna! Blessed is he who comes in the name of the Lord, even the King of Israel!' Jesus found a young ass and sat upon it; as it is written, 'Fear not, daughter of Zion; behold, your king is coming, sitting on an ass's colt!' His disciples did not understand this at first; but when Jesus was glorified, then they remembered that this had been written of him and had been done to him. The Pharisees said to one another, 'You see that you can do nothing; look, the world has gone after him.' Now among those who went up to worship at the feast were some Greeks. So these came to Philip, who was from Bethsaida in Galilee, and said, 'Sir, we wish to see Jesus.' Philip went and told Andrew; Andrew went with Philip and they told Jesus. Jesus answered, 'The hour has come for the Son of Man to be glorified. Truly, truly, I say to you, unless a grain of wheat falls into the earth and dies, it remains alone; but if it dies, it bears much fruit. He who loves his life loses it, and he who hates his life in this world will keep it for eternal life. If any one serves me, he must follow me; and where I am, there shall my servant be also; if any one serves me, the Father will honour him.' St John 12.12–26*

RESPONSE 'Ride on! ride on in majesty!
Hark! all the tribes Hosanna cry!'

Eternal God, your Son entered the holy city with meekness and he was greeted as King of the Jews – accept our homage and adoration . . .
'We wish to see Jesus' – Lord, we see you now as through a glass darkly, and we look forward with eagerness and awe to see you face to face . . .
'The hour has come for the Son of Man to be glorified' – we praise you for the victory of Christ over sin and death on the Cross . . .

INTERCESSIONS *pages 390–393* CLOSING PRAYERS *page 402–403*

8 September *The Blessed Virgin Mary*

OPENING PRAYER Eternal Father, you invite us to share in your life. Help us by the Spirit to draw near to the throne of your grace, and to offer our praise to you with the perfect praise of your Son . . . Glory be . . .

PSALMODY I will cause your name
to be celebrated in all generations;
therefore the peoples will praise you
for ever and ever. Psalm 45.17

SCRIPTURE READINGS
But you, O Bethlehem Ephrathah,
who are little to be among the clans of Judah,
from you shall come forth for me one who is to be ruler in Israel,
whose origin is from of old, from ancient days.
Therefore he shall give them up until the time
when she who is in travail has brought forth;
And he shall stand and feed his flock
in the strength of the Lord,
in the majesty of the name of the Lord his God.
Micah 5.2–4*

I saw a new heaven and a new earth; for the first heaven and first earth had passed away, and the sea was no more. And I saw the holy city, new Jerusalem, coming down out of heaven from God, prepared as a bride adorned for her husband; and I heard a loud voice from the throne saying, 'Behold, the dwelling of God is with men. He will dwell with them, and they shall be his people, and God himself will be with them; he will wipe away every tear from their eyes, and death shall be no more, neither shall there be mourning nor crying nor pain any more, for the former things have passed away.' He who sat on the throne said, 'Behold, I make all things new.' Also he said, 'Write this, for these words are trustworthy and true.' And he said to me, 'It is done! I am the Alpha and the Omega, the beginning and the end. To the thirsty I will give from the fountain of the water of life without payment. He who conquers shall have this heritage, and I will be his God and he shall be my son.' Revelation 21.1–7

RESPONSE 'Blessed be his glorious name for ever;
may his glory fill the whole earth. Amen. Amen.'

Heavenly Father, on this day your church celebrates the birth of the Blessed Virgin Mary – we honour Mary and praise her Son Jesus Christ . . .
The Word was made flesh in the womb of Mary – Lord, we rejoice in the humility and obedience of Mary . . .
Mary is most blessed among women, and blessed is Jesus, the fruit of her womb – we pray with Mary for the growth of your Kingdom . . .

INTERCESSIONS *pages 390–393* CLOSING PRAYERS *page 402–403*

9 September *Jesus Washes the Feet of the Apostles*

OPENING PRAYER Eternal Father, you invite us to share in your life. Help us by the Spirit to draw near to the throne of your grace, and to offer our praise to you with the perfect praise of your Son . . . Glory be . . .

PSALMODY Praise the Lord, all nations!
Extol him, all peoples!
For great is his steadfast love toward us;
and the faithfulness of the Lord endures for ever.
Praise the Lord! Psalm 117

SCRIPTURE READINGS Being found in human form he humbled himself and became obedient unto death, even death on a cross. Therefore God has highly exalted him and bestowed on him the name which is above every name, that at the name of Jesus every knee should bow, in heaven and on earth and under the earth, and every tongue confess that Jesus Christ is Lord, to the glory of God the Father. Philippians 2.8–11

During supper, Jesus, knowing that the Father had given all things into his hands, and that he had come from God and was going to God, rose from supper, laid aside his garments, and girded himself with a towel. Then he poured water into a basin, and began to wash the disciples' feet, and to wipe them with the towel with which he was girded. He came to Simon Peter; and Peter said, 'Lord, do you wash my feet?' Jesus answered, 'What I am doing you do not know now, but afterwards you will understand.' Peter said, 'You shall never wash my feet.' Jesus answered, 'If I do not wash you, you have no part in me.' Simon Peter said, 'Lord, not my feet only but also my hands and my head!' Jesus said, 'He who has bathed does not need to wash, except for his feet, but he is clean all over; and you are clean, but not all of you.' For he knew who was to betray him; and that was why he said, 'You are not all clean.' When he had washed their feet, and taken his garments, and resumed his place, he said, 'Do you know what I have done to you? If I then, your Lord and Teacher, have washed your feet, you also ought to wash one another's feet. For I have given you an example that you also should do as I have done to you.
St John 13.2–15*

RESPONSE 'Teach me thy way, O Lord,
that I may walk in thy truth.'

Eternal Father, your Son gave us an example of humble service – remove all pride from your Church, and fill us with your love . . .
'If I do not wash you, you have no part in me' – we thank you for forgiving us our sins, and making us members of your Body the Church . . .
'If you know these things, blessed are you if you do them' – help us to put our faith into action in loving service of you and of others . . .

INTERCESSIONS *pages 390–393* CLOSING PRAYERS *page 402–403*

10 September *One of You Will Betray Me*

OPENING PRAYER Eternal Father, you invite us to share in your life. Help us by the Spirit to draw near to the throne of your grace, and to offer our praise to you with the perfect praise of your Son . . . Glory be . . .

PSALMODY O give thanks to the Lord, for he is good;
his steadfast love endures for ever!
Let Israel say,
'His steadfast love endures for ever.' Psalm 118.1–2

SCRIPTURE READINGS 'The days are coming, says the Lord, when I will fulfil the promise I made to the house of Israel and the house of Judah. I will cause a righteous Branch to spring forth for David; and he shall execute justice and righteousness in the land.' Jeremiah 33.14–15*

Jesus said, 'I am not speaking of you all; I know whom I have chosen; it is that the scripture may be fulfilled, "He who ate my bread, has lifted his heel against me." I tell you this now, before it takes place, that when it does take place you may believe that I am he. Truly, truly, I say to you, he who receives any one whom I send receives me; and he who receives me receives him who sent me.' When Jesus had thus spoken, he was troubled in spirit, and testified, 'Truly, truly, I say to you, one of you will betray me.' The disciples looked at one another, uncertain of whom he spoke. One of his disciples, whom Jesus loved, was lying close to the breast of Jesus; so Simon Peter beckoned to him and said, 'Tell us who it is of whom he speaks.' So lying thus, close to the breast of Jesus, he said, 'Lord, who is it?' Jesus answered, 'It is he to whom I shall give this morsel when I have dipped it.' When he had dipped the morsel, he gave it to Judas, the son of Simon Iscariot. Then after the morsel, Satan entered into him, Jesus said, 'What you are going to do, do quickly.' No one at the table knew why he said this to him. Some thought that, because Judas had the money box, Jesus was telling him, 'Buy what we need for the feast'; or, that he should give something to the poor. After receiving the morsel, he immediately went out; and it was night. St John 13.18–30

RESPONSE 'The Lord is merciful and gracious,
slow to anger and abounding in steadfast love.'

Almighty God, you call us through your Son to be perfect in faith and love – we praise you for the sacrificial love of your Son . . .
'One of you will betray me' – forgive us each time we betray you, and make us aware of the price you pay for our sins . . .
'Now is the Son of Man glorified, and in him God is glorified' – praise and glory to the Father, the Son and the Holy Spirit, one God for ever . . .

INTERCESSIONS *pages 390–393* CLOSING PRAYERS *page 402–403*

11 September *I am the Way, the Truth, and the Life*

OPENING PRAYER Eternal Father, you invite us to share in your life. Help us by the Spirit to draw near to the throne of your grace, and to offer our praise to you with the perfect praise of your Son . . . Glory be . . .

PSALMODY Out of my distress I called on the Lord;
The Lord answered me and set me free.
With the Lord on my side I do not fear.
What can man do to me?
The Lord is on my side to help me;
I shall look in triumph on those who hate me. Psalm 118.5–7

SCRIPTURE READINGS Since we have the same spirit of faith as he had who wrote, 'I believed, and so I spoke,' we too believe, and so we speak, knowing that he who raised the Lord Jesus will raise us also with Jesus and bring us with you into his presence. For it is all for your sake, so that as grace extends to more and more people it may increase thanksgiving, to the glory of God. 2 Corinthians 4.13–15

Jesus said, 'Let not your hearts be troubled; believe in God, believe also in me. In my Father's house are many rooms; if it were not so, would I have told you that I go to prepare a place for you? And when I go and prepare a place for you, I will come again and will take you to myself, that where I am you may be also. And you know the way where I am going.' Thomas said, 'Lord, we do not know where you are going; how can we know the way?' Jesus said, 'I am the way, and the truth, and the life; no one comes to the Father, but by me. If you had known me, you would have known my Father also; henceforth you know him and have seen him.' Philip said, 'Lord, show us the Father, and we shall be satisfied.' Jesus said, 'Have I been with you so long, and yet you do not know me, Philip? He who has seen me has seen the Father; how can you say, "Show us the Father"? Do you not believe that I am in the Father and the Father in me? The words that I say to you I do not speak on my own authority; but the Father who dwells in me does his works. Believe me that I am in the Father and the Father in me; or else believe me for the sake of the works themselves.'
St John 14.1–11

RESPONSE 'Lead us, Heavenly Father, lead us,
o'er the world's tempestuous sea.'

Heavenly Father, your Son ascended to heaven to prepare a place for us – help us to respond to your perfect love with praise and thanksgiving . . .
'In my Father's house are many rooms' – Lord, lead us forward through each stage of our spiritual journey to union with Jesus Christ our Lord . . .
'I am the Way, the Truth and the Life' – bring us to yourself through your grace in Word and Sacrament . . .

INTERCESSIONS *pages 390–393* CLOSING PRAYERS *page 402–403*

OPENING PRAYER Eternal Father, you invite us to share in your life. Help us by the Spirit to draw near to the throne of your grace, and to offer our praise to you with the perfect praise of your Son . . . Glory be . . .

PSALMODY The Lord is my strength and my song;
he has become my salvation
Hark, glad songs of victory
in the tents of the righteous:
'The right hand of the Lord does valiantly,
the right hand of the Lord is exalted,
the right hand of the Lord does valiantly!' Psalm 118.14–16

SCRIPTURE READINGS God's love has been poured into our hearts through the Holy Spirit which has been given to us. Romans 5.5

Jesus said, 'If you love me, you will keep my commandments. And I will pray the Father, and he will give you another Counsellor, to be with you for ever, even the Spirit of truth, whom the world cannot receive, because it neither sees him nor knows him; you know him, for he dwells with you, and will be in you. I will not leave you desolate; I will come to you. Yet a little while, and the world will see me no more, but you will see me; because I live, you will live also. In that day you will know that I am in my Father, and you in me, and I in you. These things I have spoken to you, while I am still with you. But the Counsellor, the Holy Spirit, whom the Father will send in my name, he will teach you all things, and bring to your remembrance all that I have said to you. Peace I leave with you; my peace I give to you; not as the world gives do I give to you. Let not your hearts be troubled, neither let them be afraid. You heard me say to you, "I go away, and I will come to you." If you loved me, you would have rejoiced, because I go to the Father; for the Father is greater than I. And now I have told you before it takes place, so that when it does take place, you may believe. I will no longer talk much with you, for the ruler of this world is coming.' St John 14.15–31*

RESPONSE 'O Holy Spirit, Lord of grace, eternal fount of love,
inflame, we pray, our inmost hearts with fire from heaven above.'

Almighty Father, you sent the Holy Spirit to the first disciples – we praise you for the presence of your same Spirit in the Church today . . .
'I will pray the Father, and he will give you another Counsellor' – in your mercy, make known to us the nearness of your presence and love . . .
'Peace I leave with you; my peace I give to you' – cleanse us from our sins and help us to receive your gift of peace in our hearts . . .

INTERCESSIONS *pages 390–393* CLOSING PRAYERS *page 402–403*

13 September *I am the Vine*

OPENING PRAYER Eternal Father, you invite us to share in your life. Help us by the Spirit to draw near to the throne of your grace, and to offer our praise to you with the perfect praise of your Son . . . Glory be . . .

PSALMODY The stone which the builders rejected
has become the head of the corner.
This is the Lord's doing.
This is the day which the Lord has made,
let us rejoice and be glad in it. Psalm 118.19–24*

SCRIPTURE READINGS 'You have seen what I did to the Egyptians, and how I bore you on eagles' wings and brought you to myself. Now therefore, if you will obey my voice and keep my covenant, you shall be my own possession among all peoples; for all the earth is mine, and you shall be to me a kingdom of priests and a holy nation.' Exodus 19.4–6

I planted you a choice vine, wholly of pure seed.
How then have you turned degenerate and become a wild vine?
Jeremiah 2.21

Jesus said, 'I am the true vine, and my Father is the vinedresser. Every branch of mine that bears no fruit, he takes away, and every branch that does bear fruit he prunes, that it may bear more fruit. You are already made clean by the word which I have spoken to you. Abide in me, and I in you. As the branch cannot bear fruit by itself, unless it abides in the vine, neither can you, unless you abide in me. I am the vine, you are the branches. He who abides in me, and I in him, he it is that bears much fruit, for apart from me you can do nothing. If a man does not abide in me, he is cast forth as a branch and withers; and the branches are gathered, thrown into the fire and burned. If you abide in me, and my words abide in you, ask whatever you will, and it shall be done for you. By this my Father is glorified, that you bear much fruit, and so prove to be my disciples. As the Father has loved me, so have I loved you; abide in my love. If you keep my commandments, you will abide in my love, just as I have kept my Father's commandments and abide in his love.
St John 15.1–11

RESPONSE 'To thy Cross we look and live:
Jesus, may we ever be grafted, rooted, built in thee.'

Heavenly Father, your Church is like a vine reaching back into ancient Israel – we praise you for the New Covenant made by your Son . . .
'I am the vine and you are the branches' – we thank you for grafting us into Christ at our Baptism, and for feeding us at the Eucharist . . .
God is glorified when we bear much fruit – Lord, pour on us your grace so that we may bring forth the fruit of good works to your praise and glory . . .

INTERCESSIONS *pages 390–393* CLOSING PRAYERS *page 402–403*

14 September *Holy Cross Day*

OPENING PRAYER Eternal Father, you invite us to share in your life. Help us by the Spirit to draw near to the throne of your grace, and to offer our praise to you with the perfect praise of your Son . . . Glory be . . .

PSALMODY Why do the nations conspire,
and the peoples plot in vain?
The kings of the earth set themselves,
and the rulers take counsel together,
against the Lord and his anointed, saying,
'Let us burst their bonds asunder,
and cast their cords from us.' Psalm 2.1–3

SCRIPTURE READINGS Far be it from me to glory except in the cross of our Lord Jesus Christ, by which the world has been crucified to me, and I to the world. Galatians 6.14

Have this mind among yourselves, which is yours in Christ Jesus, who, though he was in the form of God, did not count equality with God a thing to be grasped, but emptied himself, taking the form of a servant, being born in the likeness of men. And being found in human form he humbled himself and became obedient unto death, even death on a cross. Therefore God has highly exalted him and bestowed on him the name which is above every name, that at the name of Jesus every knee should bow, in heaven and on earth and under the earth, and every tongue confess that Jesus Christ is Lord, to the glory of God the Father. Philippians 2.5–11

Jesus said, 'Now is the judgement of this world, now shall the ruler of this world be cast out; and I, when I am lifted up from the earth, will draw all men to myself.' He said this to show by what death he was to die. The crowd answered, 'We have heard from the law that the Christ remains for ever. How can you say that the Son of Man must be lifted up? Who is this Son of Man?' Jesus said, 'The light is with you for a little longer. Walk while you have the light, lest the darkness overtake you.'
St John 12.31–35

RESPONSE 'Lift high the Cross, the love of Christ proclaim,
till all the world adore his sacred name.'

Gracious God, you save us from our sins by the death of your Son – on this Holy Cross day, we praise you for his perfect self-offering . . .
Christ was raised high on the Cross of suffering and shame – Lord, draw all people to yourself by the mystery of your selfless love . . .
'Christ humbled himself and became obedient unto death, even death on the Cross' – give us courage to take up our cross and to follow Christ . . .

INTERCESSIONS *pages 390–393* CLOSING PRAYERS *page 402–403*

15 September *You also are My Witnesses*

OPENING PRAYER Eternal Father, you invite us to share in your life. Help us by the Spirit to draw near to the throne of your grace, and to offer our praise to you with the perfect praise of your Son . . . Glory be . . .

PSALMODY We bless you from the house of the Lord.
The Lord is God, and he has given us light.
Thou art my God, and I will give thanks to thee;
thou art my God, I will extol thee.
O give thanks to the Lord, for he is good;
for his steadfast love endures for ever! Psalm 118.26–29*

SCRIPTURE READINGS
'All our enemies rail against us;
panic and pitfall have come upon us,
devastation and destruction.
My eyes will flow without ceasing, without respite,
until the Lord from heaven looks down and sees;
Lamentations 3.46–50*

Jesus said, 'If the world hates you, know that it has hated me before it hated you. If you were of the world, the world would love its own; but because you are not of the world, but I chose you out of the world, therefore the world hates you. Remember the word that I said to you, "A servant is not greater than his master." If they persecuted me, they will persecute you; if they kept my word, they will keep yours also. But all this they will do to you on my account, because they do not know him who sent me. If I had not come and spoken to them, they would not have sin; but now they have no excuse for their sin. He who hates me hates my Father also. If I had not done among them the works which no one else did, they would not have sin; but now they have seen and hated both me and my Father. It is to fulfil the word that is written in their law, "They hated me without a cause." But when the Counsellor comes, whom I shall send to you from the Father, even the Spirit of truth, who proceeds from the Father, he will bear witness to me; and you also are witnesses, because you have been with me from the beginning.' St John 15.18–27

RESPONSE 'How precious to me are thy thoughts, O God;
how vast is the sum of them.'

Eternal Father, you are the source and strength of our lives – we praise you for your presence with us, now and always . . .
'When the Counsellor comes, whom I shall send to you from the Father' – renew your gift of the Spirit in our hearts, and make us holy . . .
'You also are my witnesses' – Lord, strengthen your Church to witness to your love for the whole world in Jesus Christ . . .

INTERCESSIONS *pages 390–393* CLOSING PRAYERS *page 402–403*

OPENING PRAYER Eternal Father, you invite us to share in your life. Help us by the Spirit to draw near to the throne of your grace, and to offer our praise to you with the perfect praise of your Son . . . Glory be . . .

PSALMODY Blessed are those whose way is blameless,
who walk in the law of the Lord! Psalm 119.1

SCRIPTURE READINGS Since then we have a great high priest who has passed through the heavens, Jesus, the Son of God, let us hold fast our confession. For we have not a high priest who is unable to sympathize with our weaknesses, but one who in every respect has been tempted as we are, yet without sinning. Let us then with confidence draw near to the throne of grace, that we may receive mercy and find grace to help in time of need.
Hebrews 4.14–16

Jesus lifted up his eyes to heaven and said, 'Father, the hour has come; glorify thy Son that the Son may glorify thee, since thou hast given him power over all flesh, to give eternal life to all whom thou hast given him. And this is eternal life, that they know thee the only true God, and Jesus Christ whom thou hast sent. I glorified thee on earth, having accomplished the work which thou gavest me to do, and now, Father, glorify thou me in thy own presence with the glory which I had with thee before the world was made. Now I am no more in the world, but they are in the world, and I am coming to thee. Holy Father, keep them in thy name, which thou hast given me, that they may be one, even as we are one. While I was with them; I kept them in thy name, which thou hast given me; I have guarded them, and none of them is lost but the son of perdition, that the scripture may be fulfilled. Sanctify them in the truth; thy word is truth. As thou didst send me into the world, so I have sent them into the world. For their sake I consecrate myself, that they also may be consecrated in truth. I do not pray for these only, but also for those who believe in me through their word, that they may all be one; even as thou, Father, art in me, and I in thee, that they also may be in us, so that the world may believe that thou hast sent me.' St John 17.1–21*

RESPONSE 'Great is the Lord, and greatly to be praised,
and his greatness is unsearchable.'

Eternal Father, your Son is our great High Priest who intercedes for us – we praise you for Christ our Prophet, Priest and King . . .
'I consecrate myself, that they also may be consecrated' – Lord, strengthen our wills and help us to grow into union with Christ . . .
'As thou didst send me into the world, so I have sent them into the world' – give your Church the grace to share in your Son's mission . . .

INTERCESSIONS *pages 390–393* CLOSING PRAYERS *page 402–403*

17 September *Jesus is Arrested*

OPENING PRAYER Eternal Father, you invite us to share in your life. Help us by the Spirit to draw near to the throne of your grace, and to offer our praise to you with the perfect praise of your Son . . . Glory be . . .

PSALMODY O that my ways may be steadfast in keeping thy statutes!
Then I shall not be put to shame,
having my eyes fixed on all thy commandments.
Psalm 119.5–6

SCRIPTURE READINGS
He was despised and rejected by men;
a man of sorrows, and acquainted with grief;
and as one from whom men hide their faces
he was despised, and we esteemed him not. Isaiah 53.3

Jesus went with his disciples across the Kidron valley, where there was a garden, which he and his disciples entered. Now Judas, who betrayed him, also knew the place; for Jesus often met there with his disciples. So Judas, procuring a band of soldiers and some officers from the chief priests and the Pharisees, went there with lanterns and torches and weapons. Jesus, knowing all that was to befall him, came forward and said, 'Whom do you seek?' They answered, 'Jesus of Nazareth.' Jesus said, 'I am he.' Judas, who betrayed him, was standing with them. When he said, 'I am he,' they drew back and fell to the ground. Again he asked them, 'Whom do you seek?' And they said, 'Jesus of Nazareth.' Jesus answered, 'I told you that I am he; so, if you seek me, let these men go.' This was to fulfil the word which he had spoken, 'Of those whom thou gavest me I lost not one.' Then Simon Peter, having a sword, drew it and struck the high priest's slave and cut off his right ear. The slave's name was Malchus. Jesus said to Peter, 'Put your sword into its sheath; shall I not drink the cup which the Father has given me?' So the band of soldiers and their captain and the officers of the Jews seized Jesus and bound him. First they led him to Annas; for he was the father-in-law of Caiaphas, who was high priest that year. It was Caiaphas who had given counsel to the Jews that it was expedient that one man should die for the people. St John 18.1–14*

RESPONSE 'The Lord is good to all,
and his compassion is over all that he has made.'

Almighty God, you are faithful and true in all your ways – we praise you for your gift of free will to all people . . .
The disciples forsook your Son and left him to the powers of this world – Lord, strengthen our desire to follow your Son faithfully . . .
'Whom do you seek?' – we seek you, Father, Son and Holy Spirit, one God to be praised and glorified for time and for eternity . . .

INTERCESSIONS *pages 390–393* CLOSING PRAYERS *page 402–403*

18 September *Peter in the Courtyard*

OPENING PRAYER Eternal Father, you invite us to share in your life. Help us by the Spirit to draw near to the throne of your grace, and to offer our praise to you with the perfect praise of your Son . . . Glory be . . .

PSALMODY How can a young man keep his way pure?
By guarding it according to thy word.
I have laid up thy word in my heart,
that I might not sin against thee. Psalm 119.9–11

SCRIPTURE READINGS 'The Son of Man came not to be served but to serve, and to give his life as a ransom for many.' St Matthew 20.28

Simon Peter followed Jesus, and so did another disciple. As this disciple was known to the high priest, he entered the court of the high priest along with Jesus, while Peter stood outside at the door. The other disciple, who was known to the high priest, went out and spoke to the man who kept the door, and brought Peter in. The maid who kept the door said to Peter, 'Are not you also one of this man's disciples?' He said, 'I am not.' Now the servants and officers had made a charcoal fire, because it was cold, and they were standing and warming themselves; Peter also was with them, standing and warming himself. The high priest then questioned Jesus about his disciples and his teaching. Jesus answered, 'I have spoken openly to the world; I have always taught in synagogues and in the temple, where all Jews come together; I have said nothing secretly. Why do you ask me? Ask those who have heard me, what I said to them; they know what I said.' When he had said this, one of the officers standing by struck Jesus with his hand, saying 'Is that how you answer the high priest?' Jesus answered, 'If I have spoken wrongly, bear witness to the wrong; but if I have spoken rightly, why do you strike me?' Annas then sent him bound to Caiaphas the high priest. Now Simon Peter was standing and warming himself. They said, 'Are not you also one of his disciples?' He denied it and said, 'I am not.' One of the servants of the high priest, a kinsman of the man whose ear Peter had cut off, asked, 'Did I not see you in the garden with him?' Peter again denied it; and at once the cock crowed. St John 18.15–27

RESPONSE 'A charge to keep I have, a God to glorify,
a never dying soul to save, and fit it for the sky.'

Heavenly Father, the mystery of your forgiveness and love is past all understanding – we praise you and we proclaim your glory . . .
'He denied it' – Lord, help us to be honest in all things, and grant us forgiveness and inner healing for all our sins and failures . . .
'Are you one of this man's disciples?' – we rejoice to be Christians . . .

INTERCESSIONS *pages 390–393* CLOSING PRAYERS *page 402–403*

OPENING PRAYER Eternal Father, you invite us to share in your life. Help us by the Spirit to draw near to the throne of your grace, and to offer our praise to you with the perfect praise of your Son . . . Glory be . . .

PSALMODY With my lips I declare all the ordinances of thy mouth.
In the way of thy testimonies I delight
as much as in all riches.
I will not forget thy word. Psalm 119.13–16*

SCRIPTURE READINGS He who did not spare his own Son, but gave him up for us all, will he not also give us all things with him? Romans 8.32

They led Jesus from the house of Caiaphas to the praetorium. It was early. They did not enter the praetorium, so that they might not be defiled, but might eat the passover. So Pilate went out and said, 'What accusation do you bring against this man?' They answered, 'If this man were not an evildoer, we would not have handed him over.' Pilate said, 'Take him yourselves and judge him by your own law.' The Jews said, 'It is not lawful for us to put any man to death.' This was to fulfil the word which Jesus had spoken to show by what death he was to die. Pilate entered the praetorium again and called Jesus, and said, 'Are you the King of the Jews?' Jesus answered, 'Do you say this of your own accord, or did others say it to you about me?' Pilate answered, 'Am I a Jew? Your own nation and the chief priests have handed you over to me; what have you done?' Jesus answered, 'My kingship is not of this world; if my kingship were of this world, my servants would fight, that I might not be handed over to the Jews; but my kingship is not from the world.' Pilate said, 'So you are a king?' Jesus answered, 'You say that I am a king. For this I was born, and for this I have come into the world, to bear witness to the truth. Every one who is of the truth hears my voice.' Pilate said, 'What is truth?' After he had said this, he went out, and told them, 'I find no crime in him. But you have a custom that I should release one man for you at the Passover; will you have me release the King of the Jews?' They cried out, 'Not this man, but Barabbas!' Barabbas was a robber. St John 18.28–40*

RESPONSE 'The Lord is faithful in all his words,
and gracious in all his deeds.'

Eternal Father, your Son is the innocent victim who dies no more – we praise you for the humility and redeeming love of your Son . . .
'Are you the King of the Jews?' – we rejoice and acclaim your Son as Lord of the universe and King of all creation . . .
'For this I have come into the world, to bear witness to the truth' – equip the Church to proclaim your message of salvation to the world . . .

INTERCESSIONS *pages 390–393* CLOSING PRAYERS *page 402–403*

20 September *Pontius Pilate*

OPENING PRAYER Eternal Father, you invite us to share in your life. Help us by the Spirit to draw near to the throne of your grace, and to offer our praise to you with the perfect praise of your Son . . . Glory be . . .

PSALMODY Deal bountifully with thy servant,
that I may live and observe thy word. Psalm 119.17

SCRIPTURE READINGS King Solomon gave to the queen of Sheba all that she desired. 1 Kings 10.13

Pilate took Jesus and scourged him. The soldiers plaited a crown of thorns, and put it on his head, and arrayed him in a purple robe; they came up to him, saying, 'Hail, King of the Jews!' and struck him with their hands. Pilate went out, and said, 'See, I am bringing him out to you, that you may know that I find no crime in him.' Jesus came out, wearing the crown of thorns and the purple robe. Pilate said, 'Behold the man!' When the chief priests and the officers saw him, they cried out, 'Crucify him, crucify him!' Pilate said, 'Take him yourselves and crucify him, for I find no crime in him.' The Jews answered, 'We have a law, and by that law he ought to die, because he has made himself the Son of God.' When Pilate heard these words, he was the more afraid; he entered the praetorium and said, 'Where are you from?' But Jesus gave no answer. Pilate said, 'You will not speak to me? Do you not know that I have power to release you, and power to crucify you?' Jesus answered, 'You would have no power over me unless it had been given you from above; therefore he who delivered me to you has the greater sin.' Upon this Pilate sought to release him, but the Jews cried out, 'If you release this man, you are not Caesar's friend; every one who makes himself a king sets himself against Caesar.' When Pilate heard these words, he brought Jesus out and sat down on the judgement seat at a place called The Pavement. It was the day of Preparation for the Passover; it was about the sixth hour. He said to the Jews, 'Here is your King!' They cried out, 'Away with him, away with him, crucify him!' Pilate said, 'Shall I crucify your King?' The chief priests answered, 'We have no king but Caesar.' Then he handed him over to be crucified. St John 19.1–16*

RESPONSE 'They shall pour forth the fame of thy abundant goodness,
and shall sing aloud of thy righteousness.'

Eternal Father, the Cross is a powerful sign of victory – we adore you and we praise you for the faithful love of Jesus . . .
'Where are you from?' – we rejoice that your Son is eternal, and that he lives and reigns with you and the Holy Spirit, one God, for ever . . .
'Behold, your King' – Lord, draw all people by the power of the sacred Cross to acknowledge Jesus as Lord and King . . .

INTERCESSIONS *pages 390–393* CLOSING PRAYERS *page 402–403*

21 September *Saint Matthew the Apostle*

OPENING PRAYER Eternal Father, you invite us to share in your life. Help us by the Spirit to draw near to the throne of your grace, and to offer our praise to you with the perfect praise of your Son . . . Glory be . . .

PSALMODY For ever, O Lord, thy word
is firmly fixed in the heavens.
If thy law had not been my delight,
I should have perished in my affliction.
I will never forget thy precepts;
for by them thou hast given me life.
I have seen a limit to all perfection,
but thy commandment is exceedingly broad.
Psalm 119.89–96*

SCRIPTURE READINGS Honour the Lord with your substance and with the first fruits of all your produce. Proverbs 3.9

Jesus saw a man called Matthew sitting at the tax office; and he said to him, 'Follow me.' He rose and followed him. Many tax-collectors and sinners came and sat down with Jesus and his disciples. When the Pharisees saw this, they said to his disciples, 'Why does your teacher eat with tax collectors and sinners?' When he heard it he said, 'Those who are well have no need of a physician, but those who are sick. Go and learn what this means, "I desire mercy, and not sacrifice." For I came not to call the righteous, but sinners.' St Matthew 9.9–13

Having this ministry by the mercy of God, we do not lose heart. We have renounced disgraceful, underhanded ways; we refuse to practise cunning or to tamper with God's word, but by the open statement of the truth we would commend ourselves to every man's conscience in the sight of God. Even if our gospel is veiled, it is veiled only to those who are perishing. For what we preach is not ourselves, but Jesus Christ as Lord, with ourselves as your servants for Jesus' sake. It is the God who said, 'Let light shine out of darkness,' who has shone in our hearts to give the light of the knowledge of the glory of God in the face of Christ. 2 Corinthians 4.1–6*

RESPONSE 'Happy is he whose help is the God of Jacob,
whose hope is in the Lord his God.'

Heavenly Father, you chose Matthew to be an Apostle and Evangelist – we join our praises with the worship of the saints in glory . . .
'Follow me' – Lord, free us from the love of money, and make us responsible stewards of all you have entrusted to us . . .
'Let light shine out of darkness' – with confidence in your goodness, we pray with Saint Matthew for the spread of the Gospel in all the world . . .

INTERCESSIONS *pages 390–393* CLOSING PRAYERS *page 402–403*

OPENING PRAYER Eternal Father, you invite us to share in your life. Help us by the Spirit to draw near to the throne of your grace, and to offer our praise to you with the perfect praise of your Son . . . Glory be . . .

PSALMODY Open my eyes, that I may behold
wondrous things out of thy law. Psalm 119.18

SCRIPTURE READINGS God shows his love for us in that while we were yet sinners Christ died for us. Romans 5.8

They took Jesus and he went out, bearing his own cross, to the place called the place of a skull, which is called in Hebrew Golgotha. There they crucified him, and with him two others, one on either side, and Jesus between them. Pilate wrote a title and put it on the cross; it read, 'Jesus of Nazareth, the King of the Jews.' Many of the Jews read this, for the place where Jesus was crucified was near the city; and it was written in Hebrew, Latin, and Greek. The chief priests of the Jews then said to Pilate, 'Do not write, "The King of the Jews," but, "This man said, I am King of the Jews."' Pilate answered, 'What I have written I have written.' When the soldiers had crucified Jesus they took his garments and made four parts, one for each soldier; also his tunic. But his tunic was without seam, woven from top to bottom; so they said to one another, 'Let us not tear it, but cast lots for it to see whose it shall be.' This was to fulfil the scripture, 'They parted my garments among them, and for my clothing they cast lots.' So the soldiers did this. But standing by the cross of Jesus were his mother, and his mother's sister, Mary the wife of Clopas, and Mary Magdalene. When Jesus saw his mother, and the disciple whom he loved standing near, he said to his mother, 'Woman, behold your son!' Then he said to the disciple, 'Behold, your mother!' From that hour the disciple took her to his own home. After this Jesus, knowing that all was now finished, said (to fulfil the scripture), 'I thirst.' A bowl full of vinegar stood there; so they put a sponge full of the vinegar on hyssop and help it to his mouth. When Jesus had received the vinegar, he said, 'It is finished'; he bowed his head and gave up his spirit. St John 19.17–30*

RESPONSE 'Fountain of goodness, Jesu, Lord and God,
cleanse us, unclean, with thy most precious Blood.'

Eternal God, great is your majesty and great is your selfless love – we thank you for your Son, who is priest and sacrifice and King . . .
The Cross is the climax in the life of Jesus – we praise you for his love without limit on the Cross for our salvation . . .
In the mystery of love, you call your church to share in the sufferings of Christ – Lord, give us courage to take up our Cross and follow Christ . . .

INTERCESSIONS *pages 390–393* CLOSING PRAYERS *page 402–403*

23 September *Joseph of Arimathea*

OPENING PRAYER Eternal Father, you invite us to share in your life. Help us by the Spirit to draw near to the throne of your grace, and to offer our praise to you with the perfect praise of your Son . . . Glory be . . .

PSALMODY Teach me, O Lord, the way of thy statutes;
and I will keep it to the end.
Give me understanding, that I may keep thy law.
Lead me in the path of thy commandments,
for I delight in it. Psalm 119.33–35*

SCRIPTURE READINGS Jesus answered, 'Destroy this temple, and in three days I will raise it up.' St John 2.19

Since it was the day of Preparation, in order to prevent the bodies from remaining on the cross on the sabbath (for that sabbath was a high day), the Jews asked Pilate that their legs might be broken, and that they might be taken away. The soldiers came and broke the legs of the first, and of the other who had been crucified with him; but when they came to Jesus and saw that he was already dead, they did not break his legs. But one of the soldiers pierced his side with a spear, and at once there came out blood and water. He who saw it has borne witness – his testimony is true, and he knows that he tells the truth – that you also may believe. For these things took place that the scripture might be fulfilled, 'Not a bone of him shall be broken.' Another scripture says, 'They shall look on him whom they have pierced.' After this Joseph of Arimathea, who was a disciple of Jesus, but secretly, for fear of the Jews, asked Pilate that he might take away the body of Jesus, and Pilate gave him leave. So he came and took away his body. Nicodemus also, who had at first come to him by night, came bringing a mixture of myrrh and aloes about a hundred pounds' weight. They took the body of Jesus, and bound it in linen cloths with the spices, as is the burial custom of the Jews. Now in the place where he was crucified there was a garden, and in the garden a new tomb where no one had ever been laid. So because of the Jewish day of Preparation, as the tomb was close at hand, they laid Jesus there. St John 19.31–42

RESPONSE 'From the rising of the sun to its setting,
the name of the Lord is to be praised.'

God our Father in heaven, you gave your Son for the salvation of the world – we rejoice in your redeeming love and we praise you . . .
'He who saw it has borne witness' – Lord, pour your Holy Spirit on the Church and help us to witness to the saving work of Christ . . .
'The souls of the righteous are in the hands of God' – in your mercy, bring our departed relatives and friends to the glory of the resurrection . . .

INTERCESSIONS *pages 390–393* CLOSING PRAYERS *page 402–403*

OPENING PRAYER Eternal Father, you invite us to share in your life. Help us by the Spirit to draw near to the throne of your grace, and to offer our praise to you with the perfect praise of your Son . . . Glory be . . .

PSALMODY Incline my heart to thy testimonies,
and not to gain!
Turn my eyes from looking at vanities;
and give me life in thy ways.
Confirm to thy servant thy promise,
which is for those who fear thee.
Turn away the reproach which I dread;
for thy ordinances are good.
Behold, I long for thy precepts
in thy righteousness give me life! Psalm 119.36–40

SCRIPTURE READINGS If you have been raised with Christ, seek the things that are above, where Christ is, seated at the right hand of God. Set your minds on things that are above, not on things that are on earth. For you have died, and your life is hid with Christ in God. Colossians 3.1–3

Now on the first day of the week Mary Magdalene came to the tomb early, while it was still dark, and saw that the stone had been taken away from the tomb. So she ran, and went to Simon Peter and the other disciple, the one whom Jesus loved, and said to them, 'They have taken the Lord out of the tomb, and we do not know where they have laid him.' Peter then came out with the other disciple, and they went toward the tomb. They both ran, but the other disciple outran Peter and reached the tomb first; stooping to look in, he saw the linen cloths lying there, but he did not go in. Then Simon Peter came, following him, and went into the tomb; he saw the linen cloths lying, and the napkin, which had been on his head, not lying with the linen cloths but rolled up in a place by itself. Then the other disciple, who reached the tomb first, also went in, and he saw and believed; for as yet they did not know the scripture, that he must rise from the dead. Then the disciples went back to their homes. St John 20.1–10

RESPONSE 'Blessed be the Lord, the God of Israel,
from everlasting to everlasting.'

Gracious God, you are the eternal Father in heaven – we join with all creation to worship and adore your holy name . . .
You give new life to us through your risen Son – we praise you for all your many blessings for us in your risen Son . . .
'They saw the stone had been taken away from the tomb' – we thank you for all the faithful witnesses of your risen Son through the centuries . . .

INTERCESSIONS *pages 390–393* CLOSING PRAYERS *page 402–403*

OPENING PRAYER Eternal Father, you invite us to share in your life. Help us by the Spirit to draw near to the throne of your grace, and to offer our praises to you with the perfect praise of your Son . . . Glory be . . .

PSALMODY Let thy steadfast love come to me, O Lord,
thy salvation according to thy promise;
then shall I have an answer for those who taunt me.
I will keep thy law continually, for ever and ever;
and I shall walk at liberty,
for I have sought thy precepts.
I will also speak of thy testimonies before kings,
and shall not be put to shame;
for I find my delight in thy commandments.
I revere thy commandments, which I love,
and I will meditate on thy statutes. Psalm 119.41–48*

SCRIPTURE READINGS Jesus said, 'Thus it is written, that the Christ should suffer and on the third day rise from the dead.' St Luke 24.46

Mary stood weeping outside the tomb, and as she wept she stooped to look into the tomb; and she saw two angels in white, sitting where the body of Jesus had lain, one at the head and one at the feet. They said, 'Woman, why are you weeping?' She said, 'Because they have taken away my Lord, and I do not know where they have laid him.' Saying this, she turned round and saw Jesus standing, but she did not know that it was Jesus. Jesus said, 'Woman, why are you weeping? Whom do you seek?' Supposing him to be the gardener, she said, 'Sir, if you have carried him away, tell me where you have laid him, and I will take him away.' Jesus said, 'Mary.' She turned and said in Hebrew, 'Rabboni!' (which means Teacher). Jesus said, 'Do not hold me, for I have not yet ascended to the Father; but go to my brethren and say to them, I am ascending to my Father and your Father, to my God and your God.' Mary Magdalene went and said to the disciples, 'I have seen the Lord'; and she told them that he had said these things to her. St John 20.11–18*

RESPONSE 'Glory in his holy name;
let the hearts of those who seek him rejoice.'

Eternal God, your Son destroyed death by dying and he restored to us eternal life – we praise you for your power and endless love . . .
'Mary stood weeping outside the tomb' – help the Church to bring the knowledge of your love to all who mourn . . .
'I am ascending to my Father and your Father' – we rejoice that you are our Father and we are your adopted children and co-heirs with Jesus . . .

INTERCESSIONS *pages 390–393* CLOSING PRAYERS *page 402–403*

26 September *Doubting Thomas*

OPENING PRAYER Eternal Father, you invite us to share in your life. Help us by the Spirit to draw near to the throne of your grace, and to offer our praise to you with the perfect praise of your Son . . . Glory be . . .

PSALMODY Remember thy word to thy servant,
in which thou hast made me hope.
This is my comfort in my affliction
that thy promise gives me life.
This blessing has fallen on me,
that I have kept thy precepts. Psalm 119.49–56*

SCRIPTURE READINGS Jesus said, 'This is the will of my Father, that every one who sees the Son and believes in him should have eternal life; and I will raise him up at the last day.' St John 6.40

On the evening of that day, the first day of the week, the doors being shut where the disciples were, for fear of the Jews, Jesus came and stood among them and said, 'Peace be with you.' When he had said this, he showed them his hands and his side. The disciples were glad when they saw the Lord. Jesus said again, 'Peace be with you. As the Father has sent me, even so I send you.' And when he had said this, he breathed on them, and said, 'Receive the Holy Spirit. If you forgive the sins of any, they are forgiven; if you retain the sins of any, they are retained.' Thomas, one of the twelve, called the Twin, was not with them when Jesus came. So the other disciples told him, 'We have seen the Lord.' But he said, 'Unless I see in his hands the print of the nails, and place my hand in his side, I will not believe.' Eight days later, his disciples were again in the house, and Thomas was with them. The doors were shut, but Jesus came and stood among them, and said, 'Peace be with you.' Then he said to Thomas, 'Put your finger here, and see my hands, and put out your hand, and place it in my side; do not be faithless, but believing.' Thomas answered, 'My Lord and my God!' Jesus said, 'Have you believed because you have seen me? Blessed are those who have not seen and yet believe.' St John 20.19–29

RESPONSE 'I will give thanks to thee, O Lord, among the peoples,
I will sing praises to thee among the nations.'

Heavenly Father, you built the Church on the sure foundation of your risen Son – we praise you for the faith of the holy apostles . . .
'Peace be with you' – cleanse our hearts so that we may receive your gift of peace . . .
'If you forgive the sins of any, they are forgiven' – we thank you for giving power and authority to the Church to forgive our sins . . .

INTERCESSIONS *pages 390–393* CLOSING PRAYERS *page 402–403*

27 September *Fishers of Men*

OPENING PRAYER Eternal Father, you invite us to share in your life. Help us by the Spirit to draw near to the throne of your grace, and to offer our praise to you with the perfect praise of your Son . . . Glory be . . .

PSALMODY When I think of thy ordinances from of old,
I take comfort, O Lord.
Hot indignation seizes me because of the wicked.
who forsake thy law. Psalm 119.52–53

SCRIPTURE READINGS You are a chosen race, a royal priesthood, a holy nation, God's own people, that you may declare the wonderful deeds of him who called you out of the darkness into his marvellous light. Once you were no people but now you are God's own people; once you had not received mercy but now you have received mercy. 1 Peter 2.9–10

Simon Peter, Thomas called the Twin, Nathanael of Cana in Galilee, the sons of Zebedee, and two others of his disciples were together. Simon Peter said, 'I am going fishing.' They said, 'We will go with you.' They got into the boat; but that night they caught nothing. Just as day was breaking, Jesus stood on the beach; yet the disciples did not know that it was Jesus. Jesus said, 'Children, have you any fish?' They answered, 'No.' He said, 'Cast the net on the right side of the boat, and you will find some.' They cast it, and they were not able to haul it in, for the quantity of fish. That disciple whom Jesus loved said to Peter, 'It is the Lord!' When Simon Peter heard that it was the Lord, he put on his clothes, for he was stripped for work, and sprang into the sea. The other disciples came in the boat, dragging the net full of fish, for they were not far from the land. When they got out on land, they saw a charcoal fire there, with fish lying on it, and bread. Jesus said, 'Bring some of the fish that you have just caught.' Simon Peter hauled the net ashore, full of large fish, a hundred and fifty-three of them; and although there were so many, the net was not torn. Jesus said, 'Come and have breakfast.' None of the disciples dared ask, 'Who are you?' They knew it was the Lord. Jesus came and took the bread and gave it to them, and so with the fish. St John 21.2–13*

RESPONSE 'Oh give thanks to the Lord, call on his name
make known his deeds among the peoples.'

Heavenly Father, it is your will to gather all people to yourself in Christ – we praise you for making us members of the Church by Baptism . . .
'The disciples did not know it was Jesus' – help us to be aware of your presence and purposes through the words and actions of other people . . .
'Cast your net on the right side' – Lord, help the Church to share with the Spirit in making Christ known to all people . . .

INTERCESSIONS *pages 390–393* CLOSING PRAYERS *page 402–403*

28 September *Do You Love Me?*

OPENING PRAYER Eternal Father, you invite us to share in your life. Help us by the Spirit to draw near to the throne of your grace, and to offer our praise to you with the perfect praise of your Son . . . Glory be . . .

PSALMODY The Lord is my portion; I promise to keep thy words.
I entreat thy favour with all my heart;
be gracious to me according to thy promise.
Psalm 119.57–58

SCRIPTURE READINGS Beloved, let us love one another; for love is of God, and he who loves is born of God and knows God. He who does not love does not know God; for God is love. 1 John 4.7–8

When they had finished breakfast, Jesus said to Simon Peter, 'Simon, son of John, do you love me more than these?' He said, 'Yes, Lord; you know that I love you.' He said, 'Feed my lambs.' A second time he said, 'Simon, son of John, do you love me?' he said, 'Yes, Lord; you know that I love you.' He said, 'Tend my sheep.' He said to him the third time, 'Simon, son of John, do you love me?' Peter was grieved because he said the third time, 'Do you love me?' He said, 'Lord, you know everything; you know that I love you.' Jesus said, 'Feed my sheep. Truly, truly, I say to you, when you were young, you girded yourself and walked where you would; but when you are old, you will stretch out your hands, and another will gird you and carry you where you do not wish to go.' (This he said to show by what death he was to glorify God.) After this he said, 'Follow me.' Peter turned and saw following them the disciple whom Jesus loved, who had lain close to his breast at the supper and had said, 'Lord, who is it that is going to betray you?' When Peter saw him, he said to Jesus, 'Lord, what about this man?' Jesus said, 'If it is my will that he remain until I come, what is that to you? Follow me!' The saying spread abroad among the brethren that this disciple was not to die; yet Jesus did not say to him that he was not to die, but, 'If it is my will that he remain until I come, what is that to you?' This is the disciple who is bearing witness to these things, and who has written these things; and we know that his testimony is true. St John 21.15–24

RESPONSE 'Lord, it is my chief complaint that my love is weak and faint;
yet I love thee, and adore; O for grace to love thee more.'

In your divine providence you raised up Peter to be the Prince of the Apostles – we praise you for your forgiveness and perfect love . . .
'Feed my sheep' – Lord, give to all bishops and priests and deacons the gifts of your grace which they need to do your work . . .
'Follow me' – call us back to yourself whenever we stray from the pathway, and enfold us in your perfect love . . .

INTERCESSIONS *pages 390–393* CLOSING PRAYERS *page 402–403*

29 September *Saint Michael and All Angels*

OPENING PRAYER Eternal Father, you invite us to share in your life. Help us by the Spirit to draw near to the throne of your grace and to offer our praise to you with the perfect praise of your Son . . . Glory be . . .

PSALMODY The Lord has established his throne in the heavens,
and his kingdom rules over all.
Bless the Lord, O you his angels,
you mighty ones who do his word,
hearkening to the voice of his word!
Bless the Lord, all his hosts,
his ministers that do his will!

Psalm 103.19–21

SCRIPTURE READINGS Elisha said, 'O Lord, I pray thee, open his eyes that he may see.' So the Lord opened the eyes of the young man, and he saw; and behold, the mountain was full of horses and chariots of fire round about Elisha.

2 Kings 6.17

War arose in heaven, Michael and his angels fighting against the dragon; and the dragon and his angels fought, but they were defeated and there was no longer any place for them in heaven. And the great dragon was thrown down, that ancient serpent, who is called the Devil and Satan, the deceiver of the whole world – he was thrown down to the earth, and his angels were thrown down with him. I heard a loud voice in heaven, saying, 'Now the salvation and the power and the kingdom of our God and the authority of his Christ have come, for the accuser of our brethren has been thrown down, who accuses them day and night before our God. They have conquered him by the blood of the Lamb and by the word of their testimony, for they loved not their lives even unto death. Rejoice then, O heaven and you that dwell therein! But woe to you, O earth and sea, for the devil has come down to you in great wrath, because he knows that his time is short!'

Revelation 12.7–12

Jesus said, 'See that you do not despise one of these little ones; for I tell you that in heaven their angels always behold the face of my Father who is in heaven.'

St Matthew 18.10

RESPONSE 'The praises of Jesus the angels proclaim
fall down on their faces, and worship the Lamb.'

Eternal God, you guide us and the angels in a special way – we praise you for the continual worship and adoration of the angels in heaven . . .
'Open his eyes that he may see' – give us spiritual understanding . . .
'Rejoice, O heavens and you that dwell therein' – Lord, we rejoice and praise you with angels and archangels, and all the company of heaven . . .

INTERCESSIONS *pages 390–393* CLOSING PRAYERS *page 402–403*

30 September *Harvest*

OPENING PRAYER Eternal Father, you invite us to share in your life. Help us by the spirit to draw near to the throne of your grace, and to offer our praise to you with the perfect praise of your Son . . . Glory be . . .

PSALMODY Thou visitest the earth and waterest it,
thou greatly enrichest it;
the river of God is full of water
thou providest their grain,
for so thou has prepared it.
Thou waterest its furrows abundantly,
settling its ridges, softening it with showers,
and blessing its growth. Psalm 65.9–10

SCRIPTURE READINGS And God said, 'Behold, I have given you every plant yielding seed which is upon the face of all the earth, and every tree with seed in its fruit; you shall have them for food.' Genesis 1.29

When you come into the land which the Lord your God gives you for an inheritance, and have taken possession of it, and live in it, you shall take some of the first of all the fruit of the ground, which you harvest from your land that the Lord your God gives you, and you shall put it in a basket, and you shall go to the place which the Lord your God will choose, to make his name to dwell there. And you shall go to the priest who is in office at that time, and say to him, 'I declare this day to the Lord your God that I have come into the land which the Lord swore to our fathers to give us.' Then the priest shall take the basket from your hand, and set it down before the altar of the Lord your God. Deuteronomy 26.1–4

Another angel came out of the temple, calling with a loud voice to him who sat upon the cloud, 'Put in your sickle, and reap, for the hour to reap has come, for the harvest of the earth is fully ripe.' Revelation 14.15

RESPONSE 'All good gifts around us are sent from heaven above,
then thank the Lord, O thank the Lord, for all his love.'

Gracious God and Father, you provide the fruits of the earth to feed our bodies – we rejoice that the whole world is a sacrament of your love . . .
'I have given you every plant yielding seed' – Lord, give us ever-grateful hearts for all your many blessings and love . . .
'The earth has yielded its harvest' – inspire the leaders of the nations to distribute your bounties in a just way . . .

INTERCESSIONS *pages 390–393* CLOSING PRAYERS *page 402–403*

1 October *(Ember Day)*

OPENING PRAYER Almighty God, you have made us and we belong to you. Help us to know the nearness of your presence as we praise you, in union with the worship of your whole Church in heaven and on earth . . . Glory be . . .

PSALMODY How lovely is thy dwelling place,
O Lord of hosts!
My soul longs, yea, faints
for the courts of the Lord;
my heart and flesh sing for joy to the living God.
Even the sparrow finds a home,
and the swallow a nest for herself,
where she may lay her young,
at thy altars, O Lord of hosts, my King and my God.
Blessed are those who dwell in thy house,
ever singing thy praise! Psalm 84.1–4

SCRIPTURE READINGS Moses did as the Lord commanded him; he took Joshua and caused him to stand before Eleazar the priest and the whole congregation, and he laid his hands upon him, and commissioned him as the Lord directed through Moses. Numbers 27.22–23

The disciples besought him, saying 'Rabbi, eat.' But he said, 'I have food to eat of which you do not know.' So the disciples said, 'Has any one brought him food?' Jesus said, 'My food is to do the will of him who sent me, and to accomplish his work. Do you not say, "There are yet four months, then comes the harvest"? I tell you, lift up your eyes, and see how the fields are already white for harvest. He who reaps receives wages, and gathers fruit for eternal life, so that sower and reaper may rejoice together. For here the saying holds true, "One sows and another reaps." I sent you to reap that for which you did not labour; others have laboured, and you have entered into their labour.' St John 4.31–38

The harvest is plentiful, but the labourers are few; pray therefore the Lord of the harvest to send labourers into his harvest. St Matthew 9.37

RESPONSE 'O Holy Spirit, Lord of grace, eternal fount of love,
inflame, we pray, our inmost hearts with fire from heaven above.'

Heavenly Father, your Son is our eternal High Priest – we rejoice that he intercedes for us at the throne of grace and we praise you . . .
You call your servants for the sacred ministry of the Church in every age – Lord, equip them for your work and make them holy . . .
'The harvest is plentiful, but the labourers are few' – inspire those whom you are calling to offer themselves to work for your Kingdom . . .

INTERCESSIONS *pages 390–393* CLOSING PRAYERS *page 402–403*

OPENING PRAYER Almighty God, you have made us and we belong to you. Help us to know the nearness of your presence as we praise you, in union with the worship of your whole Church in heaven and on earth . . . Glory be . . .

PSALMODY I am a companion of all who fear thee,
of those who keep they precepts. Psalm 119.63

SCRIPTURE READINGS David said to Ziba, 'All that belonged to Saul and to all his house I have given to your master's son. You and your sons and your servants shall till the land for him, and shall bring in the produce, that your master's son may have bread to eat; but Mephibosheth your master's son shall always eat at my table.' 2 Samuel 9.9–10*

In the first book, O Theophilus, I have dealt with all that Jesus began to do and teach, until the day when he was taken up, after he had given commandment through the Holy Spirit to the apostles whom he had chosen. To them he presented himself alive after his passion by many proofs, appearing to them during forty days, and speaking of the Kingdom of God. While staying with them he charged them not to depart from Jerusalem, but to wait for the promise of the Father, which, he said, 'you heard from me, for John baptized with water, but before many days you shall be baptized with the Holy Spirit.' So when they had come together, they asked, 'Lord, will you at this time restore the kingdom to Israel?' He said, 'It is not for you to know times or seasons which the Father has fixed by his own authority. But you shall receive power when the Holy Spirit has come upon you; and you shall be my witnesses in Jerusalem and in all Judea and Samaria and to the end of the earth.' When he had said this, as they were looking on, he was lifted up, and a cloud took him out of their sight. While they were gazing into heaven as he went, behold, two men stood by them in white robes, and said, 'Men of Galilee, why do you stand looking into heaven? This Jesus, who was taken up from you into heaven, will come in the same way as you saw him go into heaven.' They returned to Jerusalem from the mount called Olivet. All these with one accord devoted themselves to prayer. Acts 1.1–14 *

RESPONSE 'And now, Lord, for what do I wait?
My hope is in thee.'

Eternal God, your Son perfectly completed his work on earth and then he returned to the Godhead – we praise you for your redeeming love . . .
'You shall receive power when the Holy Spirit has come upon you' – transform us through the gift of the Spirit and make us holy . . .
'You shall be my witnesses' – Lord, help the Church to witness to your saving love by our words and our deeds . . .

INTERCESSIONS *pages 390–393* CLOSING PRAYERS *page 402–403*

3 October *The Coming of the Holy Spirit*

OPENING PRAYER Almighty God, you have made us and we belong to you. Help us to know the nearness of your presence as we praise you, in union with the worship of your whole Church in heaven and on earth . . . Glory be . . .

PSALMODY The earth is full of thy steadfast love.
Thou hast dealt well with thy servant,
O Lord, according to thy word. Psalm 119.64–5

SCRIPTURE READINGS God's love has been poured into our hearts through the Holy Spirit which has been given to us Romans 5.5

When the day of Pentecost had come, they were all together in one place. Suddenly a sound came from heaven like the rush of a mighty wind, and it filled all the house where they were sitting. There appeared tongues as of fire, distributed and resting on each one of them. They were all filled with the Holy Spirit and began to speak in other tongues, as the Spirit gave them utterance. Peter, standing with the eleven, lifted up his voice and addressed them, 'Men of Judea and all who dwell in Jerusalem, let this be known to you, and give ear to my words. These men are not drunk, as you suppose, since it is only the third hour of the day; but this is what was spoken by the prophet Joel: "And in the last days it shall be, God declares, that I will pour out my Spirit upon all flesh, and your sons and your daughters shall prophesy, and your young men shall see visions, and your old men shall see dreams. And it shall be that whoever calls on the name of the Lord shall be saved." Men of Israel, hear these words: Jesus of Nazareth, you crucified and killed by the hands of lawless men. But God raised him up, and has made him both Lord and Christ.' When they heard this they were cut to the heart, and said, 'Brethren, what shall we do?' Peter said, 'Repent, and be baptized every one of you in the name of Jesus Christ for the forgiveness of your sins; and you shall receive the gift of the Holy Spirit.' So those who received his word were baptized, and there were added that day about three thousand souls. They devoted themselves to the apostles' teaching and fellowship, to the breaking of bread and the prayers. Acts 2.1–42 *

RESPONSE 'Spirit of purity and grace, our weakness, pitying, see;
O make our hearts thy dwelling place, and worthier thee.'

Heavenly Father, you sent the Holy Spirit on the Apostles at Pentecost – we praise you for the presence of the same Spirit in the Church today . . .
'I will pour out my Spirit on all flesh' – Lord, purify our bodies and minds, and make us worthy temples for your Holy Spirit . . .
'Whoever calls on the name of the Lord will be saved' – renew your gift of the Spirit in all who are baptized and confirmed in the faith . . .

INTERCESSIONS *pages 390–393* CLOSING PRAYERS *page 402–403*

4 October *Saint Francis of Assisi (d 1226)*

OPENING PRAYER Almighty God, you have made us and we belong to you. Help us to know the nearness of your presence as we praise you, in union with the worship of your whole Church in heaven and on earth . . . Glory be . . .

PSALMODY I will bless the Lord at all times;
his praise shall continually be in my mouth.
Let the afflicted hear and be glad.
O magnify the Lord with me,
and let us exalt his name together!
Look to him, and be radiant;
so your faces shall never be ashamed.
This poor man cried, and the Lord heard him,
and saved him out of all his troubles. Psalm 34.1–6*

SCRIPTURE READINGS One came up to Jesus, saying, 'Teacher, what good deed must I do, to have eternal life?' And he said, 'Why do you ask me about what is good? One there is who is good. If you would enter life, keep the commandments.' He said, 'Which?' Jesus said, 'You shall not kill, You shall not commit adultery, You shall not steal, You shall not bear false witness, Honour your father and mother, and You shall love your neighbour as yourself.' The young man said, 'All these I have observed; what do I still lack?' Jesus said, 'If you would be perfect, go, sell what you possess and give to the poor, and you will have treasure in heaven; and come, follow me.' St Matthew 19.16–21

Blessed are the poor in spirit, for theirs is the kingdom of heaven.
Blessed are those who mourn, for they shall be comforted.
Blessed are the meek, for they shall inherit the earth.
Blessed are those who hunger and thirst for righteousness, for they shall be satisfied.
Blessed are the merciful, for they shall obtain mercy.
Blessed are the pure in heart, for they shall see God.
Blessed are the peacemakers, for they shall be called sons of God.
Blessed are those who are persecuted for righteousness' sake, for theirs is the kingdom of heaven. St Matthew 5.3–10

RESPONSE 'O give thanks to the Lord, for he is good;
his steadfast love endures for ever.'

Gracious God, your glory shines in the lives of your saints – we praise you on this feast day for planting the flame of love in the heart of Saint Francis . . .
You gave Francis the grace to love you and all your creatures – help us to treat all your creation with respect and care . . .

INTERCESSIONS *pages 390–393* CLOSING PRAYERS *page 402–403*

5 October *Peter and John Before the Jewish Council*

OPENING PRAYER Almighty God, you have made us and we belong to you. Help us to know the nearness of your presence as we praise you in union with the worship of your whole Church in heaven and on earth . . . Glory be . . .

PSALMODY Those who fear thee shall see me and rejoice,
because I have hoped in thy word. Psalm 119.74

SCRIPTURE READINGS The Lord Jesus was taken up into heaven, and sat down at the right hand of God. And they went forth and preached everywhere, while the Lord worked with them and confirmed the message by signs that attended it. Amen. St Mark 16.19–20*

They arrested Peter and John and put them in custody. On the morrow their rulers and elders and scribes were gathered together in Jerusalem. When they had set them in the midst, they inquired, 'By what power or by what name did you do this?' Then Peter, filled with the Holy Spirit, said, 'Rulers of the people and elders, if we are being examined today concerning a good deed done to a cripple, by what means this man has been healed, be it known to you all, that by the name of Jesus Christ of Nazareth, whom you crucified, whom God raised from the dead, by him this man is standing before you well. This is the stone which was rejected by you builders, but which has become the head of the corner. There is salvation in no one else, for there is no other name under heaven given among men by which we must be saved.' When they had commanded them to go aside, out of the council, they conferred with one another, saying, 'What shall we do with these men? For that a notable sign has been performed through them is manifest to all the inhabitants of Jerusalem, and we cannot deny it. In order that it may spread no further, let us warn them to speak no more to any one in this name.' They called them and charged them not to speak or teach in the name of Jesus. Peter and John answered, 'Whether it is right in the sight of God to listen to you rather than to God, you must judge; for we cannot but speak of what we have seen and heard.' When they had further threatened them, they let them go, finding no way to punish them, because of the people. Acts 4.3–21*

RESPONSE 'I will praise the Lord as long as I live;
I will sing praises to my God while I have my being.'

Heavenly Father, the Cross is a sign of your victory and love in the world – we praise you for the perfect and vulnerable love of your Son . . .
'They arrested Peter and John' – Lord, we thank you for the courage and faith of all who suffer to spread the Gospel . . .
'This is the stone which was rejected by you builders' – help us to build our lives on the firm foundation of faith in Christ our Lord . . .

INTERCESSIONS *pages 390–393* CLOSING PRAYERS *page 402–403*

6 October *The First Christian Martyr*

OPENING PRAYER Almighty God, you have made us and we belong to you. Help us to know the nearness of your presence as we praise you, in union with the worship of your whole Church in heaven and on earth . . Glory be . . .

PSALMODY Let thy mercy come to me, that I may live;
for thy law is my delight.
Let the godless be put to shame,
because they have subverted me with guile.
Psalm 119.76–78*

SCRIPTURE READINGS 'Be strong and of good courage; be not frightened, neither be dismayed; for the Lord your God is with you wherever you go.'
Joshua 1.9

Stephen, full of grace and power, did great wonders and signs among the people. Then some of those who belonged to the synagogue of the Freedmen (as it was called), arose and disputed with Stephen. But they could not withstand the wisdom and the Spirit with which he spoke. They seized him and brought him before the council. And gazing at him, all who sat in the council saw that his face was like the face of an angel. Stephen said, 'You stiff-necked people, uncircumcised in your heart and ears, you always resist the Holy Spirit. As your fathers did, so do you. Which of the prophets did not your fathers persecute? They killed those who announced beforehand the coming of the Righteous One, whom you have now betrayed and murdered, you who received the law as delivered by angels and did not keep it.' When they heard these things they were enraged, and they ground their teeth against him. But he, full of the Holy Spirit, gazed into heaven and saw the glory of God, and Jesus standing at the right hand of God; and he said, 'Behold, I see the heavens opened, and the Son of Man standing at the right hand of God.' They cried out with a loud voice and stopped their ears and rushed together upon him. Then they cast him out of the city and stoned him; and the witnesses laid down their garments at the feet of a young man named Saul. As they were stoning Stephen, he prayed, 'Lord, do not hold this sin against them.' When he had said this, he fell asleep. And Saul was consenting to his death. Acts 6.8–8.1*

RESPONSE 'Keep peaceful in the midst of strife, forgiving and forgiven,
O may we lead the pilgrim's life, and follow thee to heaven.'

Almighty God, you made the Cross to be a source of endless blessing for all – we thank you for the greatness of your love for us in your Son . . .
'Stephen, full of grace and power, did great wonders and signs' – Lord, give your Church the grace to take up the Cross and follow Christ . . .
'Stephen, full of the Holy Spirit, gazed into heaven and saw the glory of God' – give to the Church a greater vision of your glory . . .

INTERCESSIONS *pages 390–393* CLOSING PRAYERS *page 402–403*

7 October *The Apostles Laid Their Hands On Them*

OPENING PRAYER Almighty God, you have made us and we belong to you. Help us to know the nearness of your presence as we praise you, in union with the worship of your whole Church in heaven and on earth . . . Glory be . . .

PSALMODY My soul languishes for thy salvation; I hope in thy word.
My eyes fail with watching for thy promise. Psalm 119.81–82*

SCRIPTURE READINGS Moses said, 'See, I have set before you this day life and good, death and evil. If you obey the commandments of the Lord your God, by loving the Lord your God, by walking in his ways, and by keeping his commandments, then you shall live and multiply, and the Lord your God will bless you. But if your heart turns away, and you will not hear, I declare to you this day, that you shall perish. I call heaven and earth to witness against you this day, that I have set before you life and death, blessing and curse; therefore choose life, that you and your descendants may live, loving the Lord your God, obeying his voice and cleaving to him; for that means life to you and length of days, that you may dwell in the land which the Lord swore to your fathers, to Abraham, to Isaac, and to Jacob, to give them.' Deuteronomy 30.15–20*

Philip went to a city of Samaria, and proclaimed to them the Christ. The multitudes with one accord gave heed to what was said by Philip, when they heard him and saw the signs which he did. But there was a man named Simon who had practised magic, saying that he himself was somebody great. They all gave heed to him, from the least to the greatest, saying, 'This man is that power of God which is called Great.' But when they believed Philip as he preached good news about the Kingdom of God and the name of Jesus Christ, they were baptized, both men and women. Even Simon himself believed, and after being baptized he continued with Philip. When the apostles at Jerusalem heard that Samaria had received the word of God, they sent Peter and John, who came down and prayed for them that they might receive the Holy Spirit; for it had not yet fallen on any of them, but they had only been baptized in the name of the Lord Jesus. Then they laid their hands on them and they received the Holy Spirit.
Acts 8.5–17*

RESPONSE 'My God, accept my heart this day, and make it wholly thine;
that I from thee no more may stray, no more from thee decline.'

Almighty God, the Gospel of the risen Christ is for the salvation of all people – we praise you for the power of your Spirit in the Church . . .
'They were baptized' – Lord, I thank you for my baptism and my Godparents, and pray for the local Church and the priest who conducted the service . . .
'They laid their hands on them and they received the Holy Spirit' – help us by the power of the same Spirit to serve you in faith and love . . .

INTERCESSIONS *pages 390–393* CLOSING PRAYERS *page 402–403*

OPENING PRAYER Almighty God, you have made us and we belong to you. Help us to know the nearness of your presence as we praise you, in union with the worship of your whole Church in heaven and on earth . . . Glory be . . .

PSALMODY They persecute me with falsehood; help me!
they have almost made an end of me on earth;
but I have not forsaken thy precepts. Psalm 119.86–87*

SCRIPTURE READINGS Unless you eat the flesh of the Son of Man and drink his blood, you have no life in you. St John 6.53

Saul, breathing threats and murder against the disciples, went to the high priest and asked him for letters to the synagogues at Damascus, so that if he found any belonging to the Way, men or women, he might bring them bound to Jerusalem. Now as he journeyed he approached Damascus, and suddenly a light from heaven flashed about him. He fell to the ground and heard a voice saying, 'Saul, Saul, why do you persecute me?' He said, 'Who are you, Lord?' He said, 'I am Jesus, whom you are persecuting; but rise and enter the city, and you will be told what you are to do.' Saul arose from the ground; and when his eyes were opened, he could see nothing; so they led him by the hand and brought him into Damascus. For three days he was without sight; and neither ate nor drank. There was a disciple at Damascus named Ananias. The Lord said to him in a vision, 'Ananias.' He said, 'Here I am, Lord.' The Lord said, 'Rise and go to the street called Straight, and inquire in the house of Judas for a man of Tarsus named Saul; for behold, he is praying, and he has seen a man named Ananias come in and lay his hands on him so that he might regain his sight. He is a chosen instrument of mine to carry my name before the Gentiles and kings and the sons of Israel; for I will show him how much he must suffer for the sake of my name.' So Ananias departed and entered the house. Laying his hands on him he said, 'Brother Saul, the Lord Jesus who appeared to you on the road by which you came, has sent me that you may regain your sight and be filled with the Holy Spirit.' Immediately something like scales fell from his eyes and he regained his sight. He rose and was baptized. Acts 9.1–18*

RESPONSE 'I will give thanks to thee, O Lord, with my whole heart,
and I will glorify thy name for ever.'

Merciful Father, your Word is living and active – we praise you for accepting us by your grace and for calling us to your service . . .
'Here am I' – Lord, open our minds, and help us to receive the messages you want to give to us . . .
'He is a chosen instrument' – make us also channels of your love . . .

INTERCESSIONS *pages 390–393* CLOSING PRAYERS *page 402–403*

OPENING PRAYER Almighty God, you have made us and we belong to you. Help us to know the nearness of your presence as we praise you, in union with the worship of your whole Church in heaven and on earth. . . Glory be . . .

PSALMODY For ever, O Lord, thy word is firmly fixed in the heavens.
Thy faithfulness endures to all generations. Psalm 119.89–90

SCRIPTURE READINGS The Lord says, 'It is too light a thing that you should be my servant to raise up the tribes of Jacob and to restore the preserved of Israel; I will give you as a light to the nations, that my salvation may reach to the end of the earth.' Isaiah 49.6

The apostles and brethren in Judea heard that the Gentiles had received the word of God. When Peter went to Jerusalem, the circumcision party criticized him, saying, 'Why did you go to uncircumcised men and eat with them?' Peter explained to them in order: 'I was in the city of Joppa praying; and in a trance I saw a vision, something descending, like a great sheet, let down from heaven by four corners; and it came down to me. Looking at it closely I observed animals and beasts of prey and reptiles and birds of the air. I heard a voice saying, "Rise, Peter; kill and eat." But I said, "No, Lord; for nothing common or unclean has ever entered my mouth." The voice answered from heaven, "What God has cleansed you must not call common." This happened three times and all was drawn up again into heaven. At that very moment three men arrived at the house in which we were, sent to me from Caesarea. The Spirit told me to go with them, making no distincion. These six brethren also accompanied me, and we entered the man's house. As I began to speak, the Holy Spirit fell on them just as on us at the beginning. And I remembered the word of the Lord, how he said, "John baptized with water, but you shall be baptized with the Holy Spirit." If then God gave the same gift to them as he gave to us when we believed in the Lord Jesus Christ, who was I that I could withstand God?' When they heard this they were silenced. They glorified God, saying, 'Then to the Gentiles also God has granted repentance unto life.'
Acts 11.1–18*

RESPONSE 'Let the heavens praise thy wonders, O Lord,
thy faithfulness in the assembly of holy ones.'

Loving Father, your Son came to redeem Jews and Gentiles without distinction – we praise you for your love for all nations and races . . .
'He will declare to you a message by which you will be saved' – Lord, we thank you for those who brought us to baptism and faith in Christ . . .
'The Holy Spirit fell on them just as on us at the beginning' – we thank you for the gift of the Spirit to unite us with Christ and each other . . .

INTERCESSIONS *pages 390–393* CLOSING PRAYERS *page 402–403*

OPENING PRAYER Almighty God, you have made us and we belong to you. Help us to know the nearness of your presence as we praise you, in union with the worship of your whole Church in heaven and on earth. . . Glory be . . .

PSALMODY I will never forget thy precepts;
for by them thou hast given me life.
I am thine, save me; for I have sought thy precepts.
I have seen a limit to all perfection,
but thy commandment is exceedingly broad.
Psalm 119.93–96*

SCRIPTURE READINGS The Lord said, 'This book of the law shall not depart out of your mouth, but you shall meditate on it day and night.' Joshua 1.8

The rulers of the synagogue sent to Paul and his company, saying, 'Brethren, if you have any word of exhortation for the people, say it.' Paul stood up, and said, 'Men of Israel, and you that fear God, listen. The God of this people Israel chose our fathers and made the people great during their stay in Egypt, and with uplifted arm he led them out of it. For about forty years he bore with them in the wilderness. When he had destroyed seven nations in the land of Canaan, he gave them their land as an inheritance, for about four hundred and fifty years. After that he gave them judges until Samuel the prophet. Then they asked for a king; and God gave them Saul, for forty years. When he had removed him, he raised up David to be their king; of whom he testified and said, "I have found in David the son of Jesse a man after my heart, who will do all my will." Of this man's posterity God has brought to Israel a Saviour, Jesus, as he promised. Brethren, sons of the family of Abraham, and those among you that fear God, to us has been sent the message of this salvation. For those who live in Jerusalem and their rulers, because they did not recognise him, asked Pilate to have him killed. But God raised him from the dead, and for many days he appeared to those who came up with him from Galilee to Jerusalem, who are now his witnesses. We bring you the good news that what God promised to the fathers, this he has fulfilled to us their children by raising Jesus.' Acts 13.15–33*

RESPONSE 'Lord, thy Word abideth, and our footsteps guideth;
who its truth believeth, light and joy receiveth.'

God of Abraham, you chose the people of Israel many centuries ago – we praise you for fully revealing your love in Jesus Christ . . .
'I have found in David a man after my heart, who will do all my will' – strengthen your Church to seek and do your will in all things . . .
'To us has been given this message of salvation' – give your Church the grace to proclaim the Gospel effectively in the world . . .

INTERCESSIONS *pages 390–393* CLOSING PRAYERS *page 402–403*

11 October *Paul is Stoned at Lystra*

OPENING PRAYER Almighty God, you have made us and we belong to you. Help us to know the nearness of your presence as we praise you, in union with the worship of your whole Church in heaven and on earth . . . Glory be . . .

PSALMODY Oh, how I love thy law! It is my meditation all the day.
Thy commandment makes me wiser than my enemies.
I have more understanding than all my teachers,
for thy testimonies are my meditation. Psalm 119.97–99*

SCRIPTURE READINGS Jesus said, 'If the world hates you, know that it has hated me before it hated you.' St John 15.18

At Lystra there was a man sitting, who could not use his feet; he was a cripple from birth, who had never walked. He listened to Paul speaking; and Paul, looking intently at him and seeing that he had faith to be made well, said, 'Stand upright on your feet.' He sprang up and walked. When the crowds saw what Paul had done, they lifted up their voices, saying, 'The gods have come down to us in the likeness of men!' Barnabas they called Zeus, and Paul, because he was the chief speaker, they called Hermes. The priest of Zeus brought oxen and garlands to the gates and wanted to offer sacrifice with the people. When the apostles Barnabas and Paul heard of it, they tore their garments and rushed out, crying, 'Men, why are you doing this? We also are men, of like nature with you, and bring you good news, that you should turn from these vain things to a living God who made the heaven and the earth and the sea and all that is in them. In past generations he allowed all the nations to walk in their own ways; yet he did not leave himself without witness, for he did good and gave you from heaven rains and fruitful seasons, satisfying your hearts with food and gladness.' With these words they scarcely restrained the people from offering sacrifice to them. But Jews came there from Antioch and Iconium; and having persuaded the people, they stoned Paul and dragged him out of the city, supposing that he was dead. When the disciples gathered about him, he rose up and entered the city; on the next day he went with Barnabas to Derbe. Acts 14.8–20*

RESPONSE 'Let me live, that I may praise thee,
and let thy ordinances help me.'

Heavenly Father, the noble army of martyrs through the centuries praises you – all glory and honour and praise to your holy name . . .
'They stoned Paul' – Lord, we thank you for the courage of Saint Paul, and of all who share in the fellowship of Christ's sufferings . . .
'He did not leave himself without witness' – help us to share in your Son's priesthood to bring the Gospel of salvation to the world . . .

INTERCESSIONS *pages 390–393* CLOSING PRAYERS *page 402–403*

OPENING PRAYER Almighty God, you have made us and we belong to you. Help us to know the nearness of your presence as we praise you, in union with the worship of your whole Church in heaven and on earth . . . Glory be . . .

PSALMODY I understand more than the aged,
for I keep thy precepts.
I hold back my feet from every evil way,
in order to keep thy word.
Through thy precepts I get understanding.

Psalm 119.100–104*

SCRIPTURE READINGS Paul and Barnabas sailed to Antioch. When they arrived, they gathered the church together and declared all that God had done with them, and how he had opened a door of faith to the Gentiles. But some men came from Judea and were teaching the brethren. 'Unless you are circumcised according to the custom of Moses, you cannot be saved.' When Paul and Barnabas had no small dissension with them, Paul and Barnabas and some others were appointed to go to Jerusalem to the apostles and elders about this question. The apostles and elders were gathered together to consider the matter. After there had been much debate, Peter rose and said, 'Brethren, in the early days God made choice among you, that by my mouth the Gentiles should hear the word of the gospel and believe. God bore witness to them, giving them the Holy Spirit just as he did to us; and he made no distinction between us and them, but cleansed their hearts by faith. Now therefore why do you make trial of God by putting a yoke upon the neck of the disciples which neither our fathers nor we have been able to bear? But we believe that we shall be saved through the grace of the Lord Jesus, just as they will.' All the assembly kept silence; and they listened to Barnabas and Paul as they related what signs and wonders God had done through them among the Gentiles. After they finished, James replied, 'Brethren, listen to me. Simeon has related how God first visited the Gentiles, to take out of them a people for his name. My judgement is that we should not trouble those of the Gentiles who turn to God, but we should write to them to abstain from the pollutions of idols and from unchastity and from what is strangled, and from blood.' Acts 14.26–15.20*

RESPONSE 'Through all the changing scenes of life, in trouble and in joy,
the praises of my God shall still my heart and tongue employ.'

Eternal Father, you sent the Holy spirit to inspire the first Council of the Church – we praise you for the same Spirit in the Church today . . .
'God made no distinction between us and them' – Lord, we rejoice that the Church is universal and people of all races are equal in your sight . . .
'When two or three are gathered together in my name' – strengthen the Church and prosper the work of all Synods and Church councils . . .

INTERCESSIONS *pages 390–393* CLOSING PRAYERS *page 402–403*

13 October *Paul and Silas in Prison*

OPENING PRAYER Almighty God, you have made us and we belong to you. Help us to know the nearness of your presence as we praise you, in union with the worship of your whole Church in heaven and on earth. . . Glory be . . .

PSALMODY Thy word is a lamp to my feet
and a light to my path.
give me life, O Lord,
according to thy word! Psalm 119.105–107*

SCRIPTURE READINGS As we were going to the place of prayer, we were met by a slave girl who had a spirit of divination and brought her owners much gain by soothsaying. Paul said, 'I charge you to come out of her.' It came out that very hour. Her owners seized Paul and Silas and dragged them before the rulers; they said, 'These men are Jews and they are disturbing our city. They advocate customs which it is not lawful for us Romans to accept or practice.' The magistrates tore the garments off them and gave orders to beat them with rods. When they had inflicted many blows, they threw them into prison. About midnight Paul and Silas were praying and singing hymns to God, and the prisoners were listening, and suddenly there was a great earthquake, so that the foundations of the prison were shaken; all the doors were opened and every one's fetters were unfastened. When the jailer saw that the prison doors were open, he drew his sword and was about to kill himself, supposing that the prisoners had escaped. Paul cried with a loud voice, 'Do not harm yourself, for we are all here.' He called for lights and rushed in, and trembling with fear he fell down before Paul and Silas, and brought them out and said, 'Men, what must I do to be saved?' They said, 'Believe in the Lord Jesus, and you will be saved.' They spoke the word of the Lord to him and to all that were in his house. He took them, and washed their wounds, and he was baptized, with all his family. When it was day, the magistrates sent the police, saying, 'Let these men go.' Paul said. 'They have beaten us publicly, uncondemned, men who are Roman citizens, and have thrown us into prison, and do they now cast us out secretly? No! Let them come themselves and take us out.' They were afraid when they heard that they were Roman citizens; so they came and apologized. Acts 16.19–39*

RESPONSE 'May the Lord bless you from Zion,
he who made heaven and earth.'

Eternal God, you are our strength in time of trouble – we praise you for all who share in the fellowship of Christ's suffering . . .
'They spoke the Word of the Lord to him' – equip the Church to use each opportunity to spread the Gospel of your saving love . . .
'He was baptized' – renew your gift of the Spirit in all who are baptized . . .

INTERCESSIONS *pages 390–393* CLOSING PRAYERS *page 402–403*

14 October *Paul at Athens*

OPENING PRAYER Almighty God, you have made us and we belong to you. Help us to know the nearness of your presence as we praise you, in union with the worship of your whole Church in heaven and on earth . . . Glory be . . .

PSALMODY Thy testimonies are my heritage for ever.
yea, they are the joy of my heart. Psalm 119.111

SCRIPTURE READINGS Uzzah put his hand to the ark of God and took hold of it, for the oxen stumbled. God smote him because he put forth his hand to the ark; and he died there beside the ark of God. David was afraid of the Lord that day; and he said, 'How can the ark of the Lord come to me?' The ark of the Lord remained in the house of Obed-edom three months; and the Lord blessed Obed-edom and all his household. 2 Samuel 6.6–11*

Paul, standing in the middle of the Areopagus, said: 'Men of Athens, I perceive that in every way you are very religious. For as I passed along, and observed the objects of your worship, I found an altar with this inscription, "To an unknown god." What you worship as unknown, this I proclaim to you. The God who made the world and everything in it, being Lord of heaven and earth, does not live in shrines made by man, nor is he served by human hands, as though he needed anything, since he himself gives to all men life and breath and everything. He made from one every nation of men to live on the face of the earth, having determined allotted periods and the boundaries of their habitation, that they should seek God, in the hope that they might feel after him and find him. He is not far from us, for "In him we live and move and have our being"; as even some of your poets have said, "We are indeed his offspring." We ought not to think that the Deity is like gold, or silver, or stone, a representation by the art and imagination of man. The times of ignorance God overlooked, but now he commands all men everywhere to repent, because he has fixed a day on which he will judge the world in righteousness by a man whom he has appointed, and of this he has given assurance to all men by raising him from the dead.' When they heard of the resurrection of the dead, some mocked; but others said, 'We will hear you again about this.' Paul went out from among them. Some men joined him and believed. Acts 17.22–34*

RESPONSE 'Lead me in the path of thy commandments,
for I delight in it.'

Sovereign Lord God, in your love you created the universe out of nothing – we rejoice that all you have created is good . . .
'To an unknown god' – Lord, we rejoice that you make yourself known to us in Jesus Christ through the Scripture and the Eucharist and our prayers . . .
'In him we live and move and have our being' – Lord, we thank you . . .

INTERCESSIONS *pages 390–393* CLOSING PRAYERS *page 402–403*

OPENING PRAYER Almighty God, you have made us and we belong to you. Help us to know the nearness of your presence as we praise you, in union with the worship of your whole Church in heaven and on earth . . . Glory be . . .

PSALMODY I hate double-minded men, but I love thy law.
Depart from me, you evildoers,
that I may keep the commandments of my God.
Uphold me according to thy promise, that I may live,
and let me not be put to shame in my hope!

Psalm 119.113–116*

SCRIPTURE READINGS 'Thus it is written, that the Christ should suffer and on the third day rise from the dead, and that repentance and forgiveness of sins should be preached in his name to all nations, beginning at Jerusalem. You are witnesses of these things.' St Luke 24.46–48

Paul was occupied with preaching, testifying to the Jews that the Christ was Jesus. When they opposed and reviled him, he shook out his garments and said, 'Your blood be upon your heads! I am innocent. From now on I will go to the Gentiles.' He left there and went to the house of a man named Titius Justus, a worshipper of God. Many of the Corinthians hearing Paul believed and were baptized. And the Lord said to Paul one night in a vision, 'Do not be afraid, but speak and do not be silent; for I am with you, and no man shall attack you to harm you; for I have many people in this city.' He stayed a year and six months, teaching the word of God. But when Gallio was proconsul of Achaia, the Jews made a united attack upon Paul and brought him before the tribunal, saying, 'This man is persuading men to worship God contrary to the law.' When Paul was about to open his mouth, Gallio said to the Jews, 'If it were a matter of wrong-doing or vicious crime, I should have reason to bear with you, O Jews; but since it is a matter of questions about words and names and your own law, see to it yourselves; I refuse to be a judge of these things.' They all seized Sosthenes, the ruler of the synagogue, and beat him in front of the tribunal. Gallio paid no attention. After this Paul stayed many days longer, and then took leave of the brethren and sailed for Syria, with Priscilla and Aquila.

Acts 18.5–18*

RESPONSE 'I long for thy salvation, O Lord,
and thy law is my delight.'

God our Father, you are the source of all justice and truth – we praise you and bless you for your faithfulness in every generation . . .
'Paul was occupied with preaching' – Lord, inspire with your Spirit all who preach the Gospel of the crucified and risen Christ . . .
'This man is persuading men to worship God' – help us to share your work . . .

INTERCESSIONS *pages 390–393* CLOSING PRAYERS *page 402–403*

16 October *Baptism and Confirmation at Ephesus*

OPENING PRAYER Almighty God, you have made us and we belong to you. Help us to know the nearness of your presence as we praise you, in union with the worship of your whole Church in heaven and on earth . . . Glory be . . .

PSALMODY Hold me up, that I may be safe
and have regard for thy statutes continually!
Thou dost spurn all who go astray from thy statutes;
yea, their cunning is in vain.
My flesh trembles for fear of thee,
and I am afraid of thy judgements. Psalm 119.117–120*

SCRIPTURE READINGS Joshua said to the people, 'You are witnesses against yourselves that you have chosen the Lord, to serve him.' They said, 'We are witnesses.' He said, 'Then put away the foreign gods which are among you, and incline your heart to the Lord, the God of Israel.' The people said, 'The Lord our God we will serve, and his voice will we obey.' So Joshua made a covenant with the people that day. Joshua 24.22–25

Paul came to Ephesus. There he found some disciples. He said to them, 'Did you receive the Holy Spirit when you believed?' They said, 'No, we have never even heard that there is a Holy Spirit.' He said, 'Into what then were you baptized?' They said 'Into John's baptism.' Paul said, 'John baptized with the baptism of repentance, telling the people to believe in the one who was to come after him, that is, Jesus.' On hearing this, they were baptized in the name of the Lord Jesus. When Paul had laid his hands upon them, the Holy Spirit came on them; and they spoke with tongues and prophesied. There were about twelve of them in all. He entered the synagogue and for three months spoke boldly, arguing and pleading about the Kingdom of God; but when some were stubborn and disbelieved, speaking evil of the Way before the congregation, he withdrew from them, taking the disciples with him, and argued daily in the hall of Tyrannus. This continued for two years, so that all the residents of Asia heard the word of the Lord, both Jews and Greeks. God did extraordinary miracles by the hands of Paul. Acts 19.1–11*

RESPONSE 'Spirit of purity and grace, our weakness, pitying, see:
O make our hearts thy dwelling-place, and worthier be.'

Eternal God, you come to us in Word and Sacrament to build up our faith – we praise you for your one holy catholic and apostolic Church . . .
Those who are baptized still have to be converted – draw all people to yourself, and inspire those who teach and those who learn the faith . . .
Baptism is completed in the Sacraments of Confirmation and the Eucharist – Lord, help us by your grace to grow in faith and love . . .

INTERCESSIONS *pages 390–393* CLOSING PRAYERS *page 402–403*

OPENING PRAYER Almighty God, you have made us and we belong to you. Help us to know the nearness of your presence as we praise you, in union with the worship of your whole Church in heaven and on earth . . . Glory be . . .

PSALMODY I have done what is just and right;
do not leave me to my oppressors.
Be surety for thy servant for good;
let not the godless oppress me. Psalm 119.121–122

SCRIPTURE READINGS Jesus said, 'While I was with them, I kept them in thy name which thou hast given me; I have guarded them, and none of them is lost but the son of perdition, that the scripture might be fulfilled. But now I am coming to thee; and these things I speak in the world, that they may have my joy fulfilled in themselves.' St John 17.12–13

Paul sent to Ephesus and called to him the elders of the church. He said: 'You yourselves know how I lived among you from the first day that I set foot in Asia; testifying both to Jews and to Greeks of repentance to God and of faith in our Lord Jesus Christ. Now, I am going to Jerusalem, bound in the Spirit, not knowing what shall befall me; except that the Holy Spirit testifies in every city that imprisonment and afflictions await me. I do not account my life as precious to myself, if only I may accomplish the ministry which I received from the Lord Jesus, to testify to the gospel of the grace of God. Now, I know that you will see my face no more. Take heed to yourselves and to all the flock, in which the Holy Spirit has made you overseers, to care for the Church of God which he obtained with the blood of his own Son. Now I commend you to God and to the word of his grace, which is able to build you up and to give you the inheritance among all those who are sanctified. I have shown that by so toiling one must help the weak, remembering the words of the Lord Jesus, how he said, "It is more blessed to give than to receive."' When he had spoken, he knelt down and prayed with them. They wept and embraced Paul and kissed him, sorrowing most of all because of the word he had spoken, that they should see his face no more. And they brought him to the ship. Acts 20.17–38*

RESPONSE 'I will extol thee, my God and King,
and bless thy name for ever.'

Almighty God, you redeem us by the blood of your Son – we rejoice that nothing can separate us from your love in Christ . . .
'Imprisonment and afflictions await me' – Lord, we thank you for the faith and courage of Christians in times of persecution and trouble . . .
'It is more blessed to give than to receive' – help us to learn the meaning of these words . . .

INTERCESSIONS *pages 390–393* CLOSING PRAYERS *page 402–403*

18 October *Saint Luke the Evangelist*

OPENING PRAYER Almighty God, you have made us and we belong to you. Help us to know the nearness of your presence as we praise you, in union with the worship of your whole Church in heaven and on earth . . . Glory be . . .

PSALMODY Praise the Lord! For it is good to sing praises to our God;
for he is gracious, and a song of praise is seemly.
The Lord builds up Jerusalem;
he gathers the outcasts of Israel.
He heals the broken hearted,
and binds up their wounds.
Great is our Lord, and abundant in power;
his understanding is beyond measure.
The Lord lifts up the downtrodden,
he casts the wicked to the ground. Psalm 147.1–6*

SCRIPTURE READINGS Inasmuch as many have undertaken to compile a narrative of the things which have been accomplished among us, just as they were delivered to us by those who from the beginning were eyewitnesses and ministers of the word, it seemed good to me also, having followed all things closely for some time past, to write an orderly account for you, most excellent Theophilus, that you may know the truth concerning the things of which you have been informed. St Luke 1.1–4

How beautiful upon the mountains are the feet of him who brings good tidings. Isaiah 52.7a

I am not ashamed of the gospel; it is the power of God for salvation to every one who has faith. Romans 1.16

Luke alone is with me. 2 Timothy 4.11a

I delivered to you as of first importance what I also received, that Christ died for our sins in accordance with the scriptures, that he was buried, that he was raised on the third day in accordance with the scriptures.
1 Corinthians 15.3–4

RESPONSE 'All thy works shall give thanks to thee, O Lord,
and all thy saints shall bless thee.'

God our Father, you alone are the source of health and salvation – we celebrate this feast with your worldwide Church, and we praise you . . .
You inspired Saint Luke to write down the Gospel of your Son – we praise you for the encouragement and help you give us through the Scriptures . . .
'Heal the sick' – we pray with Saint Luke for the work of all doctors and surgeons and nurses, and for the renewal of your gift of healing in the Church.

INTERCESSIONS *pages 390–393* CLOSING PRAYERS *page 402–403*

19 October *Paul Arrives at Jerusalem*

OPENING PRAYER Almighty God, you have made us and we belong to you. Help us to know the nearness of your presence as we praise you, in union with the worship of your whole Church in heaven and on earth . . . Glory be . . .

PSALMODY My eyes fail with watching for thy salvation,
and for the fulfilment of thy righteous promise.
Deal with thy servant according to thy steadfast love,
and teach me thy statutes.
I am thy servant; give me understanding,
that I may know thy testimonies! Psalm 119.123–125

SCRIPTURE READINGS Jesus prayed, 'My Father, if it be possible, let this cup pass from me; nevertheless, not as I will, but as thou wilt.'

St Matthew 26.39

We came to Caesarea; and we entered the house of Philip the evangelist, who was one of the seven. He had four unmarried daughters, who prophesied. While we were staying for some days, a prophet named Agabus came down from Judea. And coming to us he took Paul's girdle and bound his own feet and hands, and said, 'Thus says the Holy Spirit, "So shall the Jews at Jerusalem bind the man who owns this girdle and deliver him into the hands of the Gentiles."' When we heard this, we begged him not to go to Jerusalem. Paul answered, 'What are you doing, weeping and breaking my heart? For I am ready not only to be imprisoned but even to die at Jerusalem for the name of the Lord Jesus.' When he would not be persuaded, we ceased and said, 'The will of the Lord be done.' After these days we made ready and went up to Jerusalem. Some of the disciples from Caesarea went with us, bringing us to the house of Mnason of Cyprus, an early disciple, with whom we should lodge. When we had come to Jerusalem, the brethren received us gladly. On the following day Paul went in with us to James; and all the elders were present. After greeting them, he related one by one the things that God had done among the Gentiles through his ministry. When they heard it, they glorified God.

Acts 21.7–20

RESPONSE 'Teach me the way I should go,
for to thee I lift up my soul.'

Heavenly Father, you call your Pilgrim Church to share in the mission of your Son – we praise you for the power of the Spirit in the Church . . .
'I am ready to die at Jerusalem for the name of the Lord Jesus' – Lord, inspire the Church to be courageous in its work for your Kingdom . . .
'They glorified God' – to you, Lord, be praise and glory, in the Church and in Christ Jesus, for time and for eternity. Amen . . .

INTERCESSIONS *pages 390–393* CLOSING PRAYERS *page 402–403*

20 October *Paul is Arrested*

OPENING PRAYER Almighty God, you have made us and we belong to you. Help us to know the nearness of your presence as we praise you, in union with the worship of your whole Church in heaven and on earth . . . Glory be . . .

PSALMODY It is time for the Lord to act,
for thy law has been broken.
Therefore I direct my steps by all thy precepts;
I hate every false way. Psalm 119.126–128*

SCRIPTURE READINGS King Zedekiah said, 'Behold, he is in your hands; for the king can do nothing.' So they took Jeremiah and cast him into the cistern, which was in the court of the guard. Jeremiah 38.5–6

The Jews from Asia, who had seen Paul in the temple, stirred up the crowd, and laid hands on him, crying, 'Men of Israel, help! This is the man who is teaching men everywhere against the people and the law and this place; moreover he brought Greeks into the temple, and he has defiled this holy place.' All the city was aroused, and the people ran together; they seized Paul and dragged him out of the temple, and at once the gates were shut. As they were trying to kill him, word came to the tribune of the cohort that all Jerusalem was in confusion. He took soldiers and centurions, and ran down to them; when they saw the tribune and the soldiers, they stopped beating Paul. The tribune came up and arrested him, and ordered him to be bound with two chains. He inquried who he was and what he had done. Some in the crowd shouted one thing, some another; and as he could not learn the facts because of the uproar, he ordered him to be brought into the barracks. When he came to the steps, he was carried by the soldiers because of the violence of the crowd, crying, 'Away with him!' As Paul was about to be brought into the barracks, he said to the tribune, 'May I say something to you?' He said, 'Do you know Greek? Are you not the Egyptian, then, who recently stirred up a revolt and led four thousand men of the Assassins out into the wilderness?' Paul replied, 'I am a Jew, from Tarsus in Cilicia, a citizen of no mean city; I beg you, let me speak to the people.' Paul motioned with his hand to the people; when there was a great hush, he spoke in the Hebrew language. Acts 21.27–40*

RESPONSE 'Guard me, O Lord, from the hands of wicked men,
preserve me from violent men.'

Almighty God, you are our hope and our salvation – we rejoice that nothing can separate us from your love and we praise you . . .
'I am a Jew from Tarsus' – have mercy on your ancient people the Jews, and lead us and them to the fullness of your truth . . .
'May I say something to you' – make your will known to us in all things . . .

INTERCESSIONS *pages 390–393* CLOSING PRAYERS *page 402–403*

OPENING PRAYER Almighty God, you have made us and we belong to you. Help us to know the nearness of your presence as we praise you, in union with the worship of your whole Church in heaven and on earth . . . Glory be . . .

PSALMODY Thy testimonies are wonderful; therefore my soul keeps them.
With open mouth I pant, because I long for thy commandments.
Turn to me and be gracious to me,
as is thy wont toward those who love thy name.

Psalm 119.129–132*

SCRIPTURE READING Paul spoke to the mob in Hebrew, saying, 'I am a Jew, born at Tarsus in Cilicia, but brought up in this city at the feet of Gamaliel, educated according to the strict manner of the law of our fathers. I persecuted this Way to the death, binding and delivering to prison both men and women, as the high priest and the whole council of elders bear me witness. From them I received letters, and I journeyed to Damascus to take those who were there and bring them in bonds to Jerusalem to be punished. About noon a great light from heaven suddenly shone about me. I fell to the ground and heard a voice saying, "Saul, Saul, why do you persecute me? I am Jesus of Nazareth whom you are persecuting." I said, "What shall I do, Lord?" The Lord said, "Rise, and go to Damascus, and there you will be told all that is appointed for you to do." And one Ananias said, "Brother Saul, receive your sight." In that very hour I received my sight. He said, "The God of our fathers appointed you to know his will to see the Just One and to hear a voice from his mouth; for you will be a witness for him to all men of what you have seen and heard. Why do you wait? Rise and be baptized." When I returned to Jerusalem and was praying in the temple, I fell into a trance and saw him saying to me, "They will not accept your testimony about me. Depart; for I will send you far away to the Gentiles."' To this point they listened; then they lifted up their voices, 'Away with such a fellow from the earth! For he ought not to live.' The tribune commanded him to be brought into the barracks, and ordered him to be examined by scourging, to find out why they shouted against him. Paul said, "Is it lawful to scourge a man who is a Roman citizen, and uncondemned?' Those who were about to examine him withdrew instantly; and the tribune also was afraid.

Acts 21.40–22.29*

RESPONSE 'The Lord will fulfil his purpose for me;
do not forsake the works of thy hands.'

Merciful Father, your Church is the community of all who are baptized – we praise you for the faith of all who dedicate themselves to your service . . .
'The God of our fathers appointed you to know his will' – we thank you for making your will known to us through the Old and New Testaments . . .
'You will be a witness' – inspire the Church to witness to your love . . .

INTERCESSIONS *pages 390–393* CLOSING PRAYERS *page 402–403*

OPENING PRAYER Almighty God, you have made us and we belong to you. Help us to know the nearness of your presence as we praise you, in union with the worship of your whole Church in heaven and on earth . . . Glory be . . .

PSALMODY Keep steady my steps according to thy promise,
and let no iniquity get dominion over me.
Redeem me from man's oppression,
that I may keep thy precepts.
Make thy face shine upon thy servant,
and teach me thy statutes. Psalm 119.133–135

SCRIPTURE READING On the morrow, desiring to know the real reason why the Jews accused Paul, the tribune unbound him, and commanded the chief priests and all the council to meet, and he brought Paul down and set him before them. Paul, looking intently at the council, said, 'Brethren, I have lived before God in all good conscience up to this day.' The high priest Ananias commanded those who stood by him to strike him on the mouth. Paul said, 'God shall strike you, you whitewashed wall! Are you sitting to judge me according to the law, and yet contrary to the law you order me to be struck?' Those who stood by said, 'Would you revile God's high priest?' Paul said, 'I did not know, brethren, that he was the high priest, for it is written, "You shall not speak evil of a ruler of your people."' When Paul perceived that one part were Sadducees and the other Pharisees, he cried out in the council, 'Brethren, I am a Pharisee, a son of Pharisees; with respect to the hope and the resurrection of the dead I am on trial.' When he had said this, a dissension arose between the Pharisees and the Sadducees, and the assembly was divided. For the Sadducees say that there is no resurrection, nor angel, nor spirit; but the Pharisees acknowledge them all. A great clamour arose, and some of the scribes of the Pharisees' party stood up and contended, 'We find nothing wrong in this man. What if a spirit or an angel spoke to him?' When the dissension became violent, the tribune, afraid that Paul would be torn in pieces by them, commanded the soldiers to go down and take him by force from among them and bring him into the barracks. Acts 22.30–23.10

RESPONSE 'The Lord is my light and my salvation;
whom shall I fear?'

God our Creator, you give courage to your servants to witness to your truth in every generation – to you belong the praise and the glory . . .
'I have lived before God in all good conscience up to this day' – Lord, purify our consciences, and give us inner healing, peace and joy . . .
'The Pharisees believed in the resurrection of the dead' – we thank you and bless you for the hope of eternal life in your Son . . .

INTERCESSIONS *pages 390–393* CLOSING PRAYERS *page 402–403*

OPENING PRAYER Almighty God, you have made us and we belong to you. Help us to know the nearness of your presence as we praise you, in union with the worship of your whole Church in heaven and on earth . . . Glory be . . .

PSALMODY My eyes shed streams of tears,
because men to do not keep thy law,
Righteous art thou, O Lord,
and right are thy judgements. Psalm 119.136–137

SCRIPTURE READING The following night the Lord stood by Paul and said, 'Take courage, for as you have testified about me at Jerusalem, so you must bear witness also at Rome.' When it was day, the Jews made a plot, and they went to the chief priests and elders, and said, 'We have strictly bound ourselves by an oath to taste no food till we have killed Paul.' The son of Paul's sister heard of their ambush; so he entered the barracks and told Paul. Paul called one of the centurions and said, 'Take this young man to the tribune.' The tribune took him by the hand and asked him privately, 'What is it that you have to tell me?' He said, 'The Jews have agreed to ask you to bring Paul down to the council tomorrow, as though they were going to inquire somewhat more closely about him. But do not yield to them; for more than forty of their men lie in ambush for him, having bound themselves by an oath.' The tribune dismissed the young man, charging him, 'Tell no one that you have informed me of this.' Then he called two of the centurions and said, 'At the third hour of the night get ready two hundred soldiers with seventy horsemen and two hundred spearmen to go as far as Caesarea. Provide mounts for Paul to ride, and bring him safely to Felix the governor.' He wrote a letter: 'Claudius Lysias to his Excellency the governor Felix, greeting. This man was seized by the Jews, and was about to be killed by them, when I came upon them with soldiers and rescued him, having learned that he was a Roman citizen. I found that he was accused about questions of their law, but charged with nothing deserving death or imprisonment. When it was disclosed to me that there would be a plot, I sent him to you at once, ordering his accusers to state before you what they have against him.' Acts 23.11–30*

RESPONSE Teach me thy way, O Lord;
and lead me on a level path.'

Loving God and Father, you are present with us through the Spirit in the day and the night – we thank you for your love and we praise you . . .
'You must bear witness also at Rome' – renew your gift of the Spirit in the Church and inspire us to witness to the risen Christ in the world . . .
What is it you have to tell me?' – help us to receive your messages . . .

INTERCESSIONS *pages 390–393* CLOSING PRAYERS *page 402–403*

24 October *Paul Before Felix the Governor*

OPENING PRAYER Almighty God, you have made us and we belong to you. Help us to know the nearness of your presence as we praise you, in union with the worship of your whole Church in heaven and on earth . . . Glory be . . .

PSALMODY My zeal consumes me,
because my foes forget thy words. Psalm 119.139

SCRIPTURE READING After five days the high priest Ananias came with some elders and a spokesman, one Tertullus. When he was called, Tertullus began: 'Since through you we enjoy much peace, and since by your provision, most excellent Felix, reforms are introduced on behalf of this nation, in every way and everywhere we accept this with all gratitude. But, to detain you no further, I beg you in your kindness to hear us briefly. For we have found this man a pestilent fellow, an agitator among all the Jews throughout the world, and a ringleader of the sect of the Nazarenes. By examining him yourself you will be able to learn from him about everything of which we accuse him.' When the governor motioned him to speak, Paul replied: 'Realizing that for many years you have been judge over this nation, I cheerfully make my defence. As you may ascertain, they did not find me disputing with anyone or stirring up a crowd, either in the temple or in the synagogues, or in the city. Neither can they prove to you what they now bring up against me. But this I admit, that according to the Way, which they call a sect, I worship the God of our fathers, having a hope in God which these themselves accept, that there will be a resurrection of both the just and the unjust. After some years I came to bring to my nation alms and offerings. As I was doing this, they found me purified in the temple, without any crowd or tumult. But some Jews from Asia – they ought to be here before you and to make an accusation, if they have anything against me. Or else let these men themselves say what wrongdoing they found when I stood before the council, except this one thing, which I cried out while standing among them, "With respect to the resurrection of the dead I am on trial before you this day."' But Felix, having a rather accurate knowledge of the Way, put them off, saying, 'When Lysias the tribune comes, I will decide your case.' Acts 24.1–22*

RESPONSE 'Love the Lord, all you his saints!
The Lord preserves the faithful.'

God our Saviour, you raised up Saint Paul to contend for the truth of the faith – we praise you for all who bear witness to your Son in every age . . .
'I worship the God of our fathers' – we unite our prayers with the praises of the Blessed Virgin Mary, the apostles, saints and martyrs in heaven . . .
'They found me purified in the temple' – cleanse us and make us holy . . .

INTERCESSIONS *pages 390–393* CLOSING PRAYERS *page 402–403*

OPENING PRAYER Almighty God, you have made us and we belong to you. Help us to know the nearness of your presence as we praise you, in union with the worship of your whole Church in heaven and on earth . . . . Glory be . . .

PSALMODY Righteous art thou, O Lord,
and right are thy judgements.
Thou hast appointed thy testimonies in righteousness,
and in all faithfulness.
I am small and despised,
yet I do not forget thy precepts.
With my whole heart I cry; answer me, O Lord.
I will keep thy statutes. Psalm 119.137–145*

SCRIPTURE READING When two years had elapsed, Felix was succeeded by Porcius Festus; and desiring to do the Jews a favour, Felix left Paul in prison. When Festus had come into his province, after three days he went to Jerusalem from Caesarea. The chief priests and the principal men of the Jews informed him against Paul. When he had stayed among them not more than eight or ten days, he went down to Caesarea; and the next day he took his seat on the tribunal and ordered Paul to be brought. When he had come, the Jews who had gone down from Jerusalem stood about him, bringing against him many serious charges which they could not prove. Paul said in his defence, 'Neither against the law of the Jews, nor against the temple, nor against Caesar have I offended at all.' But Festus, wishing to do the Jews a favour, said, 'Do you wish to go up to Jerusalem, and there be tried on these charges before me?' Paul said, 'I am standing before Caesar's tribunal, where I ought to be tried; to the Jews I have done no wrong, as you know very well. If then I am a wrongdoer, and have committed anything for which I deserve to die, I do not seek to escape death; but if there is nothing in their charges against me, no one can give me up to them. I appeal to Caesar.' Festus answered, 'You have appealed to Caesar; to Caesar you shall go.' Acts 24.27–25.12

RESPONSE 'Our souls wait for the Lord;
he is our help and shield.'

Eternal God, you are King of kings and all glory and power belong to you in heaven and on earth – we praise you for your power and love . . .
You are righteous and your judgements are righteous and true – help us always to seek first your kingdom and its justice and love . . .
'I appeal to Caesar' – we come to you only through the mediation of your Son, to whom, with you and the Holy Spirit, be glory for ever . . .

INTERCESSIONS *pages 390–393* CLOSING PRAYERS *page 402–403*

26 October *Paul Before King Agrippa*

OPENING PRAYER Almighty God, you have made us and we belong to you. Help us to know the nearness of your presence as we praise you, in union with the worship of your whole Church in heaven and on earth . . . Glory be . . .

PSALMODY Trouble and anguish have come upon me,
but thy commandments are my delight. Psalm 119.143

SCRIPTURE READING Agrippa the king and Bernice arrived at Caesarea to welcome Festus. Festus laid Paul's case before the king. Agrippa said, 'I should like to hear the man myself.' On the morrow, Paul made his defence: 'I think myself fortunate that it is before you, King Agrippa, I am to make my defence against the accusations of the Jews, because you are especially familiar with all customs and controversies of the Jews; therefore I beg you to listen to me patiently. I was convinced that I ought to do many things in opposing the name of Jesus of Nazareth. I not only shut up many of the saints in prison, but when they were put to death I cast my vote against them. I persecuted them even to foreign cities. I journeyed to Damascus with the authority and commission of the chief priests. At midday, O king, I saw on the way a light from heaven, brighter than the sun. I heard a voice saying, "Saul, Saul, why do you persecute me? It hurts you to kick against the goads." And I said, "Who are you, Lord?" The Lord said, "I am Jesus whom you are persecuting. I have appeared to you for this purpose, to appoint you to serve and bear witness, delivering you from the people and from the Gentiles – to whom I send you that they may receive forgiveness of sins and a place among those who are sanctified by faith in me." I stand testifying, saying nothing but what the prophets and Moses said would come to pass: that the Christ must suffer, and that, by being the first to rise from the dead, he would proclaim light both to the people and to the Gentiles.' Festus said with a loud voice, 'Paul, you are mad; your great learning is turning you mad.' But Paul said, 'I am not mad, most excellent Festus, but I am speaking the sober truth. For the king knows about these things, and to him I speak freely; King Agrippa, do you believe the prophets? I know that you believe.' Agrippa said, 'In a short time you think to make me a Christian!' Paul said, 'Whether short or long, I would to God that not only you but also all who hear me this day might become such as I am – except for these chains.' Acts 26.1–29*

RESPONSE 'Let all the earth fear the Lord,
let all the inhabitants of the world stand in awe of him.'

Lord our God, you are present everywhere in this world and the next – we rejoice that nothing can separate us from your love in Jesus Christ . . .
'I saw on the way a light from heaven' – we pray that more people will see the light of Christ through the worship and ministry of your Church . . .
'I heard a voice from heaven' – help us to be obedient to your Word . . .

INTERCESSIONS *pages 390–393* CLOSING PRAYERS *page 402–403*

27 October *Shipwrecked in the Storm*

OPENING PRAYER Almighty God, you have made us and we belong to you. Help us to know the nearness of your presence as we praise you, in union with the worship of your whole Church in heaven and on earth . . . Glory be . . .

PSALMODY I cry to thee;
save me, that I may observe thy testimonies. Psalm 119.146

SCRIPTURE READINGS Three times I have been shipwrecked.
2 Corinthians 11.25

Agrippa said to Festus, 'This man could have been set free if he had not appealed to Caesar.' When it was decided that we should sail for Italy, they delivered Paul and some other prisoners to a centurion named Julius. We sailed slowly for a number of days. But soon a tempestuous wind, called the Northeaster, struck down from the land; we gave way to it and were driven. Paul said, 'Men, you should have listened to me, and should not have sailed from Crete. I now bid you take heart; for there will be no loss of life among you, but only of the ship. This very night there stood by me an angel of God, and he said, "Do not be afraid, Paul; you must stand before Caesar; and lo, God has granted you all those who sail with you." So take heart.' They let out four anchors from the stern. And as the sailors were seeking to escape from the ship, and had lowered the boat into the sea, under pretence of laying out the anchors, Paul said to the centurion, 'Unless these men stay in the ship, you cannot be saved.' The soldiers cut the ropes of the boat and let it go. Paul urged them to take some food, saying, 'Today is the fourteenth day that you have continued in suspense and without food. I urge you to take some food.' He took bread, and giving thanks to God in the presence of all he broke it and began to eat. (We were in all two hundred and seventy-six persons in the ship.) They lightened the ship, throwing out the wheat. They cast off the anchors, and made for the beach. But striking a shoal they ran the vessel aground. The soldiers' plan was to kill the prisoners, lest any should escape; but the centurion, wishing to save Paul, kept them from carrying out their purpose. He ordered those who could swim to throw themselves overboard and make for the land, and the rest on planks or on pieces of the ship. So it was that all escaped to land. Acts 26.32–27.44*

RESPONSE 'O hear us when we call to thee,
for those in peril on the sea.'

Almighty God, you made us members of the Church through the waters of Baptism – we praise you for sending your Son to be our Redeemer . . .
'A tempestuous wind, called the Northeaster, struck down from the land' – protect and guide all who sail on, and under the seas . . .
'I bid you take heart' – fill our hearts with your love and peace . . .

INTERCESSIONS *pages 390–393* CLOSING PRAYERS *page 402–403*

28 October *Saint Simon and Saint Jude – Apostles*

OPENING PRAYER Almighty God, you have made us and we belong to you. Help us to know the nearness of your presence as we praise you, in union with the worship of your whole Church in heaven and on earth . . . Glory be . . .

PSALMODY What shall I render to the Lord
for all his bounty to me?
I will lift up the cup of salvation,
and call on the name of the Lord,
I will pay my vows to the Lord
in the presence of all his people.
Precious in the sight of the Lord
is the death of his saints. Psalm 116.12–15

SCRIPTURE READINGS 'He who has my commandments and keeps them he it is who loves me; and he who loves me will be loved by my Father, and I will love him and manifest myself to him.' Judas (not Iscariot) said, 'Lord, how is it that you will manifest yourself to us, and not to the world?' Jesus answered, 'If a man loves me, he will keep my word, and my Father will love him, and we will come to him and make our home with him.'
St John 14.21–23

You, beloved, build yourselves up on your most holy faith; pray in the Holy Spirit; keep yourselves in the love of God; wait for the mercy of our Lord Jesus Christ until eternal life. And convince some, who doubt; save some, by snatching them out of the fire; on some have mercy with fear, hating even the garment spotted by the flesh. St Jude 18–23

You are no longer strangers and sojourners, but fellow citizens with the saints and members of the household of God, built upon the foundation of the apostles and prophets, Christ Jesus himself being the cornerstone, in whom the whole structure is joined together and grows into a holy temple in the Lord; in whom you also are built into it for a dwelling place of God in the Spirit. Ephesians 2.19–22

RESPONSE 'You shall rejoice in the Lord;
in the Holy One of Israel you shall glory.'

Heavenly Father, you light the fire of your love to burn in the hearts of your servants – in union with your whole Church we praise you on this day for Saint Simon and Saint Jude . . .
'Build yourself up on your most holy faith' – Lord, increase your precious gift of faith in us, and make us strong to do your will . . .
'Pray in the Holy Spirit' – come, Holy Spirit, and sanctify your Church, and help us in our prayers . . .

INTERCESSIONS *pages 390–393* CLOSING PRAYERS *page 402–403*

OPENING PRAYER Almighty God, you have made us and we belong to you. Help us to know the nearness of your presence as we praise you, in union with the worship of your whole Church in heaven and on earth . . . Glory be . . .

PSALMODY My eyes are awake before the watches of the night,
that I may meditate upon thy promise.
Hear my voice in thy steadfast love;
O Lord, in thy justice preserve my life.
They draw near who persecute me with evil purpose;
they are far from thy law.
But thou art near, O Lord,
and all thy commandments are true. Psalm 119.148–151

SCRIPTURE READINGS Contribute to the needs of the saints, practise hospitality. Romans 12.13*

After we had escaped, we learned that the island was called Malta. The natives showed us unusual kindness, for they kindled a fire and welcomed us all, because it had begun to rain and was cold. Paul had gathered a bundle of sticks and put them on the fire, when a viper came out because of the heat and fastened on his hand. When the natives saw the creature hanging from his hand, they said, 'No doubt this man is a murderer. Though he has escaped from the sea, justice has not allowed him to live.' He shook off the creature into the fire and suffered no harm. They waited, expecting him to swell up or suddenly fall down dead; but when they had waited a long time and saw no misfortune come to him, they changed their minds and said that he was a god. Now in the neighbourhood were lands belonging to the chief man of the island, named Publius, who received us and entertained us hospitably for three days. It happened that the father of Publius lay sick with fever and dysentery; and Paul visited him and prayed, and putting his hands on him healed him. When this had taken place, the rest of the people on the island who had diseases also came and were cured. They presented many gifts to us; and when we sailed, they put on board whatever we needed. Acts 28.1–10*

RESPONSE 'Sing aloud to God our strength;
shout for joy to the God of Jacob.'

Almighty God, the holy name of Jesus is blessed for evermore – we rejoice and give thanks for your love for all people . . .
'The natives showed us unusual kindness' – Lord, fill our hearts with love and compassion, and help us to show your love to other people . . .
'Publius received us and entertained us hospitably' – deepen the love and fellowship of your whole Church, and fill us with your joy . . .

INTERCESSIONS *pages 390–393* CLOSING PRAYERS *page 402–403*

30 October *Paul Arrives at Rome*

OPENING PRAYER Almighty God, you have made us and we belong to you. Help us to know the nearness of your presence as we praise you, in union with the worship of your whole Church in heaven and on earth . . . Glory be . . .

PSALMODY Salvation is far from the wicked,
for they do not seek thy statutes. Psalm 119.155

SCRIPTURE READING Peter turned and saw following them the disciple whom Jesus loved. He said to Jesus, 'Lord, what about this man?' Jesus said, 'If it is my will that he remain until I come, what is that to you? Follow me!' The saying spread abroad among the brethren that this disciple was not to die; yet Jesus did not say he was not to die, but, 'If it is my will that he remain until I come, what is that to you?'

St John 21.20–23*

We set sail in a ship which had wintered in the island, a ship of Alexandria, with the Twin Brothers as figurehead. We came to Puteoli. There we found brethren, and were invited to stay with them for seven days. So we came to Rome. The brethren there, when they heard of us, came as far as the Forum of Appius and Three Taverns to meet us. On seeing them Paul thanked God and took courage. When we came into Rome, Paul was allowed to stay by himself with the soldier that guarded him. After three days he called together the local leaders of the Jews; he said, 'Brethren, though I had done nothing against the people or the customs of our fathers, yet I was delivered prisoner from Jerusalem into the hands of the Romans. When they had examined me, they wished to set me at liberty, because there was no reason for the death penalty in my case. When the Jews objected, I was compelled to appeal to Caesar – though I had no charge to bring against my nation. For this reason I have asked to speak with you, since it is because of the hope of Israel that I am bound with this chain.' They said, 'We have received no letter from Judea about you, and none of the brethren coming here has reported or spoken any evil about you. But we desire to hear from you what your views are; for with regard to this sect we know that everywhere it is spoken against.' Acts 28.11–22*

RESPONSE 'Help us, O God of our salvation,
for the glory of thy name.'

Almighty God, you bring joy to the world in your Son Jesus Christ – with confidence in our hearts, we praise and adore your holy name . . .
'We found brethren, and were invited to stay with them' – we thank you for the fellowship and love in your household the Church . . .
'Paul thanked God' – give us ever-grateful hearts for all the blessings you give to us through your one holy Catholic and Apostolic Church . . .

INTERCESSIONS *pages 390–393* CLOSING PRAYERS *page 402–403*

OPENING PRAYER Almighty God, you have made us and we belong to you. Help us to know the nearness of your presence as we praise you, in union with the worship of your whole Church in heaven and on earth . . . Glory be . . .

PSALMODY Many are my persecutors and my adversaries,
but I do not swerve from thy testimonies.
I look at the faithless with disgust,
because they do not keep thy commands. Psalm 119.157–158

SCRIPTURE READINGS I long to see you, that I may impart to you some spiritual gift to strengthen you, that is, that we may be mutually encouraged by each other's faith, both yours and mine. Romans 1.11–12

When they had appointed a day, the Jews came to him at his lodging in great numbers. He expounded the matter to them from morning till evening, testifying to the Kingdom of God and trying to convince them about Jesus both from the law of Moses and from the prophets. Some were convinced by what he said, while others disbelieved. So, as they disagreed among themselves, they departed, after Paul had made one statement: 'The Holy Spirit was right in saying to your fathers through Isaiah the prophet:

"Go to this people, and say
You shall indeed hear but never understand,
and you shall indeed see but never perceive.
For this people's heart has grown dull,
and their ears are heavy of hearing,
and their eyes they have closed;
lest they should perceive with their eyes,
and hear with their ears,
and understand with their hearts,
and turn for me to heal them."

Let it be known that this salvation of God has been sent to the Gentiles; they will listen.' He lived there two whole years at his own expense, and welcomed all who came to him, preaching the Kingdom of God and teaching about the Lord Jesus Christ quite openly and unhindered.
Acts 28.23–39*

RESPONSE 'The Lord reigns; let the earth rejoice;
let the many coastlands be glad.'

Gracious God, you sent your Son to gather the nations into the peace of your Kingdom – we proclaim your glory and we praise you . . .
'Some were convinced by what he said' – bless the work of theologians, and those who present the intellectual case for the Christian religion . . .
'This people's heart has grown dull' – may stubborn hearts be turned to Christ through the prayers and ministry of the Church . . .

INTERCESSIONS *pages 390–393* CLOSING PRAYERS *page 402–403*

OPENING PRAYER Almighty God, you bring our life and your life together in a marvellous way in your Son. Accept our praises offered to you with the prayers of the saints and of the hosts of heaven . . . Glory be . . .

PSALMODY Rejoice in the Lord, O you righteous!
Praise befits the upright.
He loves righteousness and justice;
the earth is full of the steadfast love of the Lord.

Psalm 33.1–5*

SCRIPTURE READINGS 'Blessed are you when men revile you and persecute you and utter all kinds of evil against you falsely on my account. Rejoice and be glad, for your reward is great in heaven, for so men persecuted the prophets before you.' St Matthew 5.11–12

You have come to Mount Zion and to the city of the living God, the heavenly Jerusalem, and to innumerable angels in festal gathering, and to the assembly of the first born who are enrolled in heaven, and to a judge who is God of all, and to the spirits of just men made perfect, and to Jesus, the mediator of a new covenant. Hebrews 12.22–24

I looked, and behold, a great multitude which no man could number, from every nation, from all tribes and peoples and tongues, standing before the throne; and before the Lamb, clothed in white robes, with palm branches in their hands, and crying out with a loud voice, 'Salvation belongs to our God who sits upon the throne, and to the Lamb!' And all the angels stood before the throne; and round the elders and the four living creatures, and they fell on their faces before the throne and worshipped God, saying, 'Amen! Blessing and glory and wisdom and thanksgiving and honour and power and might be to our God for ever and ever! Amen.' Then one of the elders addressed me, saying, 'Who are these, clothed in white robes, and whence have they come?' I said, 'Sir, you know.' And he said to me, 'These are they who have come out of the great tribulation; they have washed their robes and made them white in the blood of the Lamb.' Revelation 7.9–14

RESPONSE 'O blest communion, fellowship divine! we feebly struggle,
they in glory shine. Yet all are one in thee, for all are thine.'

Almighty God, you are the source of holiness – we praise you for all the saints in every generation . . .
Your Church on earth and in heaven is one Church – we thank you for making us one communion and fellowship in the mystical Body of your Son . . .
'We are surrounded by so great a cloud of witnesses' – we pray with all the saints in heaven for the needs of the Church on earth . . .

INTERCESSIONS *pages 390–393* CLOSING PRAYERS *page 402–403*

2 November *All Souls' Day*

OPENING PRAYER Almighty God, you bring our life and your life together in a marvellous way in your Son. Accept our praises offered to you with the prayers of the saints and of the hosts of heaven . . . Glory be . . .

PSALMODY I shall not die, but I shall live,
and recount the deeds of the Lord.
The Lord has chastened me sorely,
but he has not given me over to death.
Open to me the gates of righteousness,
that I may enter through them
and give thanks to the Lord. Psalm 118.15–19*

SCRIPTURE READINGS 'All that the Father gives me will come to me; and him who comes to me I will not cast out. For I have come down from heaven, not to do my own will, but the will of him who sent me; and this is the will of him who sent me, that I should lose nothing of all that he has given me, but raise it up at the last day. For this is the will of my Father, that everyone who sees the Son and believes in him should have eternal life; and I will raise him up at the last day.' St John 6.37–40

Blessed be the God and Father of our Lord Jesus Christ! By his great mercy we have been born anew to a living hope through the resurrection of Jesus Christ from the dead, and to an inheritance which is imperishable, undefiled, and unfading, kept in heaven for you, who by God's power are guarded through faith for a salvation ready to be revealed in the last time. In this you rejoice, though now for a little while you may have to suffer various trials, so that the genuineness of your faith, more precious than gold which though perishable is tested by fire, may redound to praise and glory and honour at the revelation of Jesus Christ. Without having seen him you love him; though you do not now see him you believe in him and rejoice with unutterable and exalted joy. As the outcome of your faith you obtain the salvation of your souls. 1 Peter 1.3–9

Christ has been raised from the dead, the first fruits of those who have fallen asleep. 1 Corinthians 15.20

RESPONSE 'Where is death's sting? Where, grave, thy victory?
I triumph still, if thou abide with me.'

Eternal God, your Church is built on faith in the risen Christ – in your mercy, grant rest and peace to our departed relatives and friends, and to all who have died in the faith of Christ . . .
You give us many joys and blessings as we travel through this life – bring us at the last to live in your peace and joy for ever . . .

INTERCESSIONS *pages 390–393* CLOSING PRAYERS *page 402–403*

3 November *I Long to See You*

OPENING PRAYER Almighty God, you bring our life and your life together in a marvellous way in your Son: Accept our praises offered to you with the prayers of the saints and of the hosts of heaven . . . Glory be . . .

PSALMODY Great peace have those who love thy law;
nothing can make them stumble.
I hope for thy salvation, O Lord. Psalm 119.165–166

SCRIPTURE READINGS The men of Nineveh will arise at the judgement with this generation and condemn it; for they repented at the preaching of Jonah, and behold, someone greater than Jonah is here. St Luke 11.32

Paul, a servant of Jesus Christ, called to be an apostle, set apart for the gospel of God which he proclaimed beforehand through his prophets in the holy scriptures, the gospel concerning his Son, who was descended from David according to the flesh, and designated Son of God in power according to the Spirit of holiness by his resurrection from the dead, Jesus Christ our Lord, through whom we have received grace and apostleship to bring about the obedience of faith for the sake of his name among all the nations, including yourselves who are called to belong to Jesus Christ; To all God's beloved in Rome, who are called to be saints: Grace to you and peace from God our Father and the Lord Jesus Christ. First, I thank my God through Jesus Christ for all of you, because your faith is proclaimed in all the world. For God is my witness, whom I serve with my spirit in the Gospel of his Son, that without ceasing I mention you always in my prayers, asking that somehow by God's will I may now at last succeed in coming to you. For I long to see you, that I may impart to you some spiritual gift to strengthen you, that is, that we may be mutually encouraged by each other's faith, both yours and mine. I want you to know, brethren, that I have often intended to come to you (but thus far have been prevented), in order that I may reap some harvest among you as well as among the rest of the Gentiles. I am under obligation both to Greeks and to barbarians, both to the wise and to the foolish: so I am eager to preach the gospel to you also who are in Rome. Romans 1.1–15

RESPONSE 'Thou, O Lord, be not far off!
O thou my help, hasten to my aid.'

Gracious God, your Church is the baptized community of believers throughout the world and the temple of the Holy Spirit – we praise you for this sign and sacrament of your salvation . . .
'Grace and peace from God our Father and the Lord Jesus Christ' – Lord, we thank you for all the blessings you give us in your Son . . .
'I thank my God' – teach us to thank you for all things . . .

INTERCESSIONS *pages 390–393* CLOSING PRAYERS *page 402–403*

OPENING PRAYER Almighty God, you bring our life and your life together in a marvellous way in your Son. Accept our praises offered to you with the prayers of the saints and of the hosts of heaven . . . Glory be . . .

PSALMODY I keep thy precepts and testimonies,
for all my ways are before thee
Let my supplication come before thee;
deliver me according to thy word.
My lips will pour forth praise
that thou dost teach me thy statutes.
My tongue will sing of thy word,
for all thy commandments are right. Psalm 119.168–172*

SCRIPTURE READINGS The Lord your God is God of gods and Lord of lords, the great, the mighty, and the terrible God, who is not partial and takes no bribe. He executes justice for the fatherless and the widow, and loves the sojourner, giving him food and clothing. Deuteronomy 10.17–18

You have no excuse, O man, whoever you are, when you judge another; for in passing judgement upon him you condemn yourself, because you, the judge, are doing the very same things. We know that the judgement of God rightly falls upon those who do such things. Do you suppose, O man, that when you judge those who do such things and yet do them yourself, you will escape the judgement of God? Or do you presume upon the riches of his kindness and forbearance and patience? Do you not know that God's kindness is meant to lead you to repentance? But by your hard and impenitent heart you are storing up wrath for yourself on the day of wrath when God's righteous judgement will be revealed. For he will render to every man according to his works: to those who by patience in well-doing seek for glory and honour and immortality, he will give eternal life; but for those who are factious and do not obey the truth, but obey wickedness, there will be wrath and fury. There will be tribulation and distress for every human being who does evil, the Jew first and also the Greek, but glory and honour and peace for every one who does good, the Jew first and also the Greek. For God shows no partiality. Romans 2.1–11

RESPONSE 'When I soar through tracts unknown, see thee on thy judgement throne; Rock of angels, cleft for me, let me hide myself in thee.'

God our Father in Heaven, you are the source of all justice and truth – purify us with the fire of your love and accept our praise . . .
'Do you suppose you will escape the judgement of God?' – have mercy on us, now and at the hour of our death . . .
'God is love' – Lord, we bless you and we rejoice in your perfect love . . .

INTERCESSIONS *pages 390–393* CLOSING PRAYERS *page 402–403*

OPENING PRAYER Almighty God, you bring our life and your life together in a marvellous way in your Son. Accept our praises offered to you with the prayers of the saints and of the hosts of heaven . . . Glory be . . .

PSALMODY I long for thy salvation, O Lord.
let me live, that I may praise thee,
seek thy servant,
for I do not forget thy commandments. Psalm 119.174–176*

SCRIPTURE READINGS Saul said, 'Cast the lot between me and my son Jonathan.' And Jonathan was taken. Saul said to Jonathan, 'Tell me what you have done.' Jonathan told him, 'I tasted a little honey with the tip of my staff that was in my hand; here I am, I will die.' And Saul said, 'God do so to me and more also; you shall surely die, Jonathan.' Then the people said, 'Shall Jonathan die, who has wrought this great victory in Israel? Far from it! As the Lord lives, there shall not one hair of his head fall to the ground; for he has wrought with God this day.' 1 Samuel 14.42–45

Since we are justified by faith, we have peace with God through our Lord Jesus Christ. Through him we have obtained access to this grace in which we stand, and we rejoice in our hope of sharing the glory of God. More than that, we rejoice in our sufferings, knowing that suffering produces endurance, and endurance produces character, and character produces hope, and hope does not disappoint us, because God's love has been poured into our hearts through the Holy Spirit which has been given to us. While we were still weak, at the right time Christ died for the ungodly. Why, one will hardly die for a righteous man – though perhaps for a good man one will dare even to die. But God shows his love for us in that while we were yet sinners Christ died for us. Since, therefore, we are now justified by his blood, much more shall we be saved by him from the wrath of God. For if while we were enemies we were reconciled to God by the death of his Son, much more, now that we are reconciled, shall we be saved by his life. Not only so, but we also rejoice in God through our Lord Jesus Christ, through whom we have now received our reconciliation. Romans 5.1–11

RESPONSE 'I will give thanks to the Lord with my whole heart;
I will tell of all thy wonderful deeds.'

Loving Father, your Son died for us while we were yet sinners – we rejoice that Christ has broken the power of sin, and we praise you . . .
'We have obtained access to this grace' – we are totally unworthy through our sins, and we praise you for your forgiveness and redeeming love . . .
'God's love has been poured into our hearts through the Holy Spirit which has been given to us' – make us worthy to receive your love . . .

INTERCESSIONS *pages 390–393* CLOSING PRAYERS *page 402–403*

OPENING PRAYER Almighty God, you bring our life and your life together in a marvellous way in your Son. Accept our praises offered to you with the prayers of the saints and of the hosts of heaven . . . Glory be . . .

PSALMODY I lift up my eyes to the hills.
From whence does my help come?
My help comes from the Lord,
who made heaven and earth.
He will not let your foot be moved,
he who keeps you will not slumber.
Behold, he who keeps Israel
will neither slumber nor sleep. Psalm 121.1–4

SCRIPTURE READINGS The tax collector, standing far off, would not even lift up his eyes to heaven, but beat his breast, saying, 'God be merciful to me a sinner!' St Luke 18.13

What shall we say then? Are we to continue in sin that grace may abound? By no means! How can we who died to sin still live in it? Do you not know that all of us who have been baptized into Christ Jesus were baptized into his death? We were buried therefore with him by baptism into death, so that as Christ was raised from the dead by the glory of the Father, we too might walk in newness of life. For if we have been united with him in a death like his, we shall certainly be united with him in a resurrection like his. We know that our old self was crucified with him so that the sinful body might be destroyed, and we might no longer be enslaved to sin. For he who has died is free from sin. But if we have died with Christ, we believe that we shall also live with him. For we know that Christ being raised from the dead will never die again; death no longer has dominion over him. The death he died he died to sin, once for all, but the life he lives he lives to God. You also must consider yourselves dead to sin and alive to God in Christ Jesus. Romans 6.1–11

RESPONSE 'Lord, there is mercy now, as ever was, with thee;
before thy throne of grace I bow; be merciful to me.'

Eternal God, your Son died for the sins of men and women in every generation – we thank you for your redeeming love . . .
'All who were baptized into Christ Jesus were baptized into his death' – Lord, help us by your grace to walk in newness of life in Christ . . .
'Yield yourselves to God' – help us to surrender more to Christ . . .

INTERCESSIONS *pages 390–393* CLOSING PRAYERS *page 402–403*

7 November *Abba! Father!*

OPENING PRAYER Almighty God, you bring our life and your life together in a marvellous way in your Son. Accept our praises offered to you with the prayers of the saints and of the hosts of heaven . . . Glory be . . .

PSALMODY The Lord is your keeper;
the Lord is your shade on your right hand.
The sun shall not smite you by day,
nor the moon by night.
The Lord will keep you from all evil;
he will keep your life.
The Lord will keep your going out
and your coming in,
from this time forth and for evermore. Psalm 121.5–8*

SCRIPTURE READINGS Unless you repent, you will all perish. St Luke 13.5

There is no condemnation for those who are in Christ Jesus. For the law of the Spirit of life in Christ Jesus has set me free from the law of sin and death. For God has done what the law, weakened by the flesh, could not do: sending his own Son in the likeness of sinful flesh and for sin, he condemned sin in the flesh, in order that the just requirement of the law might be fulfilled in us, who walk not according to the flesh but according to the Spirit. To set the mind on the flesh is death, but to set the mind on the Spirit is life and peace. If the Spirit of him who raised Jesus from the dead dwells in you, he who raised Christ Jesus from the dead will give life to your mortal bodies also through his Spirit which dwells in you. So we are debtors, not to the flesh, to live according to the flesh – for if you live according to the flesh you will die, but if by the Spirit you put to death the deeds of the body you will live. For all who are led by the Spirit of God are sons of God. You did not receive the spirit of slavery to fall back into fear, but you have received the spirit of sonship. When we cry, 'Abba! Father!' it is the Spirit himself bearing witness with our spirit that we are children of God, and if children, then heirs, heirs of God and fellow heirs with Christ, provided we suffer with him in order that we may also be glorified with him. Romans 8.1–17*

RESPONSE 'Thrice Holy! Father, Son, Spirit, mysterious Godhead, three in one,
before thy throne we bend, grace, pardon, life to us extend.'

Heavenly Father, great is the wonder of your love for us – we praise you for making us your children through the sacrament of Baptism . . .
'To set the mind on the Spirit is life and peace' – come, Holy Spirit, and kindle in us the fire of your perfect love . . .
'Abba! Father' – Holy Father, Holy God, we worship your holy name . . .

INTERCESSIONS *pages 390–393* CLOSING PRAYERS *page 402–403*

8 November *Who Shall Separate Us From The Love of God?*

OPENING PRAYER Almighty God, you bring our life and your life together in a marvellous way in your Son. Accept our praises offered to you with the prayers of the saints and of the hosts of heaven . . . Glory be . . .

PSALMODY I was glad when they said,
'Let us go to the house of the Lord!'
Our feet have been standing
within your gates, O Jerusalem!
Jerusalem, built as a city
which is bound firmly together,
to which the tribes go up, the tribes of the Lord
as was decreed for Israel,
to give thanks to the name of the Lord.
There thrones for judgment were set,
the thrones of the house of David. Psalm 122.1–5*

SCRIPTURE READINGS We told the king, 'The hand of our God is for good upon all that seek him.' Ezra 8.22

In everything God works for good with those who love him, who are called according to his purpose. What then shall we say? If God is for us, who is against us? He who did not spare his own Son but gave him up for us all, will he not also give us all things with him? Who shall bring any charge against God's elect? It is God who justifies; who is to condemn? Is it Christ Jesus, who died, yes, who was raised from the dead, who is at the right hand of God, who indeed intercedes for us? Who shall separate us from the love of Christ? Shall tribulation, or distress, or persecution, or famine, or nakedness, or peril, or sword? As it is written, 'For thy sake we are being killed all the day long; we are regarded as sheep to be slaughtered.' No, in all these things we are more than conquerors through him who loved us. For I am sure that neither death, nor life, nor angels, nor principalities, nor things present, nor things to come, nor powers, nor height, nor depth, nor anything else in all creation, will be able to separate us from the love of God in Christ Jesus our Lord. Romans 8.28–39*

RESPONSE 'Jesu, thou art all compassion, pure unbounded love thou art,
visit us with thy salvation, enter every trembling heart.'

Almighty God, you show us the true nature of your love on the Cross – we rejoice that you are Creator, Lover and Sustainer of all life . . .
'We are more than conquerors through him who loved us' – help us to respond more fully to your great love in your Son . . .
'Nothing can separate us from the love of God' – we rejoice in this assurance of your love, and we praise and bless your holy name . . .

INTERCESSIONS *pages 390–393* CLOSING PRAYERS *page 402–403*

9 November *The Stumbling Stone*

OPENING PRAYER Almighty God, you bring our life and your life together in a marvellous way in your Son. Accept our praises offered to you with the prayers of the saints and of the hosts of heaven . . . Glory be . . .

PSALMODY Pray for the peace of Jerusalem!
'May they prosper who love you!
Peace be within your walls,
and security within your towers!'
For the sake of the house of the Lord our God,
I will seek your good. Psalm 122.6–9*

SCRIPTURE READINGS Moses said, 'I besought the Lord, saying, 'O Lord God, thou hast only begun to show thy greatness and thy mighty hand. Let me go over and see the good land beyond the Jordan.' The Lord was angry with me on your account; and the Lord said, 'Let it suffice you. Go to the top of Pisgah, and behold it with your eyes; for you shall not go over the Jordan. Charge Joshua, and strengthen him, for he shall go over at the head of this people and put them in possession of the land.
Deuteronomy 3.23–28

I am speaking the truth in Christ, I am not lying; my conscience bears me witness in the Holy Spirit, that I have great sorrow and unceasing anguish in my heart. For I could wish that I myself were accursed and cut off from Christ for the sake of my brethren, my kinsmen by race. They are Israelites, and to them belong the sonship, the glory, the covenants, the giving of the law, the worship, and the promises; to them belong the patriarchs, and of their race, according to the flesh, is the Christ. God who is over all be blessed for ever. Amen. Isaiah cries out concerning Israel: 'Though the number of the sons of Israel be as the sand of the sea, only a remnant of them will be saved; for the Lord will execute his sentence upon the earth with rigour and dispatch.' They have stumbled over the stumbling stone, as it is written, 'Behold, I am laying in Zion a stone that will make men stumble; and he who believes in him will not be put to shame.' Brethren, my heart's desire and prayer to God is that they may be saved.
Romans 9.1–10.1*

RESPONSE 'The Lord lives; and blessed be my rock,
and exalted be the God of my salvation.'

Almighty God, you invite all people to share your glory in your Son – with thankful hearts, we ascribe all praise to your holy name . . .
You chose the Jewish people to receive your messages – may all people come to know your love in Jesus Christ . . .
'My prayer is for them to be saved' – may all people of all nations come to accept your Word, and be led to rejoice in Christ as Lord . . .

INTERCESSIONS *pages 390–393* CLOSING PRAYERS *page 402–403*

10 November *How Inscrutable His Ways*

OPENING PRAYER Almighty God, you bring our life and your life together in a marvellous way in your Son. Accept our praises offered to you with the prayers of the saints and of the hosts of heaven . . . Glory be . . .

PSALMODY If it had not been the Lord who was on our side.
when men rose up against us,
then they would have swallowed us up alive,
when their anger was kindled against us;
then the flood would have swept us away. Psalm 124.1–4

SCRIPTURE READINGS One of the twelve, who was called Judas Iscariot, went to the chief priests and said, 'What will you give me if I deliver him to you?' And they paid him thirty pieces of silver. St Matthew 26.14–15

I ask, then, has God rejected his people? By no means! I myself am an Israelite, a descendant of Abraham, a member of the tribe of Benjamin. God has not rejected his people whom he foreknew. Lest you be wise in your own conceits, I want you to understand this mystery, brethren: a hardening has come upon part of Israel, until the full number of the Gentiles come in, and so all Israel will be saved; as it is written, 'The Deliverer will come from Zion, he will banish ungodliness from Jacob'; and 'this will be my covenant with them when I take away their sins.' As regards the gospel they are enemies of God, for your sake; but as regards election they are beloved for the sake of their forefathers. For the gifts and the call of God are irrevocable. Just as you were once disobedient to God but now have received mercy because of their disobedience, so they have now been disobedient in order that by the mercy shown to you they also may receive mercy. For God has consigned all men to disobedience, that he may have mercy upon all. O the depth of the riches and wisdom and knowledge of God! How unsearchable are his judgements and how inscrutable his ways! 'For who has known the mind of the Lord, or who has been his counsellor?' 'Or who has given a gift to him that he might be repaid?' For from him and through him and to him are all things. To him be glory for ever. Amen. Romans 11.1–36*

RESPONSE 'Praise to the Holiest in the height, and in the depth be praise:
in all his works most wonderful, most sure in all his ways.'

Heavenly Father, you revealed the mystery of your love in your Son – we rejoice that one day, all creation will be united in Christ . . .
'The gifts and the call of God are irrevocable' – Lord, give us a deeper understanding of your goodness and love . . .
'You were once disobedient to God' – forgive us our former sins, and help us to seek your will in all things . . .

INTERCESSIONS *pages 390–393* CLOSING PRAYERS *page 402–403*

OPENING PRAYER Almighty God, you bring our life and your life together in a marvellous way in your Son. Accept our praises offered to you with the prayers of the saints and of the hosts of heaven . . . Glory be . . .

PSALMODY God is our refuge and strength,
a very present help in trouble. Psalm 46.1

SCRIPTURE READINGS
He shall judge between many peoples,
and shall decide for strong nations afar off;
and they shall beat their swords into ploughshares,
and their spears into pruning hooks;
nation shall not lift up sword against nation,
neither shall they learn war any more. Micah 4.2–3

I urge that supplications, prayers, intercessions, and thanksgivings be made for all men, for kings and all who are in high positions, that we may lead a quiet and peaceable life. 1 Timothy 2.1–2

You have heard that it was said, You shall love your neighbour and hate your enemy. But I say to you, Love your enemies and pray for those who persecute you, so that you may be sons of your Father who is in heaven, for he makes his sun rise on the evil and on the good, and sends rain on the just and on the unjust. For if you love those who love you, what reward have you? Do not even the tax collectors do the same? And if you salute only your brethren, what more are you doing than others? Do not even the Gentiles do the same? You, therefore, must be perfect, as your heavenly Father is perfect. St Matthew 5.43–48

Peace I leave with you; my peace I give to you; not as the world gives do I give to you. Let not your hearts be troubled, neither let them be afraid. St John 14.27

RESPONSE 'Peace, perfect peace, with loved ones far away?
In Jesus' keeping we are safe and they.'

Almighty God, your Son sacrificed his life on the Cross for the salvation of the world – Lord, unite all people in your love . . .
Our hope of resurrection to eternal life is in Jesus Christ – Lord, grant eternal rest and peace to those who died in war . . .
'The Lord is my shepherd' – we pray for the sorrowful relatives of all who died in war, and for all who still suffer from their wounds . . .
'Live in peace' – inspire a genuine desire for justice and peace in the hearts of all people, and fill us with your love . . .

INTERCESSIONS *pages 390–393* CLOSING PRAYERS *page 402–403*

OPENING PRAYER Almighty God, you bring our life and your life together in a marvellous way in your Son. Accept our praises offered to you with the prayers of the saints and of the hosts of heaven . . . Glory be . . .

PSALMODY Our help is in the name of the Lord,
who made heaven and earth. Psalm 124.8

SCRIPTURE READINGS Jesus said, 'One of you will betray me.'
St Matthew 26.21

I appeal to you by the mercies of God, to present your bodies as a living sacrifice, holy and acceptable to God, which is your spiritual worship. Do not be conformed to this world, but be transformed by the renewal of your mind, that you may prove what is the will of God, what is good and acceptable and perfect. I bid everyone among you not to think of himself more highly than he ought to think, but to think with sober judgement, each according to the measure of faith which God has assigned him. For as in one body we have many members, and all the members do not have the same function, so we, though many, are one body in Christ, and individually members one of another. Having gifts that differ according to the grace given to us, let us use them: if prophecy, in proportion to our faith; if service, in our serving; he who teaches, in his teaching; he who exhorts, in his exhortation; he who contributes, in liberality; he who gives aid, with zeal; he who does acts of mercy, with cheerfulness. Let love be genuine; hate what is evil, hold fast to what is good; love one another with brotherly affection; outdo one another in showing honour. Never flag in zeal, be aglow with the Spirit, serve the Lord. Rejoice in your hope, be patient in tribulation, be constant in prayer. Contribute to the needs of the saints, practise hospitality. Bless those who persecute you; bless and do not curse them. Rejoice with those who rejoice, weep with those who weep. Live in harmony with one another; do not be haughty, but associate with the lowly; never be conceited. Repay no one evil for evil, but take thought for what is noble in the sight of all. If possible, so far as it depends upon you, live peaceably with all. Beloved, never avenge yourselves, but leave it to the wrath of God. Romans 12.1–19*

RESPONSE 'Where is thy reign of peace and purity and love?
when shall all hatred cease, as in the realms above?'

Eternal Saviour, you set before us the perfect example of love in your Son – we celebrate your glory and we bless your holy name . . .
'Present your bodies as a living sacrifice, holy and acceptable to God' – purify us, and help us to grow in holiness and love . . .
'Let love be genuine' – Lord, help us to learn more about your love from the Cross and the Crib of Bethlehem . . .

INTERCESSIONS *pages 390–393* CLOSING PRAYERS *page 402–403*

OPENING PRAYER Almighty God, you bring our life and your life together in a marvellous way in your Son. Accept our praises offered to you with the prayers of the saints and of the hosts of heaven . . . Glory be . . .

PSALMODY Those who trust in the Lord are like Mount Zion,
which cannot be moved, but abides for ever. Psalm 125.1

SCRIPTURE READINGS Joshua summoned the inhabitants of Gibeon, and said to them, 'Why did you deceive us, saying, "We are very far from you," when you dwell among us?' They answered, 'Because the Lord your God had commanded his servant Moses to give you all the land, and to destroy all the inhabitants of the land before you; so we feared greatly for our lives. Now we are in your hand; do as it seems good and right in your sight to do to us.' So he did to them and delivered them out of the hand of the people of Israel; and they did not kill them. But Joshua made them hewers of wood and drawers of water for the congregation and for the altar of the Lord, to continue to this day. Joshua 9.22–27*

Welcome one another, as Christ has welcomed you, for the glory of God. For I tell you that Christ became a servant to the circumcised to show God's truthfulness, in order to confirm the promises given to the patriarchs, and in order that the Gentiles might glorify God for his mercy. It is written, 'Therefore I will praise thee among the Gentiles, and sing to thy name.' And again it is said, 'Rejoice, O Gentiles, with his people'; and further Isaiah says, 'The root of Jesse shall come, he who rises to rule the Gentiles; in him shall the Gentiles hope.' May the God of hope fill you with all joy and peace in believing, so that by the power of the Holy Spirit you may abound in hope. Now to him who is able to strengthen you according to my gospel and the preaching of Jesus Christ, according to the revelation of the mystery which was kept secret for long ages but is now disclosed and through the prophetic writing is made known to all nations, according to the command of the eternal God, to bring about the obedience of faith – to the only wise God be glory for evermore through Jesus Christ! Amen. Romans 15.7–16.27*

RESPONSE 'Rejoice, the Lord is King!
Your Lord and King adore.'

Almighty God, you share in our sufferings and in our joy – we raise our voices to re-echo the triumphal praise of heaven . . .
'May the God of hope fill you with all joy and peace in believing' – we praise you for all your blessings and we rejoice in Christ our Saviour . . .
'To the only wise God be glory for evermore through Jesus Christ' – we praise you for your glory in the Church and in Christ Jesus . . .

INTERCESSIONS *pages 390–393* CLOSING PRAYERS *page 402–403*

OPENING PRAYER Almighty God, you bring our life and your life together in a marvellous way in your Son. Accept our praises offered to you with the prayers of the saints and of the hosts of heaven . . . Glory be . . .

PSALMODY When the Lord restored the fortunes of Zion,
we were like those who dream.
Then our mouth was filled with laughter,
and our tongue with shouts of joy;
then they said among the nations,
'The Lord has done great things for them.'
The Lord has done great things for us. Psalm 126.1–3

SCRIPTURE READINGS 'Holy Father, keep them in thy name which thou hast given me, that they may be one, even as we are one.' St John 17.11

I give thanks to God always for you because of the grace of God which was given you in Christ Jesus, that in every way you were enriched in him with all speech and all knowledge – even as the testimony to Christ was confirmed among you – so that you are not lacking in any spiritual gift, as you wait for the revealing of our Lord Jesus Christ; who will sustain you to the end, guiltless in the day of our Lord Jesus Christ. God is faithful, by whom you were called into the fellowship of his Son, Jesus Christ our Lord. I appeal to you, brethren, by the name of our Lord Jesus Christ, that all of you agree and that there be no dissensions among you, but that you be united in the same mind and the same judgement. For it has been reported to me by Chloe's people that there is quarrelling among you, my brethren. What I mean is that each one of you says, 'I belong to Paul,' or 'I belong to Apollos,' or 'I belong to Cephas,' or 'I belong to Christ.' Is Christ divided? Was Paul crucified for you? Or were you baptized in the name of Paul? I am thankful that I baptized none of you except Crispus and Gaius; lest any one should say that you were baptized in my name. For Christ did not send me to baptize but to preach the Gospel, and not with eloquent wisdom, lest the cross of Christ be emptied of its power. 1 Corinthians 1.4–17*

RESPONSE 'The Church's one foundation is Jesus Christ her Lord;
she is his new creation by water and the word.'

Almighty God, you call us into the fellowship of those who are baptized in Christ's name – we praise you for your gift of grace . . .
'Be united in the same mind' – fill us with your love, and help us to make real the unity we share in the one Spirit . . .
'Lest the Cross of Christ be emptied of its power' – send the Spirit to make present the redeeming work of Christ through the Church . . .

INTERCESSIONS *pages 390–393* CLOSING PRAYERS *page 402–403*

15 November *The Power of the Cross*

OPENING PRAYER Almighty God, you bring our life and your life together in a marvellous way in your Son. Accept our praises offered to you with the prayers of the saints and of the hosts of heaven . . . Glory be . . .

PSALMODY Restore our fortunes, O Lord,
like the watercourses in the Negeb!
May those who sow in tears
reap with shouts of joy!
He that goes forth weeping,
shall come home with shouts of joy. Psalm 126.4–6

SCRIPTURE READINGS In him all the fulness of God was pleased to dwell, and through him to reconcile to himself all things, whether on earth or in heaven, making peace by the blood of his cross. Colossians 1.19–20

The word of the cross is folly to those who are perishing, but to us who are being saved it is the power of God. It is written, 'I will destroy the wisdom of the wise, and the cleverness of the clever I will thwart.' Has not God made foolish the wisdom of the world? For since, in the wisdom of God, the world did not know God through wisdom, it pleased God through the folly of what we preach to save those who believe. For Jews demand signs and Greeks seek wisdom, but we preach Christ crucified, a stumbling block to Jews and folly to Gentiles, but to those who are called, both Jews and Greeks, Christ the power of God and the wisdom of God. For the foolishness of God is wiser than men, and the weakness of God is stronger than men. For consider your call, brethren; not many of you were wise according to worldly standards, not many were powerful, not many were of noble birth; but God chose what is foolish in the world to shame the wise, God chose what is weak in the world to shame the strong. God chose what is low and despised in the world, even things that are not, to bring to nothing the things that are, so that no human being might boast in the presence of God. He is the source of your life in Christ Jesus, whom God made our wisdom, our righteousness and sanctification and redemption; therefore, 'Let him who boasts, boast of the Lord.'
1 Corinthians 1.18–31*

RESPONSE 'Thy blest Cross which doth for all atone,
creation's praises rise before thy throne.'

Almighty God, the Cross is a sign of triumph over sin and death – we thank you for the victory of your Son at Calvary and we praise you . . .
'The word of the Cross is the power of God' – Lord, draw all people to yourself through the selfless love of Jesus Christ on the Cross . . .
'Consider your call' – help us to understand what you want us to do, and give us strength to do it for your glory and the good of your Church . . .

INTERCESSIONS *pages 390–393* CLOSING PRAYERS *page 402–403*

16 November *A Secret and Hidden Wisdom of God*

OPENING PRAYER Almighty God, you bring our life and your life together in a marvellous way in your Son. Accept our praises offered to you with the prayers of the saints and of the hosts of heaven . . . Glory be . . .

PSALMODY Unless the Lord builds the house,
those who build it labour in vain.
Unless the Lord watches over the city,
the watchman stays awake in vain. Psalm 127.1–2

SCRIPTURE READINGS The messenger who went to summon Micaiah said to him, 'Behold, the words of the prophets with one accord are favourable to the king; let your word be like the word of one of them, and speak favourably.' But Micaiah said, 'As the Lord lives, what the Lord says to me, that I will speak.' 1 Kings 22.13–14

When I came to you, I did not come proclaiming to you the testimony of God in lofty words or wisdom. For I decided to know nothing among you except Jesus Christ and him crucified. I was with you in weakness and in much fear and trembling; and my speech and my message were not in plausible words of wisdom, but in demonstration of the Spirit and of power, that your faith might not rest in the wisdom of men but in the power of God. Yet among the mature we do impart wisdom, although it is not a wisdom of this age or of the rulers of this age, who are doomed to pass away. We impart a secret and hidden wisdom of God, which God decreed before the ages for our glorification. None of the rulers of this age understood this; for if they had, they would not have crucified the Lord of glory. As it is written, 'What no eye has seen, or ear heard, nor the heart of man conceived, what God has prepared for those who love him,' God has revealed to us through the Spirit. For the Spirit searches everything, even the depths of God. For what person knows a man's thoughts except the spirit of the man which is in him? No one comprehends the thoughts of God except the Spirit of God. We have received not the spirit of the world, but the Spirit which is from God, that we might understand the gifts bestowed on us by God. We impart this in words taught by the Spirit, interpreting spiritual truths to those who possess the Spirit.
1 Corinthians 2.1–13*

RESPONSE 'I will give to the Lord the thanks due to his righteousness,
and I will sing praises to the name of the Lord, the Most High.'

Eternal God, your majesty and power are beyond our knowledge – we praise you for revealing the mystery of your love in your Son . . .
'We impart a secret and hidden wisdom of God' – enlighten our minds and give us grace to come to your Kingdom . . .
'The Spirit searches everything' – purify us and make us holy . . .

INTERCESSIONS *pages 390–393* CLOSING PRAYERS *page 402–403*

17 November *You Are God's Building*

OPENING PRAYER Almighty God, you bring our life and your life together in a marvellous way in your Son. Accept our praises offered to you with the prayers of the saints and of the hosts of heaven . . . Glory be . . .

PSALMODY Blessed is every one who fears the Lord.
You shall eat the fruit of the labour of your hands;
you shall be happy, and it shall be well with you.
Your wife will be like a fruitful vine within your house;
your children will be like olive shoots around your table.
The Lord bless you from Zion!
May you see the prosperity of Jerusalem
all the days of your life!
May you see your children's children!
Peace be upon Israel! Psalm 128.1–6*

SCRIPTURE READINGS Come to him, to that living stone, rejected by men but in God's sight chosen and precious; and like living stones be yourselves built into a spiritual house, to be a holy priesthood, to offer spiritual sacrifices acceptable to God through Jesus Christ. 1 Peter 2.4–5

We are fellow workmen for God; you are God's field, God's building. According to the commission of God given to me, like a skilled master builder, I laid a foundation, and another man is building upon it. Let each man take care how he builds upon it. For no other foundation can any one lay than that which is laid, which is Jesus Christ. If anyone builds on the foundation with gold, silver, precious stones, wood, hay, stubble – each man's work will become manifest; for the Day will disclose it, because it will be revealed with fire, and the fire will test what sort of work each one has done. If the work which any man has built on the foundation survives, he will receive a reward. If any man's work is burned up he will suffer loss, though he himself will be saved, but only as through fire. Do you not know that you are God's temple and that God's Spirit dwells in you?
1 Corinthians 3.9–16

RESPONSE 'Christ is our corner-stone, on him alone we build;
with his true saints alone the courts of heaven are filled.'

Almighty God, you are building the Church as a spiritual temple – we praise you for the foundations laid by the Apostles long ago . . .
'We are fellow workers for God' – teach us to co-operate with the Holy Spirit to build your Church and Kingdom . . .
'You are God's temple, and God's Spirit dwells in you' – cleanse our souls and bodies, and make us worthy dwelling places for your eternal Spirit . . .

INTERCESSIONS *pages 390–393* CLOSING PRAYERS *page 402–403*

18 November *Stewards of the Mysteries of God*

OPENING PRAYER Almighty God, you bring our life and your life together in a marvellous way in your Son. Accept our praises offered to you with the prayers of the saints and of the hosts of heaven . . . Glory be . . .

PSALMODY 'Sorely have they afflicted me from my youth,'
let Israel now say –
'Sorely have they afflicted me from my youth,
yet they have not prevailed against me.
The ploughers ploughed upon my back;
they made long their furrows.'
The Lord is righteous;
he has cut the cords of the wicked. Psalm 129.1–4

SCRIPTURE READINGS Woe to those who are wise in their own eyes,
and shrewd in their own sight! Isaiah 5.21

Let no one deceive himself. If any one among you thinks that he is wise in this age, let him become a fool that he may become wise. For the wisdom of this world is folly with God. For it is written, 'He catches the wise in their craftiness', and again 'The Lord knows that the thoughts of the wise are futile.' So let no one boast of men. For all things are yours, whether Paul or Apollos or Cephas or the world or life or death or the present or the future, all are yours; and you are Christ's; and Christ is God's. This is how one should regard us, as servants of Christ and stewards of the mysteries of God. Moreover it is required of stewards that they be found trustworthy. But with me it is a very small thing that I should be judged by you or by any human court. I do not even judge myself. I am not aware of anything against myself, but I am not thereby acquitted. It is the Lord who judges me. Therefore do not pronounce judgement before the time, before the Lord comes, who will bring to light the things now hidden in darkness and will disclose the purposes of the heart. Then every man will receive his commendation from God. 1 Corinthians 3.18–4.5

RESPONSE 'Take my life, and let it be consecrated, Lord, to thee;
take my moments and my days, let them flow in ceaseless praise.'

Almighty God, you gather disciples in every generation to be agents of your love – we praise you for the richness of your mercy and love . . .
'It is required of stewards that they be found trustworthy' – bless the ordained ministry and give them grace to be holy and faithful . . .
Your continual presence with us is both judgement and grace – forgive us all our sins and renew our union with Christ our Lord . . .

INTERCESSIONS *pages 390–393* CLOSING PRAYERS *page 402–403*

19 November *Spiritual Gifts From God*

OPENING PRAYER Almighty God, you bring our life and your life together in a marvellous way in your Son. Accept our praises offered to you with the prayers of the saints and of the hosts of heaven . . . Glory be . . .

PSALMODY If thou, O Lord, shouldst mark iniquities,
Lord, who could stand?
But there is forgiveness with thee. Psalm 130.3–4

SCRIPTURE READINGS King Josiah commanded the high priest to bring out of the temple of the Lord all the vessels made for Baal; he burned them outside Jerusalem in the fields of Kidron. He deposed the idolatrous priests, and the king commanded all people, 'Keep the Passover of the Lord your God, as it is written in this book of the Covenant.' 2 Kings 23.4–21*

Concerning spiritual gifts, I do not want you to be uninformed. You know that when you were heathen, you were led astray to dumb idols, however you may have been moved. Therefore I want you to understand that no one speaking by the Spirit of God ever says, 'Jesus be cursed!' and no one can say 'Jesus is Lord' except by the Holy Spirit. Now there are varieties of gifts but the same Spirit; and there are varieties of service, but the same Lord; and there are varieties of working, but it is the same God who inspires them all in every one. To each is given the manifestation of the Spirit for the common good. To one is given through the Spirit the utterance of wisdom, and to another the utterance of knowledge according to the same Spirit, and to another faith by the same Spirit, to another gifts of healing by the one Spirit, to another the working of miracles, to another prophecy, to another the ability to distinguish between spirits, to another various kinds of tongues, to another the interpretation of tongues. All these are inspired by one and the same Spirit, who apportions to each one individually as he wills. For just as the body is one and has many members, and all the members of the body, though many, are one body, so it is with Christ. For by one Spirit we were all baptized into one body – Jews or Greeks, slaves or free – and all were made to drink of one Spirit.

1 Corinthians 12.1–13

RESPONSE 'Gracious Spirit, Holy Ghost, taught by thee, we covet most of thy gifts at Pentecost, Holy, heavenly love.'

Heavenly Father, you pour out your blessings on the Church – we rejoice that the Church is the temple of the Spirit and a sign of salvation . . .
'All these are inspired by one and the same Spirit' – Lord, renew your gift of the Spirit in the Church and fill us with your joy and peace . . .
'By one Spirit we were all baptized into one body' – thank you, Lord, for uniting us in an unseen way with Christ in his death and resurrection . . .

INTERCESSIONS *pages 390–393* CLOSING PRAYERS *page 402–403*

OPENING PRAYER Almighty God, you bring our life and your life together in a marvellous way in your Son. Accept our praises offered to you with the prayers of the saints and of the hosts of heaven . . . Glory be . . .

PSALMODY O Israel, hope in the Lord!
For with the Lord there is steadfast love.
And he will redeem Israel from all his iniquities.
Psalm 130.7–8*

SCRIPTURE READINGS He is the head of the body, the Church.
Colossians 1.18

The body does not consist of one member but of many. If the foot should say, 'Because I am not a hand, I do not belong to the body,' that would not make it any less a part of the body. If the ear should say, 'Because I am not an eye, I do not belong to the body,' that would not make it any less a part of the body. If the whole body were an eye, where would be the hearing? If the whole body were an ear, where would be the sense of smell? As it is, God arranged the organs in the body, each one of them, as he chose. If all were a single organ, where would the body be? As it is, there are many parts, yet one body. The eye cannot say to the hand, 'I have no need of you,' nor again the head to the feet, 'I have no need of you.' On the contrary, the parts of the body which seem to be weaker are indispensable, and those parts of the body which we think less honourable we invest with the greater honour, and our unpresentable parts are treated with greater modesty, which our more presentable parts do not require. God has so composed the body, giving the greater honour to the inferior part, that there may be no discord in the body, but that the members may have the same care for one another. If one member suffers, all suffer together; if one member is honoured, all rejoice together. You are the body of Christ and individually members of it. God has appointed in the Church first apostles, second prophets, third teachers, then workers of miracles, then healers, helpers, administrators, speakers in various kinds of tongues. Are all apostles? Are all prophets? Are all teachers? Do all work miracles? Do all possess gifts of healing? Do all speak with tongues? Do all interpret? But earnestly desire the higher gifts. 1 Corinthians 12.14–30

RESPONSE 'O happy band of pilgrims, if onward ye will tread,
with Jesus as your fellow, to Jesus as your Head.'

Heavenly God, you created the Church to share in the mission of your Son – we praise you for the one holy catholic and apostolic Church . . .
'God has appointed in the Church first apostles' – we praise you for the glorious company of the apostles, and their successors through the ages . . .
'You are the body of Christ and individually members of it' – help all who are baptized to seek and do your will in their lives . . .

INTERCESSIONS *pages 390–393* CLOSING PRAYERS *page 402–403*

21 November *The Greatest is Love*

OPENING PRAYER Almighty God, you bring our life and your life together in a marvellous way in your Son. Accept our praises offered to you with the prayers of the saints and of the hosts of heaven . . . Glory be . . .

PSALMODY Remember, O Lord, in David's favour,
all the hardships he endured;
how he swore to the Lord,
'I will not enter my house or get into my bed;
until I find a place for the Lord,
a dwelling place for the Mighty One of Jacob.'
'Let us go to his dwelling place;
Let us worship at his footstool!' Psalm 132.1–7*

SCRIPTURE READINGS God so loved the world that he gave his only Son, that whoever believes in him should not perish but have eternal life.
St John 3.16

I will show you a still more excellent way. If I speak in the tongues of men and of angels, but have not love, I am a noisy gong or a clanging cymbal. And if I have prophetic powers, and understand all mysteries and all knowledge, and if I have all faith, so as to remove mountains, but have not love, I am nothing. If I give away all I have, and if I deliver my body to be burned, but have not love, I gain nothing. Love is patient and kind; love is not jealous or boastful; it is not arrogant or rude. Love does not insist on its own way; it is not irritable or resentful; it does not rejoice at wrong, but rejoices in the right. Love bears all things, believes all things, hopes all things, endures all things. Love never ends; as for prophecies, they will pass away; as for tongues, they will cease; as for knowledge, it will pass away. For our knowledge is imperfect and our prophecy is imperfect; but when the perfect comes, the imperfect will pass away. When I was a child, I spoke like a child, I thought like a child, I reasoned like a child; when I became a man, I gave up childish ways. For now we see in a mirror dimly, but then face to face. Now I know in part; then I shall understand fully, even as I have been fully understood. So faith, hope, love abide, these three; but the greatest of these is love. 1 Corinthians 12.31–13.13

RESPONSE 'Faith and hope and love we see, joining hand in hand agree;
but the greatest of the three, and the best, is love.'

Heavenly Father, you are the source of that wonderful gift of love – we praise you for your perfect gift of love in Jesus Christ our Lord . . .
'Love is patient and kind' – make your love perfect in the Church, and help us to spread your love in the world by our words and actions . . .
'Love never ends' – Lord, we rejoice in your eternal love . . .

INTERCESSIONS *pages 390–393* CLOSING PRAYERS *page 402–403*

OPENING PRAYER Almighty God, you bring our life and your life together in a marvellous way in your Son. Accept our praises offered to you with the prayers of the saints and of the hosts of heaven . . . Glory be . . .

PSALMODY Arise, O Lord, and go to thy resting place,
thou and the ark of thy might.
Let thy priests be clothed with righteousness,
and let thy saints shout for joy.
For thy servant David's sake
do not turn away the face of thy anointed one.
The Lord swore to David a sure oath
'One of the sons of your body I will set on your throne.
If your sons keep my covenant, their sons also for ever
shall sit upon your throne.' Psalm 132.8–12*

SCRIPTURE READINGS Since we believe that Jesus died and rose again, even so, through Jesus, God will bring with him those who have fallen asleep.
1 Thessalonians 4.14

I would remind you, brethren, in what terms I preached to you the gospel, which you recieved, in which you stand, by which you are saved, if you hold it fast – unless you believed in vain. For I delivered to you as of first importance what I also received, that Christ died for our sins in accordance with the scriptures, that he was buried, that he was raised on the third day in accordance with the scriptures, and that he appeared to Cephas, then to the twelve. Then he appeared to more than five hundred brethren at one time, most of whom are still alive, though some have fallen asleep. Then he appeared to James, then to all the apostles. Last of all, as to one untimely born, he appeared also to me. For I am the least of the apostles, unfit to be called an apostle, because I persecuted the church of God. But by the grace of God I am what I am, and his grace toward me was not in vain. On the contrary, I worked harder than any of them, though it was not I, but the grace of God which is with me. Whether it was I or they, so we preach and so you believed. 1 Corinthians 15.1–11

RESPONSE 'He who on the Cross a Victim for the world's salvation bled,
Jesus Christ, the King of Glory, now is raised from the dead.'

Eternal Father, you give joy to the world through the glorious resurrection of your Son – we rejoice and proclaim your glory . . .
'He was raised on the third day in accordance with the Scriptures' – we rejoice that our life in Christ is stronger than death . . .
'I worked harder than any of them' – fill your Church with your grace, and inspire us to bear witness to your risen Son in the world . . .

INTERCESSIONS *pages 390–393* CLOSING PRAYERS *page 402–403*

23 November *The Last enemy to be Destroyed*

OPENING PRAYER Almighty God, you bring our life and your life together in a marvellous way in your Son. Accept our praises offered to you with the prayers of the saints and of the hosts of heaven . . . Glory be . . .

PSALMODY The Lord has chosen Zion;
he has desired it for his habitation Psalm 132.13

SCRIPTURE READINGS Nebuzaradan, the captain of the bodyguard, a servant of the king of Babylon, came to Jerusalem. He burned the house of the Lord, and the king's house and all the houses of Jerusalem. And all the army of the Chaldeans, who were with the captain of the guard, broke down the walls around Jerusalem. And the rest of the people who were left in the city, Nebuzaradan carried into exile. 2 Kings 24.8–11*

Now if Christ is preached as raised from the dead, how can some of you say that there is no resurrection of the dead? But if there is no resurrection of the dead, then Christ has not been raised. If Christ has not been raised, then our preaching is in vain and your faith is in vain. We are even found to be misrepresenting God, because we testified of God that he raised Christ, whom he did not raise if it is true that the dead are not raised. For if the dead are not raised, then Christ has not been raised. If Christ has not been raised, your faith is futile and you are still in your sins. Then those also who have fallen asleep in Christ have perished. If for this life only we have hoped in Christ, we are of all men most to be pitied. But in fact Christ has been raised from the dead, the first fruits of those who have fallen asleep. For as by a man came death, by a man has come also the resurrection of the dead. For as in Adam all die, so also in Christ shall all be made alive. But each in his own order: Christ the first fruits, then at his coming those who belong to Christ. Then comes the end, when he delivers the Kingdom to God the Father after destroying every rule and every authority and power. For he must reign until he has put all his enemies under his feet. The last enemy to be destroyed is death. 'For God has put all things in subjection under his feet.' 1 Corinthians 15.12–27

RESPONSE 'When other helpers fail, and comforts flee,
Help of the helpless, O abide with me.'

God our Father, you give hope to the world by the resurrection of your Son – we praise you for the faith of the Church through the centuries . . .
You call us to yourself in death – Lord, we trust in your goodness and love in Jesus Christ, and we praise you . . .
'By a man has come the resurrection of the dead' – we rejoice that your Son opened the gate of eternal life to all believers, and we thank you . . .

INTERCESSIONS *pages 390–393* CLOSING PRAYERS *page 402–403*

OPENING PRAYER Almighty God, you bring our life and your life together in a marvellous way in your Son. Accept our praises offered to you with the prayers of the saints and of the hosts of heaven . . . Glory be . . .

PSALMODY Behold, how good and pleasant it is
when brothers dwell in unity!
It is like the precious oil upon the head,
running down upon the beard, upon the beard of Aaron.
It is like the dew of Hermon.
For there the Lord has commanded the blessing,
life for evermore. Psalm 133*

Come bless the Lord, all you servants of the Lord,
who stand by night in the house of the Lord!
Lift up your hands to the holy place, and bless the Lord.
May the Lord bless you from Zion,
who has made heaven and earth! Psalm 134

SCRIPTURE READING What do I gain if, humanly speaking, I fought with beasts at Ephesus? If the dead are not raised, 'Let us eat and drink, for tomorrow we die.' Do not be decieved: 'Bad company ruins good morals.' Come to your right mind, and sin no more. For some have no knowledge of God. I say this to your shame. But some one will ask, 'How are the dead raised? With what kind of body do they come?' You foolish man! What you sow does not come to life unless it dies. And what you sow is not the body which is to be, but a bare kernel, perhaps of wheat or of some other grain. But God gives it a body as he has chosen, and to each kind of seed its own body. For not all flesh is alike, but there is one kind for men, another for animals, another for birds, and another for fish. There are celestial bodies and there are terrestrial bodies; but the glory of the celestial is one, and the glory of the terrestrial is another. There is one glory of the sun, and another glory of the moon, and another glory of the stars; for star differs from star in glory. So it is with the resurrection of the dead.
1 Corinthians 15.32–42

RESPONSE 'Jesus lives! to him the throne over all the world is given;
may we go where he is gone, rest and reign with him in heaven.'

Almighty God, you sent your Son to share in our human nature – we thank you and praise you for inviting us to share in your divine nature . . .
'Some have no knowledge of God' – equip the Church through the power of the Spirit to bring the redeeming work of Christ to all the world . . .
'How are the dead raised up? With what body do they come?' – we rejoice in your power, and we trust in your goodness and love . . .

INTERCESSIONS *pages 390–393* CLOSING PRAYERS *page 402–403*

25 November — *God Gives Us the Victory*

OPENING PRAYER Almighty God, you bring our life and your life together in a marvellous way in your Son. Accept our praises offered to you with the prayers of the saints and of the hosts of heaven . . . Glory be . . .

PSALMODY Praise the Lord. Praise the name of the Lord,
give praise, O servants of the Lord. Psalm 135.1

SCRIPTURE READINGS

How lonely sits the city that was full of people!
How like a widow has she become.
She weeps bitterly in the night, tears on her cheeks;
she has none to comfort her. Lamentations 1.1–2

Come to me, all who labour and are heavy-laden, and I will give you rest. Take my yoke upon you, and learn from me; for I am gentle and lowly in heart, and you will find rest for your souls. St Matthew 11.28–29

If there is a physical body, there is also a spiritual body. But it is not the spiritual which is first but the physical, and then the spiritual. The first man was from the earth, a man of dust; the second man is from heaven. As was the man of dust, so are those who are of the dust; and as is the man of heaven, so are those who are of heaven. Flesh and blood cannot inherit the Kingdom of God, nor does the perishable inherit the imperishable. I tell you a mystery. We shall not all sleep, but we shall all be changed, in a moment, in the twinkling of an eye, at the last trumpet. For the trumpet will sound, and the dead will be raised imperishable, and we shall be changed. For this perishable nature must put on the imperishable, and this mortal nature must put on immortality. When the perishable puts on the imperishable, and the mortal puts on immortality, then shall come to pass the saying that is written: 'Death is swallowed up in victory.' O death, where is thy victory? O death, where is thy sting? The sting of death is sin, and the power of sin is the law. But thanks be to God, who gives us the victory through our Lord Jesus Christ. Therefore, be steadfast, immovable, always abounding in the work of the Lord, knowing that in the Lord your labour is not in vain. 1 Corinthians 15.44–58*

RESPONSE 'Jesus lives!
Henceforth is death but the gate of life immortal.'

Heavenly Father, your Son won the victory over sin and death – fill us with the joy of his life-giving resurrection and accept our praise . . .
'Thanks be to God, who gives us the victory through our Lord Jesus Christ' – help us by the Spirit to make known the saving love of Christ . . .
'Be steadfast, immovable, always abounding in the work of the Lord' – strengthen the faith of the Church and give us ever-grateful hearts.

INTERCESSIONS *pages 390–393* CLOSING PRAYERS *page 402–403*

26 November *Sharing in Christ's Sufferings*

OPENING PRAYER Almighty God, you bring our life and your life together in a marvellous way in your Son. Accept our praises offered to you with the prayers of the saints and of the hosts of heaven . . . Glory be . . .

PSALMODY Praise the Lord, for the Lord is good;
sing to his name, for he is gracious!
For I know that the Lord is great,
and that our Lord is above all gods. Psalm 135.3–5*

SCRIPTURE READINGS
Surely he has borne our griefs
and carried our sorrows. Isaiah 53.4

Blessed be the God and Father of our Lord Jesus Christ, the Father of mercies and God of all comfort; who comforts us in all our affliction, so that we may be able to comfort those who are in any affliction, with the comfort with which we ourselves are comforted by God. For as we share abundantly in Christ's sufferings, so through Christ we share abundantly in comfort too. If we are afflicted, it is for your comfort and salvation; and if we are comforted, it is for your comfort, which you experience when you patiently endure the same sufferings that we suffer. Our hope for you is unshaken; for we know that as you share in our sufferings, you will also share in our comfort. For we do not want you to be ignorant, brethren, of the affliction we experienced in Asia; for we were so utterly, unbearably crushed that we despaired of life itself. Why, we felt that we had received the sentence of death; but that was to make us rely not on ourselves but on God who raises the dead; he delivered us from so deadly a peril, and he will deliver us; on him we have set our hope that he will deliver us again. You also must help us by prayer, so that many will give thanks on our behalf for the blessing granted us in answer to many prayers. For our boast is this, the testimony of our conscience that we have behaved in the world, and still more toward you, with holiness and godly sincerity, not by earthly wisdom but by the grace of God. For we write you nothing but what you can read and understand; I hope you will understand fully.
2 Corinthians 1.3–13

RESPONSE 'Take up thy Cross, and follow Christ.
Only he who bears the Cross may hope to wear the glorious crown.'

Loving Father, your Son knew suffering and pain for our salvation – we rejoice that the tree of shame has become the tree of glory . . .
'That was to make us rely not on ourselves but on God' – strengthen and uphold all who share in the fellowship of Christ's suffering . . .
'We write you nothing but what you can read and understand' – help us to understand more of the mystery of your love . . .

INTERCESSIONS *pages 390–393* CLOSING PRAYERS *page 402–403*

27 November *Treasure in Earthen Vessels*

OPENING PRAYER Almighty God, you bring our life and your life together in a marvellous way in your Son. Accept our praises offered to you with the prayers of the saints and of the hosts of heaven . . . Glory be . . .

PSALMODY Whatever the Lord pleases he does, in heaven and on earth.
He it is who makes the clouds rise at the end of the earth,
who makes lightnings for the rain
and brings forth the wind from his storehouses.
Psalm 135.6–7*

SCRIPTURE READINGS The word of the Lord came to me: 'O house of Israel, can I not do with you as this potter has done? says the Lord. Behold, like the clay in the potter's hand, so are you in my hand.' Jeremiah 18.5–6

Having this ministry by the mercy of God, we do not lose heart. Even if our gospel is veiled, it is veiled only to those who are perishing. In their case the god of this world has blinded the minds of the unbelievers, to keep them from seeing the light of the gospel of the glory of Christ, who is the likeness of God. For what we preach is not ourselves, but Jesus Christ as Lord, with ourselves as your servants for Jesus' sake. For it is the God who said, 'Let light shine out of darkness,' who has shone in our hearts to give the light of the knowledge of the glory of God in the face of Christ. But we have this treasure in earthen vessels, to show that the transcendent power belongs to God and not to us. We are afflicted in every way, but not crushed; perplexed, but not driven to despair; persecuted, but not forsaken; struck down, but not destroyed; always carrying in the body the death of Jesus, so that the life of Jesus may also be manifested in our bodies. For while we live we are always being given up to death for Jesus' sake, so that the life of Jesus may be manifested in our mortal flesh. So death is at work in us, but life in you. Since we have the same spirit of faith as he had who wrote, 'I believed, and so I spoke,' we too believe, and so we speak, knowing that he who raised the Lord Jesus will raise us also with Jesus and bring us with you into his presence. For it is all for your sake, so that as grace extends to more and more people it may increase thanksgiving, to the glory of God. 2 Corinthians 4.1–15*

RESPONSE 'Thy mercies how tender, how firm to the end!
Our Maker, Defender, Redeemer and Friend.'

Almighty God, in your love you entrusted the Gospel of Christ to the Church on earth – we praise you for your light in the Church today . . .
'We have this treasure in earthen vessels' – Lord, cleanse us and make us worthy to receive the infinite riches of your grace . . .
'I believe and so I spoke' – send the Spirit and help us to do your work . . .

INTERCESSIONS *pages 390–393* CLOSING PRAYERS *page 402–403*

28 November *In Christ a New Creation*

OPENING PRAYER Almighty God, you bring our life and your life together in a marvellous way in your Son. Accept our praises offered to you with the prayers of the saints and of the hosts of heaven . . . Glory be . . .

PSALMODY He it was who smote the first-born of Egypt,
both of man and of beast;
who in thy midst, O Egypt,
sent signs and wonders against Pharaoh and all his servants;
who smote many nations and slew mighty kings,
and gave their land as a heritage,
a heritage to his people Israel. Psalm 135.8–12*

SCRIPTURE READINGS He who sat upon the throne said, 'Behold, I make all things new.' Revelation 21.5

We know that if the earthly tent we live in is destroyed, we have a building from God, a house not made with hands, eternal in the heavens. He who has prepared us for this very thing is God, who has given us the Spirit as a guarantee. For we must all appear before the judgement seat of Christ, so that each one may receive good or evil, according to what he has done in the body. Therefore, knowing the fear of the Lord, we persuade men; but what we are is known to God, and I hope it is known also to your conscience. For the love of Christ controls us, because we are convinced that one has died for all; therefore all have died. And he died for all, that those who live might live no longer for themselves but for him who for their sake died and was raised. From now on, we regard no one from a human point of view; even though we once regarded Christ from a human point of view, we regard him thus no longer. Therefore, if any one is in Christ, he is a new creation, the old has passed away, behold, the new has come. All this is from God, who through Christ reconciled us to himself and gave us the ministry of reconciliation; that is, in Christ God was reconciling the world to himself, not counting their trespasses against them, and entrusting to us the message of reconciliation. So we are ambassadors for Christ, God making his appeal through us. We beseech you on behalf of Christ, be reconciled to God. 2 Corinthians 5.1–20*

RESPONSE 'New every morning is the love,
our waking and uprising prove.'

God of eternal glory, you create us in your own image – we praise you for all your blessings and goodness to us and to all people . . .
'If anyone is in Christ, he is a new creation' – we rejoice that we are born again in Christ, and we pray that he may live and grow in us . . .
'We are ambassadors for Christ' – Lord, make us worthy of your calling . . .

INTERCESSIONS *pages 390–393* CLOSING PRAYERS *page 402–403*

29 November *Christian Giving*

OPENING PRAYER Almighty God, you bring our life and your life together in a marvellous way in your Son. Accept our praises offered to you with the prayers of the saints and of the hosts of heaven . . . Glory be . . .

PSALMODY The idols of the nations are silver and gold.
They have mouths, but they speak not,
they have eyes, but they see not.
Blessed be the Lord from Zion,
he who dwells in Jerusalem! Praise the Lord!

Psalm 135.15–21*

SCRIPTURE READINGS Every man shall give as he is able, according to the blessing of the Lord your God which he has given you.

Deuteronomy 16.17

You know the grace of our Lord Jesus Christ, that though he was rich, yet for your sake he became poor, so that by his poverty you might become rich. And in this matter I give my advice: it is best for you now to complete what a year ago you began not only to do but to desire, so that your readiness in desiring it may be matched by your completing it out of what you have. For if the readiness is there, it is acceptable according to what a man has, not according to what he has not. I do not mean the others should be eased and you burdened, but that as a matter of equality your abundance at the present time should supply their want, so that their abundance may supply your want, that there may be equality. It is written, 'He who gathered much had nothing over, and he who gathered little had no lack.' The point is this: he who sows sparingly will also reap sparingly, and he who sows bountifully will also reap bountifully. Each one must do as he has made up his mind, not reluctantly or under compulsion, for God loves a cheerful giver. God is able to provide you with every blessing in abundance, so that you may always have enough of everything and may provide in abundance for every good work. It is written, 'He scatters abroad, he gives to the poor; his righteousness endures for ever.' He who supplies seed to the sower and bread for food will supply and multiply your resources and increase the harvest of your righteousness.

2 Corinthians 8.9–9.10*

RESPONSE 'Take my love; my Lord, I pour at thy feet its treasure store.
Take myself, and I will be ever, only, all for thee.'

God of eternal glory, your Son was rich but for our sake he became poor – we praise you for his total giving of himself on the Cross for us . . .
'God loves a cheerful giver' – inspire us to give back to you a responsible proportion of our time and money for the work of your Church . . .
'God is able to provide you with every blessing in abundance' – we thank you for all your blessings and your loving kindness . . .

INTERCESSIONS *pages 390–393* CLOSING PRAYERS *page 402–403*

30 November *Saint Andrew the Apostle*

OPENING PRAYER Almighty God, you bring our life and your life together in a marvellous way in your Son. Accept our praises offered to you with the prayers of the saints and of the hosts of heaven . . . Glory be . . .

PSALMODY It is good to give thanks to the Lord,
to sing praises to thy name, O Most High;
to declare thy steadfast love in the morning,
and thy faithfulness by night.
For thou, O Lord, hast made me glad by thy work;
at the works of thy hands I sing for joy. Psalm 92.1–4*

SCRIPTURE READINGS 'Thus says the Lord of Hosts: Peoples shall yet come, even the inhabitants of many cities; the inhabitants of one city shall go to another, saying, "Let us go at once to entreat the favour of the Lord, and to seek the Lord of hosts: I am going." Many peoples and strong nations shall come to seek the Lord of hosts in Jerusalem, and to entreat the favour of the Lord. Zechariah 8.20–22

From that time Jesus began to preach, saying, 'Repent, for the Kingdom of heaven is at hand.' As he walked by the Sea of Galilee, he saw two brothers, Simon who is called Peter and Andrew his brother, casting a net into the sea; for they were fishermen. And he said to them, 'Follow me, and I will make you fishers of men.' St Matthew 4.17–19

'Every one who calls upon the name of the Lord will be saved.' But how are men to call upon him in whom they have not believed? And how are they to believe in him of whom they have never heard? And how are they to hear without a preacher? And how can men preach unless they are sent? As it is written, 'How beautiful are the feet of those who preach good news?' But they have not all heeded the gospel; for Isaiah says, 'Lord, who has believed what he has heard from us?' So faith comes from what is heard, and what is heard comes by the preaching of Christ.
Romans 10.13–17

RESPONSE 'Jesus calls us! By his mercies, Saviour, make us hear his call;
Give our hearts to thine obedience, serve and love thee best of all.'

Eternal Father, you raise up your servants to witness to your saving grace in your Son – we praise you as we celebrate this feast of Saint Andrew . . .
'Faith comes from what is heard' – Lord, give the power of your Holy Spirit to all who proclaim the Gospel message in the world . . .
'Follow me, and I will make you fishers of men' – we pray with Saint Andrew that you will help the Church to share in the mission of your Son . . .

INTERCESSIONS *pages 390–393* CLOSING PRAYERS *page 402–403*

OPENING PRAYER Holy Father, holy and almighty, holy and eternal, come to our aid and save us, for you are our God. Help us in your mercy to look forward in hope, and to prepare our hearts for the coming of our Saviour . . .

PSALMODY The Mighty One, God the Lord, speaks
and summons the earth
from the rising of the sun to its setting.
Our God comes, he does not keep silence,
before him is a devouring fire,
round about him a mighty tempest.
He calls to the heavens above and to the earth,
that he may judge his people.
'Gather to me my faithful ones
who made a covenant with me by sacrifice.'
The heavens declared his righteousness,
our God himself is judge. Psalm 50.1–6*

SCRIPTURE READINGS
They shall see the glory of the Lord,
the majesty of our God.
Strengthen the weak hands,
and make firm the feeble knees.
Say to those who are of a fearful heart,
'Be strong, fear not!
Behold your God will come with vengeance,
with the recompense of God.
He will come and save you.' Isaiah 35.2–4

'Take heed, watch; for you do not know when the time will come. It is like a man going on a journey, when he leaves home and puts his servants in charge, each with his work, and commands the doorkeeper to be on watch. Watch therefore – for you do not know when the master of the house will come, in the evening, or at midnight, or at cockcrow, or in the morning – lest he come suddenly and find you asleep. And what I say to you I say to all. Watch.' St Mark 13.33–37

RESPONSE 'Cast away the dreams of darkness,
of ye children of the day.'

Almighty God, you alone give us grace to turn away from sin – strengthen our wills and help us to use Advent to grow in holiness and love . . .
'They shall see the glory of the Lord, and the majesty of our God' – Lord, have mercy on us when your Son comes to judge the living and the dead . . .
'Salvation is nearer to us now than when we first believed' – stir in our hearts the desire to grow into union with your Son . . .

INTERCESSIONS *pages 390–393* CLOSING PRAYERS *page 402–403*

2 December *The Coming Kingdom*

OPENING PRAYER Holy Father, holy and almighty, holy and eternal, come to our aid and save us, for you are our God. Help us in your mercy to look forward in hope, and to prepare our hearts for the coming of our Saviour . . .

PSALMODY By the waters of Babylon, there we sat down and wept,
when we remembered Zion.
On the willows there we hung up our lyres.
For there our captors required of us songs,
and our tormentors, mirth, saying,
'Sing us one of the songs of Zion!' Psalm 137.1–3

SCRIPTURE READINGS
'It shall come to pass in the latter days
that the mountain of the house of the Lord
shall be established as the highest of the mountains,
and shall be raised above the hills;
and all the nations shall flow to it,
and many peoples shall come, and say:
"Come, let us go up to the mountain of the Lord,
to the house of the God of Jacob;
that he may teach us his ways
and that we may walk in his paths."
For out of Zion shall go forth the law,
and the word of the Lord from Jerusalem.
He shall judge between the nations,
and shall decide for many peoples;
and they shall beat their swords into ploughshares,
and their spears into pruning hooks;
nation shall not lift up sword against nation,
neither shall they learn war any more.
O house of Jacob, come,
let us walk in the light of the Lord.' Isaiah 2.2–5

Jesus said, 'Truly, I say, not even in Israel have I found such faith. Many will come from the east and west and sit at table with Abraham, Isaac, and Jacob in the kingdom of heaven.' St Matthew 8.10–11

RESPONSE 'Hear, above all, hear thy Lord;
hide within thy heart his word: "Watch and pray."'

Lord God of Israel, your Kingdom is eternal and your power is infinite – give us grace to lift our souls to you in prayer through your Son . . .
'All nations shall flow to it' – teach all people the knowledge of your truth in Christ through the work and mission of your Church . . .
'Let us go to the house of the God of Jacob' – sustain us with your love in Jesus Christ, and lead us in the way of eternal salvation . . .

INTERCESSIONS *pages 390–393* CLOSING PRAYERS *page 402–403*

OPENING PRAYER Holy Father, holy and almighty, holy and eternal, come to our aid and save us, for you are our God. Help us in your mercy to look forward in hope, and to prepare our hearts for the coming of our Saviour . . .

PSALMODY How shall we sing the Lord's song in a foreign land?
If I forget you, O Jerusalem, let my right hand wither!
Let my tongue cleave to the roof of my mouth,
if I do not remember you;
if I do not set Jerusalem above my highest joy! Psalm 137.4–6

SCRIPTURE READINGS

There shall come forth a shoot from the stump of Jesse,
and a branch shall grow out of his roots.
And the Spirit of the Lord shall rest upon him,
the spirit of wisdom and understanding,
the spirit of counsel and might,
the spirit of knowledge and the fear of the Lord.
And his delight shall be in the fear of the Lord.
He shall not judge by what his eyes see,
but with righteousness he shall judge the poor;
and he shall smite the earth with the rod of his mouth,
and with the breath of his lips he shall slay the wicked.
Righteousness shall be the girdle of his waist,
and faithfulness the girdle of his loins.
The wolf shall dwell with the lamb,
and the leopard shall lie down with the kid,
and the calf and the lion and the fatling together,
and a little child shall lead them.
They shall not hurt or destroy in all my holy mountain;
for the earth shall be full of the knowledge of the Lord
as the waters cover the sea. Isaiah 11.1–9*

He rejoiced in the Holy Spirit and said, 'I thank thee, Father, Lord of heaven and earth, that thou hast hidden these things from the wise and understanding and revealed them to babes.' St Luke 10.21

RESPONSE 'The advent of our God with eager prayers we greet,
and singing, haste upon his road his glorious gift to meet.'

God of our fathers, you fulfilled all your promises in your Son – come to our hearts, and bring us to your salvation in Christ . . .
You promised to send a king to reign with justice and righteousness – Lord, come and reign in your Church and fill us with your eternal love . . .
'The earth shall be filled with the knowledge of the Lord' – help the Church to spread the knowledge of your love in all the world . . .

INTERCESSIONS *pages 390–393* CLOSING PRAYERS *page 402–403*

OPENING PRAYER Holy Father, holy and almighty, holy and eternal, come to our aid and save us, for you are our God. Help us in your mercy to look forward in hope, and to prepare our hearts for the coming of our Saviour . . .

PSALMODY I will give thanks to thee, O Lord, with my whole heart;
before the gods I sing thy praise.
I bow down toward thy holy temple
and give thanks to thy name
for thy steadfast love and thy faithfulness;
for thou hast exalted above everything
thy name and thy work.
On the day I called, thou didst answer me,
my strength of soul thou didst increase. Psalm 138.1–3

SCRIPTURE READINGS On this mountain the Lord of hosts will make for all peoples a feast of fat things, a feast of wine on the lees, of fat things full of marrow, of wine on the lees well refined. And he will destroy on this mountain the covering that is cast over all peoples, the veil that is spread over all nations. He will swallow up death for ever, and the Lord God will wipe away tears from all faces, and the reproach of his people he will take away from all the earth; for the Lord has spoken. It will be said on that day, 'Lo, this is our God; we have waited for him, that he might save us. This is the Lord; we have waited for him; let us be glad and rejoice in his salvation.' Isaiah 25.6–9

I thank my God in all my rememberance of you, always in every prayer of mine for you all making my prayer with joy, thankful for your partnership in the gospel from the first day until now. And I am sure that he who began a good work in you will bring it to completion at the day of Jesus Christ. And it is my prayer that your love may abound more and more, with knowledge and all discernment, so that you may approve what is excellent, and may be pure and blameless for the day of Christ, filled with the fruits of righteousness which come through Jesus Christ, to the glory and praise of God. Philippians 1.3–11*

RESPONSE 'Hear, above all, hear thy Lord;
hide within thy heart his word: Watch and pray.'

Lord God of Israel, you are the God and Father of our Lord Jesus Christ – we acknowledge our total dependence on your mercy and love . . .
You invite us to share in your heavenly banquet – Lord, forgive us our sins and make us worthy of your love . . .
You give us a share in the spiritual inheritance of your chosen people the Jews – help us to respond to your gift by doing your will . . .

INTERCESSIONS *pages 390–393* CLOSING PRAYERS *page 402–403*

5 December *How to Enter the Kingdom*

OPENING PRAYER Holy Father, holy and almighty, holy and eternal, come to our aid and save us, for you are our God. Help us in your mercy to look forward in hope, and to prepare our hearts for the coming of our Saviour . . .

PSALMODY All the kings of the earth shall praise thee, O Lord,
for they have heard the words of thy mouth;
and they shall sing of the ways of the Lord,
for great is the glory of the Lord.
For though the Lord is high, he regards the lowly;
but the haughty he regards from afar. Psalm 138.4–6

SCRIPTURE READINGS

In that day
this song will be sung in the land of Judah:
'We have a strong city;
he sets up salvation as walls and bulwarks.
Open the gates,
that the righteous nation which keeps faith may enter in.
Thou dost keep him in perfect peace,
whose mind is stayed on thee,
because he trusts in thee.
Trust in the Lord for ever,
for the Lord God is an everlasting rock.

'Isaiah 26.1–4*

'Not everyone who says, "Lord, Lord," shall enter the kingdom of heaven, but he who does the will of my Father who is in heaven. Everyone who hears these words of mine and does them will be like a wise man who built his house upon the rock; and the rain fell, and the floods came, and the winds blew and beat upon that house, but it did not fall, because it had been founded on the rock. And everyone who hears these words of mine and does not do them will be like a foolish man who built his house upon the sand; and the rain fell, and the floods came, and the winds blew and beat against that house, and it fell; and great was the fall of it.

St Matthew 7.21–27*

RESPONSE 'Thy kingdom come, O God, thy rule, O Christ begin;
break with thine iron rod the tyrannies of sin.'

Eternal God, you chose the Jewish people to receive the revelations of your love – help us to seek your will, and give us grace to love you . . .
'Thou didst keep him in perfect peace whose mind is stayed on thee' – keep us steadfast in the faith, and lead us to your eternal kingdom . . .
'Trust in the Lord for ever' – Lord, help us to put our whole trust and confidence in the promises of your Son . . .

INTERCESSIONS *pages 390–393* CLOSING PRAYERS *page 402–403*

6 December *A Great Light*

OPENING PRAYER Holy Father, holy and almighty, holy and eternal, come to our aid and save us, for you are our God. Help us in your mercy to look forward in hope, and to prepare our hearts for the coming of our Saviour . . .

PSALMODY Though I walk in the midst of trouble,
thou dost preserve my life;
thou dost stretch out thy hand
against the wrath of my enemies,
and thy right hand delivers me.
The Lord will fulfil his purposes for me;
thy steadfast love, O Lord, endures for ever.
Do not forsake the work of thy hands. Psalm 138.7–8

SCRIPTURE READING

In that day the deaf shall hear the words of a book,
and out of their gloom and darkness
the eyes of the blind man shall see.
The meek shall obtain fresh joy in the Lord,
and the poor shall exult in the Holy One of Israel.
Therefore thus says the Lord,
'Jacob shall no more be ashamed,
no more shall his face grow pale.
For when he sees his children,
the work of my hands, in his midst,
they will sanctify my name;
they will sanctify the Holy One of Jacob,
and will stand in awe of the God of Israel.
And those who err in spirit will come to understanding,
and those who murmur will accept instruction.'

Isaiah 29.18–24*

Two blind men followed Jesus, crying aloud, 'Have mercy on us, Son of David.' When he entered the house, the blind men came to him; and Jesus said, 'Do you believe that I am able to do this?' They said, 'Yes, Lord.' Then he touched their eyes, saying, 'According to your faith be it done to you.' And their eyes were opened. Jesus sternly charged them, 'See that no one knows it.' But they went away and spread his fame through all that district.

St Matthew 9.27–31

RESPONSE 'In clouds of awful light, as Judge he comes again,
his scattered people to unite, with them in heaven to reign.'

Almighty God and Father, you dwell in eternal light – shed the light of Christ in our hearts and show us the way to perfect grace . . .
You revealed your will to us through the prophets – help us to seek your will in our daily lives . . .
You first made known the light of your truth under the old covenant – free us from sin and help us to reflect the light of Christ in the world . . .

INTERCESSIONS *pages 390–393* CLOSING PRAYERS *page 402–403*

7 December *This is the Way*

OPENING PRAYER Holy Father, holy and almighty, holy and eternal, come to our aid and save us, for you are our God. Help us in your mercy to look forward in hope, and to prepare our hearts for the coming of our Saviour . . .

PSALMODY O Lord, thou hast searched me and known me!
Thou knowest when I sit down and when I rise up;
thou discernest my thoughts from afar.
thou searchest out my path and my lying down,
thou art acquainted with all my ways.
Even before a word is on my tongue,
lo, O Lord, thou knowest it altogether. Psalm 139.1–4

SCRIPTURE READINGS O people in Zion, who dwell at Jerusalem; you shall weep no more. He will surely be gracious to you at the sound of your cry; when he hears it, he will answer you. And though the Lord gives you bread of adversity and the water of affliction, yet your Teacher will not hide himself any more, but your eyes shall see your Teacher. Your ears shall hear a word behind you, saying, 'This is the way, walk in it,' when you turn to the right or when you turn to the left. He will give rain for the seed with which you sow the ground, and grain, and produce of the ground which will be rich and plenteous. In that day your cattle will graze in large pastures. And upon every lofty mountain and every high hill there will be brooks running with water, in the day of the great slaughter, when the towers fall. Moreover the light of the moon will be as the light of the sun, and the light of the sun will be sevenfold, as the light of seven days, in the day when the Lord binds up the hurt of his people and heals the wounds inflicted by his blows. Isaiah 30.19–26*

Jesus went about all the cities and villages, teaching in their synagogues and preaching the gospel of the kingdom, and healing every disease and every infirmity. He called to him his twelve disciples, and sent them out, charging them, 'Go nowhere among the Gentiles, but go rather to the lost sheep of the house of Israel. Preach as you go, saying, "The kingdom of heaven is at hand."' St Matthew 9.35–10.7*

RESPONSE 'Gird up your loins, ye prophet souls,
proclaim the day is near.'

Almighty God, you called the Jews to make known your salvation in the world – enrich us with your grace, and incline our hearts to seek your perfect love in Jesus Christ . . .
'This is the way, walk in it' – guide us by your Spirit in all things . . .
'The kingdom of heaven is at hand' – in your mercy, help us to look forward in hope to that day when all will be gathered up in Christ . . .

INTERCESSIONS *pages 390–393* CLOSING PRAYERS *page 402–403*

OPENING PRAYER Holy Father, holy and almighty, holy and eternal, come to our aid and save us, for you are our God. Help us in your mercy to look forward in hope, and to prepare our hearts for the coming of our Saviour . . .

PSALMODY Praise the Lord!
Praise, O servants of the Lord,
praise the name of the Lord!
Who is like the Lord our God,
who is seated on high?
He raises the poor from the dust,
and lifts the needy from the ash heap,
to make them sit with princes,
with the princes of his people.
He gives the barren woman a home,
making her the joyous mother of children.
Praise the Lord! Psalm 113.1–9*

SCRIPTURE READINGS Fear not, for I have redeemed you; I have called you by name, you are mine. Isaiah 43.1

Sin came into the world through one man and death through sin, and so death spread to all men because all men sinned. Romans 5.12

Blessed be the God and Father of our Lord Jesus Christ, who has blessed us in Christ with every spiritual blessing in the heavenly places, even as he chose us in him before the foundation of the world, that we should be holy and blameless before him. He destined us in love to be his sons through Jesus Christ, according to the purpose of his will, to the praise of his glorious grace which he freely bestowed on us in the Beloved. In him, according to the purpose of him who accomplishes all things according to the counsel of his will, we who first hoped in Christ have been destined and appointed to live for the praise of his glory. Ephesians 1.3–12*

Behold, henceforth all generations will call me blessed. St Luke 1.48b

RESPONSE 'What Christ's Mother sang in gladness,
Let Christ's people sing the same.'

Heavenly Father, you prepared Mary to be the Mother of our Redeemer – we sing to your eternal glory on this Feast of the Blessed Virgin Mary . . . It was by your will and by the work of the Spirit that the Word became flesh in the womb of Mary – Lord, bless the Church, and make us holy . . . 'Behold, henceforth, all generations will call me blessed' – we rejoice with your universal Church in the love and obedience of Mary . . .

INTERCESSIONS *pages 390–393* CLOSING PRAYERS *page 402–403*

9 December *Prepare the Way of the Lord*

OPENING PRAYER Holy Father, holy and almighty, holy and eternal, in your great mercy come to our aid and save us. You are our God and our Saviour, and we wait in hope for the fulfilling of your promises in Christ . . .

PSALMODY Whither shall I go from thy Spirit?
or wither shall I flee from thy presence?
If I ascend to heaven, thou art there!
If I make my bed in Sheol, thou art there!
If I take the wings of the morning
and dwell in the uttermost parts of the sea,
even there thy hand shall lead me. Psalm 139.7–10*

SCRIPTURE READINGS
A voice cries:
'In the wilderness prepare the way of the Lord,
make straight in the desert a highway for our God.
Every valley shall be lifted up,
and every mountain and hill be made low;
and the rough places a plain.
And the glory of the Lord shall be revealed,
and all flesh shall see it together,
for the mouth of the Lord has spoken.'
A voice says, 'Cry!' And I said, 'What shall I cry?'
All flesh is grass,
and all its beauty is like the flower of the field.
The grass withers, the flower fades;
but the word of our God will stand for ever.
O Zion, herald of good tidings,
say to the cities of Judah, 'Behold your God!'
Behold, the Lord God comes with might,
and his arm rules for him;
behold, his reward is with him,
and his recompense before him. Isaiah 40.1–10

'Look up and raise your heads, because your redemption is drawing near.'
St Luke 21.28

RESPONSE 'Let us each our hearts prepare
for Christ to come and enter there.'

Eternal God, you promised Abraham that his descendants would be a nation under your special care – continue your same mercy and love in the Church . . .
'The word of our God will stand for ever' – we thank you for the help and encouragement you give to us through the Scriptures . . .
'Your redemption is drawing near' – Lord, make us worthy of your love . . .

INTERCESSIONS *pages 390–393* CLOSING PRAYERS *page 402–403*

10 December *To Whom Will You Compare Me?*

OPENING PRAYER Holy Father, holy and almighty, holy and eternal, in your great mercy come to our aid and save us. You are our God and our Saviour, and we wait in hope for the fulfilling of your promises in Christ . . .

PSALMODY Thou didst knit me together in my mother's womb.
I praise thee, for thou art fearful and wonderful.
Wonderful are thy works. Psalm 139.13–14*

SCRIPTURE READING

To whom then will you compare me,
that I should be like him? says the Holy One.
Lift up your eyes on high and see:
who created these?
He who brings out their host by number,
calling them all by name;
by the greatness of his might,
and because he is strong in power not one is missing.
Why do you say, O Jacob, and speak, O Israel,
'My way is hid from the Lord,
and my right is disregarded by my God'?
Have you not known? Have you not heard?
The Lord is the everlasting God,
the Creator of the ends of the earth.
He does not faint or grow weary,
his understanding is unsearchable.
He gives power to the faint,
and to him who has no might he increases strength.
Even youths shall faint and be weary;
but they who wait for the Lord
shall renew their strength,
they shall mount up with wings like eagles,
they shall run and not be weary,
they shall walk and not faint. Isaiah 40.25–31*

'Take my yoke upon you, and learn from me; for I am gentle and lowly in heart, and you will find rest for your souls. For my yoke is easy, and my burden is light.' St Matthew 11.29–30

RESPONSE 'Praise to the Incarnate Son, who comes to set us free,
with God the Father, ever one, to all eternity.'

Lord God of Israel, you alone are unique and uncreated – incline our hearts to love you with the perfect love of your only Son, Jesus Christ . . .
In your love, you created the universe out of nothing, and you sustain it by your power – Lord, in your mercy, come to our aid . . .

INTERCESSIONS *pages 390–393* CLOSING PRAYERS *page 402–403*

11 December *Your Redeemer is the Holy One of Israel*

OPENING PRAYER Holy Father, holy and almighty, holy and eternal, in your great mercy come to our aid and save us. You are our God and our Saviour, and we wait in hope for the fulfilling of your promises in Christ . . .

PSALMODY How precious to me are thy thoughts, O God!
How vast is the sum of them! Psalm 139.17

SCRIPTURE READINGS
I will help you, says the Lord;
your Redeemer is the Holy One of Israel.
Behold, I will make of you a threshing sledge,
and you shall make the hills like chaff.
You shall winnow them
and the wind shall carry them away.
And you shall rejoice in the Lord;
in the Holy One of Israel you shall glory.
When the poor and needy seek water, and there is none;
and their tongue is parched with thirst,
I the Lord will answer them,
I the God of Israel will not forsake them.
I will open rivers on the bare heights,
and fountains in the midst of the valleys;
I will put in the wilderness the cedar,
the acacia, the myrtle, and the olive,
that men may see and know,
that the hand of the Lord has done this,
the Holy One of Israel has created it. Isaiah 41.14–20*

'Among those born of women there has risen no one greater than John the Baptist; yet he who is least in the kingdom of heaven is greater than he. From the days of John the Baptist until now the kingdom of heaven has suffered violence, and men of violence take it by force. For all the prophets and the law prophesied until John; and if you are willing to accept it, he is Elijah who is to come. He who has ears to hear, let him hear.'
St Matthew 11.11–15

RESPONSE 'Hark the glad sound; the Saviour comes.
Let every heart prepare a throne, and every voice a song.'

Lord God, your ways are mysterious and you are wonderful in all your works – open our hearts to understand the light of your truth in Christ . . .
'I will help you, says the Lord' – help us to have a deeper understanding of your will, and a deeper awareness of your love for us in your Son . . .

INTERCESSIONS *pages 390–393* CLOSING PRAYERS *page 402–403*

OPENING PRAYER Holy Father, holy and almighty, holy and eternal, in your great mercy come to our aid and save us. You are our God and our Saviour, and we wait in hope for the fulfilling of your promises in Christ . . .

PSALMODY Deliver me, O Lord, from evil men;
preserve me from violent men,
who plan evil things in their heart,
and stir up wars continually.
Guard me, O Lord, from the hands of the wicked;
preserve me from men of violence.
I say to the Lord, Thou art God;
give ear to the voice of my supplications, O Lord.
Psalm 140.1–6*

SCRIPTURE READINGS
Thus says the Lord, your Redeemer,
the Holy One of Israel:
'I am the Lord your God,
who teaches you to profit,
who leads you in the way you should go.
O that you had harkened to my commandments!
Then your peace would have been like a river,
and your righteousness like the waves of the sea;
your offspring would have been like the sand,
and your descendents like its grains;
their name would never be cut off
or destroyed from before me.' Isaiah 48.17–19

But to what shall I compare this generation? It is like children sitting in the market places and calling to their playmates,

"We piped to you, and you did not dance;
we wailed, and you did not mourn."

For John came neither eating nor drinking, and they say, "He has a demon"; the Son of Man came eating and drinking, and they say, "Behold, a glutton and a drunkard, a friend of tax collectors and sinners!" Yet wisdom is justified by her deeds.' St Matthew 11.16–19

RESPONSE 'Saviour, take the power and the glory:
claim the kingdom for thine own. Alleluia! Come, Lord, come.'

Eternal God, you are the source of our peace and reconciliation – help us to draw near in penitence and faith to the throne of your grace . . .
'To whom shall I compare this generation?' – Lord, in your mercy, forgive us our sins, and help us to grow into union with Christ . . .
Your character and your purposes are made plain to us in the Word made flesh – in your mercy, help us to prepare for the coming of your Son . . .

INTERCESSIONS *pages 390–393* CLOSING PRAYERS *page 402–403*

OPENING PRAYER Holy Father, holy and almighty, holy and eternal, in your great mercy come to our aid and save us. You are our God and our Saviour, and we wait in hope for the fulfilling of your promises in Christ . . .

PSALMODY I call upon thee, O Lord; make haste to me!
Give ear to my voice, when I call to thee!
and the lifting up of my hands as an evening sacrifice!
Set a guard over my mouth, O Lord,
keep watch over the door of my lips! Psalm 141.1–3

SCRIPTURE READINGS Balaam lifted up his eyes, and saw Israel encamping tribe by tribe. And the Spirit of God came upon him, and he said,

'The oracle of Balaam the son of Beor,
who sees the vision of the Almighty:
how fair are your tents, O Jacob,
your encampments, O Israel!
Blessed be every one who blesses you,
and cursed be every one who curses you.'

Balak's anger was kindled against Balaam, and Balak said,
'I called you to curse my enemies, and behold, you have blessed them these three times. Therefore flee to your place.' Balaam said, 'If Balak should give me his house full of silver and gold, I would not be able to go beyond the word of the Lord.' He took up his discourse and said,

'The oracle of Balaam the son of Beor,
who sees the vision of the Almighty,
falling down, but having his eyes uncovered:
I see him, but not now;
I behold him, but not nigh:
a star shall come forth out of Jacob;
and a sceptre shall rise out of Israel.' Numbers 24.2–17*

The chief priests and elders came to Jesus and said, 'By what authority are you doing these things, and who gave you this authority?'
St Matthew 21.23

RESPONSE 'Alleluia! Sing to Jesus! – his the sceptre, his the throne;
Alleluia! His the triumph, his the victory alone.'

Almighty God; you rule your universe with perfect love from everlasting to everlasting – come and rule in our hearts as Lord and King . . .
You raised the sceptre of your kingdom long ago in Israel – renew your gift of faith in the Church as we wait for the coming of your Son . . .
You call us to be faithful and to work for the coming of your Kingdom – help us, Lord, to fulfil your will in our lives . . .

INTERCESSIONS *pages 390–393* CLOSING PRAYERS *page 402–403*

14 December *The Humble and Lowly*

OPENING PRAYER Holy Father, holy and almighty, holy and eternal, in your great mercy come to our aid and save us. Your are our God and our Saviour, and we wait in hope for the fulfilling of your promises in Christ . . .

PSALMODY Incline not my heart to any evil,
to busy myself with wicked deeds
in company with men who work iniquity;
and let me not eat of their dainties!
When they are given over to those who shall condemn them,
then they shall learn that the word of the Lord is true.

Psalm 141.4–6

SCRIPTURE READING

Woe to her that is rebellious and defiled,
the oppressing city!
She listens to no voice, she accepts no correction.
She does not trust in the Lord,
she does not draw near to her God.
At that time I will change the speech of the people
to a pure speech,
that all of them may call on the name of the Lord
and serve him with one accord.
For I will leave in the midst of you
a people humble and lowly.
They shall seek refuge in the name of the Lord.
They shall do no wrong and utter no lies,
nor shall there be found in their mouth
a deceitful tongue.
For they shall pasture and lie down,
and none shall make them afraid.' Zephaniah 3.1–13*

Jesus said, 'The tax collectors and the harlots go into the Kingdom of God before you. For John came in the way of righteousness, and you did not believe him, but the tax collectors and the harlots believed him; and even when you saw it, you did not repent and believe him.

St Matthew 21.31–32*

RESPONSE 'Once more upon thy people shine,
and fill the world with love divine.'

Almighty God, you perfectly fulfilled all your promises in your Son – help us to prepare our hearts to celebrate the mystery of your love . . .
Your Son is our Redeemer and Judge and King – send your Spirit to us to cleanse us, so that we may give birth to your Son in our hearts . . .
You call your Church to prepare the way for your Son – come, Lord, and reign in our hearts . . .

INTERCESSIONS *pages 390–393* CLOSING PRAYERS *page 402–403*

15 December *Turn to Me and be Saved*

OPENING PRAYER Holy Father, holy and almighty, holy and eternal, in your great mercy come to our aid and save us. You are our God and our Saviour, and we wait in hope for the fulfilling of your promises in Christ . . .

PSALMODY Deliver me, O Lord, from my enemies!
I have fled to thee for refuge!
Teach me to do thy will, for thou art my God!
Let thy good spirit lead me on a level path!
For thy name's sake, O Lord, preserve my life!
In thy righteousness bring me out of trouble! Psalm 143.9–11

SCRIPTURE READING
I am the Lord, and there is no other,
besides me there is no God;
I gird you, though you do not know me,
that men may know, from the rising of the sun,
and from the west, that there is none besides me;
I form light and create darkness,
I make weal and create woe,
I am the Lord, who do all these things.
I do not speak in secret, in a land of darkness;
I the Lord speak the truth, I declare what is right.
Declare and present your case.
Who told this long ago? Who declared it of old?
Was it not I, the Lord?
And there is no other god besides me, in our land,
a righteous God and a Saviour.
'Turn to me and be saved, all the ends of the earth!
From my mouth has gone forth in righteousness
a word that shall not return:
"To me every knee shall bow, every tongue shall swear."
In the Lord all the offspring of Israel
shall triumph and glory.' Isaiah 45.5–25*

John sent two of his disciples to the Lord, saying, 'Are you he who is to come, or shall we look for another?' St Luke 7.19*

RESPONSE 'Lo, he comes with clouds descending.
God appears on earth to reign.'

Eternal Father, you are the hope of the nations and the origin of our redemption – in your mercy, direct us in the way of your salvation . . .
You break down all barriers with your love – Lord, pour out your Spirit on your Church and help us to grow in holiness and love . . .
Your Son will come again in glory with all your saints made perfect – fill us with your grace and bring us into unity with your Beloved Son . . .

INTERCESSIONS *pages 390–393* CLOSING PRAYERS *page 402–403*

16 December *Steadfast Love*

OPENING PRAYER Holy Father, holy and almighty, holy and eternal, in your great mercy come to our aid and save us. You are our God and our Saviour, and we wait in hope for the fulfilling of your promises in Christ . . .

PSALMODY Blessed be the Lord, my rock, who trains my hands for war,
my shield and he in whom I take refuge.
O Lord, what is man that thou dost regard him?
Man is like a breath,
his days are like a passing shadow. Psalm 144.1–4*

SCRIPTURE READING
'Fear not, for you will not be ashamed;
for you will forget the shame of your youth,
and the reproach of your widowhood
you will remember no more.
For your Maker is your husband,
the Lord of Hosts is his name;
and the Holy One of Israel is your Redeemer,
the God of the whole earth he is called.
For the Lord has called you
like a wife forsaken and grieved in spirit,
like a wife of youth when she is cast off.
For the mountains may depart and the hills be removed,
but my steadfast love shall not depart from you,
and my covenant of peace shall not be removed,
says the Lord, who has compassion on you.' Isaiah 54.4–10*

Jesus said to the crowds concerning John, 'What did you go out into the wilderness to behold? A reed shaken by the wind? What then did you go out to see? A man clothed in soft raiment? Behold, those who are gorgeously apparelled and live in luxury are in Kings' courts. What then did you go out to see? A prophet? Yes, I tell you, and more than a prophet. This is he of whom it is written,

'Behold, I sent my messenger before thy face,
who shall prepare thy way before thee.' St Luke 7.24–27

RESPONSE 'O Wisdom, which camest out of the Mouth of the Most High,
come and teach us the way of prudence.'

God of measureless love, you have made us in your own image – give us grace to prepare for the coming of your Son . . .
You called Mary and you filled her with the fullness of your grace – Lord, we rejoice with Mary at the greatness of your perfect love . . .
You call us to be faithful – increase your gift of faith and hope and love in the Church, and unite us in your eternal love . . .

INTERCESSIONS *pages 390–393* CLOSING PRAYERS *page 402–403*

17 December *A Light*

OPENING PRAYER Lord God of Israel, you are the God and Father of our Lord Jesus Christ. We praise you for sending your Son to take flesh in the womb of Mary. Make us worthy of your redeeming love . . . Glory be . . .

PSALMODY I will extol thee, my God and King,
and bless thy name for ever and ever.
Every day I will bless thee,
and praise thy name for ever and ever.
Great is the Lord, and greatly to be praised,
and his greatness is unsearchable. Psalm 145.1–3

SCRIPTURE READING
Thus says the Lord:
'Keep justice, and do righteousness,
for soon my salvation will come,
and my deliverance be revealed.
Blessed is the man who does this.
And the foreigners who join themselves to the Lord,
to minister to him, to love the name of the Lord,
and to be his servants,
everyone who keeps the sabbath, and does not profane it,
and holds fast my covenant –
these I will bring to my holy mountain
and make them joyful in my house of prayer. Isaiah 56.1–7*

Jesus said, 'You sent to John, and he has borne witness to the truth. Not that the testimony which I receive is from man; but I say this that you may be saved. He was a burning and shining lamp, and you were willing to rejoice for a while in his light. But the testimony which I have is greater than that of John; for the works which the Father has granted me to accomplish, these very works which I am doing, bear me witness that the Father has sent me.' St John 5.33–36

RESPONSE 'O Adonai, and Leader of the house of Israel,
come and deliver us with an outstretched arm.'

Father in glory, your light shines in the darkness of the world – we praise you for the new light of the Word made flesh . . .
'He was a burning and shining lamp' – help us to dispel the dark areas of our lives and to reflect your light in the world . . .
'These very works which I am doing, bear witness that the Father has sent me' – may all our words and actions bear witness to your love . . .

INTERCESSIONS *pages 390–393* CLOSING PRAYERS *page 402–403*

18 December

Emmanuel

OPENING PRAYER Lord God of Israel, you are the God and Father of our Lord Jesus Christ. We praise you for sending your Son to take flesh in the womb of Mary. Make us worthy of your redeeming love . . . Glory be . . .

PSALMODY One generation shall laud thy works to another,
and shall declare thy mighty acts.
On the glorious splendour of thy majesty,
and on thy wondrous works, I will meditate.
Men shall proclaim the might of thy terrible acts,
and I will declare thy greatness.
They shall pour forth the fame of thy abundant goodness,
and shall sing aloud of thy righteousness. Psalm 145.4–7

SCRIPTURE READING 'Behold, the days are coming, says the Lord, when I will raise up for David a righteous branch, and he shall reign as king and deal wisely, and shall execute justice and righteousness in the land. Judah will be saved, and Israel will dwell securely. This is the name by which he will be called: 'The Lord is our righteousness.' Jeremiah 23.5–6

The birth of Jesus Christ took place in this way. When his mother Mary had been betrothed to Joseph, before they came together, she was found to be with child of the Holy Spirit; and her husband Joseph, being a just man and unwilling to put her to shame, resolved to divorce her quietly. But as he considered this, behold, an angel of the Lord appeared to him in a dream, saying, 'Joseph, son of David, do not fear to take Mary your wife, for that which is conceived in her is of the Holy Spirit; she will bear a son, and you shall call his name Jesus, for he will save his people from their sins.' All this took place to fulfil what the Lord had spoken by the prophet:

'Behold, a virgin shall conceive and bear a son,
and his name shall be called Emmanuel'
(which means, God with us).

When Joseph woke from sleep, he did as the angel of the Lord commanded him; he took his wife, but knew her not until she had borne a son; and called his name Jesus. St Matthew 1.18–24

RESPONSE 'O root of Jesse, which standest for an ensign of the people,
come and deliver us, and tarry not.'

Almighty God, you emptied yourself of your glory and took human nature for our salvation – let every age adore the mystery of your love . . .
You raised up a mighty Saviour for us in the royal house of David – let every heart rejoice and praise the sacred name of Jesus . . .
Jesus Christ is our Emmanuel – we rejoice with great joy that you are with us always, and we thank you for your love . . .

INTERCESSIONS *pages 390–393* CLOSING PRAYERS *page 402–403*

19 December *Announcing the Birth of John the Baptist*

OPENING PRAYER Lord God of Israel, you are the God and Father of our Lord Jesus Christ. We praise you for sending your Son to take flesh in the womb of Mary. Make us worthy of your redeeming love . . . Glory be . . .

PSALMODY The Lord is gracious and merciful,
slow to anger and abounding in steadfast love.
The Lord is good to all,
and his compassion is over all that he has made.
All thy works shall give thanks to thee O Lord
and all thy saints shall bless thee!
They shall speak of the glory of thy kingdom,
and tell of thy power,
to make known to the sons of men thy mighty deeds,
and the glorious splendour of thy kingdom. Psalm 145.8–12

SCRIPTURE READINGS The woman said to her husband Manoah, 'A man of God came to me, and said, "Behold, you shall conceive and bear a son; so then drink no wine or strong drink, and eat nothing unclean, for the boy shall be a Nazerite to God from birth to the day of his death."' The woman bore a son, and called his name Sampson; and the boy grew, and the Lord blessed him. And the Spirit of the Lord began to stir in him.
Judges 13.6–25*

Zechariah was serving as priest before God when his division was on duty. There appeared to him an angel of the Lord standing on the right side of the altar of incense. Zechariah was troubled, and fear fell upon him. The angel said. 'Do not be afraid, Zechariah, for your prayer is heard, and your wife Elizabeth will bear you a son, and you shall call his name John. You will have joy and gladness, and many will rejoice at his birth; for he will be great before the Lord, and he shall drink no wine nor strong drink, and he will be filled with the Holy Spirit, even from his mother's womb. He will turn many of the sons of Israel to the Lord their God, and he will go before him in the spirit and power of Elijah, to turn the hearts of the fathers to the children, and the disobedient to the wisdom of the just, to make ready for the Lord a people prepared.' St Luke 1.8–17*

RESPONSE 'O Key of David, and Sceptre of the house of Israel,
come and set us free.'

Eternal God, you created the Church as a new Israel through your Son – we thank you for both the continuity and the new creation in Christ . . .
'Zechariah was serving as priest before God' – pour out your grace on the bishops and clergy of the Church, and strengthen them for their work . . .
'He will be filled with the Holy Spirit, even from his mother's womb' – Lord, pour out your Spirit on the Church, and make us holy . . .

INTERCESSIONS *pages 390–393* CLOSING PRAYERS *page 402–403*

20 December *Announcing the Birth of Jesus*

OPENING PRAYER Lord God of Israel, you are the God and Father of our Lord Jesus Christ. We praise you for sending your Son to take flesh in the womb of Mary. Make us worthy of your redeeming love . . . Glory be . . .

PSALMODY Thy Kingdom is an everlasting kingdom,
and thy dominion endures throughout all generations.
The Lord is faithful in all his words,
and gracious in all his deeds.
The Lord upholds all who are falling,
and raises up all who are bowed down.
Thou openest thy hand,
thou satisfiest the desire of every living thing.

Psalm 145.13–16*

SCRIPTURE READINGS The Lord spoke to Ahaz, 'Ask a sign of the Lord your God.' Ahaz said, 'I will not ask, and I will not put the Lord to the test.' He said, 'Hear, then, O house of David! Is it too little for you to weary men, that you weary my God also? Therefore the Lord himself will give you a sign. Behold, a young woman shall conceive and bear a son, and shall call his name Immanuel.' Isaiah 7.10–14

The angel Gabriel came to Mary and said, 'Hail, O favoured one, the Lord is with you!' She was greatly troubled. The angel said, 'Do not be afraid, Mary, for you have found favour with God. Behold, you will conceive in your womb and bear a Son, and you shall call his name Jesus. He will be great, and will be called the Son of the Most High; and the Lord God will give to him the throne of his father David, and he will reign over the House of Jacob for ever; and of his kingdom there will be no end.' Mary said to the angel, 'How shall this be, since I have no husband?' The angel said, 'The Holy Spirit will come upon you, and the power of the Most High will overshadow you; therefore the child to be born will be called holy, the Son of God. And behold, your kinswoman Elizabeth in her old age has also conceived a son; this is the sixth month with her who is called barren. For with God nothing will be impossible.' Mary said, 'Behold, I am the handmaid of the Lord; let it be to me according to your word.' And the angel departed from her. St Luke 1.26–38

RESPONSE 'O Day-spring, Brightness of Light Everlasting, come,
and enlighten him that sitteth in darkness and the shadow of death.'

Gracious God, you chose Mary as the mother of the Messiah – we praise you for her willingness to accept your plan for our salvation . . .
The coming of your Son is the turning point in history – we bless you and praise you for the wondrous day of his birth . . .
Mary responded with joy to your call – give us grace to do your will like Mary, and to share in your redeeming work in the world . . .

INTERCESSIONS *pages 390–393* CLOSING PRAYERS *page 402–403*

21 December *Most Blessed of all Women*

OPENING PRAYER Lord God of Israel, you are the God and Father of our Lord Jesus Christ. We praise you for sending your Son to take flesh in the womb of Mary. Make us worthy of your redeeming love . . . Glory be . . .

PSALMODY The Lord is near to all who call upon him.
He fulfils the desire of all who fear him.
My mouth will speak the praise of the Lord.
and let all flesh bless his holy name for ever and ever.
Psalm 145.17–21*

SCRIPTURE READINGS
The voice of my beloved!
Behold, he comes, leaping upon the mountains,
bounding over the hills.
My beloved is like a gazelle, or a young stag.
Behold, there he stands behind our wall,
gazing in at the windows.
My beloved speaks and says to me:
'Arise, my love, my fair one, and come away;
for lo, the winter is past.
The flowers appear on the earth,
the time of singing has come,
the voice of the turtledove is heard in our land.
Arise, my love, my fair one, and come away.
O my dove, in the clefts of the rock,
in the covet of the cliff, let me see your face,
let me hear your voice, for your voice is sweet,
and your face is comely. Song of Solomon 2.8–14*

Mary entered the house and greeted Elizabeth. When Elizabeth heard the greeting, the babe leaped in her womb; and Elizabeth was filled with the Holy Spirit and she exclaimed, 'Blessed are you among women, and blessed is the fruit of your womb! Why is this granted me, that the mother of my Lord should come to me? Behold, when the voice of your greeting came to my ears, the babe in my womb leaped for joy. Blessed is she who believed that there would be a fulfilment of what was spoken to her from the Lord.'
St Luke 1.39–45

RESPONSE 'O King of the Nations, and their desire,
come and save mankind, whom thou formest of clay.'

Heavenly Father, you are the lover of souls and the source of all love – purify our hearts and bring our love to perfection in your Son . . .
'Blessed are you among women and blessed is the fruit of your womb' – we honour Mary and we worship her incarnate Son . . .

INTERCESSIONS *pages 390–393* CLOSING PRAYERS *page 402–403*

22 December *The Magnificat (Song of Mary)*

OPENING PRAYER Lord God of Israel, you are the God and Father of our Lord Jesus Christ. We praise you for sending your Son to take flesh in the womb of Mary. Make us worthy of your redeeming love . . . Glory be . . .

PSALMODY Praise the Lord! Praise the Lord, O my soul!
Put not your trust in princes,
in a son of man, in whom there is no help.
When his breath departs he returns to his earth;
on that very day his plans perish.
Happy is he whose help is the God of Jacob,
whose hope is in the Lord his God. Psalm 146.1–5*

SCRIPTURE READINGS Hannah said to Eli, 'My Lord, I am the woman who was standing here in your presence, praying to the Lord. For this child I prayed; and the Lord has granted me my petition which I made to him. Therefore I have lent him to the Lord; as long as he lives he is lent to the Lord.' 1 Samuel 1.26–28

Mary said, 'My soul magnifies the Lord,
and my spirit rejoices in God my Saviour,
for he has regarded the low estate of his handmaiden.
For behold, henceforth all generations will call me blessed;
for he who is mighty has done great things for me,
and holy is his name.
And his mercy is on those who fear him
from generation to generation.
He has shown strength with his arm,
he has scattered the proud in the imagination of their hearts,
he has put down the mighty from their thrones,
and exalted those of low degree;
he has filled the hungry with good things,
and the rich he has sent empty away.
He has helped his servant Israel, in remembrance of his mercy,
as he spoke to our fathers,
to Abraham and his posterity for ever.' St Luke 1.46–55

RESPONSE 'O Emmanuel, our King and Lawgiver,
come and save us, O Lord our God.'

Eternal God, your Son took flesh in the womb of Mary – we praise you for exalting the humble and meek by choosing Mary as his mother . . .
'All generations shall call me blessed' – we praise you for your gift of grace to Mary, and we thank you for your love . . .

INTERCESSIONS *pages 390–393* CLOSING PRAYERS *page 402–403*

23 December *The Birth of Saint John the Baptist*

OPENING PRAYER Lord God of Israel, you are the God and Father of our Lord Jesus Christ. We praise you for sending your Son to take flesh in the womb of Mary. Make us worthy of your redeeming love . . . Glory be . . .

PSALMODY Happy is he whose help is the God of Jacob,
whose hope is in the Lord his God,
who made heaven and earth,
the sea, and all that is in them;
who keeps faith for ever,
who executes justice for the oppressed;
who gives food to the hungry. Psalm 146.5–7

SCRIPTURE READINGS The messenger of the covenant in whom you delight, behold, he is coming, says the Lord of hosts. But who can endure the day of his coming, and who can stand when he appears? For he is like a refiner's fire and like fullers' soap; he will sit as a refiner and purifier of silver, and he will purify the sons of Levi and refine them like gold and silver, till they present right offerings to the Lord. Then the offerings of Judah and Jerusalem will be pleasing to the Lord as in the days of old and as in former years.' Malachi 3.1–4

Now the time came for Elizabeth to be delivered, and she gave birth to her son. Her neighbours and kinsfold heard that the Lord had shown great mercy to her, and they rejoiced with her. On the eighth day they came to circumcise the child; and they would have named him Zechariah after his father, but his mother said, 'Not so; he shall be called John.' They said, 'None of your kindred is called by this name.' They made signs to his father, enquiring what he would have him called. He asked for a writing tablet, and wrote, 'His name is John.' They all marvelled. Immediately his mouth was opened and his tongue loosed, and he spoke, blessing God. And fear came on all their neighbours. All these things were talked about through all the hill country of Judea; and all who heard them laid them up in their hearts, saying, 'What then will this child be?' For the hand of the Lord was with him. St Luke 1.57–66

RESPONSE 'Daughters of Jerusalem, why marvel at me?
The thing which ye behold is a divine mystery.'

Eternal God, you chose John the Baptist to prepare for the coming of your Son – accept our praises and re-create us in the image of your Son . . .
'The offering of Judah and Jerusalem will be pleasing to the Lord' – purify our prayers and praises, and make them a worthy offering in your sight . . .
'The hand of the Lord was with him' – Lord, help us to be more aware of your presence with us, day by day . . .

INTERCESSIONS *pages 390–393* CLOSING PRAYERS *page 402–403*

OPENING PRAYER Lord God of Israel, you are the God and Father of our Lord Jesus Christ. We praise you for sending your Son to take flesh in the womb of Mary. Make us worthy of your redeeming love . . . Glory be . . .

PSALMODY 'I have made a covenant with my chosen one,
I have sworn to David my servant:
"I will establish your descendants for ever,
and build your throne for all generations."'
Let the heavens praise thy wonders O Lord,
thy faithfulness in the assembly of the holy ones.

Psalm 89.3–5

SCRIPTURE READINGS Nathan said to David, 'Your house and your kingdom shall be made sure for ever before me; your throne shall be established for ever.' 2 Samuel 7.16*

Zechariah was filled with the Holy Spirit, and prophesied, saying,

'Blessed be the Lord God of Israel,
for he has visited and redeemed his people,
and has raised up a horn of salvation for us
in the house of his servant David,
as he spoke by the mouth of his holy prophets from of old,
that we should be saved from our enemies,
and from the hand of all that hate us;
to perform the mercy promised to our fathers,
and to remember his holy covenant,
the oath which he swore to our father Abraham, to grant us,
that we, being delivered from the hand of our enemies,
might serve him without fear,
in holiness and righteousness before him all the days of our life.
And you, child, will be called the prophet of the Most High;
for you will go before the Lord to prepare his ways,
to give knowledge of salvation to his people
in the forgiveness of their sins, through the tender mercy of our God, when the day shall dawn upon us from on high
to give light to those who sit in darkness and in the shadow of death,
to guide our feet in the way of peace.' St Luke 1.67–79

RESPONSE 'O come to us, abide with us,
our Lord Emmanuel.'

Lord God of Israel, you revealed your love for us in the birth of your Son – fill us with your love until we overflow with joy and thanksgiving . . .
You sent your Son to save us from our sins – bless your Church, and make us worthy to celebrate the mystery of your love . . .

INTERCESSIONS *pages 390–393* CLOSING PRAYERS *page 402–403*

25 December *The Nativity of Our Lord Jesus Christ*

OPENING PRAYER Glory to God in the highest, and peace to his people on earth. The Word became flesh and lived among us. Bless the Lord, O my soul, and praise him for ever, Alleluia . . . Glory be . . .

PSALMODY O sing to the Lord a new song;
sing to the Lord, all the earth!
Sing to the Lord, bless his name;
tell of his salvation from day to day.
Declare his glory among the nations,
his marvellous works among all the peoples!
For great is the Lord, and greatly to be praised.
Honour and majesty are before him;
strength and beauty are in his sanctuary.
Ascribe to the Lord, O families of the peoples,
ascribe to the Lord glory and strength!
Ascribe to the Lord the glory due to his name;
bring an offering, and come into his courts!
Worship the Lord in holy array;
tremble before him, all the earth! Psalm 96.1–9*

SCRIPTURE READINGS
'Behold, your salvation comes;
behold, his reward is with him,
and his recompense before him.'
And they shall be called the holy people,
The redeemed of the Lord. Isaiah 62.11–12*

Joseph went up from Nazareth, to the city of David, which is called Bethlehem, because he was of the house and lineage of David, to be enrolled with Mary, his betrothed, who was with child. While they were there, the time came for her to be delivered. She gave birth to her first-born son and wrapped him in swaddling cloths and laid him in a manger because there was no place for them in the inn. St Luke 2.4–7*

RESPONSE 'Christians, awake, salute the happy morn,
whereon the Saviour of the world was born.'

Blessed are you, Heavenly Father, and blessed is your Son, the Holy Child of Bethlehem – Alleluia, Alleluia, Alleluia . . .
Your Son is Lord at his birth – with the angels, we sing to his eternal glory, Alleluia, Alleluia, Alleluia . . .
Blessed is Mary, his holy Mother and highly favoured lady – Alleluia . . .
The coming of Christ gives joy to the world – Lord, we rejoice with your whole Church on earth and in heaven . . .
'There was no place at the inn' – bless and comfort all who are lonely . . .

INTERCESSIONS *pages 390–393* CLOSING PRAYERS *page 402–403*

OPENING PRAYER Glory to God in the highest, and peace to his people on earth. The Word became flesh and lived among us. Bless the Lord, O my soul, and praise him for ever, Alleluia . . . Glory be . . .

PSALMODY Praise the Lord!
For it is good to sing praises to our God;
for he is gracious, and a song of praise is seemly.
The Lord builds up Jerusalem;
he gathers the outcasts of Israel.
He heals the broken-hearted, and binds up their wounds.
He determines the number of the stars,
he gives to all of them their names.
Great is our Lord, and abundant in power.
Sing to the Lord with thanksgiving;
make melody to our God upon the lyre! Psalm 147.1–7*

SCRIPTURE READINGS
You, O Bethlehem,
from you shall come forth for me
one who is to be ruler in Israel.
You shall stand and feed his flock
in the strength of the Lord. Micah 5.2–4*

There were shepherds out in the fields, keeping watch over their flock by night. And an angel of the Lord appeared to them, and the glory of the Lord shone around them, and they were filled with fear. And the angel said to them, 'Be not afraid; for behold, I bring you good news of a great joy which will come to all the people; for to you is born this day in the city of David a Saviour, who is Christ the Lord. And this will be a sign for you: you will find a babe wrapped in swaddling cloths and lying in a manger.' And suddenly there was with the angel a multitude of the heavenly host praising God and saying, 'Glory to God in the highest, and on earth peace among men with whom he is pleased!' St Luke 2.8–15*

RESPONSE 'The praises of redeeming love they sang,
and heaven's whole orb with Alleluyas rang.'

Loving Father, you wonderfully restored our human nature in your Son – with Mary and Joseph and your whole Church, we praise your holy name . . .
On this day, your Church remembers Saint Stephen, the first martyr – help us to forgive others as you forgive us, and give us your peace . . .
'Glory to God in the highest, and on earth peace among men with whom he is well pleased' – we rejoice and adore the new born King . . .
'I bring you good news of a great joy' – Alleluia, Alleluia, Alleluia . . .

INTERCESSIONS *pages 390–393* CLOSING PRAYERS *page 402–403*

27 December *St John the Evangelist*

OPENING PRAYER Praise the Lord. May your name be blessed for ever. Angels and archangels rejoice because your Son has brought eternal salvation to the people on earth . . . Glory be . . .

PSALMODY The righteous flourish like the palm tree,
and grow like a cedar in Lebanon.
They are planted in the house of the Lord,
they flourish in the courts of our God.
They still bring forth fruit in old age,
they are ever full of sap and green,
to show that the Lord is upright;
he is my rock
and there is no unrighteousness in him. Psalm 92.12–15

SCRIPTURE READINGS That which was from the beginning, which we have heard, which we have seen with our eyes, which we have looked upon and touched with our hands, concerning the word of life – the life was made manifest, and we saw it, and testify to it, and proclaim to you the eternal life which was with the Father and was made manifest to us – that which we have seen and heard we proclaim also to you, so that you may have fellowship with us; and our fellowship is with the Father and with his Son Jesus Christ. We are writing this that our joy may be complete.
1 John 1.1–4

On the first day of the week, Mary Magdalene came to Simon Peter and the other disciple, the one whom Jesus loved, and said, 'They have taken the Lord out of the tomb, and we do not know where they have laid him.' Peter then came out with the other disciple, and they went toward the tomb. They both ran, but the other disciple outran Peter and reached the tomb first; and stooping to look in, he saw the linen cloths lying there, but he did not go in. Then Simon Peter came, following him, and he went into the tomb; he saw the linen cloths lying, and the napkin, which had been on his head, not lying with the linen cloths but rolled up in a place by itself. Then the other disciple, who reached the tomb first, also went in, and he saw and believed. St John 20.1–8*

RESPONSE 'Glad tidings of great joy I bring,
to you and all mankind.'

Gracious God, you revealed the mystery of your divine love to your Apostle and Evangelist Saint John – we praise you as we celebrate this feast . . .
'We are writing this that our joy may be complete' – we rejoice with your Church in heaven and on earth, and we praise your holy name, Alleluia . . .
The Gospel is a living person – we praise you for the Word made flesh in the womb of Mary . . .

INTERCESSIONS *pages 390–393* CLOSING PRAYERS *page 402–403*

OPENING PRAYER To us a child is born. To us a Son is given. Blessed be your name, because your Son appeared with grace and healing for all people. To you be glory for time and for eternity . . . Glory be . . .

PSALMODY Young men and maidens together, old men and children!
Let them praise the name of the Lord;
his glory is above earth and heaven.
He has raised up a horn for his people,
praise for all his saints,
for the people of Israel who are near him.
Praise the Lord. Psalm 148.12–15*

SCRIPTURE READINGS In many and various ways God spoke of old to our fathers by the prophets; but in these last days he has spoken to us by a Son, whom he appointed the heir of all things, through whom also he created the world. He reflects the glory of God and bears the very stamp of his nature, upholding the universe by his word of power. When he had made purification for sins, he sat down at the right hand of the Majesty on high, having become as much superior to angels as the name he has obtained is more excellent than theirs. For to what angel did God ever say, 'Thou art my Son, today I have begotten thee'? or again, 'I will be to him a father, and he shall be to me a Son'? Hebrews 1.1–5

When the Wise Men departed, an angel of the Lord appeared to Joseph in a dream and said, 'Rise, take the child and his mother, and flee to Egypt, and remain there till I tell you; for Herod is about to search for the child, to destroy him.' He rose and took the child and his mother by night, and departed to Egypt, and remained there until the death of Herod. This was to fulfil what the Lord had spoken by the prophet, 'Out of Egypt have I called my son.' Then Herod, when he saw that he had been tricked by the wise men, was in a furious rage, and he sent and killed all the male children in Bethlehem and in all that region, who were two years old or under, according to the time which he had ascertained from the wise men.
St Matthew 2.13–18*

RESPONSE 'Be near me, Lord Jesus; I ask you to stay close by me for ever, and love me, I pray. Bless all the dear children in thy tender care, and fit us for heaven, to live with thee there.'

Loving Father, the life of your Son began in dangerous times – help us to put to death all evil thoughts, and to praise you in all our actions . . .
Your Church remembers the death of the Holy Innocents on this day – we pray for all who suffer cruelty and injustice . . .
Your love and mercy never fail – Lord, bless all children, and especially those in hospitals, hospices, and children's homes . . .

INTERCESSIONS *pages 390–393* CLOSING PRAYERS *page 402–403*

OPENING PRAYER All praise and honour to the God of eternal glory. You sent your only begotten Son with healing for all peoples and races. Lift our souls into your presence and hear our prayer . . . Glory be . . .

PSALMODY Praise the Lord!
Sing to the Lord a new song,
his praise in the assembly of the faithful!
Let them praise his name with dancing.
Let the faithful exult in glory;
let them sing for joy on their couches. Psalm 149.1–5*

SCRIPTURE READING Blessed be the God and Father of our Lord Jesus Christ, who has blessed us in Christ with every spiritual blessing in the heavenly places, even as he chose us in him before the foundation of the world, that we should be holy and blameless before him. He destined us in love to be his sons through Jesus Christ, according to the purpose of his will, to the praise of his glorious grace which he freely bestowed on us in the Beloved. Ephesians 1.3–6

In the beginning was the Word, and the Word was with God, and the Word was God. He was in the beginning with God; all things were made through him, and without him was not anything made that was made. In him was life, and the life was the light of men. The light shines in the darkness, and the darkness has not overcome it. There was a man sent from God, whose name was John. He came for testimony, to bear witness to the light, that all might believe through him. He was not the light, but came to bear witness to the light. The true light that enlightens every man was coming into the world. He was in the world, and the world was made through him, yet the world knew him not. He came to his own home, and his own people received him not. But to all who received him, who believed in his name, he gave power to become children of God; who were born, not of blood, nor of the will of the flesh, nor of the will of man, but of God. The Word became flesh and dwelt among us, full of grace and truth; we have behold his glory, glory as of the only Son from the Father. St John 1.1–14

RESPONSE 'Word of the Father, now in flesh appearing;
O come, let us adore him, Christ the Lord.'

Eternal God, you are Spirit – we praise you for taking flesh and blood in the womb of Mary for the salvation of the world . . .
Your Son became man to give us a share in your glory – Lord, bring to completion the work you have started in us . . .
You give joy to the world in the mystery of your Word made flesh – Blessed is your holy name, for you reign from eternity to eternity . . .

INTERCESSIONS *pages 390–393* CLOSING PRAYERS *page 402–403*

OPENING PRAYER Blessed are you, God and Father of our Lord Jesus Christ. To us a Son is given. to us a Son is born. The Word became flesh and lived among us . . . Glory be . . .

PSALMODY Praise the Lord!
Praise God in his sanctuary;
praise him in his mighty firmament!
Praise him for his mighty deeds;
praise him according to his exceeding greatness!
Praise him with trumpet sound;
praise him with lute and harp!
Praise him with timbrel and dance;
praise him with strings and pipe!
Praise him with sounding cymbals!
praise him with loud clashing symbals!
Let everything that breathes praise the Lord!
Praise the Lord! Psalm 150

SCRIPTURE READING When Herod died, an angel of the Lord appeared in a dream to Joseph in Egypt, saying, 'Rise, take the child and his mother, and go to the land of Israel, for those who sought the child's life are dead.' He took the child and his mother, and went to the land of Israel. But when he heard that Archelaus reigned over Judea in place of his father Herod, he was afraid to go there, and being warned in a dream he withdrew to the district of Galilee. He went and dwelt in the city called Nazareth, that what was spoken by the prophets might be fulfilled, 'He shall be called a Nazarene.' St Matthew 2.19–23*

RESPONSE 'Like Mary, let us ponder in our minds
God's wondrous love in saving lost mankind.'

Heavenly Father, your Son shared in the family life at the home of Mary and Joseph – we praise you for sharing the same love with us today . . .
The Church is one family in Jesus Christ through baptism – Lord, we pray for all our sisters and brothers in Christ, and for all who are lonely . . .
God still loves those who forsake his family – help us to learn both love and obedience from the perfect example of your Son . . .

INTERCESSIONS *pages 390–393* CLOSING PRAYERS *page 402–403*

31 December *New year's Eve*

OPENING PRAYER Eternal Father, you are our helper and refuge from generation to generation. You have created us, and brought us to this hour. To you be praise and glory for time and for eternity . . . Glory be . . .

PSALMODY The years of our life are threescore and ten,
or even by reason of strength fourscore;
yet their span is but toil and trouble;
they are soon gone, and we fly away.
So teach us to number our days
that we may get a heart of wisdom.
Satisfy us in the morning
with thy steadfast love,
that we may rejoice and be glad all our days.
Psalm 90.10–14*

SCRIPTURE READINGS
For everything there is a season,
and a time for every matter under heaven:
a time to be born, and a time to die;
a time to plant,
and a time to pluck up what is planted;
a time to kill, and a time to heal;
a time to break down, and a time to build up;
a time to weep, and a time to laugh;
a time to mourn, and a time to dance;
a time to embrace,
and a time to refrain from embracing;
a time to keep silence, and a time to speak;
a time to love; and a time to hate;
a time for war, and a time for peace. Ecclesiastes. 3.1–8*

With the Lord one day is as a thousand years, and a thousand years as one day. 2 Peter 3.8

RESPONSE 'O God, our help in ages past, our hope for years to come,
our shelter from the stormy blast, and our eternal home.'

Eternal God, you created time and you are Lord of the years – forgive all our sins and confirm all the good we have done in the past year . . .
A thousand years in your sight are but as yesterday – help us to be good stewards of the time you have allotted to us here on earth . . .
'There is a time for everything under the sun' – help us to be happy and to rejoice in your love year by year, and give us ever-grateful hearts . . .

INTERCESSIONS *pages 390–393* CLOSING PRAYERS *page 402–403*

(*Perhaps this is a good time to re-read 'Thoughts about the Spiritual Life' on page xii*)

Moveable Seasons and Holy Days

Ash Wednesday *The Beginning of Lent*

OPENING PRAYER Almighty God, help us by your Spirit to draw near to you in penitence and faith. Be with us in our Lenten observance, and inspire us to follow more closely in the way of your Son Jesus Christ . . .

PSALMODY Have mercy on me, O God, according to thy steadfast love;
according to thy abundant mercy blot out my transgressions.
Wash me thoroughly from my iniquity,
and cleanse me from my sin!
For I know my transgressions,
and my sin is ever before me.
Behold, thou desirest truth in the inward being;
therefore teach me wisdom in my secret heart.
Fill me with joy and gladness.
Create in me a clean heart, O God,
and put a new and right spirit within me. Psalm 51.1–10*

SCRIPTURE READINGS I will judge you, O house of Israel, everyone according to his ways, says the Lord God. Repent and turn from all your transgressions, lest iniquity be your ruin. Cast away from you all the transgressions which you have committed against me, and get yourselves a new heart and a new spirit! Why will you die, O house of Israel? For I have no pleasure in the death of any one, says the Lord God; so turn, and live.
Ezekiel 18.30–32

We are ambassadors for Christ, God making his appeal through us. We beseech you on behalf of Christ, be reconciled to God. For our sake he made him to be sin who knew no sin, so that in him we might become the righteousness of God. Working together with him, then, we entreat you not to accept the grace of God in vain. For he says, 'At the acceptable time I have listened to you, and helped you on the day of salvation.' Behold, now is the acceptable time; behold, now is the day of salvation.
2 Corinthians 5.20–6.2

RESPONSE 'The sacrifice acceptable to God is a broken spirit;
a broken and contrite heart, O God, thou wilt not despise.'

Loving Father, you inspire the Church to keep Lent as a time of spiritual renewal – help us in these forty days to grow in holiness and love . . .
Our sins separate us from you – Lord, help us to fight against our sins, and give us grace to overcome them in this holy season . . .
'Every athlete exercises self-control' – renew your Church and help us to change our lives through the power of Christ's victory on the Cross . . .

INTERCESSIONS *pages 390–393* CLOSING PRAYERS *page 402–403*

(THE LENT OPENING PRAYER IS USED UNTIL PALM SUNDAY. NO 'GLORY BE . . .' DURING LENT)

Palm (Passion) Sunday *Jesus enters Jerusalem*

OPENING PRAYER Heavenly Father, you reveal the mystery of your love on the Cross. Give us a deeper understanding of the death and resurrection of your Son, and help us to reflect it in our lives . . .

PSALMODY Who is the King of glory?
The Lord, strong and mighty,
the Lord mighty in battle!
Lift up your heads, O gates!
and be lifted up, O ancient doors!
that the King of glory may come in.
Who is this King of glory?
The Lord of hosts, he is the King of glory. Psalm 24.8–10

SCRIPTURE READINGS As Jesus rode along, they spread their garments on the road. As he was now drawing near, at the descent of the Mount of Olives, the whole multitude of the disciples began to rejoice and praise God with a loud voice for all the mighty works that they had seen, saying, 'Blessed is the King who comes in the name of the Lord! Peace in heaven and glory in the highest!' And some of the Pharisees in the multitude said to him, 'Teacher, rebuke your disciples.' He answered, 'I tell you, if these were silent, the very stones would cry out.' St Luke 19.29–40

Have this mind among yourselves which you have in Christ Jesus, who, though he was in the form of God, did not count equality with God a thing to be grasped, but emptied himself, taking the form of a servant, being born in the likeness of men. And being found in human form he humbled himself and became obedient unto death, even death on a cross. Therefore God has highly exalted him and bestowed on him the name which is above every name, that at the name of Jesus every knee should bow, in heaven and on earth and under the earth, and every tongue confess that Jesus Christ is Lord, to the glory of God the Father. Philippians 2.5–11

The word of the cross is folly to those who are perishing, but to us who are being saved it is the power of God. 1 Corinthians 1.18

RESPONSE 'O Saviour of the world, who by thy Cross and precious blood hast redeemed us, save us and help us, we beseech thee, O Lord.'

Eternal God, you sent your Son to take our flesh and suffer death for our redemption – help us to follow his example of humility and love . . .
Your Son surrendered his life in loving obedience on the Cross – unite the Church with Christ in his passion . . .
The crowds expected a military Saviour – help us to overcome sin and death through the power of Christ's redeeming love . . .

INTERCESSIONS *pages 390–393* CLOSING PRAYERS *page 402–403*

Monday in Holy Week *Jesus is Anointed*

OPENING PRAYER Heavenly Father, you reveal the mystery of your love on the Cross. Give us a deeper understanding of the death and resurrection of your Son, and help us to reflect it in our lives . . .

PSALMODY The Lord is my light and my salvation;
whom then shall I fear?
The Lord is the stronghold of my life;
of whom shall I be afraid?
When evildoers assail me,
uttering slanders against me,
my adversaries and foes,
they shall stumble and fall.
Yet will I be confident. Psalm 27.1–3*

SCRIPTURE READING
Behold, my servant, whom I uphold,
my chosen, in whom my soul delights;
I will put my spirit upon him,
He will not fail or be discouraged,
till he has established justice in the earth.
'I have given you as a covenant to the people,
a light to the nations.' Isaiah 42.1–6*

Six days before the Passover, Jesus came to Bethany, where Lazarus was, whom Jesus had raised from the dead. There they made him a supper; Martha served, but Lazarus was one of those at table with him. Mary took a pound of costly ointment of pure nard and anointed the feet of Jesus and wiped his feet with her hair; and the house was filled with the fragrance of the ointment. But Judas Iscariot, one of his disciples (he who was to betray him), said, 'Why was this ointment not sold for three hundred denarii and given to the poor?' This he said, not that he cared for the poor but because he was a thief, and as he had the money box he used to take what was put into it. Jesus said, 'Let her alone, let her keep it for the day of my burial. The poor you always have with you, but you do not always have me.'
St John 12.1–8

RESPONSE 'Look, Father, look on his anointed face,
and only look on us as found in him.'

God our Father, your Son was anointed with oil to prepare his body for burial – make us worthy of his death for our salvation . . .
The Cross is the way of life and salvation for all who put their trust in Christ – transform our lives through the redeeming love of your Son . . .
Your Son entered glory through suffering – help us to share his sufferings, and in your mercy, bring us to partake in his resurrection . . .

INTERCESSIONS *pages 390–393* CLOSING PRAYERS *page 402–403*

Tuesday in Holy Week *Now is My Soul Troubled*

OPENING PRAYER Heavenly Father, you reveal the mystery of your love on the Cross. Give us a deeper understanding of the death and resurrection of your Son, and help us to reflect it in our lives . . .

PSALMODY In thee, O Lord, do I take refuge;
let me never be put to shame!
In thy righteousness deliver me and rescue me;
incline thy ear to me, and save me! Psalm 71.1–2

SCRIPTURE READINGS
The Lord says, 'It is too light a thing that you should
be my servant to raise up the tribe of Jacob
and to restore the preserved of Israel;
I will give you as a light to the nations;
that my salvation may reach to the ends of the earth.'
Isaiah 49.6

Some Greeks came to Philip and said, 'Sir, we wish to see Jesus.' Philip went and told Andrew; Andrew went with Philip and they told Jesus. And Jesus answered them, 'The hour has come for the Son of Man to be glorified. Truly, I say to you, unless a grain of wheat falls into the earth and dies, it remains alone; but if it dies, it bears much fruit. He who loves his life loses it, and he who hates his life in this world will keep it for eternal life. If anyone serves me, he must follow me; and where I am, there shall my servant be also; if any one serves me, the Father will honour him. Now is my soul troubled. And what shall I say, "Father, save me from this hour"? No, for this purpose I have come to this hour. Father, glorify thy name.' Then a voice came from heaven, 'I have glorified it, and I will glorify it again.' The crowd heard it and said that it had thundered. Others said, 'An angel has spoken to him.' Jesus answered, 'This voice has come for your sake, not for mine. Now is the judgement of this world, now shall the ruler of this world be cast out; and I, when I am lifted up from the earth, will draw all men to myself.' He said this to show by what death he had to die. St John 12.20–33*

RESPONSE 'Forbid it, Lord, that I should boast,
save in the death of Christ my God.'

Almighty God, your Beloved Son was raised on the Cross before he entered his glory – help us to share in the victory of his passion . . .
'I, when I am lifted up, will draw all men to myself' – give your Church grace to grow in holiness, and make us channels of your love . . .
You gave us an example of selfless love in Jesus – strengthen our faith and lead us in the way of salvation . . .

INTERCESSIONS *pages 390–393* CLOSING PRAYERS *page 402–403*

Wednesday in Holy Week *Thirty Pieces of Silver*

OPENING PRAYER Heavenly Father, you reveal the mystery of your love on the Cross. Give us a deeper understanding of the death and resurrection of your Son, and help us to reflect it in our lives . . .

PSALMODY Be pleased, O God, to deliver me!
O Lord, make haste to help me!
Let them be turned back and brought to dishonour
who desire my hurt! Psalm 70.1–2

SCRIPTURE READINGS

Who will contend with me? Let us stand up together.
Who is my adversary? Let him come near to me.
Behold, the Lord God helps me;
who will declare me guilty?
Behold, all of them will wear out like a garment;
the moth will eat them up. Isaiah 50.8–9

Let us lay aside every weight, and sin which clings so closely, and let us run with perseverance the race that is set before us, looking to Jesus the pioneer and perfecter of our faith, who for the joy that was set before him endured the cross, despising the shame, and is seated at the right hand of the throne of God. Hebrews 12.1–2*

One of the twelve, called Judas Iscariot, went to the chief priests and said, 'What will you give me if I deliver him to you?' And they paid him thirty pieces of silver. And from that moment he sought an opportunity to betray him. When it was evening, Jesus sat with the twelve disciples; and as they were eating, he said, 'Truly, I say to you, one of you will betray me.' And they were very sorrowful, and began to say to him one after another, 'Is it I, Lord?' He answered, 'He who has dipped his hand in the dish with me, will betray me. The Son of Man goes as it is written of him, but woe to that man by whom the Son of Man is betrayed! It would have been better for that man if he had not been born.' Judas, who betrayed him, said, 'Is it I, Master?' He said, 'You have said so.' St Matthew 26.14–26*

RESPONSE 'I believe I shall see the goodness of the Lord
in the land of the living.'

Lord God, your Son allowed himself to be condemned to death for our salvation – help us to die to sin and live in newness of life in Christ . . .
The death of your Son at Calvary is the pivot of history – Lord, draw all people to yourself through the power of the Holy Cross . . .
Your Son was betrayed by his friend Judas – help us to be faithful disciples of Christ and to grow in holiness and love . . .

INTERCESSIONS *pages 390–393* CLOSING PRAYERS *page 402–403*

Maundy Thursday *Feet Washing and the Last Supper*

OPENING PRAYER Heavenly Father, you reveal the mystery of your love on the Cross. Give us a deeper understanding of the death and resurrection of your Son, and help us to reflect it in our lives . . .

PSALMODY What shall I render to the Lord
for all his bounty to me?
I will lift up the cup of salvation
and call on the name of the Lord.
I will pay my vows to the Lord.
Precious in the sight of the Lord
is the death of his saints.
I will offer to thee the sacrifice of thanksgiving
and call on the name of the Lord.
I will pay my vows to the Lord
in the presence of all his people. Psalm 116.12–18*

SCRIPTURE READINGS Jesus, knowing that the Father had given all things into his hands, and that he had come from God and was going to God, rose from supper, laid aside his garments, and girded himself with a towel. Then he poured water into a basin, and began to wash the disciples' feet, and to wipe them with the towel with which he was girded.

St John 13.3–5

I received from the Lord what I also delivered to you, that the Lord Jesus on the night when he was betrayed took bread, and when he had given thanks, he broke it, and said, 'This is my body which is for you. Do this in remembrance of me.' In the same way also the cup, after supper, saying, 'This cup is the new covenant in my blood. Do this, as often as you drink it, in remembrance of me.' For as often as you eat this bread and drink the cup, you proclaim the Lord's death until he comes.

1 Corinthians 11.23–26

RESPONSE 'My God, and is thy Table spread,
and does thy Cup with love o'erflow?'

Eternal Father, your Son gave the Eucharist to the Church as a memorial of his death and resurrection – we worship and praise your holy name . . .
Bread is broken at the altar, as Christ's body was broken on the Cross – we thank you for sharing your life with us in the Sacrament of unity . . .
'Jesus girded himself with a towel, and began to wash the disciples' feet' – inspire your Church to follow his example of humility and love . . .

INTERCESSIONS *pages 390–393* CLOSING PRAYERS *page 402–403*

OPENING PRAYER Heavenly Father, you reveal the mystery of your love on the Cross. Give us a deeper understanding of the death and resurrection of your Son, and help us to reflect it in our lives . . .

PSALMODY All who see me mock at me,
they make mouths at me, they wag their heads,
'He committed his cause to the Lord;
let him deliver him,
let him rescue him, for he delights in him!' Psalm 22.7–8

SCRIPTURE READINGS
Surely he has borne our griefs
and carried our sorrows.
He was wounded for our transgressions.
All we like sheep have gone astray;
and the Lord has laid on him the iniquity of us all.
He poured out his soul to death,
and was numbered with the transgressors;
yet he bore the sin of many,
and made intercession for the transgressors. Isaiah 53.4–12*

When the soldiers came to the place which is called The Skull, they crucified Jesus, and the criminals, one on the right and one on the left. Jesus said, 'Father, forgive them; for they know not what they do.' They cast lots to divide his garments. One of the criminals who were hanged railed at him, saying, 'Are you not the Christ? Save yourself and us!' The other rebuked him, saying 'Do you not fear God, since you are under the same sentence of condemnation? We indeed justly; for we are receiving the due reward of our deeds; but this man has done nothing wrong.' He said, 'Jesus, remember me when you come into your kingdom.' He said, 'Truly, I say to you, today you will be with me in Paradise.' It was about the sixth hour, and there was darkness over the whole land until the ninth hour, while the sun's light failed; and the curtain of the temple was torn in two. Jesus, crying with a loud voice, said, 'Father, into thy hands I commit my spirit!' Having said this he breathed his last. St Luke 23.33–46*

RESPONSE 'Love so amazing, so divine,
demands my soul, my life, my all.'

Ever-living God, your Son is the suffering Servant who offered his life as an atoning sacrifice for the sins of all – we praise your holy name . . .
From the silent pulpit of the Cross, you draw your family together in every age – help us to share his cup so that we may share his glory . . .
Your Son died and now lives and reigns with you and the Holy Spirit, one God for ever – Lord, have mercy on your Church and make us holy . . .

INTERCESSIONS *pages 390–393* CLOSING PRAYERS *page 402–403*

OPENING PRAYER Heavenly Father, you reveal the mystery of your love on the Cross. Grant us a deeper understanding of the death and resurrection of your Son, and help us to reflect it in our lives . . .

PSALMODY I cry with my voice to the Lord,
with my voice I make supplication to the Lord.
I pour out my complaint before him.
I cry to thee, O Lord; I say, thou art my refuge,
my portion in the land of the living.
Give heed to my cry; for I am brought very low.
Bring me out of prison,
that I may give thanks to thy name!
The righteous will surround me;
for thou wilt deal bountifully with me. Psalm 142.1–7*

SCRIPTURE READINGS Now there was a man named Joseph from the Jewish town of Arimathea. He was a member of the council, a good and righteous man, who had not consented to their purpose and deed, and he was looking for the kingdom of God. This man went to Pilate and asked for the body of Jesus. Then he took it down and wrapped it in a linen shroud, and laid him in a rock-hewn tomb, where no one had ever yet been laid. It was the day of Preparation, and the sabbath was beginning. The women who had come with him from Galilee followed, and saw the tomb, and how his body was laid; then they returned, and prepared spices and ointments. On the sabbath they rested according to the commandment. St Luke 23.50–56

The Jews said to Jesus, 'What sign have you to show us for doing this?' Jesus answered them, 'Destroy this temple, and in three days I will raise it up.' The Jews then said, 'It has taken forty-six years to build this temple, and will you raise it up in three days?' But he spoke of the temple of his body. St John 2.18–21

'Unless a grain of wheat falls into the earth and dies, it remains alone; but if it dies, it bears much fruit.' St John 12.24b

RESPONSE 'He died that we might be forgiven, he died to make us good;
that we might go at last to heaven, saved by his precious blood.'

Loving Father, your Son passed from death to new life in this coming night – bring us to share in his victory and to partake of his glory . . .
'Unless a grain of wheat falls into the earth and dies, it remains alone' – give us the comfort of your Spirit as we wait for Easter . . .
'It was the Day of Preparation' – cleanse us from the stain of sin, and prepare us to receive the risen Christ in the Eucharist . . .

INTERCESSIONS *pages 390–393* CLOSING PRAYERS *page 402–403*

EASTER ANTHEMS

Christ, our paschal lamb, has been sacrificed.
Let us, therefore, celebrate the festival,
not with the old leaven, the leaven of malice and evil,
but with the unleavened bread of sincerity and truth.
For we know that Christ being raised from the dead
will never die again;
death no longer has dominion over him.
the death he died he died to sin, once for all,
but the life he lives he lives to God.
So you must also consider yourselves dead to sin
and alive to God in Christ Jesus.
Christ has been raised from the dead,
the first fruits of those who have fallen asleep.
For as by a man came death,
by a man has come also the resurrection of the dead.
For as in Adam all die,
so also in Christ shall all be made alive . . . Glory be . . .

PSALMODY The Lord is my strength and my song,
he has become my salvation.
Hark, glad songs of victory in the tents of the righteous.
This is the Lord's doing; it is marvellous in our eyes.
Psalm 118.14–23*

SCRIPTURE READING On the first day of the week Mary Magdalene came to the tomb early, while it was still dark, and saw that the stone had been taken away. She ran to Simon Peter and the other disciple, the one whom Jesus loved, and said, 'They have taken the Lord out of the tomb, and we do not know where they have laid him.' Peter came with the other disciple, and they went toward the tomb. They both ran, but the other disciple outran Peter and reached the tomb first; and stooping to look in, he saw the linen cloths, but he did not go in. Simon Peter came, following him, and he went into the tomb; he saw the linen cloths lying, and the napkin, which had been on his head, not lying with the linen cloths, but rolled up in a place by itself. The other disciple, who reached the tomb first, also went in, and he saw and believed; for as yet they did not know the scripture that he must rise from the dead. St John 20.1–9*

RESPONSE 'The Day of Resurrection! Earth tell it out abroad.
The Passover of gladness, the Passover of God.'

Eternal Father, you make all things new by the resurrection of your Son – renew your Church as we celebrate this passover mystery with praise . . .
You defeated the power of sin and death by raising your Son from the dead – renew our faith and bring us to share in his glorious resurrection . . .
Your risen Son is active in the Church through the Spirit – we rejoice that his death and resurrection are made effective for us in baptism . . .

INTERCESSIONS *pages 390–393* CLOSING PRAYERS *page 402–403*

Monday in Easter Week — *A Living Hope*

OPENING PRAYER Eternal Father, your holy Church in all the world rejoices at the glorious resurrection of your Son. To you be endless glory in the Church and in Christ Jesus from generation to generation. Alleluia. Alleluia . . . Glory be . . .

PSALMODY O sing to the Lord a new song,
for he has done marvellous things!
His right hand and his holy arm have gotten him victory.
The Lord has made known his victory,
he has revealed his vindication in the sight of the nations.
He has remembered his steadfast love and faithfulness
to the house of Israel.
All the ends of the earth have seen the victory of our God.
Make a joyful noise to the Lord, all the earth;
break forth into joyous song and sing praises! Psalm 98.1–4*

SCRIPTURE READINGS
Sing to the Lord a new song,
his praise from the end of the earth!
Let the sea roar and all that fills it,
Let them shout from the top of the mountains;
Let them give glory to the Lord. Isaiah 42.10–12*

Blessed be the God and Father of our Lord Jesus Christ! By his great mercy we have been born anew to a living hope through the resurrection of Jesus Christ from the dead, and to an inheritance which is imperishable, undefiled, and unfading, kept in heaven for you, who by God's power are guarded through faith for a salvation ready to be revealed in the last time. In this you rejoice, though now for a while you may have to suffer various trials, so that the genuineness of your faith, more precious than gold which though perishable is tested by fire, may redound to praise and glory and honour at the revelation of Jesus Christ. Without having seen him you love him; though you do not now see him you believe in him and rejoice with unutterable and exalted joy. As the outcome of your faith you obtain the salvation of your souls. 1 Peter 1.3–9

RESPONSE 'Christ the Lord is risen again! Christ hath broken every chain. Hark, the angels shout for joy, singing evermore on high. Alleluia.'

Heavenly Father, your holy Church in all the world celebrates the powerful resurrection of your Son – we praise you with joy and gladness . . .
Your Son fulfilled his promise to the disciples – Lord, we rejoice that your Son gives joy to the Church and hope to the world . . .
Your Son conquered death and opened the way to eternal life – we rejoice at the wonder of your redeeming love, Alleluia, Alleluia . . .

INTERCESSIONS *pages 390–393* CLOSING PRAYERS *page 402–403*

Tuesday in Easter Week *A Great Multitude*

OPENING PRAYER Eternal Father, your holy Church in all the world rejoices at the glorious resurrection of your Son. To you be endless glory in the Church and in Christ Jesus from generation to generation, Alleluia, Alleluia . . . Glory be . . .

PSALMODY Thou hast turned for me my mourning into dancing;
thou hast loosed my sackcloth
and girded me with gladness,
that my soul may praise thee and not be silent.
O Lord my god,
I will give thanks to thee for ever. Psalm 30.11–12

SCRIPTURE READINGS The Lord said to Moses and Aaron in the land of Egypt, 'You shall observe the feast of unleavened bread, for on this very day I brought your hosts out of the land of Egypt.' Then Moses called all the elders of Israel, and said to them, 'Select lambs for your selves according to your families, and kill the passover lamb. Take a bunch of hyssop and dip it in the blood which is in the basin, and touch the lintel and the two doorposts with the blood which is in the basin; and none of you shall go out of the door of his house until the morning. And when you come to the land which the Lord will give you, as he has promised, you shall keep this service. And when your children say to you, "What do you mean by this service?" you shall say, "It is the sacrifice of the Lord's passover, for he passed over the houses of the people of Israel in Egypt, when he slew the Egyptians but spared our houses."' Exodus 12.17–27*

I looked, and behold, a great multitude which no man could number, from every nation, from all tribes and peoples and tongues, standing before the throne and before the Lamb, clothed in white robes, with palm branches in their hands, and crying out with a loud voice, 'Salvation belongs to our God who sits upon the throne, and to the Lamb!' And all the angels stood round the throne and round the elders and the four living creatures, and they fell on their faces before the throne and worshipped God, saying, 'Amen! Blessing and glory and wisdom and thanksgiving and honour and power and might be to our God for ever and ever! Amen.'
Revelation 7.9–12

RESPONSE 'Hearts to heaven and voices raise,
singing to God a hymn of praise.'

Eternal God, you freed the Israelites from slavery in Egypt – we praise you for freeing us from the slavery of sin through your risen Son . . .
The power of the resurrection remains strong today in the Church – we praise and magnify you for the miracle of Easter, Alleluia, Alleluia . . .
'Salvation belongs to our God' – bring us to union with your risen Son . . .

INTERCESSIONS *pages 390–393* CLOSING PRAYERS *page 402–403*

Wednesday in Easter Week *Every Knee Shall Bow*

OPENING PRAYER Eternal Father, your holy Church in all the world rejoices at the glorious resurrection of your Son. To you be endless glory in the Church and in Christ Jesus from generation to generation, Alleluia, Alleluia . . . Glory be . . .

PSALMODY I will extol thee, my God and King,
and bless thy name for ever and ever.
Every day I will bless thee,
and praise thy name for ever and ever.
Great is the Lord, and greatly to be praised,
and his greatness is unsearchable.
One generation shall laud thy works to another,
and shall declare thy mighty acts.
Men shall proclaim the might of thy terrible acts.
They shall pour forth the fame of thy abundant goodness,
and shall sing aloud of thy righteousness. Psalm 145.1–7*

SCRIPTURE READINGS
As for me, I will look to the Lord,
I will wait for the God of my salvation;
my God will hear me.
Rejoice not over me, O my enemy;
when I fall, I shall rise;
when I sit in darkness,
the Lord will be a light to me. Micah 7.7–8

Have this mind among yourselves, which you have in Christ Jesus, who, though he was in the form of God, did not count equality with God a thing to be grasped, but emptied himself, taking the form of a servant, being born in the likeness of men. And being found in human form he humbled himself and became obedient unto death, even death on a cross. Therefore God has highly exalted him and bestowed on him the name which is above every name, that at the name of Jesus every knee should bow, in heaven and on earth and under the earth, and every tongue confess that Jesus Christ is Lord, to the glory of God the Father. Philippians 2.5–11

RESPONSE 'At the name of Jesus every knee shall bow,
every tongue confess him King of glory now.'

Eternal God, you opened the gate of eternal life through the death and resurrection of your Son – we praise you for your redeeming love . . .
You make all things new in your risen Son – let all the world proclaim the glory of your sacred name . . .
Your Son has broken the power of death – raise us up with Christ, and strengthen us to serve you in the joy and power of his risen life . . .

INTERCESSIONS *pages 390–393* CLOSING PRAYERS *page 402–403*

Thursday in Easter Week *The Blood of the Eternal Covenant*

OPENING PRAYER Eternal Father, your holy Church in all the world rejoices at the glorious resurrection of your Son. To you be endless glory in the Church and in Christ Jesus from generation to generation, Alleluia, Alleluia . . . Glory be . . .

PSALMODY Return, O my soul, to your rest;
for the Lord has dealt bountifully with you.
For thou hast delivered my soul from death,
my eyes from tears, my feet from stumbling;
I walk before the Lord in the land of the living.
I kept my faith, even when I said, 'I am greatly afflicted.'
Psalm 116.7–10

SCRIPTURE READINGS
You will say in that day:
'I will give thanks to thee, O Lord,
for though thou wast angry with me,
and thou didst comfort me.
Behold, God is my salvation;
I will trust, and will not be afraid;
for the Lord God is my strength and my song,
and he has become my salvation.'
'Give thanks to the Lord, call upon his name;
make known his deeds among the nations,
proclaim that his name is exalted.
Sing praises to the Lord, for he has done gloriously;
let this be known in all the earth.
Shout, and sing for joy, O inhabitant of Zion,
for great in your midst is the Holy One of Israel.'
Isaiah 12.1–6*

Now may the God of peace who brought again from the dead our Lord Jesus Christ, the great shepherd of the sheep, by the blood of the eternal covenant, equip you with everything good that you may do his will, working in you that which is pleasing in his sight, through Jesus Christ; to whom be glory for ever and ever. Amen. Hebrews 13.20–21

RESPONSE 'God is working his purpose out,
as year succeeds to year.'

Eternal God, you made a covenant with the Israelites – we praise you for the new and everlasting covenant sealed in the blood of Christ . . .
You overcame the power of sin and death – Lord, raise us to new life and make us more aware of all your blessings for us in Jesus Christ . . .
'May God equip you with everything good that you may do his will' – give the Church all the graces needed to witness to the Risen Christ . . .

INTERCESSIONS *pages 390–393* CLOSING PRAYERS *page 402–403*

Friday in Easter Week *Raised with Christ*

OPENING PRAYER Eternal Father, your holy Church in all the world rejoices at the glorious resurrection of your Son. To you be endless glory in the Church and in Christ Jesus from generation to generation, Alleluia, Alleluia . . . Glory be . . .

PSALMODY The heavens are the Lord's heavens,
but the earth he has given to the sons of men.
The dead do not praise the Lord,
nor do any that go down into silence.
But we will bless the Lord from this time forth
and for evermore. Praise the Lord. Psalm 115.16–18

SCRIPTURE READINGS
'For there is hope for a tree,
if it be cut down, that it will sprout again,
and that its shoots will not cease.
Though its root grow old in the earth,
and its stump die in the ground,
yet at the scent of water it will bud
and put forth branches like a young plant.
But man dies, and is laid low;
man breathes his last, and where is he?
As waters fail from a lake,
and a river wastes away and dries up,
so man lies down and rises not again;
till the heavens are no more he will not awake,
or be roused out of his sleep.
If a man die, shall he live again?
All the days of my service I would wait,
till my release should come. Job 14.7–14*

If then you have been raised with Christ, seek the things that are above, where Christ is, seated at the right hand of God. Set your minds on things that are above, not on things that are on earth. For you have died, and your life is hid with Christ in God. When Christ who is our life appears, then you also will appear with him in glory. Colossians 3.1–4

RESPONSE 'May we go where he is gone,
rest and reign with him in heaven.'

Heavenly Father, you invite us to share in the life of your risen Son – with Easter joy and confidence we praise and magnify your holy name . . .
You redeemed us by the blood of your Son – Lord, we praise you and thank you for the Paschal sacrifice of your beloved Son . . .

INTERCESSIONS *pages 390–393* CLOSING PRAYERS *page 402–403*

Saturday in Easter Week *The Valley of Dry Bones*

OPENING PRAYER Eternal Father, your holy Church in all the world rejoices at the glorious resurrection of your Son. To you be endless glory in the Church and in Christ Jesus from generation to generation, Alleluia, Alleluia . . . Glory be . . .

PSALMODY I shall not die, but I shall live,
and recount the deeds of the Lord.
Open to me the gates of righteousness,
that I may enter through them
and give thanks to the Lord. Psalm 118.17 & 19

SCRIPTURE READINGS The hand of the Lord was upon me, and he brought me out by the Spirit of the Lord, and set me down in the midst of the valley; it was full of bones. And he said to me, 'Son of man, can these bones live?' And I answered, 'O Lord God, thou knowest.' Again he said to me, 'Prophesy to these bones, and say to them, O dry bones, hear the word of the Lord. Thus says the Lord God to these bones: Behold, I will cause breath to enter you, and you shall live. And I will lay sinews upon you, and will cause flesh to come upon you, and cover you with skin, and put breath in you, and you shall live; and you shall know that I am the Lord.' So I prophesied as I was commanded; and as I prophesied, there was a noise, and behold, a rattling; and the bones came together, bone to its bone. And as I looked, there were sinews on them, and flesh had come upon them, and skin had covered them; but there was no breath in them. Then he said to me, 'Prophesy to the breath, prophesy, son of man and say to the breath, Thus says the Lord God: Come from the four winds, O breath, and breathe upon these slain, that they may live.' So I prophesied as he commanded me, and the breath came into them, and they lived, and stood upon their feet, an exceedingly great host. Then he said to me, 'Son of man, these bones are the whole house of Israel.' Ezekiel 37.1–11*

We know that Christ being raised from the dead will never die again; death no longer has dominion over him. The death he died he died to sin, once for all, but the life he lives he lives to God. So you also must consider yourselves dead to sin and alive to God in Christ Jesus. Romans 6.9–11

RESPONSE 'Ye choirs of new Jerusalem, your sweetest notes employ,
the Paschal victory to hymn in strains of holy joy.'

Eternal Lord, you forgive our sins and bring us to new birth by the power of the Spirit – we praise you for redeeming us by the blood of Christ . . . 'Christ is risen indeed' – we ask you to live in us and use us to bring new life to those around us in our daily lives . . .

INTERCESSIONS *pages 390–393* CLOSING PRAYERS *page 402–403*

(TOMORROW USE APPROPRIATE 'DATE' AND EASTERTIDE OPENING PRAYER ON BOOKMARKER)

Ascension Day *King of Eternal Glory*

OPENING PRAYER Almighty God, your Church rejoices that you have exalted your only Son to glory. Have mercy on us and make us worthy to offer this sacrifice of praise and thanksgiving to you . . . Glory be . . .

PSALMODY Lift up your heads, O gates!
and be lifted up, O ancient doors!
that the King of Glory may come in.
Who is the King of glory?
The Lord, strong and mighty, the Lord, mighty in battle!
Lift up your heads, O gates!
and be lifted up, O ancient doors!
Who is this King of glory?
The Lord of hosts, he is the King of glory! Psalm 24.7–10

SCRIPTURE READINGS Then Jesus said to them, 'These are my words which I spoke to you, while I was still with you, that everything written about me in the law of Moses and the prophets and the psalms must be fulfilled.' Then he opened their minds to understand the scriptures, and said to them, 'Thus it is written, that the Christ should suffer and on the third day rise from the dead; and that repentance and forgiveness of sins should be preached in his name to all nations, beginning from Jerusalem. You are witnesses of these things. And behold, I send the promise of my Father upon you; but stay in the city, until you are clothed with power from on high.' Then he led them out as far as Bethany, and lifting up his hands he blessed them. While he blessed them, he parted from them; and was carried up into heaven. And they returned to Jerusalem with great joy, and were continually in the temple blessing God. St Luke 24.45–53

Men of Galilee, why do you stand looking into heaven? This Jesus, who was taken up from you into heaven, will come in the same way as you saw him go into heaven. Acts 1.11

Since then we have a great high priest who has passed through the heavens, Jesus, the Son of God, let us hold fast our confession. Hebrews 4.14

RESPONSE 'Lift up your hearts, lift up your voice,
rejoice, again, I say, rejoice.'

Eternal God, your Son is seated at your right hand in glory – in union with your universal Church, we celebrate this feast with praise . . .
Your Son completed his work in a perfect way, and returned to his place in the Godhead – give us grace to share in his work in the world . . .
Christ is our great High Priest, and he intercedes for us in heaven – Lord, we rejoice that Christ is our King in glory . . .

INTERCESSIONS *pages 390–393* CLOSING PRAYERS *page 402–403*

(TOMORROW USE NORMAL 'DATE' AND ASCENSION OPENING PRAYER UNTIL PENTECOST)

Pentecost (Whitsun) *The Holy Spirit*

OPENING PRAYER Heavenly Father, you poured out your Spirit on the Church at Pentecost to begin the proclamation of the Gospel. Fill us with the same Spirit to continue your work, and make yourself known to us in this time of prayer . . . Glory be . . .

PSALMODY Bless the Lord, O my soul;
O Lord my God, thou art very great!
O Lord, how manifold are thy works!
In wisdom hast thou made them all.
When thou sendest forth thy Spirit, they are created;
and thou renewest the face of the ground.
May the glory of the Lord endure for ever,
may the Lord rejoice in his works Psalm 103.1–31*

SCRIPTURE READINGS When the day of Pentecost had come, they were all together in one place. Suddenly a sound came from heaven like the rush of a mighty wind, and it filled all the house where they were sitting. There appeared to them tongues as of fire, distributed and resting on each one of them. And they were all filled with the Holy Spirit and began to speak in other tongues, as the Spirit gave them utterance. Acts 2.1–4

If you love me, you will keep my commandments. I will pray the Father, and he will give you another Counsellor, to be with you for ever, even the Spirit of truth, whom the world cannot receive, because it neither sees him nor knows him; you know him, for he dwells with you, and will be in you. St John 14.15–17

Jesus came and stood among them and said, 'Peace be with you.' He showed them his hands and side. Then the disciples were glad when they saw the Lord. Jesus said, 'Peace be with you. As the Father has sent me, even so I send you.' When he had said this, he breathed on them, and said, 'Receive the Holy Spirit. If you forgive the sins of any, they are forgiven, if you retain the sins of any, they are retained.' St John 20.19–23*

RESPONSE 'Gracious Spirit, Holy Ghost, taught by thee we covet most of thy gifts at Pentecost, holy, heavenly love.'

Eternal God, you sent the Spirit to the Church at Pentecost – we rejoice that the same Spirit continues to sanctify the Church today . . .
You send forth your Spirit to renew the face of the earth – renew your gift of life in us, and give us grateful hearts for all your blessings . . .
Your Son commissioned his disciples to proclaim the Good News – fill us with the fire of your love, and help us to share in the same mission . . .

INTERCESSIONS *pages 390–393* CLOSING PRAYERS *page 402–403*

(TOMORROW USE NORMAL 'DATE' WITH THE PENTECOST OPENING PRAYER UNTIL TRINITY)

Trinity Sunday *The Nature of God*

OPENING PRAYER Blessed and eternal God, three Persons in a Trinity of unity and love, you are the Lord from everlasting to everlasting. In your mercy, accept our praise and prayers . . . Glory be . . .

PSALMODY The Lord reigns; he is robed in majesty;
the Lord is robed, he is girded with strength.
Yea, the world is established; it shall never be moved;
thy throne is established from of old;
thou art from everlasting.
Thy decrees are very sure;
holiness befits thy house, O Lord, for evermore.

Psalm 93.1–5*

SCRIPTURE READINGS Holy, holy, holy, is the Lord God Almighty, who was and is and is to come. Revelation 4.8

O the depth of the riches and wisdom and knowledge of God! How unsearchable are his judgements and how inscrutable his ways! 'For who has known the mind of the Lord, or who has been his counsellor?' 'Or who has given a gift to him that he might be repaid?' For from him and through him and to him are all things. To him be glory for ever. Amen.

Romans 11.33–36

The grace of the Lord Jesus Christ and the love of God and fellowship of the Holy Spirit be with you all. 2 Corinthians 13.14

Philip said to Jesus, 'Lord, show us the Father, and we shall be satisfied.' Jesus said to him, 'Have I been with you so long, and yet you do not know me, Philip? He who has seen me has seen the Father; how can you say, "Show us the Father?". Do you not believe that I am in the Father and the Father in me? The words that I say to you I do not speak on my own authority; but the Father who dwells in me does his works. Believe me that I am in the Father and the Father in me; or else believe me for the sake of the works themselves.' St John 14.8–11

RESPONSE 'Holy, Holy, Holy, merciful and mighty!
God in three persons, blessed Trinity.'

Lord God, you make yourself known to us as Father, Son and Holy Spirit – we worship and adore the Blessed and Eternal Trinity, one God for ever . . .
The Father creates us, and the Son redeems us and the Holy Spirit sanctifies us – Lord, we worship you, three Persons in one God . . .
You are undivided in splendour and co-eternal in majesty and glory – Lord, we praise your holy name for time and eternity . . .

INTERCESSIONS *pages 390–393* CLOSING PRAYERS *page 402–403*

Corpus Christi *The Body and Blood of Christ*

(Thursday after Trinity Sunday)

OPENING PRAYER Blessed and eternal God, three Persons in a Trinity of unity and love, you are the Lord from everlasting to everlasting. In your mercy, accept our praise and prayers . . . Glory be . . .

PSALMODY Oh send out thy light and thy truth; let them lead me,
let them bring me to thy holy hill
and to thy dwelling!
Then I will go to the altar of God,
to God my exceeding joy;
and I will praise thee with the lyre, O God, my God.
Why are you cast down, O my soul,
and why are you disquieted within me?
Hope in God; for I shall again praise him,
my help and my God. Psalm 43.3–5

SCRIPTURE READINGS The cup of blessing which we bless, is it not a participation in the blood of Christ? The bread which we break, is it not a participation in the body of Christ. Because there is one bread, we who are many are one body, for we all partake of the one bread.

1 Corinthians 10.16–17

As the disciples were eating, Jesus took bread, and blessed, and broke it, and gave it to them, and said, 'Take; this is my body.' And he took a cup, and when he had given thanks he gave it to them, and they all drank of it. And he said to them, 'This is my blood of the covenant; which is poured out for many. Truly, I say to you, I shall not drink again of the fruit of the vine until that day when I drink it new in the kingdom of God.' And when they had sung a hymn, they went out to the Mount of Olives.

St Mark 14.22–26

Jesus said, 'Truly, truly, I say to you, unless you eat the flesh of the Son of man and drink his blood, you have no life in you; he who eats my flesh and drinks my blood has eternal life, and I will raise him up at the last day.

St John 6.53–54

RESPONSE 'Thou spread'st a table in my sight, thy unction grace bestoweth,
and O what transport of delight from thy pure chalice floweth.'

Heavenly Father, you provide the Eucharist as a memorial of the death of your Son – we praise you for this wonderful sacrament of love . . .
Your Son is the unseen host who feeds us in the Eucharist – we praise you for the mystery of our salvation in the death and resurrection of Christ . . .
Your Son is both priest and victim, who made the perfect offering to you – we praise you for uniting us in this sacrament of love . . .

INTERCESSIONS *pages 390–393* CLOSING PRAYERS *page 402–403*

Intercessions

SUGGESTIONS FOR A 31 DAY CYCLE OF PRAYER

DAY 1

A The Archbishop of . . . The Church in this Parish. *(N)* Our Priest.
B Peace and justice in the world.
C The Church in the British Isles.
D . . . .

DAY 2

A All who receive Communion at home or in hospital. *(N)* Our Bishop.
B The leaders of the nations, especially . . .
C The Church in Western Europe.
D . . . .

DAY 3

A All who use this prayer book. The unity of all Christians.
B All involved in local and national government, especially . . .
C The Church in Eastern Europe.
D . . . .

DAY 4

A PCC members and clergy of the Deanery. The mission of the Church.
B Scientists and their families and their work.
C The Church in Russia.
D . . . .

DAY 5

A Spiritual growth of the congregation and of the priest. Church unity.
B Writers, journalists, all involved in broadcasting and entertainment.
C The Church in Scandinavia.
D . . . .

DAY 6

A Sunday School children, teachers, and parents in the Deanery.
B Police, Prison and Probation Officers. Priests who minister to them.
C The Church in the Far East.
D . . . .

DAY 7

A Diocesan Synod and General Synod members. The Church in this parish.
B All members of the Armed Services. Service Chaplains.
C The Church in China.
D . . . .

DAY 8

A The mission of the Church in this parish. *(N)* Our Priest.
B Prisoners and hostages, and their families.
C The Church in Japan.
D . . . .

DAY 9

A *(N)* Our Bishop. The Church in the Diocese. Unity of all Christians.
B The Royal Family.
C The Church in India.
D . . . .

DAY 10

A Present and former choristers and organists. *(N)* Our Priest.
B All who are disabled. Their families. All who help them.
C The Church in Pakistan.
D . . . .

DAY 11

A Students and Staff at Theological Colleges and Training Courses.
B All who are employed and their families.
C The Church in Burma and Ceylon.
D . . . .

DAY 12

A All who work to maintain the life of the Church in the parish.
B The poor and needy of the world. Homeless people. Refugees.
C The Church in the Pacific Ocean Islands.
D . . . .

DAY 13

A Those whom we find it difficult to love, (especially . . .)
B All who are retired. The elderly.
C The Church in the Punjab and Kashmir.
D . . . .

DAY 14

A Present and former Sidesmen and Churchwardens. The unity of the Church. *(N)* Our Priest.
B Young families and children. Single parent families.
C The Church in the Middle East.
D . . . .

DAY 15

A Those who lead the worship of the Church in the parish.
B All who are separated or divorced. Children of broken homes.
C The church in South East Asia.
D . . . .

DAY 16

A Those for whom we have promised to pray. All who need our prayers.
B Single parent families. All who live alone.
C The Church in North Africa.
D . . . .

DAY 17

A Church organizations in the parish. Clergy of the Diocese. Their families.
B All who are married. The strengthening of home and family life.
C The Church in Central Africa.
D . . . .

DAY 18

A Vocations to the Sacred Ministry. Those not accepted. The Selectors.
B Victims of crime. Those who care for them.
C The Church in Southern Africa.
D . . . .

DAY 19

A Retired Bishops and Clergy of the Diocese. Their families.
B Students, staff and governors of Schools, Colleges and Universities.
C The Church in Canada.
D . . . .

DAY 20

A Christian writers, broadcasters and theologians. *(N)* Our Priest.
B All who work in industry, commerce and finance.
C The Church in North America.
D . . . .

DAY 21

A The sick. Those who care for them. Their families. *(N)* Our Bishop.
B All Trades Union officials and members.
C The Church in Central America.
D . . . .

DAY 22

A Church Schools in the Diocese. Mothers' Union branches in the Deanery. *(N)* Our Priest.
B All who travel by land or sea or air.
C The Church in South America.
D . . . .

DAY 23

A All who are baptized. Parents and Godparents. Their spiritual growth.
B Those who help to maintain the life of the community.
C The Church in Australia.
D . . . .

DAY 24

A The preparation by the congregation to receive Communion. Church unity. *(N)* Our Priest.
B All who are blind. Their families. Those who care for them.
C The Church in New Zealand.
D . . . .

DAY 25
A The Dean/Provost. Cathedral staff and congregation. *(N)* Our Priest.
B Doctors, surgeons, nurses, hospital staff, hospices, medical research.
C The Church in the Atlantic Ocean Islands.
D . . . .

DAY 26
A Nuns, monks and friars. For an increase in vocations. *(N)* Our Bishop.
B Drug addicts. Their families. All who help them.
C The Church in the Artic and the Antarctic.
D . . . .

DAY 27
A All confirmed in the parish. Their spiritual growth. *(N)* Our Bishop.
B All with an incurable disease. Their families. Those who care for them
C The Church in Scotland.
D . . . .

DAY 28
A The renewal of the gift of the Spirit in those who have lapsed.
B Funeral directors. Cemetery and crematorium staff.
C The Church in Ireland.
D . . . .

DAY 29
A The Dying. The Bereaved. Those who minister to them. The Departed. *(N)* Our Priest.
B All who work during the night.
C The Church in England and Wales.
D . . . .

DAY 30
A Deanery and Diocesan officials and committee members. *(N)* Our Priest.
B The deaf. Their families. All who care for them.
C Missionary Societies in this country.
D . . . .

DAY 31
A Accredited Lay Workers and Lay Readers. Work and mission of the PCC. *(N)* Our Bishop.
B Criminals and wicked people, that their hearts may be turned to good.
C The Church in places which are hostile to the Christian faith.
D . . . .

The Canticles

Sunday – *Te Deum*

You are God and we praise you:
  you are the Lord and we acclaim you;
you are the eternal Father:
  all creation worships you.
To you all angels, all the powers of heaven:
  cherubim and seraphim sing in endless praise,
Holy, holy, holy Lord, God of power and might:
  heaven and earth are full of your glory.
The glorious company of apostles praise you:
  the noble fellowship of prophets praise you,
  the white-robed army of martyrs praise you.
Throughout the world the holy Church acclaims you:
  Father of majesty unbounded;
your true and only Son, worthy of all worship:
  and the Holy Spirit, advocate and guide.
You, Christ, are the King of glory:
  the eternal Son of the Father.
When you became man to set us free:
  you did not abhor the Virgin's womb,
You overcame the sting of death:
  and opened the kingdom of heaven to all believers.
You are seated at God's right hand in glory:
  we believe that you will come, and be our judge.
Come then, Lord, and help your people:
  bought with the price of your own blood:
and bring us with your saints:
  to glory everlasting.
Save your people, Lord, and bless your inheritance:
  govern and uphold them now and always.
Day by day we bless you:
  we praise your name for ever.
Keep us today, Lord, from all sin:
  have mercy on us, Lord, have mercy.
Lord, show us your love and mercy:
  for we put our trust in you.
In you, Lord, is our hope:
  let us not be confounded at the last.

Monday – *Magnificat*

My soul proclaims the greatness of the Lord:
  my spirit rejoices in God my saviour;
for he has looked with favour on his lowly servant:
  from this day all generations will call me blessed;
the Almighty has done great things for me:
  and holy is his name.
He has mercy on those who fear him:
  in every generation.
He has shown the strength of his arm:
  he has scattered the proud in their conceit.
He has cast down the mighty from their thrones:
  and has lifted up the lowly.
He has filled the hungry with good things:
  and the rich he has sent away empty.
He has come to the help of his servant Israel:
  for he has remembered his promise of mercy,
the promise he made to our fathers:
  to Abraham and his children for ever.
Glory be . . .

Tuesday – *Glory and Honour*

Glory and honour and power:
  are yours by right, O Lord our God:
for you created all things:
  and by your will they have their being.
Glory and honour and power:
  are yours by right, O Lamb who was slain;
for by your blood you ransomed men for God:
  from every race and language, from every people and nation,
to make them a kingdom of priests:
  to stand and serve before our God.
To him who sits on the throne and to the Lamb:
  be praise and honour, glory and might,
for ever and ever. Amen.

Wednesday – *Benedictus*

Blessed be the Lord, the God of Israel:
 for he has come to his people and set them free.
He has raised up for us a mighty saviour:
 born of the house of his servant David.
Through his holy prophets he promised of old:
 that he would save us from our enemies,
 from the hands of all that hate us.
He promised to show mercy to our fathers:
 and to remember his holy covenant.
This was the oath he swore to our father Abraham:
 to set us free from the hands of our enemies,
free to worship him without fear:
 holy and righteous in his sight all the days of our life.
You, my child, shall be called the prophet of the Most High:
 for you will go before the Lord to prepare his way,
to give his people knowledge of salvation:
 by the forgiveness of all their sins.
In the tender compassion of our God:
 the dawn from on high shall break upon us,
to shine on those who dwell in darkness and in the shadow of death:
 and to guide our feet into the way of peace.
Glory be . . .

Thursday – *The Song of Christ's Glory*

Christ Jesus was in the form of God:
 but he did not cling to equality with God.
He emptied himself, taking the form of a servant:
 and was born in the likeness of men.
Being found in human form, he humbled himself:
 and became obedient unto death, even death on a cross.
Therefore God has highly exalted him:
 and bestowed on him the name above every name,
that at the name of Jesus every knee should bow:
 in heaven and on earth and under the earth;
and every tongue confess that Jesus Christ is Lord:
 to the glory of God the Father.
Glory be . . .

Friday – *Saviour of the World*

Jesus, saviour of the world, come to us in your mercy:
 we look to you to save and help us.
By your cross and your life laid down you set your people free:
 we look to you to save and help us.
When they were ready to perish you saved your disciples:
 we look to you to come to our help.
In the greatness of your mercy loose us from our chains:
 forgive the sins of all your people.
Make yourself known as our saviour and mighty deliverer:
 save and help us that we may praise you.
Come now and dwell with us, Lord Christ Jesus:
 hear our prayer and be with us always.
And when you come in your glory:
 make us to be one with you and to share the life of your kingdom.

Saturday – *Great and Wonderful*

Great and wonderful are your deeds, Lord God the Almighty:
 just and true are your ways, O King of the nations.
Who shall not revere and praise your name, O Lord?
 for you alone are holy.
All nations shall come and worship in your presence:
 for your just dealings have been revealed.
To him who sits on the throne and to the Lamb:
 be praise and honour, glory and might, for ever and ever. Amen.

Closing Prayers

The Lord's Prayer

Our Father, who art in heaven,
hallowed be thy name;
thy kingdom come,
thy will be done
on earth as it is in heaven.
Give us this day our daily bread.
And forgive us our trespasses,
as we forgive those who trespass against us.
And lead us not into temptation,
but deliver us from evil.
For thine is the kingdom, the power and the glory,
for ever and ever. Amen.

Seasonal Endings

ADVENT (*1–16 December*)
May Christ, the Light of the world, scatter all darkness from our path. May he strengthen the hope which we have, and give us his peace. Amen.

ADVENT (*17–24 December*)
May the God of peace sanctify us, and may our spirits and souls and bodies be kept sound and blameless at the coming of our Lord Jesus Christ. Amen.

CHRISTMAS (*25 December–5 January*)
Christ himself gathered together all things in heaven and on earth by his incarnation. May he fill us with his love and joy and peace. Amen.

EPIPHANY (*6–31 January*)
May Christ, the eternal Son of God, make us glad with the Good News of his Kingdom, and may he fill us with his love. Amen.

FEBRUARY
May Christ give us grace to take up our Cross and follow him, and may he give us his peace. Amen.

MARCH
May God, in his great mercy and love, strengthen our faith and guide us in the way of peace and truth. Amen.

ASH WEDNESDAY AND LENT
May God give us grace to grow in holiness and love. May he give us grace to take up our Cross and follow him. Amen.

HOLY WEEK (*Palm Sunday to Easter Eve*)
May the crucified Christ draw us to himself, and may we find in him a firm foundation for our faith, and a strong support for our hope. Amen.

EASTER (*use until eve of the Ascension*)
May God our Father, who raised the Lord Jesus Christ from the dead, give us joy and peace in our Christian faith. Amen.

ASCENSION (*use until the eve of Pentecost*)
May Christ our exulted King strengthen our faith, so that we may carry out his will, and come to reign with him in glory. Amen.

PENTECOST (*use until the eve of Trinity*)
May the Lord pour out his Spirit upon us, and bring us to the fullness of all truth, and give us grace to proclaim Jesus as Lord. Amen.

TRINITY SUNDAY
May the holy and undivided Trinity strengthen our faith, give us grace to do his will, and lead us in the way of peace. Amen.

CORPUS CHRISTI
May the grace of Christ our Saviour, and the Father's eternal love, and the power of the Holy Spirit, be with us and remain with us, always. Amen.

SAINTS DAYS
May God help us to follow the example of his saints, and bring us to share with them in his eternal glory. Amen.

Other Endings

(General)
May the grace of our Lord Jesus Christ, and the love of God, and the fellowship of the Holy Spirit, be with us now and always. Amen.

APRIL
May the God of peace give us his blessing, protect us from all evil, and bring us to life eternal. Amen.

MAY
May the God of hope reign in our hearts, and fill us with all joy and peace in believing. Amen.

JUNE
May the Lord bless us and keep us. May the Lord make his face to shine upon us, and be gracious to us. May the Lord give us his peace. Amen.

JULY
Now to him who is able to do more abundantly than all we can ask or think, to him be glory in the Church and in Christ Jesus, for ever. Amen.

AUGUST
May God grant us to live in harmony, in accord with Christ Jesus, that together we may glorify the God and Father of our Lord Jesus Christ. Amen.

SEPTEMBER
May the Lord grant us to be strengthened with might through his Spirit. May he grant that we be filled with all the fullness of God. Amen.

OCTOBER
Now may the Lord of peace himself give us peace at all times, and in all ways. May the Lord be with us always. Amen.

NOVEMBER
Thine, O Lord, is the greatness, and the power, and the glory, and the victory, and the majesty, for time and for eternity. Amen.